BAD FAITH

BAD FAITH
TEACHERS, LIBERALISM, AND THE ORIGINS OF McCARTHYISM

ANDREW FEFFER

Empire State Editions
An imprint of Fordham University Press
New York 2019

Copyright © 2019 Fordham University Press

All rights reserved. No part of this publication may be reproduced, stored in a retrieval system, or transmitted in any form or by any means—electronic, mechanical, photocopy, recording, or any other—except for brief quotations in printed reviews, without the prior permission of the publisher.

Fordham University Press has no responsibility for the persistence or accuracy of URLs for external or third-party Internet websites referred to in this publication and does not guarantee that any content on such websites is, or will remain, accurate or appropriate.

Fordham University Press also publishes its books in a variety of electronic formats. Some content that appears in print may not be available in electronic books.

Visit us online:
www.empirestateeditions.com
www.fordhampress.com

Library of Congress Cataloging-in-Publication Data

Names: Feffer, Andrew, 1954– author.
Title: Bad faith : teachers, liberalism, and the origins of McCarthyism / Andrew Feffer.
Description: First edition. | New York : Empire State Editions, an imprint of Fordham University Press, 2019. | Includes bibliographical references and index.
Identifiers: LCCN 2018025301 | ISBN 9780823281169 (cloth : alk. paper) | ISBN 9780823281152 (pbk. : alk. paper)
Subjects: LCSH: Public schools—New York (State)—New York—History—20th century. | Community colleges—New York (State)—New York—History—20th century. | Communism and education—New York (State)—New York—History—20th century. | Anti-communist movements—New York (State)—New York—History—20th century. | New York (State). Legislature. Joint Legislative Committee to Investigate the Educational System of the State of New York.
Classification: LCC LA339.N5 F44 2019 | DDC 371.0109747—dc23
LC record available at https://lccn.loc.gov/2018025301

Printed in the United States of America

21 20 19   5 4 3 2 1
First edition

for Michelle

Contents

Introduction   1

PART I: The Hearings

1. The Threshold   21
2. The Stooge Grebanier   36
3. Coudertism   54
4. Vichy's Lawyer?   70

PART II: Class War

5. The Dewey Trial   85
6. The Educational Front   108
7. Far from the Ivory Tower   129

PART III: The Mortal Storm

8. Bad Faith   149
9. CCNY   174
10. Flirting with the Right   195
11. Communism on Trial   212

12 Aftermath	227
Conclusion: The Coudert Legacy	241
Acknowledgments	*255*
Abbreviations Used in the Endnotes	*259*
Notes	*265*
Index	*317*

Lisez avec vos yeux frais et votre esprit libre.
—*Leon Blum, 1917*

Introduction

It was the first week of December 1940, a year before Pearl Harbor. Franklin Delano Roosevelt had just won an unprecedented third term after ten years of the deepest and most prolonged economic crisis in modern history. Crushed by catastrophic unemployment, the nation had suffered the collapse of the farm economy and industrial upheaval approaching insurrection in several major cities. Unemployment in 1940 remained high, yet for the first time in a decade, economic recovery seemed to be on the horizon. In fifteen months, the Nazi blitzkrieg had overrun most of Western Europe, reaching the English Channel. Roosevelt successfully campaigned on military preparedness, and mounting war production already promised a steadier flow of jobs; defense appropriations reached $17 billion by that October. The war was coming to America, and the Great Depression was about to end.[1]

With the Christmas season approaching, New York was buoyed up on the rising tide of new employment. Manhattan's avenues swelled with shoppers, while the city's department stores reported a ten percent increase in sales over the previous year. Times Square offered one picture of growing consumer optimism: Bond's opened its "cathedral of clothing"—the world's largest men's store—employing hundreds to sell suits and accessories to Manhattan's rejuvenated white-collar workforce.[2] The *New York Times* reported that rising employment lifted the city's stagnant real estate market. Urban planners presented optimistic projections of a city of the future, built around a network of highways crisscrossing the region, moving commuters, consumers, and the products of a burgeoning defense industry across the revitalized metropolitan landscape. The city's economy was no longer shrinking. And although it was already darkened by the shadow of war, New York seemed to be on the threshold of a new era.[3]

Rapp-Coudert

Yet, as the revived economy brightened the city's prospects, a darker drama unfolded in lower Manhattan. Several hundred teachers, students, and their supporters jammed the hallway outside a tiny room in the federal courthouse on Foley Square. They had been closed out of the first day of state legislative hearings of the so-called Rapp-Coudert committee that was investigating subversion in New York City's public schools and colleges. As the bundled-up crowd pressed against police barricades, the committee packed the chamber with sympathizers and friends, leaving only thirty open seats. There was shouting and pushing. Scores of indignant people lingered by the door through the afternoon.[4]

Inside the atmosphere was even more tense—"sulpherous" according to the *PM* reporter on the scene.[5] Just three months into their investigation, the committee presented unsubstantiated preliminary findings, but they did so with headline-grabbing certainty: "Fostering discontent" among the city's students, Communist teachers sought to "undermine American youth by spreading [communism's] alien and subversive principles among them," the committee's chief of staff Paul Windels asserted. They had conspired systematically over the previous decade, he added, to foment revolution in New York City schools and colleges using the party's strategic control of the city's main teachers unions. Windels then released the names of twenty-three municipal college faculty and staff suspected of classroom subversion who had refused to testify, presumably because they had something to hide. The *New York Times*, which would credulously report almost all of the committee's allegations, predicted that the "intensive skirmishing" over testimony and subpoenas in the previous months of investigation would "flare into open battle." They were right. When the meeting opened, William Mulligan, attorney for the accused teachers, called from the audience for the committee to follow due process. Committee chair Frederick Coudert, Jr., Republican state senator from the city's posh Upper East Side, had the police drag him out.[6]

So began one of the most methodically conducted and documented local investigations in the chain of anticommunist witch hunts lasting into the 1960s that we have come to call "McCarthyism." Authorized in March 1940 by the New York state legislature, the Rapp-Coudert investigation had by that December probed aggressively for evidence of communist subversion at Brooklyn College (BC), which was perceived by many to be the center of Communist Party activity in the city's recently consolidated municipal college system. Through the fall, dozens of faculty, staff, and students were interrogated in preparation for the December hearings, which opened on Monday, December 2. When the Coudert committee officially completed its work in early 1942, it had spent more than $500,000[7] interrogating over five hundred witnesses in private and public hearings for which more than ten thousand pages of transcripts were recorded. Committee staffers informally interviewed approximately seven hundred more in homes and offices around the city and elsewhere. The committee claimed to have exposed sixty-nine members of the Communist Party and to have brought about the firing, suspension, or resignation of roughly fifty employees, mainly at City College of New York (CCNY) and BC. One CCNY professor went to prison for perjuring himself in testimony before the committee. Others, members of the large group of part-time faculty without permanent positions or contracts, merely melted away after being dropped from instruction rosters. In addition, the committee compiled the names of over six hundred suspected communists and sympathizers in what amounted to a blacklist, made available to state police, city officials, and, eventually, federal investigators who used that list along with Rapp-Coudert transcripts to draw the net around dozens of other faculty, staff, and public-school teachers in inquisitions a decade later.[8] Finally, the Coudert investigation, together with a concerted campaign on the part of anticommunists in the American Federation of Teachers (AFT) and its parent, the American Federation of Labor (AFL), pursued and severely crippled the two most powerful and pioneering teachers unions in the city, AFT's Local 5, representing public-school teachers, and its spinoff, Local 537 or the College Teachers Union (CTU), representing faculty and staff from New York City's municipal colleges, as well as from colleges and universities in the New York metropolitan area.

Rapp-Coudert had a profound impact on the intellectual and political life of New York, the nation's largest city, its center of high culture and an engine of social and political transformation. With other such countersubversive investigations, Rapp-Coudert sent a chill through American higher education. "Fear stalks the classroom," wrote Supreme Court Justice William O. Douglas in a related case. "Where suspicion fills the air and holds scholars in line for fear of their jobs, there can be no exercise of the free intellect.... A deadening dogma takes the place of free inquiry."[9]

People writing the history of political inquisitions similarly note their long-term effect on teaching, including shifts in curriculum away from controversial subjects and toward conventional ways of thinking. According to a 1958 study by Columbia University sociologists, "the difficult years" of Cold War hysteria made forty-six percent of social science faculty interviewed "apprehensive" about some aspect of their academic work. Around a tenth acknowledged that they "toned down their writings." The same proportion hesitated to assign "potentially controversial works" to their students, and twenty-seven percent felt "obliged to go out of [their] way to express [their] loyalty." Faculty avoided doing research on the Soviet Union or China for fear of raising suspicions or because they did not want to risk using proscribed sources. One historian stopped a book he was writing at the year 1945 so as not to address the Cold War; an economist told his interviewers that "I just limit my writings to things that Congressmen can't understand."[10] Similar effects were almost immediately evident in the wake of Rapp-Coudert. Howard Selsam, forced from his job teaching philosophy at BC in June 1941, observed that the New York investigation made his colleagues "fearful even to be seen speaking to one who had been subpoenaed." Rapp-Coudert investigators gave them good reason to be afraid, calling in for interrogation Selsam's noncommunist colleagues for such telltale associations as having Selsam's signature on their union membership cards, or in the case of one young faculty member, for telling her class she respected Selsam for standing up to the committee. Ultimately, the effect of the purges on surviving municipal college faculty included, in Selsam's words, "timidity, servility, seclusion, pre-censored and self-censored teaching and research."[11]

Prelude to McCarthyism

In addition to troubling us morally and constitutionally, Rapp-Coudert upsets the popular narrative of the era's history, which tends to focus on the antics of Senator Joseph McCarthy a decade later and to treat the red scare as a phenomenon of the Cold War, a reaction to the perceived Soviet threat against the United States after 1945. Yet Rapp-Coudert long preceded the Cold War, as one of several inquisitions conducted just before World War II in what some historians have termed the "Little Red Scares." Spurred in part by the Dies committee in the House of Representatives, that wave of xenophobic, anticommunist hysteria included the passage of the Hatch Act in 1939 barring federal employees from belonging to revolutionary organizations, the 1940 Smith Act criminalizing subversive activities at the federal level, attacks on radicals and communists by legislatures and police across the United States, and the spate of local investigations and prosecutions that, in addition to Rapp-Coudert, included others in Michigan, Wisconsin, and California. Like many such outbreaks of anticommunist hysteria in the twentieth century, Rapp-Coudert had relatively little to do with Soviet belligerence toward the United States. It and other prewar inquisitions were driven by dynamics that were largely domestic in origin, born not only of the social and political conflicts of the Depression years, but also of deeper and more-enduring currents in American culture.[12]

Rapp-Coudert was a pivotal event in that longer history—a "prelude to McCarthyism," according to some. And in its long-term consequences, Rapp-Coudert does look very much like a test run for the full-blown postwar red scare. In addition to drawing out testimony that would be used in later cases, it set legal precedents for the subsequent firing of teachers and staff across the nation. It tested and expanded the power of legislative committees to force teachers and other public employees to acknowledge their political associations. Rapp-Coudert made "conduct unbecoming a professor" the preferred charge against suspected Communists in higher education, evading the question of whether membership in the Communist Party was sufficient grounds for dismissal (technically, it was not at the time, since the party was legal in most states) or even whether suspects were being persecuted for their political views. Moreover, as historian Stephen Leberstein points out, Rapp-Coudert "marked a turning point away from the virulent and energetic but blundering attacks of the past decades ... toward the more systematic repression of the McCarthy era."[13] It methodically built cases against suspects using multiple witnesses in a seemingly legal framework of accusation and proof. It used existing municipal and state law to force faculty to inform on their colleagues or face the consequences of "non-cooperation." And as it tightened that noose, Rapp-Coudert drove suspected Communists to lie about their political associations in order to avoid naming names, the ostensible reason that New York's boards of education gave for eventually firing accused teachers and staff. At the same time, Rapp-Coudert investigators significantly strengthened the case for criminalizing communism on the alleged grounds that, regardless of its statements and official policies to the contrary, the Communist Party of the United States was engaged in the process of overthrowing our democratically elected government by "force and violence." One could justly argue that in its open-ended investigation of subversion in the city's schools, Rapp-Coudert essentially authorized itself to find a crime where none yet existed—and to make that crime the crime of the century.[14]

The Countersubversive Tradition

One of the striking things about the Rapp-Coudert inquiry is the extent to which it was conceived and run by liberals, including most of the Rapp-Coudert staffers and many of its supporters—key among whom were former office-holders and organizers of the Fusion administration of Mayor Fiorello La Guardia—which brought Republicans, Democrats, and independents together to back a local version of FDR's New Deal.[15] The involvement of these liberals, some of them Republicans, others from the anti-Tammany wing of the Democratic Party, confounds another prevailing assumption about McCarthyism, held not just by the general public but by many historians and social scientists as well—that it thundered in from the right, from the illiberal populist movements and quasireligious enthusiasms that periodically upend American society. This assumption was first fixed in our historical consciousness during the McCarthy era by liberals themselves, such as historian Richard Hofstadter and his colleague at Columbia University, sociologist Daniel Bell.

For Hofstadter and Bell, McCarthyism was just the most recent expression of the average American's recurrent anxiety over perceived inequalities of status and power, which were especially prevalent in those parts of the country outside the centers of political and economic authority such as Washington and New York. Status anxiety led populations dislocated by industrial development, declining agricultural prices, and periodic market collapse to blame their misfortunes on those distant sources of authority and on the people who lived there in, as Hofstadter famously put it, a "paranoid style" of bigoted and irrational attack driven by "restlessness, suspicion, and fear." Yet during periods of prosperity, status anxiety over potential failure and occupational mobility mounted as well, only this time in proportion to the *rising* fortunes of the very same social groups. Regardless of their socioeconomic origins, such "pseudo-conservative" reactions, with their "widespread latent hostility toward American institutions," tended toward violence, and Hofstadter considered them to that degree to be beyond the responsible politics that are required to run a modern nation. Bell similarly traced the "momentary range of support and intense emotional heat" of McCarthyism and its "damage to the democratic fabric" to "prosperity-created," status-oriented social movements that generated a "strange coalition" of "soured patricians," the nouveau riche, and the rising ethnic middle class on the one hand, and, on the other, "cankered ex-Communists" who "opened up an attack on liberalism in general." Bell traced the moralistic orientation of contemporary status groups to the "peculiar evangelicalism" of the American heartland "with its high emotionalism, its fervor, enthusiasm and excitement."[16]

These arguments about the origins of McCarthyism contrasted it sharply with the rational pluralism supposedly practiced by legitimate conservatives and liberals in the major national parties. Only the geographical scope, inclusiveness, and flexibility of American representative government, its essentially liberal character, Bell argued, saved the body politic from such violently paroxysmal tendencies in the political culture. The Hofstadter-Bell thesis fits with the related tendency to consider McCarthyism a single front in a much broader attack by "conservative coalitions" on the regulatory policies and entitlement programs that started with the New Deal.[17] McCarthy's own rhetoric as well as the postwar machinations of key anticommunist institutions such as the House Committee on Un-American Activities targeting New Deal agencies and programs lend weight to this explanation, which was popular especially among liberal and left-wing defenders of Roosevelt's legacy.

The Rapp-Coudert inquiry, however, complicates this picture of "reactionary" McCarthyism attacking "progressive" social policies and responsibly democratic institutions. Its history instead confirms political scientist Michael Paul Rogin's argument that midcentury anticommunism was as much the work of elites, including liberal architects and managers of postwar political institutions, as it was of the anti-intellectual, neopopulist right wing, onto whom Hofstadter and Bell so effectively shifted sole responsibility.[18] Situating McCarthyism in a "countersubversive tradition" at the heart of the national culture, a "continuing feature of American politics" from the conquest of the New World to the Reagan administration and beyond, Rogin tended to explain McCarthyism in psychoanalytic terms that identified it with other kinds of "countersubversive" demonization—namely the exclusion and punishment of indigenous peoples, ethnocultural and racial minorities, women, and other groups considered "responsible for American weakness." Rogin treats this politics of "demonization" as cinematic in conception and practice, with McCarthyism as just another episode in a series culminating (Rogin published his study in 1987) with "Ronald Reagan: The Movie," a national story of unbridled yet wounded individuality wrestling with its demons.[19]

I find Rogin's insights into American countersubversion's dark and obsessive past compelling, but as a historian I think it slights the more direct and obvious connections to people and groups acting in historical time. In the case of McCarthyism, Rogin connected it formally and symbolically to Hollywood's postwar dreamscape of perceived enemies, Soviet spies, labor racketeers, and controlling mothers as Freudian cinematic types, rather than to the real people who fashioned those illusions in the world of politics as well as film.[20] Yet, in that analysis, one can also find a clue to Rapp-Coudert's historical significance: Rogin recognized McCarthyism's conservatism, its resistance to change and difference, its exceptionalism, and its bigotry, yet he also traced it to a dark side of American liberalism, to the liberal's habitual need to regulate and purify a social and cultural landscape that is constantly disordered by the pursuit of individual gain and corporate profit margins in an expanding market economy that liberals as a matter of principle also embraced. Or, equally, to the liberal's need to stabilize a political order that is constantly disrupted by democratic impulses, whether on a national or local scale. This was the paradox of American liberalism in the twentieth century, a politics that endorsed social planning without violating the basic norms of modern industrial capitalism in the name of democratic impulses that liberals themselves often defeated.

In one chapter especially, Rogin points obliquely to the manner in which liberal elites, notably those with an investment in the economic reforms and regulatory framework of the New Deal, contributed in the 1930s to the rising tide of anticommunism. There he offers a critique of the interest-group theories of political scientist David Truman, which are treated as the primary theoretical framework for liberal politics after the war. Rogin suggests that liberals believed communism undermined the institutional order on which they hoped to erect a more stable and rational democracy, a "non-partisan" framework of regulation and social welfare built on voluntary organizations and government institutions that presumably enabled ordinary people to participate in social reform and political management without resorting to violence, rebellion or revolution to resolve their differences. But, as Rogin points out, this liberal presumption of democratic governance within each organization was a mere convenience. In such cases, nonpartisanship served as a guise behind which bureaucratic leadership exercised undemocratic authority—a latter-day example of Robert Michels's "iron law of oligarchy."[21]

Some of these organizations, moreover, were the ones the communist left was active in throughout the Depression era—notably teachers unions, student and parent associations, and the institutions that those organizations acted in, such as schools and universities—in extended and bitter contests over the democratic character of those bodies—exactly the matter, as Rogin pointed out for the postwar era, that liberals took for granted. It is those organizations and institutions, and the growing conflicts within them over the meaning and practice of democracy, which this book explores as it reconstructs the history and genealogy of Rapp-Coudert.

From the point of view of communists who were active in trade unions or school reform in the 1930s, at stake in this struggle was the future of a real economic democracy, as well as the ability of unions and related organizations to represent working-class interests effectively as matters of "class struggle," rather than just the particular interests of this or that social group. From the point of view of liberals trying to build a framework in which social groups could negotiate particular needs and common interests, these disputes over the meaning of democracy and the measure of class conflict, promoted by partisans of the "extreme left," merely disrupted the orderly deliberations on which a modern democracy must be founded. For those institutions to function the way liberals wanted and expected them to, Rogin pointed out, stubbornly dissenting voices had to be excluded, demonized, and expelled, much as Native Americans had to be pushed from the western landscape before Europeans could take it over. And this countersubversive imperative is exactly what drove liberals, who were committed at the height of the Depression to building a pluralist society and regulatory state out of the wreckage of the American economy, to endorse, guide and even direct the Rapp-Coudert inquiry. Thus, in 1940 at least, organized and official anticommunism, rather than merely a conservative pretext for attacking liberal achievements served also as a means of purging inconveniently dissenting voices from supposedly democratic pluralistic organizations and institutions, such as unions and schools, on which many liberals expected to erect a stable and prosperous political order.[22]

In key respects, the Rapp-Coudert version of the red scare, what its opponents at the time aptly called "Coudertism," after Rapp-Coudert committee chair Frederic R. Coudert, Jr., emerged from an already well-formed liberal intellectual and political movement, which had been building over the previous ten years and which had already put communists in its sights by the middle years of the Depression. Among those abetting Coudertism, one could find liberal, socialist, and social-democratic labor leaders, including former officers and activists of the teachers union and functionaries of the AFL. They were joined (as early as 1935) by insurgent reformers headquartered at Columbia Teachers College and guided by the progressive educational theories of John Dewey. When one puts the Rapp-Coudert drama in its proper historical context, one sees that prominent liberals played a surprisingly central role as ideological guides and mouthpieces for a new kind of liberal anticommunism that was expressed in Coudertism. One sees as well the truth of historian Ellen Schrecker's recent observation that there were "many McCarthyisms," conservative, liberal, and left-wing, whose diversity of approaches to anticommunism helped ensure its durability and virulence.[23]

This historical association of liberals with anticommunism, extending back into the Depression years, confounds yet another conventional view—of liberals as reluctant latecomers who acquiesced to conservative pressure for action as they came to recognize that the Soviets posed a real threat, whether after the war or in the wake of the 1936 Moscow Trials and the 1939 Hitler-Stalin Pact.[24] Once again, Rapp-Coudert suggests a more complicated story, and once again the chronology is important: Liberals and conservative socialists (many of whom would later call themselves "social democrats") crusaded against communist teachers as early as 1932, when the former first attempted to purge the latter from the New York local of the AFT. That conflict led to a split in 1935 and the founding of an explicitly anticommunist union that spent the next five years trying to destroy its left-wing rivals. Anticommunism in the schools and teachers unions, then, preceded the Moscow Trials by several years, finding support in liberal intellectual circles as early as 1934.

My point is not to deny the trials and the pact as contributing factors, but rather to reconsider the way in which we recount the history of liberal anticommunism as a story of collective apostasy that privileges the influence of foreign affairs. As other historians have recently made clear, anticommunism between the world wars flowed in part from liberal and social-democratic currents in the American labor movement. Moreover, one finds in those early expressions of anticommunism much of the extremist rhetoric and many of the methods from which later liberals such as Bell, trying to distance themselves from a political phenomenon at least in part of their own creation, blamed primarily on "pseudo-conservative" populists such as Joe McCarthy. By the time in 1950 when McCarthy, before an audience in Wheeling, West Virginia, waved his list of two hundred or so alleged Communists in the State Department, the anticommunist crusade was already more than a decade and a half old, and part of it was decidedly liberal and social democratic in origin.

Thus, the story of Rapp-Coudert underscores the extent to which liberals actively developed and promoted late twentieth-century anticommunism, which we tend exclusively to associate with the extreme right as "McCarthyism." For Americans accustomed to thinking of liberals as communist sympathizers, such an observation might seem to violate common sense. In part, that misperception follows from the confused definition of "liberal" in American political culture, which tends to lump all parts of the left—communist, socialist, social democratic, and liberal—together under the rubric "liberal," as generically the politics favoring state ownership and regulation of large parts of a mixed economy. One point of this study is to end that loose association of a generic left under the terms "liberal" and "progressive," commonplaces that served the temporary rhetorical strategies during the 1930s of both the liberal New Deal and the communist Popular Front against fascism. Whatever alliances there were between liberals and the left already had begun to come apart, however, in the middle of the Depression. After the war, these terms served instead to mark the boundaries of a supposedly rational discourse from which communists and much of the Marxist left were excluded. As I use the term in this book, "liberal" will mean those advocates of limited state ownership and regulation who accept the basic terms of capitalist economic relations, disavow the politics of class and mass mobilization, and think of American political culture as uniquely pluralistic, bipartisan, and capable of negotiating and solving social and economic differences through democratic deliberation and reform. That definition includes conservative socialists and social democrats (and some ex-communists) that came to call themselves "liberal" after the war, as they increasingly distanced themselves from Marxism, communism, and more radically militant forms of socialism. As I hope this study will show, the direction by liberals of the Rapp-Coudert inquisition not only marks the fundamental ideological incompatibility of liberalism and communism; it also suggests a deeper and more complicated origin for McCarthyism in American political culture with roots not only in conservative hostility to government spending and market regulation, but also in a chronic distemper over the very thing that liberals hold closest to their hearts: the democratic tradition.

Nor am I blaming liberals for a historical phenomenon driven by many historical forces. Rather, I would argue that the growing hostility of liberal intellectuals toward communism, besides the obvious and oft-cited ideological incompatibilities, followed from their investment in building a pluralist democracy based on the sorts of interest groups that were conceived by people such as David Truman and criticized by Michael Rogin. That sort of pluralism could not tolerate the political style, practices, and beliefs of Communists, who, while they espoused a democratic socialism (in the

Popular Front period at least) conceived of democracy in agonistic terms and thought of social progress as necessarily tied to unavoidable class antagonism at odds with the negotiation of interests among presumptively democratic organizations and institutions.

Key liberals strenuously objected to this "class war view," as they became attached to an emerging social and political order that they uniquely if only dimly perceived. Dewey, who is considered an intellectual leader of the new state-oriented form of liberalism and who joined other liberals in resigning from Local 5 in 1935, summed up the pluralist objections to Communist Party activism in the union and in the Popular Front against fascism, as it unfolded from 1934 on. The "dogma" about class struggle, he asserted in his influential 1935 manifesto, *Liberalism and Social Action*, "generates violent strife" because it fails "to bring the conflict into the light of intelligence where the conflicting interests can be adjudicated in behalf of the interest of the great majority."[25]

In their dedication to this "class war" dogma, Dewey argued, communists (of all the several types active in the mid-1930s) inevitably practice misrepresentation, subterfuge and other forms of "bad faith," as they make themselves appear to be responsible participants in democratic deliberations over common concerns. As his protégé Sidney Hook famously declared, communists instead enter into schools and unions in a "Trojan horse," planning subversion and conquest, lying about their true intentions and, as individuals, about their membership in communist organizations. Hook insisted and Dewey and others agreed that by acting in bad faith, communists disqualified themselves from being teachers or even members of ostensibly democratic organizations, which they, like David Truman, considered to be the pillars of a modern pluralism. Liberal anticommunists returned to communist bad faith as the primary rationale for purging communists from schools and universities. As it pursued Communist Party members in New York's educational system, the Rapp-Coudert committee followed suit, invoking Dewey and other liberals in justifying its inquisition.[26]

One could argue as well that the prospects of a growth economy and the hope of realizing its potential—a dream partially realized during and after the war—helped split liberals decisively from the Marxist left. As historian Athan Theoharis long ago pointed out, during the McCarthy era proper, anticommunist liberals such as historian Arthur Schlesinger, Jr., whose 1949 book *The Vital Center* offered a manifesto of centrist, anticommunist liberalism, found in the mixed economy already emerging at the end of the 1930s, "the dual advantage of ensuring prosperity and providing the means to avoid class conflict ... through economic growth," as the war economy spread employment and consumer confidence across the nation.[27] When the Rapp-Coudert committee opened its public hearings in December 1940, the United States was on the cusp of that new social and political reality. Though few could imagine at the time, the economic revival evident on the streets and in the workplaces of New York City that Christmas season prefigured a postwar economy based on high wages, an expanding and increasingly homogenous, middle-class consumer culture, moderate forms of state regulation, conciliatory labor relations, open international markets, and a reliable source of permanent demand from the military.

Some Additional Thoughts

As I am sure readers are well aware, the study of anticommunism is riddled with controversy and conflict. Conservatives, along with many liberals, who consider the occasional excesses of anticommunist crusades to be the price of defending liberty and democracy, might ask of this book: why criticize an investigation that was justified on its face and that exposed actual members of the Communist Party subverting the nation's schools and universities? Many find confirmation of this view, moreover, in the fact that some members of the Communist Party engaged in an active conspiracy to spy on behalf of the Soviet Union, a long-standing accusation reinforced in the late 1990s by the declassification of the United States military's VENONA files, which uncovered ongoing communications between Soviet handlers and their operatives in the United States. Even before VENONA, it would have been hard to deny the evidence that some members of the American Communist Party engaged in espionage for the Soviets during the 1930s, 1940s, and 1950s.[28]

Yet one must put the Soviet use of a few Communists as spies in proper historical perspective: Of the tens of thousands of Americans who passed through the ranks of the Communist Party between 1919 and 1989, no more than a couple of hundred have been plausibly accused of spying.[29] For the vast majority, the motives for joining the party were entirely consistent with American political values and constitutional law. They were subversive, perhaps, but only in the broadest (and healthiest) sense, not in a manner that is contrary to a robust conception of American democracy—of the sort endorsed by most of the nation's founders, who not only allowed for but encouraged political dissent. Those few historians who have documented the political activism of the party's rank and file have reconstructed a very different picture of American communism than one sees in the VENONA files, showing instead how tens of thousands of Communists actively contributed to the growth of American democracy in the civil rights and labor movements, and even eventually in the pursuit of gender equality.[30] Such was also the case in the New York City schools, where Communist teachers enhanced rather than undermined American education, promoting both a broader, more egalitarian curriculum with an emphasis on the social and natural sciences, and progressive pedagogies that broke down the rigid authoritarianism and racism of prevailing instructional practices.[31]

A similar perspective needs to be gained about the fact that many Communists lied to federal and state investigators when asked about their party membership, which for many Americans seemed to confirm the complicity of the accused in Soviet spying. If Communists had nothing to hide, why lie? As it did in 1941, such misrepresentation seemed to many to be symptomatic of a politics of bad faith and deceit, suggesting a broad, party-based conspiracy as well as disloyalty to American values and institutions. But, once we shed the tunnel vision of VENONA and broaden our view of communism's history, the misrepresentation and perjury of Communists before the bar of justice and in the court of public opinion begin to look much more mundane, as examples of what ordinary people do when they are framed and boxed in by hostile inquisitors.

As for accusations such as Sidney Hook's that Communist teachers used their classrooms to indoctrinate students, virtually none of the teachers and staff under investigation by Rapp-Coudert used the city's schools and colleges to promote communism or even just Marxism. One's judgment on this question depends in part on what one means by "indoctrination." If, as some insisted, any point of view that challenged moral, educational, or political conventions amounted to "indoctrination," then yes, Communists, like many dissenters, tended to teach their students to think for themselves and to challenge authority. But if what was meant by indoctrination was teaching Communist doctrine, then the Rapp-Coudert investigation turned up no substantial evidence of Communists indoctrinating students, though that did not stop the committee and the press from making those accusations and using them to justify dismissing professors and staff at the municipal colleges. In the chapters that follow, the evidence (or lack of it) concerning "Communist indoctrination" will speak for itself.

One additional point needs to be added here, and it is one that gets to the heart of the book's argument. Many Americans express remorse at the excesses of McCarthyism, but only to the extent that it was an overblown and indiscriminate reaction to a real threat—that its objectives were good, while only its methods were a problem. To the degree that McCarthyism did any damage, from this perspective (for the most part a liberal one, though many conservatives and libertarians agree), it was mainly to the constitutional protection of civil liberties and to the liberal practices of an open society that is predicated on the protection of individual rights.[32] Similarly, much of the indignation over McCarthyism focuses on the personal costs of political repression, the loss of jobs and careers, imprisonment, the breakup of families, and the exclusion from public life that were suffered by the accused.

There is no question that legislative inquisitions such as Rapp-Coudert and broader campaigns after the war posed a substantial threat to civil liberties. One merely has to read through the committee's own record to see rights violated profoundly and repeatedly. Aided by municipal law, the committee forced New York City employees to incriminate themselves, stripping them of protection under the Fifth Amendment to the Constitution. Demanding membership lists of the teachers unions and using them to flush out suspects, the Rapp-Coudert inquisition made association evidence of guilt, violating the fundamental principle of the First Amendment defending one's right of assembly. Using signatures on petitions to harangue witnesses into confessing Communist sympathies or party membership also violated the First Amendment protection of the right to free speech. One can read the effects of such actions in the cowed and terrified testimony of former party members brought before Coudert's and later tribunals, even some of the best and most resolute champions in earlier campaigns for social justice or against international fascism. Or in the many ruined careers and broken families among the committee's targets.

Yet, however damaging these violations were to the Constitution and however much individuals suffered from them, I would argue that even more important was the loss of the communist tradition itself; its exclusion from public life and from those institutions like the university, the school, and the trade union in which the vocabulary of political debate is forged severely compromised our ability in the United States to conceive of and practice a real democracy.

There is of course much more to say about Rapp-Coudert than will be recounted in this study, and I gladly point the reader to other works, including those that explore "Little Red Scares" elsewhere. While I conceived this book as a basic history of the Coudert inquisition, grounded in a systematic reading of the committee's records, I am especially interested in what that history reveals about the gravitational pull that anticommunism exerted on American political culture through the late twentieth century. I have constructed the book accordingly, around the practical and ideological attachment of liberals to the investigation. The first section of the book (Chapters 1 through 4) starts with Rapp-Coudert's public debut on that cold December morning when the committee held its first open hearings into communist subversion at BC (Chapters 1 and 2), moves on to recall the political struggle the previous year leading to the probe's authorization by the state legislature (Chapter 3), and finishes with an appraisal of the hand liberals such as Windels had in the investigation (Chapter 4). The second section of the book is a flashback to the early 1930s and the origins of the probe, as the Depression heightened conflicts over schooling in New York City, deepening already-strong hostilities that pitted liberals and social democrats in the teachers union against teacher-activists involved in the growing communist movement. Chapter 5 recounts the history of the Dewey Trial, an internal investigation of communists in the New York City local of the AFT in April 1933, an event that foreshadowed later anticommunist probes, introduced the liberal notion of communist "bad faith," and figured prominently in the Coudert investigation and its deliberations, as the Coudert staff traced the history of subversion in the municipal colleges and schools back to that conflict in the union. Chapters 6 and 7 explore the ideological and political differences between liberal reformers of education such as Dewey and his followers at Columbia University, and communist activists who "democratized" the municipal colleges, introducing tenure and faculty governance into a system run capriciously by New York's political machine, Tammany Hall.

Part III returns to the immediate context of the Coudert probe, with Chapter 8 recounting the campaign begun by liberals in 1935 to oust communists from the AFT and AFL, culminating in the 1939 coup against the left at the AFT national convention. Chapter 9 chronicles the Coudert investigation's next and most sensational phase, which unfolded in spring 1941—namely, the probe of communist activism at CCNY that forced out dozens of faculty and staff from the municipal colleges. Chapter 10 pauses to evaluate accusations that anti-Semitism motivated the Coudert committee. Chapter 11 assesses the real motives behind the investigation—that rather than merely judging the "bad faith" of alleged communists in hiding their political affiliations, Coudertism put communism itself on trial, while lying about its intentions—a consummate act of *liberal* bad faith.

Chapter 12 traces the aftermath of the investigation. The study concludes with its legacy for the history of McCarthyism and for the political culture of postwar America.

A Note on Terminology

Some terminological ambiguities in the history of American communism have led me to use a couple of spelling conventions in this study. When speaking of members of the Communist Party of the United States, I have capitalized the word "Communist." However, there were other political and labor activists, intellectuals, and writers in related parties—including, for instance, the followers of Jay Lovestone and Leon Trotsky—who laid claim to that label, especially in the early years of the Depression. As former members of the official Communist Party, Trotskyists and Lovestoneites (as they were also called) shared much in common in theory and practice with their former comrades, and were regularly lumped together with them as versions of the same un-Americanism by conservative and liberal opponents. Together with members of the Communist Party, they form the category "communists" (without capitalization). The general political theory derived from the theories of Karl Marx through the experience of the Bolshevik Revolution, regardless of the party to which it was attached in the United States, I am calling "communism" (without capitalization). The official doctrines of the Communist Party, whether originating in the Soviet Union or in the United States, I will identify as just that—"official doctrines." Obviously, since politics is often the art of misrepresentation, such terminological vagaries can never be fully sorted out.

As for the relation of individuals to various parties, that is an evidentiary rather than lexical question. I have tried to be as specific as possible when discussing the association of any particular person with the Communist Party or any other party for that matter. While the grounds used by Coudert's committee to establish membership in the Communist Party were not completely irresponsible, because of what I know about the committee's methods I cannot consider them reliable. Unless membership was acknowledged freely—perhaps even under oath—and under what might be considered noncoercive circumstances, I will address someone's party membership as a matter of relative probability.

PART I
The Hearings

> Make no mistake about it. The Soviet invasion of the United States has already taken place.
>
> —*Martin Dies,* The Trojan Horse in America *(1940)*

1
The Threshold

When the Rapp-Coudert hearings opened in December, the front pages of the daily newspapers were filled with accounts of dogfights over England, German submarines sinking British merchant ships, and the Greek army routing the Italians in Albania.[1] A whole new kind of war was unfolding across the Atlantic, riveting public attention. Even Ralph Ingersoll's politically sophisticated progressive weekly *PM* fixated on events at the front, discussing such details of combat as the relative merits of British and German fighter planes. The public hearings on subversion in the schools, scheduled for the afternoon of Monday, December 2, would have to reach a comparable pitch to attract the attention of a public sated on sensation. Thanks to Paul Windels, the Rapp-Coudert committee's chief of staff, they did.

It was Windels, a liberal Republican, who set the public hearings on their course for the next three days, and he, with a young and largely liberal staff, shaped the entire investigation. His role in the process underscores how mistaken the assumption is that the repression we call "McCarthyism" was a right-wing movement on which liberals merely tagged along in the chill of the Cold War. These proceedings were run and supported by liberal reformers who well before 1940 had acquired a stake in repressing communism.

In many respects, this public role suited Windels perfectly. Fifty-five years old, born and bred in Brooklyn, Paul Windels was "a tall, stocky man, with thinning graying hair atop a strong head."[2] By 1940 he was a prominent fixture in New York City politics. Now he is largely forgotten. Like many of the era's reform-minded Republicans, he had impeccable liberal credentials. He was a key player in the bipartisan Fusion movement that had been attempting since the 1890s to depose the Tammany Hall political machine, which had run city government like a cash box since before the Civil War. Windels earned his reputation in part by managing the electoral campaigns of celebrated reform mayor Fiorello La Guardia, beginning with his unsuccessful run for president of the New York City Board of Aldermen in 1919. A solid loyalist, Windels masterminded La Guardia's successful bid for Congress the next year by mobilizing Italian and other ethnic voters in East Harlem and effectively maneuvering financial support from the national GOP. After that, according to Windels's son, the two "were absolutely inseparable."[3] Windels stuck with the "Little Flower" through congressional, city council, and mayoral campaigns, and he and his family remained close friends with the La Guardias (they vacationed together at adjacent homes in Westport, Connecticut, and shared spaghetti dinners) until a falling out over the Mayor's support for Franklin Delano Roosevelt in the 1940 presidential elections.[4] When La Guardia took over city hall in 1934, Windels agreed to serve as his first corporation counsel (the city's chief lawyer), sweeping the accumulation of grafters and Tammany drones out of the office of legal affairs and shaping La Guardia's legislative agenda in Albany, including the rewriting of the city charter in 1936. "The housecleaning was swift and complete," Windels recalled of his initial impact as corporation counsel. "Even the offices themselves were filthy and had to be cleaned."[5] Windels also had a major hand in building New York City's transportation infrastructure, and thus its modern geography, a rival to the more notorious (and more powerful) Robert Moses, whom he opposed in GOP and Fusion circles. In this role, Windels crafted the landmark legislation and interstate agreements that enabled the construction of the Holland Tunnel and the creation of the Port Authority in the 1920s.[6]

Once teachers-union attorney William Mulligan had been ejected from the courtroom, Windels launched into his opening statement. High-minded from the start, he assured the public the investigation would not be a smear campaign; it would have none of the indiscriminate naming of suspects on the basis of "gossip, rumor or hearsay" that had been seen in earlier antisubversive investigations such as those run by the Dies committee in Washington, D.C. In the two years of its existence, Congressman Martin Dies's investigation had acquired a reputation for making reckless and unsubstantiated charges against suspected Communists and fascists. Thanks in part to Dies, the threat of communism had been in the national news for most of that year, from the indictment and prosecution of Communist Party leader Earl Browder to FBI raids on party offices in February to the passage of the Smith Act in June. Unlike the grandstanding coming out of Washington, D.C., however, the Rapp-Coudert investigation would operate under "self-imposed limitations" that would allow it "to proceed with complete objectivity." Windels insisted that it would "present only such evidence as may be relevant by legal standards" and "only such evidence as would be accepted in a court of law."[7]

Yet beneath this respectable façade, Windels also harbored a penchant for the theatrical and a reputation for suddenly shifting gears to drive home an argument in a sensationalistic prosecutorial style.[8] While in one breath, he promised to "refrain from making charges in the public press," in the next Windels offered a "résumé" of the committee's accusations against the Communist Party and the teachers suspected of belonging to it, knowing full well that his remarks would appear in the evening papers. "In the case of the pupils," Windels asserted (on the basis of as-yet undisclosed evidence), "the Communist lends the aid of his counsel and guidance to the task of organizing them for the class struggle." As its "basic creed," communism advocated "a forcible and violent revolution by the workers to overthrow the existing form of government." Communists advance that goal by "fostering discontent" through "strategically located members" including those who sought "to undermine American youth by spreading its alien and subversive principles among them."[9]

Windels's performance won over the press. Quoting him at length the next day, a *New York Times* editorial endorsed his management of the investigation. He "could easily have entered on a typical 'Red hunt,'" the editors noted. Instead he was "willing to draw the line between 'the right of private political beliefs,' which cannot be interfered with in a democratic society, and 'improper methods of political action,' which no democratic society can tolerate, least of all in its schools." Windels aimed "properly" at those who "inject communism 'into their teaching at the least risk of exposure'" and "conduct struggles around the schools in a truly Bolshevik manner."[10] For the editors of the *Times*, First Amendment rights of speech and association did not take precedence in cases such as this one, even when the association and speech in question belonged to a political party as legal as the Republicans and the Democrats. The line was drawn, they argued, at the schoolhouse door. Moreover, the *Times* approved the principle on which Windels would rest much of his inquiry— that in practicing bad faith, Communists lost the protection of the First Amendment. As Windels declared in his introduction, "there is no civil liberty to commit a breach of trust; there is no academic freedom to be

24 The Hearings

one thing and pretend to be something else; there is no freedom in this country to poison the rising generation in the name of any political philosophy which practices hypocrisy and deception, as a part of its central and vital doctrine."[11]

The accused teachers, however, were hardly reassured, especially as Windels flagrantly exposed suspects and presented the investigation's findings as foregone conclusions before the public hearings had even taken place. They, their union, and that small part of the press that backed them not surprisingly viewed the conduct of the hearings with dismay. Later that first afternoon, incensed by his treatment at the hands of the committee and shocked by the license Windels was taking with civil liberties, Mulligan described the proceedings as a "totalitarian way of trial." It was a "star chamber proceeding," declared teachers-union president Charles Hendley during his interrogation the following day.[12] Windels was conducting a trial without trial procedure and without constitutional restraint, whose judgments would have real consequences: teachers could be suspended or fired for what was said in the hearings, and yet they would not have the opportunity to defend themselves properly against their accusers, even as those accusations appeared in the daily press. "Despite a pious preliminary statement by Windels that he would rigorously exclude from testimony anything except evidence permissible in a court of law," wrote Simon Gerson in the Communist-affiliated weekly *New Masses*, "everything except the proverbial kitchen sink has been tossed into the record.... Far from following the laws of evidence, the committee has permitted surmise, guess, estimate, and hearsay."[13]

Even though Gerson was right, Windels acted within his constitutional authority as it was understood at the time. The Rapp-Coudert investigation was a legislative inquiry, authorized to gather information that supported the writing of more effective laws, among other things. Until the 1960s, when the Supreme Court began imposing stronger constitutional guidelines, such investigations operated with great latitude, which Windels used freely and effectively. He could subpoena witnesses and documents. He could compel those witnesses to testify under threat of punishment (for contempt of the state legislature if they refused). He could indirectly threaten them with prosecution for perjuring themselves under oath. He could deny them the counsel of a lawyer while he was interrogating them. He could draw conclusions from their testimony and make those conclusions public, even though those findings were still, from a legal perspective, mere allegations. Almost the only thing Windels and the Rapp-Coudert committee could not do was convict a suspect of a statutory crime (that is, a crime other than contempt) and impose a punishment on him or her, something allowed only within the powers of a properly constituted court.[14]

At the same time, this lack of judicial authority worked to Windels's advantage. He could, as he did, profess respect for trial procedure and rules of evidence, yet he did not have to observe any trial rules at all. And he in fact did not. To be sure, Windels and his staff—a group of young lawyers, some recently out of law school, others with substantial legal and investigative experience—superficially followed something resembling courtroom process. And Windels conducted the kind of investigation one would expect to find in a well-run district attorney's office, by collecting an enormous amount of evidence that would eventually find its way into legal proceedings of one sort or another, including trials and Supreme Court reviews. At its core were a series of interviews and private depositions collected and methodically organized over sixteen months by staff members who were following leads on communist activities in the schools and colleges and in the teachers unions that represented New York City faculty and staff. The committee would disclose many of those findings in the series of public hearings that started that afternoon and ended the following year, and in a series of reports prepared for the state legislature and released to the press through 1942.

All the trappings of courtroom procedure and decorum, however, were merely superficial. And for the teachers and their union, the effects of the investigation were catastrophic: by the time the Rapp-Coudert committee was done, dozens of municipal college faculty and staff as well as a handful of public-school teachers had been fired or forced to resign because of alleged association with the Communist Party or their unwillingness to disavow it. Additionally, the investigation crippled the unions that represented those teachers by vilifying them in the press as "communist dominated" and by coordinating that attack with a successful campaign to throw the New York City locals out of the American Federation of Teachers (AFT), which represented teachers nationally and in the American Federation of Labor (AFL). And while many of those teachers and their unions had some sort of day in court by being run through the Board of Higher Education's (BHE) judicial process (required in the dismissal of tenured faculty), it was the Rapp-Coudert inquiry, unrestricted by courtroom rules and almost completely indifferent to constitutional rights, that really put them on trial.

Public Opinion

Windels did observe the rules of one powerful court—the court of public opinion. He set very strict guidelines on the conduct of the inquiry, not to insure rights were protected or even to guarantee convictions would be upheld, but in order to manage the investigation's public relations effectively, the political influences on its outcome, and the political impact of its judgments. It was those measures that the accused teachers and their supporters, communist or not, came especially to resent.

In putting the manipulation of public opinion at the core of his strategy, Windels followed his mentor, Judge Samuel Seabury, who led the liberal and bipartisan reform movement that installed La Guardia in the mayor's office seven years earlier. A follower of the radical economist Henry George, Seabury won a city court judgeship in 1901, eventually sitting on both the New York Supreme Court (the lowest of the state courts at the time, despite its name) and the state court of appeals, from which he resigned to run unsuccessfully for governor in 1916.[15] He then largely stayed out of the political limelight until 1930, when then-governor Franklin Delano Roosevelt appointed him to deal with a corruption scandal in New York City's court system. Seabury reestablished his reputation as a reformer in those investigations, going on to run as a dark horse candidate against FDR for the Democratic Party's presidential nomination in 1932, then helping to resurrect the Fusion movement that elected La Guardia in 1933 from constituencies spread across all the major parties. Thereafter he concentrated on other aspects of municipal reform—notably, the unification of the New York subway lines under municipal ownership.[16]

Seabury's inquiry cracked open the rotten machinery of Tammany Hall, which had bought and sold public offices in Manhattan and the surrounding boroughs for decades. Running from 1930 through 1932, the Seabury Commission's work began with an inquiry into the city's Magistrates Courts (its lowest judicial body), many of which were run by judges not much more observant of the law than were the political hacks and thugs lodged in the Democratic Party clubs throughout the city that formed Tammany's field of operations. While the initial impetus for the investigation was the association of the courts with organized crime, the most alarming element of the court's corruption was its use by policemen and their informers to shake down innocent citizens, many of them women, by falsely accusing them of crimes such as prostitution and then dragging them before cooperating judges to buy back their freedom (and, less reliably, their reputations). The Seabury Commission shifted focus the following year to the Manhattan District Attorney's office and then to the overwhelmingly popular Mayor Jimmy Walker, elected with the support of the Tammany machine in 1925.[17]

Like Windels's investigation, Seabury's was a legislative inquiry without the judicial authority of courtroom trials, but with none of the restrictions, either. Unlike previous legislative probes, Seabury's also had additional coercive means at its disposal. Tammany had for years evaded the cleansing action of Progressive reform, and through the 1920s it continued to run the city like a gambling house. Until the 1929 crash brought down the speculative frenzy of the previous decade along with the fortunes of middle-class Americans, Tammany enjoyed widespread support from a public willing to tolerate a little corruption if some of the profits returned to them as the patronage and informal services that the machine spread through city neighborhoods.[18] Such support was evident at the polls and invested in figures such as Walker, a flamboyantly corrupt yet charming man of the people, who spent more time on Broadway in the company of beautiful women than in the mayor's office. The Depression, however, wore out public tolerance for graft and inefficiency not to mention outright criminality and violence, and liberal reformers found that by 1930 their demands for action gained traction among economically distressed New Yorkers. Meanwhile, FDR, considering a bid for the presidency and weighed down like most New York Democrats by his electoral dependency on the city's Tammany kingpins, wanted a high-profile housecleaning. So, Seabury devised an approach that appeared high-minded and reasonable yet, at the same time, used public sentiment to exert considerable pressure on witnesses who, despite the fact that they were not yet officially being accused of crimes, were widely considered criminals.[19]

Seabury understood that in dealing with Tammany Hall, he would need to overcome the machine's influence in the courts and police precincts as well as the sway of its graft and patronage. And he expected the usual evasions of Tammany figures on the witness stand. To increase his leverage over them, he first deposed witnesses under oath in private hearings, where they would be less conscious of public reaction to what they said and unaware how their statements would figure into Seabury's line of inquiry or the relationship they would have to the revelations of others. He would then use the private statements to box witnesses into admissions of guilt or culpability in public hearings, at which all of the evidence would be at Seabury's disposal and none of it available to the

28 The Hearings

witnesses themselves. So that the witnesses, who had practiced lives of criminal conspiracy as they ran the affairs of the city, could not compare notes, Seabury's staff kept the private transcripts locked away in a safe in the commission's office, unavailable even to committee members. Seabury was further aided in his investigation when, in 1931, he and FDR pushed through the state legislature a bill that allowed Seabury to force waivers of immunity on public employees (which included most Tammany grafters) so that they could no longer avoid answering questions by invoking their Fifth Amendment right against self-incrimination.[20] While such laws were questionable even at the time, they remained on the books until the 1960s.

These were the sorts of measures considered necessary for dealing with criminal conspiracies like Tammany's. And they succeeded. Seabury's investigation crippled the machine, forcing Walker out of office with sensational revelations of bribes taken in exchange for signing private bus and trolley contracts. It seemed common sense to apply Seabury's successful methods to investigate Communist activities, since many viewed the party as a similar sort of conspiracy.[21] Moreover, as he had to operate in a setting controlled by the state legislature, Windels also had to deal with the machinations of rival Republicans and Democrats on the committee, including, in the latter case, assemblymen and senators with ties to the still-functioning Tammany organization. While both of the major parties shared hostility toward communists and other socialist parties and organizations, the Democrats especially did not want their rivals to gain political advantage from the investigations. Those rivals included adherents of the anti-Tammany Fusion movement such as Windels and La Guardia, whose control of city government recently had been undercut by Tammany's triumph (after eight years of declining fortunes) in the 1939 city-council elections.[22]

To fend off such interference, Windels demanded, as terms of his appointment, arrangements that were modeled on the Seabury Commission. Like Seabury, Windels carefully guarded evidence and set strict limits on conduct and decorum. A single representative from the larger legislative committee generally would preside in the private hearings so that staff would not be outnumbered by legislators. Senators and assemblymen attended the private depositions only "by invitation" from staff. All transcripts from the private hearings would be controlled by Windels and only made available to the elected committee members at his discretion, and then very rarely. In this way, Windels could minimize political obstruction by officials who might have reasons to help specific witnesses evade scrutiny by, for instance, leaking private transcripts to the press. Nor would those transcripts be released to witnesses, who would not be allowed to have lawyers or advocates of any sort present in the private interrogations or the public hearings. At the public hearings, all interrogation was run by Windels and his senior staff without interruption from committee members. Any questions from committee members had to be approved by him beforehand. Only Windels would be allowed to call witnesses, and no "third parties" would be allowed to participate. Nor was evidence used in the public interrogations to be released to witnesses or accused teachers. Once entered into the public record, it either appeared in the committee reports or was sequestered in the committee's voluminous files.[23] Like Seabury, Windels could also deny many witnesses the protection of the Fifth Amendment. In the aftermath of the Seabury investigations, the City of New York revised its charter to require that all public employees cooperate with legislative and similar investigations. To this end, Windels asked teachers, professors, and staff at the public schools and municipal colleges to sign waivers of immunity before testifying.

When William Mulligan voiced his objections at the public hearings, he had in mind the basic framework of legislative investigations as well as the many restrictions and requirements Windels imposed on this particular one. Ironically, Mulligan earlier had prominently advocated (in a *Columbia Law Review* article cowritten with Seabury) amplifying the power of legislative committees, largely because of his experience serving as one of "Seabury's boys," the young lawyers on the staff of the Seabury Commission.[24] But by 1940, Mulligan clearly had changed his mind, finding Windels's treatment of witnesses potentially unconstitutional as well as contrary to the public sense of justice and decency. Hoping the public and the courts would support them, Mulligan advised the teachers not to testify in either the private or public hearings under the conditions set by Windels on grounds that Mulligan would have strongly rejected only a few years earlier. Many of the teachers followed this advice, leading to a series of court cases that dragged on for the next year. For some of them, that failure to cooperate led to their dismissals.

At the heart of Mulligan's objections was Windels's denial of legal counsel to witnesses called before the committee, his prohibition of any cross-examination and his tight control of evidence, especially the transcripts of the private depositions collected over the previous several months. As Mulligan well knew, legislative committees often proceeded without allowing witnesses to have immediate access to a lawyer (the witness could always talk to one before or after hearings or depositions), but it was a matter of discretion that to some extent depended upon the nature of the investigation and the status of the witness. Windels merely took advantage of the fact that the practice of excluding lawyers had not yet been explicitly challenged in the courts.[25] For his part, Windels justified the practice by likening legislative committees to grand juries, the investigative side of the American legal process in which a group of citizens are selected to decide whether there is enough evidence that a law has been broken to warrant bringing charges and going to trial. Normally, a grand jury deliberates without the presence of a defense lawyer—justified by the fact that no one has yet been accused of a crime. For the same reason, witnesses before grand juries are not questioned by any other legal advocates than the prosecution (acting for the state and the public), since there is as yet no defendant for whom a defense lawyer's advocacy is necessary. According to Windels, as in a grand jury, his committee would investigate whether there were grounds for believing a crime had been committed (in this case, some kind of subversion), and then the courts would take on the task of determining the guilt or innocence of specific individuals, at which point they would have the right to counsel, with all the other protections afforded defendants.[26]

But if Windels thought he was running a grand jury, Mulligan and others recognized that something else was going on. Those differences are instructive. First, as in all criminal proceedings, witnesses facing grand juries can invoke the Fifth Amendment protection against self-incrimination. In the Rapp-Coudert inquiry, teachers and other city employees could not, thanks to municipal and state law.[27] Second, grand juries are supposed to be secret, and necessarily so. Accusations and suspicions raised in them may not be warranted, and the case may never go to trial. In such instances, the collected evidence in principle never sees the light of day, and whoever is alleged to have committed a crime leaves with his record unchanged and his reputation intact. If the grand jury decides to indict a suspect, then the allegations are not revealed to the public until a trial is actually expected. At that point, other rules prevail, including allowing defendants all the protections of the law and the Constitution that are familiar elements of courtroom procedure: the defendant has the right to a lawyer who can challenge what is declared in court; the defense has the power to cross-examine any witness called to the stand; and whatever evidence the prosecution brings before the court (including previously secret grand-jury testimony) must be provided to the defense so it can prepare its case. The protection of an individual's rights in grand juries depends in large part upon their secrecy; once charges against a person are made public, his or her rights count upon, among other things, their equal access to the public forum—namely, the court—in which those charges are discussed. People accused of crimes depend as well upon the presumption of their innocence—that they can only be considered guilty if proven so in an open court of law. The presumption of innocence, moreover, applies not only to what is said in court, but also to what is said in public—that the newspapers, for instance, will treat an allegation of guilt as no more than that. Even with all of these protections that are afforded the accused in the courtroom, grand juries still have an inherent tendency toward constitutional abuse, largely because the secrecy to which they are sworn is often violated.[28]

Legislative inquiries, in contrast, are already public forums. Whatever they reveal enters into the public record, often damaging the reputations of the individuals and groups under investigation. This is one of the main reasons that they are constitutionally dangerous. As Mulligan reminded Coudert and his colleagues, "these teachers are no mere witnesses before your Committee. They are the very subject of the inquisition."[29] Though aware of this danger, both Seabury and Windels also understood that their investigative power depended on publicity. Seabury instructed his young staff on the virtues of unedited public testimony:

> There is more eloquence in the testimony of an illiterate witness telling of oppression suffered from legal processes than in the greatest sermon, editorial, or address ever written. Where preachers, editors, and lawyers have failed in arousing the public to a consciousness of unjust conditions these simple, unlearned witnesses will succeed.[30]

Similarly, the Coudert committee's success hinged on Windels's ability to expose Communists and their party to negative publicity. In part, Windels did this because membership in the Communist Party at that time was perfectly legal. The party published a daily newspaper, it held meetings openly, it ran candidates for public office, and it collected signatures for political campaigns. While the state and the federal government had laws against subversive activities, in early 1940 none of those laws yet specifically mentioned the Communist Party, and the party had explicitly distanced itself from the acts covered by those laws. Moreover, affiliation with political organizations such as the Communist Party was protected by the Constitution under the First Amendment rights of assembly and free speech. Clearly the state legislature, which had debated the subject for over twenty years, considered it part of the committee's job to determine not only whether laws had been broken, but also whether a new law was needed that would penalize actions not covered by existing criminal statutes. Coudert and Windels, for their part, wanted to convince the public, elected representatives, and other public officials that in fact the Communist Party and its members operated in a fashion that violated American democracy and that it should be proscribed.[31]

Yet it would have been one thing if the Rapp-Coudert hearings provided an open, many-sided discussion about the role of communists and the Communist Party in American politics. It was another to drag people before a public tribunal for crimes that did not yet exist in order to interrogate and threaten them about membership in a perfectly legal party. Mulligan and the teachers he represented understood the difference. "The totalitarian way of trial is not our way, certainly," he reminded the committee, alluding to the Soviet show trials held three years before. "We permit both sides to be heard. That is the democratic way of trial, and the only way we know. Counsel to your Committee makes up but one side. On the other side are 7,500 professors and teachers."[32] The investigation, in this sense, did not open debate but closed it. While Windels subpoenaed teachers accused of Communist subversion to testify at private and public hearings, he did not invite them to challenge those accusations in a timely fashion. And he would not provide a forum for lawyers such as Mulligan to question his line of argument, his witnesses' testimony, or his evidence.

Myths of Subversion

And there was an important reason why Windels did not want both sides of the story told: much of what he presented before the public was not true. Windels had sworn testimony that most of the people named as Communists by the committee indeed belonged to the party. And in many of those cases, the testimony was reliable. Quite a few Communists worked in New York City's public schools and municipal colleges; estimates range from a couple of hundred to a thousand out of well over thirty thousand faculty and staff. But the central piece of Windels's case against Communist teachers was not just that they were Communists, but that as Communists they subverted the educational system and indoctrinated students, fomenting rebellion among them as well as among their fellow teachers in order to serve the Communist Party's larger purpose of overthrowing the government of the United States. It was that claim that was false, a "countersubversive" myth. And once this myth was firmly established in the public mind as a bit of modern folklore, once the public had been convinced that Communist teachers indoctrinated their students and fomented student rebellion, one could easily argue that even though membership in the Communist Party was presently legal, it should not be. Or that, in the absence of more repressive laws, Communists at least should be denied employment as teachers.[33]

Not only was the evidence of indoctrination and subversion thin, but Windels almost certainly knew that it was. He had substantial documentation and testimony to the contrary that he never disclosed to the public or much less offered to Mulligan and the teachers as support for their side of the story, as he would in a real court of law.[34] Instead, Windels based his case on the poorly substantiated and fabricated testimony of a handful of witnesses and on a few Communist Party publications that, freely interpreted, seemed to preach subversion in educational institutions. With this evidence, much of it the "gossip, rumor or hearsay" that he disavowed in his opening statement, he proceeded to convince the public of the myth that subversive communist teachers endangered public education and threatened democratic government.

To take one example of how such countersubversive myth-making worked, the Communist Party text on which Windels and his staff primarily relied was a 1937 article written for *The Communist,* the party's journal of political theory and debate, by Richard Frank, the *nom de plume* of Francis Franklin, the former education director of the Young Communist League (YCL), the party's youth organization.[35] Windels asserted that Frank's text demonstrated that the Communist teacher is required to "inject Marxism and Leninism into the classroom while concealing his party affiliation," and that it was "the policy of the Communist Party to attempt to use the youth movement to bring young people into the class war." Heavily inflected with party rhetoric, Frank's essay certainly had the tone of a revolutionary document. And it did indeed interpret schooling in terms of class conflict and what Communists at the time understood as the relentless historical trend toward revolution. Windels cited the following offending passage as proof of the party's intention to plant ideologues in the classroom: "Only when teachers have really mastered Marxism-Leninism will they be able skillfully to inject it into their teachings at the least risk of exposure, and at the same time to conduct struggles around the schools in a truly Bolshevik manner."[36]

But as he selectively read sections of the essay into the record, Windels ignored its main point, which was to counsel teachers to cooperate with administrators, parents, and students to promote an educational system that would be most beneficial to working-class families and their children, including the child-centered curriculum favored at the time by mainstream progressive and liberal educators. Contrary to Windels's notion that Communists imposed class divisions on the educational system, Frank urged teachers to view administrators, students and parents as potential allies in the struggle to fund public schooling and give it a less authoritarian pedagogy. "There must be no mechanical analogy drawn between the class struggle of workers and capitalists on one side and of students and administrators on the other," Frank insisted.[37] The less mechanical approach to the educational crisis was a large part of what Frank meant by the "Marxist-Leninist" education that teachers were supposed to "inject" into schooling. Upon closer examination, Frank's pedagogical views appeared to be much closer to John Dewey's "child-centered" theories than to Marx's or Lenin's, both of whom (to the extent that they addressed pedagogy at all) tended to favor more-regimented forms of instruction. Frank also suggested that party goals would be served better if teachers organized the "already existing rebelliousness of students" in order to "guide and direct that spirit," giving it "definite and effective direction."[38] Far from fomenting rebellion for rebellion's sake, Frank's Communist program might even have been doing the public-school system a favor, taking the unbridled discontent of Depression-era students and constructively channeling it into such actions as demanding that the federal government provide more subsidies for in-school lunch and milk programs. While some of what Frank recommended did appear to fit the bill of "indoctrinating students," the specifics of a "Marxist-Leninist" approach to teaching were less threatening—compensating for "bourgeois omissions and distortions" in the curriculum "by means of discussion, brochures, etc."[39]

Frank's rhetoric surely threatened many who read or heard of it, but even if it were the case that the text in question or the handful of others cited by Windels counseled subversion by teachers, there was no clear evidence that any suspected teachers read such texts or followed their recommendations. Communist teachers interviewed by Windels's staff, including one open member of the party, either were unaware of Frank's essay or repudiated it, objecting that it had no relationship to the actual experience of teachers in American schools. Moreover, *The Communist* was not the most popular reading among party members, though they subscribed to it dutifully. Mulligan argued this point to no avail before the appellate courts. In the absence of cross-examination during the public hearings, such points could become part of the public record only with great difficulty. Instead, Windels effectively conveyed the impression to the public that Communist Party officials dictated a "party line" to public-school teachers through such organs as *The Communist* and the *Daily Worker*.⁴⁰

As we will see, however, it was with his star witness that Windels clinched the countersubversive myth that Communists infiltrated educational institutions to indoctrinate and foment rebellion. And he did so with the deviousness and misrepresentation that would become the hallmarks of the Rapp-Coudert inquiry.

2
The Stooge Grebanier

Suppose you describe the process or technique employed by your colleagues to interest you in the Communist Party." Bernard Grebanier nervously asked his interrogator to repeat the proposition. Described as "tall, fleshy, [and] dark," Grebanier occupied the witness stand for all of the first day of public testimony before the Rapp-Coudert Committee. He wrung his hands, knit his brow, and stared at the floor as Windels pried from him the names of alleged Communists among his fellow Brooklyn College (BC) professors. His foot jiggled. Grebanier's testimony would go on this way for the rest of the afternoon. Asked who recruited him to the party, Grebanier derided the naiveté and simplicity of the question: "Rather than say that I was asked by him to join the Party I will say that for him I signed a card of the Communist Party."[1]

Colleagues were not surprised to see Grebanier testifying against former comrades. The Communist teachers and their supporters considered him a coward and betrayer, a liar driven by self-interest. Some, largely as cover for their own misrepresentations, called him "emotionally disturbed" and "hysterical." Brooklyn's left-wing students labeled him a "stooge" of homegrown fascists such as Martin Dies for his public attacks on the Popular Front.[2] Simon Gerson, one of the best left-wing observers of the New York political scene at the time, recognized something more complex in Grebanier: "None of your vulgar gut-spilling a la Dies committee witnesses. The Grebanier performance had, as the dramatic critics say, restraint, point, counterpoint, the understatement of genius, the controlled passion of the artist attaining new heights."[3]

Hired into the BC English department in 1927 at the age of twenty-four, Grebanier specialized in Shakespeare and English poetry. He retired in the mid-1960s with a substantial resume of publications, some of them quite influential, and a strong reputation as an inspiring and entertaining teacher. Married to novelist and biographer Frances Winwar (whose first husband, V. J. Jerome, became the American Communist Party's cultural commissar), Grebanier maintained a close connection to New York's literary and theatrical community. His skills as a pianist were well known, though that reputation may just as well have been due to his equally well-known capacity for self-aggrandizement. Later in life, he directed off-Broadway Shakespeare revivals.[4] As a young man Grebanier kept a relatively low profile politically until he called the American Legion "a bunch of morons" in one of his classes. Forty years later, he was still proud that the Legion pressured the BC administration and the board of education (one of whose members was the head of the Kings County lodge) to have him fired.[5]

The Legion's campaign against Grebanier, which made the news, typified the relationship between BC and its surrounding community. Brooklyn had no public university instruction until 1926, when the city's newly established Board of Higher Education (BHE) opened extension courses for City and Hunter Colleges on several rented floors at Willoughby and Bridge streets a few blocks from Brooklyn's Borough Hall. That program was upgraded in 1930 to an independent institution, at the head of which the BHE installed William A. Boylan, who had served the public schools as an associate superintendent in charge of buildings. Harry Gideonse, his successor, regarded Boylan to be "a political appointee, without experience or academic qualifications." That judgment was not entirely fair. As someone who managed school construction for the entire system, Boylan presumably was well suited to one of his main tasks as president: moving BC from its rented space, which had quickly expanded to several buildings in the borough's downtown, onto its own campus. Boylan's reputation as a property administrator, however, was tarnished by allegations of real-estate "racketeering," in which the school system purchased land at inflated prices from Tammany loyalists.[6]

The new campus opened in fall 1937 on an abandoned golf course in Flatbush. The building project was heavily financed by Washington, D.C. and lubricated, according to some, by graft. A Tammany ally who counted Mayor Jimmy Walker, a former pupil, among his close friends, Boylan reportedly took referrals from the Brooklyn machine when faculty positions needed to be filled, appointing and promoting clearly unqualified people, including a politically connected switchboard operator with no teaching qualifications, an elementary school arithmetic teacher whom Boylan forced on the history department, and a Tammany hack who had already been fired from several other schools where he had abused and harangued students with obscenities and racial slurs to the point that everyone except the American Legion agreed he had to be dismissed. According to Grebanier, who called Boylan's presidency a "silent reign of terror," members of the BHE took bribes for arranging faculty appointments through the president's office, which had absolute authority over departmental hiring. Faculty at BC consequently did not hold their president in very high regard. Nor did BC's Communists, who spent a good part of the decade calling for his dismissal, which they got in 1938, when the BHE forced Boylan to retire, and for limits on the authority of the president's office, which were achieved the following year.[7]

While City College of New York (CCNY) was earning itself a sterling academic reputation, BC became known for fostering student radicalism, though that reputation was overblown. The students, who were mainly commuters who lived at home and often worked full-time jobs, came from the borough's vast working-class and immigrant communities. As one dean pointed out, BC students did not have to be taught radicalism in the classroom. They absorbed it at home and in their neighborhoods—they learned the value of labor solidarity and the practicality of striking from their relatives, many of whom were union members or in one of the city's many left-wing groups, or from their own experiences working in factories and offices. BC students regularly supported local workers, often going to jail for picketing nearby restaurants and businesses during union organizing drives. When communists recruited students, BC was a good target. But while anticommunists ranted about the school's radical reputation, in fact only a relatively small percentage of the student body belonged to left-wing parties. At its height, Brooklyn's Communists amounted to only three dozen on a faculty of hundreds and only a hundred or so in a student body of close to ten thousand.[8]

Grebanier's attraction to the Communist Party reflected the changing political attitudes of BC faculty and students in the mid-1930s as well as the shifting doctrines of the international Communist movement. By the time he joined, Communists had abandoned the revolutionary rhetoric and sectarianism that guided and isolated them during the so-called "Third Period," launched in 1928. Mistaking the world-wide Depression for what they liked to call the "death knell of capitalism," Communist parties here and elsewhere followed the Soviet lead in agitating for a revolution against existing capitalist governments, including the parliamentary democracies in modern industrial nations such as the United States, Great Britain, and France. Under those conditions, Communists refused to work with liberals and the noncommunist left on common projects, forming organizations such as unions under their own control. Notoriously, German Communists in the early 1930s refused to cooperate with the rival Social Democratic party to defeat Adolph Hitler's growing National Socialist movement, instead making the fatal decision to oppose other socialist and liberal parties as representatives of a dying capitalism. The American Communist Party, recently split apart by internal Soviet power struggles and local sectarian disputes and still with few adherents, followed suit.[9]

By 1934, however, American Communists, under the leadership of Earl Browder, recognizing the shortcomings of this strategy, began returning to mainstream trade unions to collaborate with socialists and liberals, first in the American Federation of Labor then in the Congress of Industrial Organizations after it split from its parent labor federation in 1935. The Soviets made this programmatic shift official in 1935, with the declaration of the "Popular Front" against fascism, the abandonment of parallel trade unions, and the expressed willingness to join coalitions to defeat fascism internationally and build democracy at home. Turning away from the revolutionary fervor of the Third Period and embracing democratic institutions, Browder encouraged American party members to promote communism as "twentieth-century Americanism" in the tradition of Tom Paine, Thomas Jefferson, Frederick Douglass, and Abraham Lincoln. In building the Popular Front, the American party joined forces on the left to address a range of issues from within organizations such as the American Writers Union and the American League Against War and Fascism that were dedicated at once to specific causes and grand ideas. Some of these organizations were genuinely collaborative; others drew together a mélange of activists, party members and so-called "fellow travelers," into a "cultural front" loosely guided by communist, socialist, and liberal principles. Some were tightly controlled by Communists—what anticommunists liked to call "front organizations." The Writers Union and the League Against War and Fascism roughly fit the front stereotype. The American Student Union (ASU), to which belonged many of the students targeted by the Coudert investigation as Communist agitators, did not. Instead, the ASU comprised an alliance of several student organizations that emerged out of the student rights and antiwar movements of the mid-1930s. It was run by Socialists, Communists, and liberals who managed to work through their doctrinal and political differences until the late 1930s.[10]

As the Popular Front became official Communist policy, Brooklyn students and faculty increasingly joined the party and its allied organizations. Grebanier drifted into the party after Hitler's rise to power in 1934, propelled like many others by mounting concerns about the impending war in Europe. At American colleges and universities, a growing antiwar movement took shape around the Oxford Pledge to disavow militarism and war; eventually, the movement drew in students and faculty with campaigns against German remilitarization and Italian expansionism, especially after Mussolini's invasion and annexation of Ethiopia in 1935. Such pacifist and seemingly isolationist sentiments were not as alien to American political culture as one might imagine looking back through the filter of McCarthyism and the Cold War, as suspicions about American motives for joining the debacle of World War I still influenced American public opinion. Furthermore, tensions grew on American campuses as conservative faculty and administrators, some of them openly sympathetic to fascist and Nazi regimes, sustained and even strengthened ties with sister institutions in Italy and Germany.[11]

As did many of the faculty investigated by the Coudert committee, Grebanier entered the party through antifascist and other Popular Front organizations. Grebanier belonged to several Communist-related groups that concentrated on antifascist campaigns. He was a "very active member" of the League of American Writers, though perhaps not so prominent as his wife, Frances Winwar, who was born in Italy as Francesca Vinciguerra and was one of the most outspoken critics of the Mussolini regime on the American literary scene. Grebanier at one point also became active in a Communist-led organization called the American Society for Race Tolerance.[12] It seems, however, to have been the party's leadership of the union and their willingness to challenge patronage and graft in the municipal colleges that clinched Grebanier's commitment. "There was a peculiar situation ... at Brooklyn College," he recalled. "A great many incompetent people were being given positions without any academic standing, and the only people, it seemed to me, in the college who were putting up a front against that were some of the people whom I later knew to be Communists."[13]

Recruited to the party by colleagues in 1935, Grebanier erratically joined in Communist projects, paying his dues (he complained that they cost ten percent of his salary) and buying his monthly allotment of official party publications, as required of all members.[14] At one point, he took on the responsibility of leading the unit at its regular Tuesday meetings, but that lasted only a couple of weeks. And though still strongly resentful of the college's administrative corruption, his involvement in the union also remained spotty. He knew little about the local's affairs and even less, it seems, about Communist involvement in them. "I have always been bored with these matters, and I have been very negligent," he admitted when asked about party efforts to have members elected to leadership positions in the union.[15]

Grebanier officially left the party in 1939, although he insisted that he was out a year earlier and that party officials ignored his resignation. The reasons that he gave for leaving were not especially clear: Stalin's nonaggression pact with Hitler (announced in late August of 1939) had not yet betrayed the antifascist movement. Grebanier cited as the "last nail that hammered in the coffin-lid" the Communist treatment of Boris Krivitsky, a Soviet defector and former intelligence officer who was vilified and harassed by American Communists when he was used in anticommunist propaganda. Grebanier's reaction to the Krivitsky affair reflected his and others' discomfort with excuses American Communists made for Stalinist repression.[16] But, according to Grebanier, one could not resign from the party; one could only be expelled. This notion, which would circulate through the Rapp-Coudert investigation for the next year and a half, was regularly posed as a question in private and public interrogations, and often cited as evidence of the party's authoritarianism, though it might just as well have been a symptom of the party's desperation to inflate membership. At least one other faculty member who was brought before Coudert likewise reported the party's reluctance to let him go—after three inconclusive heresy trials and a rather abusive campaign against him.[17]

It was only after threatening to publish a letter attacking Communism that Grebanier got the reaction he wanted. In June, the BC branch branded him "a counter-revolutionary enemy of the working class and of the Party" for "disseminating the poisonous ideas of Trotsky, fascist ideas." They forbade "any personal or social connections with such an individual" as "incompatible with the honor and self-respect of a conscious and politically developed revolutionist."[18] The party informed Grebanier of his expulsion in a letter posted in mid-August, just a few days before the politically disastrous revelation of the Hitler-Stalin Pact. "To be 'expelled' after one has resigned is a piece of felicitous humor which only you seem likely to miss," Grebanier responded with relish. "Expelled or dismissed, it is a pleasure to be disassociated from a movement that finds the building of a 'democratic front' best achieved through an alliance with Hitler."[19]

So Grebanier was no accidental witness against former comrades, discovered at the last minute by the Coudert committee; by 1939, he had overtly enlisted in the anticommunist ranks. In an open letter to Brooklyn students that appeared in the campus newspaper in early October, Grebanier confessed to feeling betrayed by official Communism and expressed his belief that even under the Popular Front, the party was lying about its adherence to democratic values: "It is time that we reexamined our talk about liberty and freedom and be sure that we are not actually trying to further totalitarian success by a dishonest use of these words." He signed on to the emerging liberal consensus that Stalin's dictatorship and Communism in general were as totalitarian as Europe's fascist regimes. The Nazi invasion of Poland and its partition with the Soviets demonstrated "the menace of totalitarianism of both right and left to civilization," showing that "no man or woman can with integrity hereafter cooperate with either brand and pretend to be furthering the interests of American democracy."[20] By the time Grebanier appeared on Windels's witness stand, he had considered cooperating with the Dies committee, granted interviews to the conservative Hearst press, written anti-Stalinist tracts for the right-wing socialist weekly *The New Leader*, and joined perhaps the most important liberal anticommunist organization at the time, the short-lived Committee for Cultural Freedom (CCF), formed in spring 1939.[21] He played the unwilling witness, dragged before the public by state investigators, but in fact he was as Gerson noted "brimming over with reluctance" as he named eight of his colleagues as members of the party.[22]

Playing the Stooge

Most of Grebanier's testimony about BC Communists was vague and much of it hearsay; this was not surprising, since by his own admission he was indifferent to the week-to-week management of party affairs and largely ignorant of specific policies. Some of the people he named undoubtedly were in the party. Yet Windels had bigger goals than just rooting out hidden Communists, and used Grebanier to trump up his case that Communist subversives preached revolution in their classrooms. Windels emulated the Seabury model, wielding Grebanier's private hearing testimony to back him into definitive statements that were on the record, ready to be picked up by the press and disseminated to the public.

Unlike Seabury, he did not intend to get at the truth, but rather to obscure and misrepresent it in order to build, in the manner of a show trial, the countersubversive myth.

It is worth spending some time with Grebanier's testimony to see the method of Windels's misrepresentations. In the private hearings, Grebanier had spoken loosely but evasively about the practices of his faculty comrades. He claimed not to have had direct knowledge of classroom subversion; he indicated instead that it was unlikely to have occurred. "I was sometimes rather amused, for instance," he remarked, "at the extent to which some of them [his colleagues] apparently leaned backward in order to avoid any impression among the students, people that I knew to be Communists, and of whom the students had no conception, apparently, because of the position they took in the classroom." Staffer Phillip W. Haberman, Jr., pressed Grebanier, citing Richard Frank as an authority, "that it is the part of the Communist teacher to be thoroughly steeped in Marxist-Leninist philosophy" to "lead the student body" toward "a spirit of dissatisfaction with the existing state of things." Grebanier responded that "most people probably who really were students of Marxism, in connection with their study, would not have felt that that was what was meant by Marxist teaching." Had BC Communists, Haberman asked, "attempted to inculcate students with [Marxist-Leninist] principles in [extracurricular] seminars or private discussions?" "Well, no," Grebanier responded. "I should imagine that was left entirely to whatever single link they may have had with some student. In other words, the students, they used to make a great point about the student initiative and student democracy, and so forth."[23] At most, Grebanier merely had "suspicions" of such extracurricular connections and few of them at that. He could not name a colleague who cultivated political protégés among the students. Moreover, though an admitted member of the BC Communist Party, Grebanier at that point could not or would not name a Communist student, either.[24]

There were other instances in which Grebanier disavowed that the BC party unit manipulated students. In late April 1937, the Brooklyn campus was rocked first by an antiwar strike that brought thousands of students out in a show of impressive strength, then again a few days later by a disruptive protest against the firing of Henry Klein, a popular history instructor active in the peace movement. To support Klein, students staged a sit-in at the offices of President Boylan. The BHE, relatively more liberal than the system's administrative staff, reinstated Klein in May. Coudert committee investigators, prompted by administrators and right-wing faculty, assumed the Communist Party organized the demonstrations. While there was little doubt that Young Communist League (YCL) activists were involved, Klein had a following among a broad spectrum of students. Questioned *in camera* by Coudert staff on the matter, Grebanier judged "that [the protest] was pretty well engineered. Of course, it wasn't spontaneous." But he did not mean that faculty had promoted it. "You mean the student agitation was engineered by your unit?" Haberman asked. "Not by my unit as such," Grebanier responded, but by the party more generally. Yet, when pressed further, Grebanier revealed that he had no idea of the relationship between the party apparatus that he believed had "engineered" the protest and what happened thereafter. "I have no proof that it was [instigated by Communists], except the general appearance of the thing." Concerning the peace demonstrations, Grebanier was similarly noncommittal and vague.[25]

As such an indefinite witness in the private depositions, Grebanier presented a challenge for Windels as the December public hearings approached. Instead of simply letting him testify, Windels subtly distorted the transcript of Grebanier's earlier testimony, to which only he and his staff had access, so that he would confirm Windels's accusations. Windels's trial brief, a set of notes that guided his questioning in the public hearings and included the responses he expected from Grebanier, clearly show that he intended to force his witness's speculation and hearsay into definitive statements that faculty and staff "work[ed] through the students," and that the "Communist party unit would communicate with students through the Young Communist League at Brooklyn college" as "the channel through which the Communist Party's point of view was expressed among the students."[26] Grebanier had not said either of these things in the private depositions and would not at first in the public hearings, either. Asked whether there "were ... young Communists in Brooklyn College," he continued to be evasive, probably because he could not or would not name any: "There have been students who issued leaflets under the name of the Young Communists [sic] League" and "it can be taken for granted" that the YCL was "used to spread the Communist Party" on campus. Grebanier even retreated from his private testimony about the Klein protests, now remembering only "some of the details." He had "never witnessed, but ... certainly heard of" the student demonstrations against the Klein firing. To make matters worse for Windels, Grebanier added, "I cannot pretend to know what I do not know."[27]

At this point, Windels picked up his copy of the private testimony, turning to selections on the Klein demonstrations. He read a bit to remind Grebanier of his reported familiarity with the scene at Brooklyn;

then he asked, "Was this student demonstration in connection with the Klein case a spontaneous demonstration?" Here, Grebanier seemed to get back on track: "I should doubt it." But when Windels asked, "Do you know?" all Grebanier could say was, "I know nothing about the machinations by which the demonstrations were organized." An interrogator more interested in the truth might have left it at that. However, at this point, Windels put the words that he wanted into Grebanier's mouth, by quoting *himself* from the private interrogation: in "a situation like this Klein case, the communication then would be right from some members of the unit to the Young Communists [*sic*] League in the college [and] they set the machinery at work among the students." To that statement, Grebanier originally responded that he did not know that his faculty unit actually communicated with the students involved in the Klein demonstrations. He had only surmised that the party did, "from the general appearance of the thing." In Windels's edited version, Grebanier's vague conjectures and hearsay had been boiled down for the public to a confirmation of faculty incitement and subversion beyond a shadow of a doubt.[28]

That evening, the *Brooklyn Eagle's* front-page banner headline screamed "Red Tutors Incited Students in Outbreaks, Quiz Reveals." The *Eagle* dutifully reported the "truth" that Windels drew out of Grebanier about Communist incitement, citing the very moment in which Windels misrepresented Grebanier's earlier testimony about the sit-in at Boylan's office.[29] The following day's lead editorial expressed confidence in Grebanier's testimony, or rather Windels's staging of it. "There is no question in our mind of its complete reliability," the editors declared, basing their conclusion on the flood of documents that Windels entered into evidence as if before a court of law. "Dr. Grebanier has revealed how faculty members directed Communist students to stage demonstrations" as part of the general Communist project "to poison the minds of students with propaganda for a foreign totalitarian doctrine." It was "high time" for a "showdown" on the bad faith of Communist teachers, the editorial concluded: "This business of stealthily spreading Marxism in our public schools and colleges is nothing more than a fraud ... on the State for whom the teachers are trustees." The *Eagle* added a cartoon of a hand labeled "Coudert School Inquiry" stripping a mask of academic gentility with wire-rimmed glasses perched on an aquiline nose from the swarthy, brutal face of "COMMUNISM" whose big ears, full lips, wiry beard, and nappy hair embellished the editors' point with a visual ethnic slur.[30]

Similar headlines graced the *New York Sun* that Monday evening, declaring that Windels had revealed to the public "How Reds Seek to Bore

46 The Hearings

Editorial cartoon, *Brooklyn Daily Eagle*, 4 December 1940, p. 14. (Reproduced with permission of *Brooklyn Daily Eagle*.)

into City's Schools." A Communist "Fifth Column" was "working under cover" to "implant the idea of the class struggle and proletarian revolution in the minds both of teachers and pupils," according to the *Sun*.[31] The *New York Times*, a bit less inflammatory than the *Sun* or the *Eagle*, nonetheless bought Windels's argument, declaring in faux legal language that it had "been established beyond reasonable doubt" that some Brooklyn faculty and teachers-union members "have been working underhandedly to advance the cause of communism." Though the *Times* editors acknowledged that it was legal "for any person in this State, whether or not he or she is a teacher, to believe in communism and to vote for it," they reminded their readers that "it is not proper for them to violate their trust as teachers by surreptitiously indoctrinating their students."[32]

And so the news media recycled Windels's lie as if it were the finding of a court. There had been no substantive evidence presented before the committee of incitement or indoctrination. This was the very situation Mulligan had warned against—the Communist Party, the College Teachers Union (CTU) that supposedly was being run by the Communist Party, and the professors named by Grebanier were effectively being put on trial in the press for indoctrinating students. And Windels declared for the whole process the legitimacy of a trial in a court of law, with documents and testimony entered into evidence and with trial-like interrogations from a well-known and highly respected attorney. Yet if Windels's inquiry reached conclusions that seemed like legitimate legal judgments, it did so without the essential ingredient of all American courts of law— the inclusion of an advocate on the side of the accused who could raise the obvious and sometimes not so obvious questions about testimony, evidence, and lines of argument that are necessary for finding out the truth. Clearly, if Mulligan had been allowed to, he would have pressed Grebanier on the many vague conjectures about what he thought his fellow Communists were doing. Most important, he would have challenged Windels's reading of the evidence, offered his own evidence to the contrary, as well as alternative explanations for what happened. Some of those explanations could be found in Grebanier's private testimony and even in those public remarks that everyone chose to ignore.

Such misrepresentations persisted through the months of the investigation, with Mulligan and others repeatedly trying to force the Coudert committee, through the courts, in the press, and by intervening directly, to adopt fairer practices consistent with the spirit of the Constitution, including letting a lawyer represent the accused teachers and allowing someone to cross-examine witnesses. Meanwhile, Windels and his staff published reports, one in March of 1941 and another in February of 1942, which continued on the basis of negligible evidence to accuse teachers of indoctrination and subversion as part of the Communist Party's "ambitious scheme" to establish "an elaborate system of conniving, masquerading, interlocking directorates, agitation and propaganda" in the city school system and on its municipal college campuses. Even as cases went to court or to administrative review, Mulligan and other lawyers who acted on behalf of accused teachers found that they had very little access to the evidence referred to in the public hearings or used in Coudert committee reports, limited opportunities to challenge public hearing testimony, and no option at all of seeing depositions and documents archived by the committee that might have told a different story. Any efforts on the part of the teachers, their union or the lawyers representing them to challenge the Rapp-Coudert committee's constitutionality and fairness were dismissed by Windels and his staff as attempts to "obstruct the inquiry."[33]

The Private Record

In fact, if Mulligan had been able to obtain evidence collected by the Rapp-Coudert staff, he would have found, in addition to Grebanier's evasive private testimony, quite a few documents that offered a different picture of what Communists did in their classes and at their institutions—which might have persuaded the public that Communist teachers were no more involved than Democrats or Republicans in classroom subversion, indoctrination, and incitement.

In the first place, most of the private testimony alleging classroom indoctrination was as vague as Grebanier's and, like it, hearsay. Ben Gitlow, an early teachers-union activist and a prominent Communist official in the 1920s who had become a radical anticommunist by the time Rapp-Coudert staff interviewed him, could only "recollect" that indoctrination of students was "discussed from time to time" among Communist teachers, but he offered no specifics.[34] The same was true of friendly witness Mark Graubard, who taught at Columbia until 1938 and suffered through three "trials" in which Communist Party officials considered his expulsion for making unorthodox public statements, including one judging party chairman Earl Browder to be a bad speaker. Graubard privately complained of a "folk lore of radicalism in the air [at the municipal colleges] on account of the few Communists among the students, and the faculty perhaps, too." He was "amazed, at the facility with which [many students] repeat phrases like class struggle, imperialism, and things like that." But when pressed by the Coudert interviewer, he offered no evidence that faculty actually introduced that rhetoric to the students, who as others pointed out had access to it from many public sources, including the widely available literature of the Communists and other left-wing parties, some of it for sale at newsstands throughout the city.[35]

New York University philosophy professor Sidney Hook, who was just acquiring his reputation for virulent anticommunist attacks, was another source on faculty indoctrination. Hook complained of a "special type of abuse of trust" in which Communist teachers "get to know" students and "cultivate them," inviting them "out to tea or ... to their homes." They "establish these personal relationships when they really flatter the students by the attention and the sedulous care which they give them. Then the students are likely to acquire, almost by a process of intellectual osmosis, their attitudes." Yet, when asked by staffer George Shea if he had any "personal knowledge" of direct connection between faculty and the YCL or ASU as vehicles for indoctrination in coordination with faculty "cultivation," Hook responded that he had none; he knew it only from unidentified students who had broken with the Communists. And he could name no specific teachers who engaged in such practices. "It is common knowledge," he weakly offered, insisting, "I am confident these are the facts," but also confessing that "I couldn't establish them by saying that at such and such a place this meeting occurred." Nor would Hook offer these opinions in public testimony.[36]

Other documents collected by the Coudert staff suggested that Communists did in fact "bend over backwards," as Grebanier said, to avoid the impression among students that they were being taught a Communist point of view. Granville Hicks, who served as the book review editor of the *New Masses* yet publicly and quite bitterly quit the party in fall 1939 because of the Hitler-Stalin pact, granted Shea a very long and frank background interview on the practices of academic party members. Hicks had taught at Harvard and Rensselaer Polytechnic Institute before being fired from RPI in 1935 for his political views. Hicks dispelled the notion that Communist faculty cultivated protégés among the students. Even Harvard's YCL chapter was considered too risky, according to Hicks, for faculty to approach without endangering their jobs. "I can tell you frankly that so far as our group at Harvard was concerned, it was felt that the YCL was a very rapidly shifting group, and that it simply was not safe for a member of the Harvard faculty to be known to the membership of the YCL as a party member." Hicks suggested that such was the case for the relations between the YCL and Communist Party faculty generally, as "kids pop in and out of the YCL all the time." Instead of being directed by faculty Communists, the YCL activists at Harvard worked with the main Boston office of the Communist Party.[37]

Grebanier similarly testified privately that he and his colleagues kept a distance from the BC YCL chapter, with whom the faculty Communists communicated sporadically through liaisons. Pressed to admit that faculty comrades "gave instruction" to YCL students, Grebanier insisted that the BC YCL chapter was given directions by the borough's YCL headquarters. When Grebanier briefly served as the BC unit's liaison, attending occasional YCL meetings, he "understood [his] duties to be chiefly that of an observer who gave advice when it was asked for," and that students in the BC YCL chapter "on no occasion that I can remember took any direct orders transmitted through me, though ... to make comments upon the wisdom of some campaign they were carrying out or whether they had done the job well, and so on." Such comments, however, were "not in the spirit of an order. It was in the spirit of criticism. Everywhere was an insistence upon their autonomy. They had direction much more particularly, you see, from the [Brooklyn] offices of the Young Communist League." While such testimony might not diminish worry over the influence of the party's Boston or Brooklyn headquarters, it significantly cut faculty out of the picture of Communists steering student agitation.[38]

Noncommunist administrators, faculty, and students confirmed that if there were Communists who tried to indoctrinate students in class, they were the exception rather than the rule. A painstaking 1939 investigation conducted by a committee of Brooklyn citizens in response to earlier accusations by right-wing faculty of Communist subversion found no evidence of classroom propagandizing, and it concluded based on interviews across the campus and the community that the Communist Party had relatively limited influence and numbers among the Brooklyn faculty and students.[39] Brooklyn Dean Mario Cosenza likewise diminished the extent of "communist infiltration" and attributed student interest in left-wing politics to their social backgrounds, including having parents in trade unions and socialist parties, and the political life of the city in those waning years of the Depression. "Our students are part of our city population," he reminded Windels, "and they are the result of the social, political, and economic conditions which have surrounded them from childhood."[40]

Later, as the BHE began its disciplinary hearings against Brooklyn and CCNY staff, students sent in petitions and letters supporting accused or dismissed teachers. While such campaigns arguably reflected student political alignments, in many instances entire classes signed petitions attesting to the professor's impartiality and fairness. Almost all the students in five classes being taught that spring by Howard Selsam, a philosophy professor whom Grebanier called the "Stalin" of BC, gave him unqualified support. They found him "stimulating, but even more important—

fair. Impartial discussion on all related topics has been encouraged." He had "at all times been objective" and "intellectually honest."[41]

Other evidence was similarly filtered. While the Coudert staff selected and misread party publications that they believed revealed a policy of student indoctrination, they ignored others stating precisely the opposite. One example, an editorial comment on an address by New York state party leader Israel Amter, appeared in the January 1936 newsletter of the BC Communist faculty, *The Staff*, a publication that Windels's investigators methodically combed through for incriminating evidence. Amter defended the pedagogical integrity of Communist teachers, pointing out that as a matter of policy they would not teach communism in the public schools. The party maintained its own instructional staff for that purpose at independent workers' schools. The editorial then asked,

> does not every teacher interpret his subject from some standpoint (in fact he cannot be a good teacher if he does not do so)? As Communists we exercise only the same right exercised consciously or unconsciously, by all teachers, whether Democratic or Republican, Protestant or Catholic.... We seek to throw the fullest and best knowledge on whatever comes before us and to present the various points of view to our students for their criticism and analysis.[42]

Harry Gideonse

To bolster Grebanier's testimony, Windels brought Harry Gideonse to the witness stand on Wednesday, the third day of the hearings. Appointed president of BC in 1939, Gideonse cut a charming and impressive figure with the press, which regarded his "slightly graying black hair, snapping black eyes, eyebrows which are at least half as beetling as John L. Lewis's and a devastating dimple on his chin" as if Gideonse were the latest movie idol. Not yet forty years old when he took Brooklyn's helm, Gideonse had experienced a meteoric rise in the American academy. After immigrating as a boy to the United States from his native Holland and taking advanced degrees in economics at American graduate schools, Gideonse ended up teaching for eight years at the University of Chicago. There, he locked horns with another young and influential college president, Robert Maynard Hutchins, over the introduction of a conservative core curriculum based on classics and the great books. That conflict as well as his service on American Association of University Professors (AAUP) academic freedom committees earned Gideonse a reputation as "an outstanding liberal," as the *Brooklyn Eagle* put it.⁴³ Besides opposing Hutchins, he prominently supported the appointment of the radically nonconformist and politically outspoken philosopher Bertrand Russell to a position at CCNY, a controversy that some argued precipitated the formation of the Rapp-Coudert committee. Yet Gideonse also was a protégé of free-market economist Ferdinand von Hayek, helping found the archconservative Mont Pelerin Institute that promoted Hayek's laissez-faire views.⁴⁴

Gideonse's liberal bona fides added credibility to his complaints about Communist agitation on campus. Moreover, Gideonse had been hired not only to clean up the detritus of Tammany's campus corruption, but to bring student activism and faculty radicalism under control. As he informed Windels, he made a study of the Communist Party's role in the college's political scene for two months before accepting the job, even going so far as to attend student meetings incognito.⁴⁵ In addition to claiming a special expertise about Communist agitation on campus, Gideonse credited himself with almost single-handedly loosening the party's grip on Brooklyn students by reengineering student government elections and precipitating a confrontation between left-wing students and the campus administration. That conflict led to the month-long suspension of the ASU and a series of demonstrations in late spring 1940, including the picketing of Gideonse's house by several hundred students, some of them wearing gas masks. In the retelling, Gideonse exploited these events for their most sensational effect, calling the demonstrations "Prussian" and claiming that the masks terrorized his two young sons, as he and Windels made it look like BC was being bullied by a gang of thugs.

Gideonse's most damaging testimony, however, was the most speculative— that the disruption of the college and the "organized effort to intimidate" him had been engineered by Communist faculty: "In my judgment the leadership of the picket line [at his home] did not at all look like student leadership. It was a sort of person that one sees in pictures of mass meetings at Madison Square Garden." Gideonse, of course, may have been right—he had alienated faculty as well as students as he tried to whip the college into shape, and at least one faculty member was present among the several hundred people in front of Gideonse's house, though there was no indication that he led the action. But Gideonse could provide little evidence that faculty guidance was needed for the student agitation to occur, or that it was even offered, or that it was provided by the Communist Party, officially or unofficially.⁴⁶

By the third day of testimony, public reaction was already swiftly overtaking the hearings. Conservatives of both parties immediately began a drive for more repressive legislation targeting Communists not only for overt acts but also for mere party membership. The refusal of nearly two dozen teachers and staff to cooperate with the committee, well publicized by Windels with the release of their names, cast a pall of suspicion over their academic careers and their activities in the union.

Windels, however, had one more major witness to interrogate. The tone of that exchange would be different from the testimony of Grebanier and Gideonse. But it did little to dampen the rising tide of public opinion.

3
Coudertism

One common question in the study of McCarthyism concerns how to best defend oneself against punitive investigations like Rapp-Coudert. Most Americans consider constitutional rights the most reliable legal recourse, and through the 1950s, accused Communists invoked both Fifth Amendment protection against self-incrimination and First Amendment guarantees of free speech and assembly in order to back refusals to cooperate with the witch hunt. Until 1956, when the Supreme Court threw out restrictions on use of the Fifth Amendment, neither strategy was successful. Additional constitutional issues also mattered. As union attorney William Mulligan pointed out, legislative investigations, with consequences equal to those of a real prosecution, seldom followed the due process of law that ensured individuals their day in court. Such rights as protected under the Sixth and Fourteenth Amendments were at the heart of the teachers union's initial legal challenges to Coudertism.

Critics of red scares are justified in expressing indignation over such violations of individual rights, for they are central to the problem of political inquisition. However, making such points on constitutional grounds does not necessarily lead to a successful defense against the kinds of repression practiced during the era, which operated in the realm of sleazy publicity and legislative intimidation even more effectively than they did in the world of courtrooms and constitutional debate. People were fired, financially ruined, and vilified long before they could bring their cases before judges and juries, and even longer before their cases or similar ones worked their way through the federal courts toward definitive judgments made by the nation's highest court.[1] And while the federal bench eventually applied some basic due-process protections to legislative inquiries, the Constitution still cannot effectively protect against a concerted political campaign like Rapp-Coudert or its offspring, McCarthyism. Something more is needed.

The teachers union and the Communist activists in its leadership understood the fundamentally political character of the conflict unfolding in and around the Rapp-Coudert investigation. They not only had to conduct a legal defense of individually accused teachers; they had to build a political defense of the union as well. For this reason, the union and its legal advisers, including those provided by the Communist Party, mounted in addition to constitutional challenges a campaign that was based on their understanding of the broader political and social motives behind the unfolding repression.[2] A crucial part of this strategy was for individuals to deny Communist membership or to refuse to cooperate with the investigation and for the representatives of the teachers-union locals to deny Communist involvement in the union's leadership. There were good reasons for pursuing this strategy: Individuals who admitted membership and acknowledged the presence of Communists in the union could immediately be pressured by the boards of education and under threat of legislative contempt to reveal the identities of other party members (to "name names") or be put in the position of having to lie under oath about friends and colleagues. Moreover, Communist teachers knew that even if in good faith they disclosed their political views and affiliations, the city would dismiss them on some pretext, or the state would pass laws allowing it to do so specifically because they were Communists. Such laws were debated in the legislature as the Rapp-Coudert investigation unfolded, just as they had already been considered several times in New York's recent past.

So a good number of the accused teachers, many of whom were certainly Communists, lied under oath, denying membership in the party and denying the party's involvement in the union. Such misrepresentations were understandable given the circumstances, and they worked for many teachers who, though interrogated in closed sessions, escaped being called before the committee's public tribunals. Many of these suspects made it through this early round of McCarthyism by refusing to cooperate until the investigation ran out of steam in 1942.[3] But for those publicly accused in December 1940 or in the spring of 1941, lying was fatal. Inevitably, the Rapp-Coudert committee found enough former Communists like Grebanier who would name names, confirm each others' testimony, and expose Communist and non-Communist colleagues to charges of perjury and "conduct unbecoming a teacher." Such exposure especially condemned Communists in the eyes of liberals, both among their colleagues and in the broader public. Once the city's predominantly liberal boards of education, many of whose members had been appointed by La Guardia, concluded on the basis of public disclosures that teachers had lied or refused to cooperate, they had little choice according to their own rules and sensibilities but to publicly condemn the accused and begin dismissal proceedings, which is what they did in spring 1941.

As others have cogently argued concerning the Communist Party's response to McCarthyism, such subterfuge became a self-defeating strategy for individual Communists, for the Communist Party, and for the unions in which Communists were active. Accurate charges of misrepresentation reinforced the false charges of subversion and incitement made by Windels and others, calling into question the good faith of accused individuals, of communism as a social movement, and of the Communist Party as a legitimate political organization. Moreover, while the double bind over personal exposure may have forced teachers to misrepresent the truth about their personal beliefs, and while it may have been good practical advice for individuals to stonewall, it was a mistake for the union and the party to deny the positive role of Communists and communism in building the teachers union or their contribution to the broader currents of American political life. In some sense, it was this political lie that served the repression most effectively and durably. For Communist teachers—once they were exposed and shown to be "hiding something"—could no longer claim, as they might have, that as part of a social movement and as members of a party, they had helped create a democratic union that supported strong public education, encouraged pedagogical innovation, and served the public interest by advancing the "educational front."

Hillbilly from Carolina

Charles Hendley's testimony on the third day of the December hearings was caught on the horns of this political dilemma. A "hillbilly from the poor eroded hills of North Carolina," Hendley retained his southern drawl even after almost twenty years teaching history and economics in New York City high schools. He described himself as a "polite and somewhat timid classroom teacher," yet on the witness stand he seemed anything but that.[4] A Socialist through most of the 1930s, Hendley did not agree with much of the Communist Party's ideology and platform at the time of the investigation. Yet he saw nothing wrong in working with or defending fellow teachers who happened to be Communists, and cultivated the same level of tolerance in his students. "In discussing current issues in a class of high school students," he retorted to a principal investigating charges of communist sympathy against Hendley in 1930, "I think it would be just as atrocious to try to develop in them an intolerance against communism as it would be to try to make them converts to it."[5] For that openmindedness, Hendley was expelled from the Socialist Party in 1938 (much as Bernard Grebanier would be from the Communist Party a year later). It is also one of the reasons that he served as president of Local 5 at that moment in its history, representing a coalition in the union of communists, left-wing socialists, and liberals.[6]

Hendley credited his rural, southern, working-class background for cultivating in him both a deep resentment of economic injustice and an openness to views that were different from his own. He grew up the son of a railway section boss, "a pioneer in organizing maintenance of way workers in the south," including African Americans, whose endurance of Jim Crow made an enormous impression on Hendley as a young boy. As a teenager, Hendley helped his semiliterate father draft the demands and negotiating positions of the workers he represented.[7] Besides building a strong attachment to the trade-union movement, this experience launched Hendley on a career in teaching, especially of people like his parents. After working his way through the University of North Carolina as a dishwasher, Hendley taught in mill towns around the state before moving to New York for a master of history at Columbia University. There, he studied under Charles Beard, serving as his research assistant not long before the infamously iconoclastic historian was forced out for opposing American entry into World War I. After receiving his degree, Hendley joined the educational staff of the Amalgamated Textile Workers Union in Paterson, New Jersey, where he also helped set up that city's first local of the American Federation of Teachers (AFT) in 1919. From there, Hendley moved on to offer labor classes to union organizers and strikers in Pennsylvania mining and steel towns before finally settling in 1921 into his first job at George Washington High School, at the northern end of Manhattan. Hendley naturally joined the fledgling teachers union, which elected him treasurer in 1925 and then president in 1935.[8]

In the public hearings, Paul Windels tried to expose Hendley as a willing dupe of Communist handlers; his pliability could serve as demonstrable evidence of the party's control over union affairs. Still quoting from the same Communist texts that he had used over the previous two days,

Windels pressed Hendley to admit that the union harbored teachers who followed party orders to "inject Marxism and Leninism into the classroom while concealing [their] party affiliation" (135).[9] Windels's strategy, however, backfired: Hendley scolded Windels for twisting his words into "a most vicious distortion of the truth" (130). There was no more reason to suspect Communist teachers of classroom subversion, he pointed out, than to suspect it of any other teacher who belongs to a group or organization with strong principles and a mission such as, for instance, Jehovah's Witnesses (137). Later in the interrogation, Hendley provocatively expanded on this allusion to religious persecution in Nazi Germany.

> You condemn the Communists, you liquidate the Communists and then you turn your attention to the most progressive element on the left. That is what happened in Germany, a terrific hew [sic] and cry against the Communists. They liquidated the Communists and then turned their attention to the most conservative trade unions. (233)

This was not the testimony that Windels expected, serving a show trial like the one Seabury mounted against Tammany a decade earlier, with political hacks, their fingers still in the public till, broken under relentless questioning and the weight of evidence.

Hendley also asked to read a prepared statement. At first, the committee would have nothing of it. "I noticed this morning you let Dr. Gideonse talk on and on and on," Hendley acidly remarked after being thwarted several times. "He was never shut off at any time during the testimony."[10] Eventually Windels relented, reckoning that stifling the mild-mannered Hendley would cost too much politically. After some minutes pleading his case that "labor has been the most consistent friend of public education ever since a century ago," (244) Hendley in frustration attacked the investigation as a "star chamber proceeding" that took testimony in secret, prosecuted without a jury, and interrogated suspects without a lawyer present. In the end, Windels had little to worry about: The press barely reported Hendley's remarks, even though Local 5 widely distributed copies before and after the hearings. Relegated to the inner pages of the news, his defense was buried under Harry Gideonse's sensational and self-aggrandizing tales about mopping up the remains of the student left on the Brooklyn campus.

More important than his earnest invocations of union democracy and human rights, however, was what Hendley left unsaid. He wanted to launch a stronger, more politically minded defense of the union and the left. "So what if there were Communists in the union?" he considered asking Windels. But as he told Communist writer Mike Gold a few years later, "the lawyers and everybody else advised me that it was not the time to put up such a fight."[11] That reluctance to defend Communist trade unionism on political grounds would be damaging for Communists and teachers alike.

Instead, the union and the Communist Party pursued a strategy of shifting public attention from the issue of Communist teachers to what they perceived as the real dynamic behind the inquiry: the relentless right-wing effort over the previous quarter of a century to cut budgets and bend public institutions to the will of corporate and banking interests. The Coudert subcommittee's job, the union argued, was "discrediting the schools, the teachers and the character of education. By a campaign of red-labeling and witch-hunting they hope to destroy public confidence in the school system and thus make it easier to cut State aid and salaries."[12] Over the two years of the investigation, the union and its supporters pursued this argument under the auspices of the ad hoc Citizens Committee to Defend Public Education (CDPE), formed at a protest meeting in late March 1940 and headed by the legislative representative for the New York City teachers' locals, Bella Dodd. On behalf of the union and (without acknowledging it) the Communist Party, Dodd ran the project until the Coudert committee officially wrapped up in 1942.[13] Under Dodd's direction, the CDPE traced the inquiry back through the GOP to initiatives by right-wing organizations that were clamoring for tax cuts and promoting union busting. "The budget cutters are out to destroy the confidence which 13 million citizens of New York State have in their public school system," the CDPE warned. "All effective defenders of State aid, tenure and salary standards may expect to be labeled and attacked as 'subversive and un-American.'"[14]

The CDPE was not completely wrong, but in treating the extreme right as the main force behind the witch hunt, Dodd and her committee inadvertently obscured other motives that could not be traced to conservative origins. And so they made the same mistake that later critics made with McCarthyism, treating red scares as expressions of marginal currents in American political culture rather than its mainstream.

Bella Dodd

At the center of the campaign against Rapp-Coudert, Dodd set the posture of both union and party toward the unfolding political repression. She had ascended to the leadership of the union in the early years of the Depression as she became increasingly involved in Communist Party affairs. Though she did not officially join the party until 1943, according to her later testimony before the United States Senate, while working for the union she had access to the party's highest circles and served as one of Communism's most valuable assets in the schools and the trade-union movement.¹⁵ In many ways, she was the ideal party activist for that era, combining humble beginnings with sophistication and political ambition.

Born Maria Assunta Isabella Visono in southern Italy in 1904, Dodd was brought to the United States at age five and raised in Harlem and the Bronx. After graduating from Evander Childs High School, Dodd enrolled at Hunter College in Manhattan on a state scholarship, living at home and taking the subway on the recently constructed Pelham Line to classes every day. Hunter at that time was just beginning to make its transition from a teachers' training school for middle-class women into a more academically serious institution. When she started teaching after her 1925 graduation, first in the public high schools and then in the political science department at Hunter, she found herself drifting without clear political or moral conviction. Later in her life, after she had been drawn back into the Catholic church, she would regard that condition as an absence of spiritual direction, but it prepared her to embrace the unrelenting and uncompromising theory and practice of the Communist Party. During this period, Dodd took a master's degree in political science at Columbia, studying with future Roosevelt Brain Truster Raymond Moley and others in a new pragmatically oriented approach to the discipline. She also earned a law degree at New York University.¹⁶

Like Grebanier, with whom she was acquainted in high school, Dodd entered the orbit of the Communist Party through the antifascist movement. Long opposed to Mussolini's regime in her native Italy, she was newly moved by the terrifying effects of authoritarian movements that she experienced during a trip to Europe in 1932. In Berlin, she witnessed violence tearing through the city and the university, with Nazis, Communists, and Socialists in constant struggle. Returning to Hunter that fall, she found a growing interest in communism among students hard-bitten by the Depression; they drew faculty into the movement rather than the other way around. "We had no known members of the Communist Party among us [the faculty]," Dodd recalled. "But communist students went into action and before long had a tremendous impact on ... young teachers."¹⁷

It is impossible to disentangle Dodd's recruitment to the party from her involvement in the teachers union, which began around the same time. On the boat home from Europe, Dodd met a group of New York City public-school teachers who persuaded her to join Local 5, which at that

Bella V. Dodd, legislative representative for Local 5 and related AFT locals in New York City, 1936–1941. Dodd here is speaking at the May Day rally 1938. (New York State Archives, Albany.)

point was actively recruiting faculty and staff from area colleges, public and private. She and several colleagues began organizing the Hunter College Instructors Association, which Dodd later described as "a grass-roots organization for immediate action on important questions of privilege and one in which discussion was uninhibited." The association would eventually evolve into the Hunter chapter of the College Teachers Union (CTU), AFT Local 537. Through the College Instructors Association, Dodd came into contact with linguist Margaret Schlauch, who from her post in the English department at NYU coordinated union organizing among the city's college faculty and staff. In Schlauch's network, she met other young professors who would form the core of New York's party academics as well as much of the leadership first of the college section of Local 5 and then of the CTU, when it was split off of the main local in 1938. When the effort to organize college instructors hit a snag, Schlauch brought its remnants together into a new, collegiate antifascist organization. It was through her participation in that group that Dodd became one of the party's most effective fund-raisers and organizers.[18]

Meanwhile, the efforts of Dodd and her colleagues to organize Hunter College were boosted by the appointment to president of Eugene Colligan, a young recruit from public-school administration who like Brooklyn College (BC) President William Boylan had close ties to the Tammany machine. Colligan antagonized Hunter students and most of the faculty just at the moment when Tammany, weakened by scandal and economic collapse, was defeated in the election of Fiorello La Guardia in 1933.[19] With Colligan as a convenient foil, Dodd's work organizing the Hunter staff revived, spreading to other municipal and private colleges in the area. Eventually Dodd introduced a bill into the state legislature that initiated tenure rights for college teachers. It was partly because of her success with that bill that the teachers union made Dodd its legislative representative in Albany in spring 1936. They chose well. Through the late 1930s, Dodd mounted aggressive and successful union campaigns to defend salaries and school funding by placing teachers in charge of assembly-district committees to exert through parents and other residents constituent pressure on legislative representatives.[20]

Creating Rapp-Coudert

Dodd's work as a legislative representative pitted her against fiscal conservatives in Albany whose persistent and often vicious opposition to school spending framed her interpretation of school politics generally. So her perspective on the Rapp-Coudert investigation, like that of other teachers union and party activists, had some foundation in past experience. As Dodd and the CDPE contended, conservative budget-cutters across the state did indeed quite vocally support the witch hunt. Right-wing antitax activist Merwin K. Hart, chair of the New York Economic Council, and Milo MacDonald, who headed the Christian Front–aligned American Education Association, produced reams of propaganda supporting the investigation, as did the state Chamber of Commerce, which had been captured by conservative extremists earlier in the decade. Hart considered the Rapp-Coudert inquiry to be "one of the Economic Council's chief objectives."[21] The extreme right also made clear that at the heart of their crusade against school budgets lay a contempt for democratic institutions like public higher education, which the Chamber of Commerce reportedly had proposed ending earlier that year: "It seems to us there is a definite line which must be recognized, and that is the line between the amount of education it requires to kill illiteracy and the amount of education we give beyond that point.... In not carrying students too far and in having parents who are able to do so pay the cost of all education beyond illiteracy, is found a means of reducing the cost."[22]

An especially contentious battle over school spending and the state budget in winter 1940 similarly reinforced Dodd's and the CDPE's interpretation of the political alignments behind the Coudert committee. Between January and March, the union spearheaded a massive public campaign to save state school budgets from being axed by a newly elected Republican majority in the state legislature. The success of that campaign and its close proximity to the passage of the bill authorizing the Rapp-Coudert committee tends to support Dodd's and the CDPE's interpretation that the witch hunt was motivated by conservative budgetary retrenchment. But the tale is more complicated than the one outlined by the teachers; it involved an almost comical yet punishing fight between the GOP-controlled legislature, La Guardia's Fusion-GOP government in New York City, Tammany's representatives in Albany, and Democratic Governor Herbert Lehman that was worthy of New York state's reputation for byzantine legislative politics. The story of that budget fight exposes other motives behind the investigation involving a mobilization against the Communist Party and the union of forces and interests far more diverse than the party or Dodd were willing to acknowledge. Significantly, that full-blown anticommunist coalition included liberals, among them veterans of earlier conflicts with the Communist Party in the New York City teachers locals and elsewhere.

It is important first to recognize that in the decade before the budget battle during the winter of 1940, the New York City school system had had its share of local financial disasters that were largely unrelated to events in Albany. Declining real-estate values through the 1930s reduced city tax revenues while skyrocketing unemployment and local relief demands increasingly strained the municipal treasury. Additionally, La Guardia came into office in 1934 saddled by his spendthrift Tammany predecessors with a "Bankers Agreement," a stopgap measure brokered with the banks by Governor Lehman that forced the city to maintain balanced budgets under the gun of high-interest loans and low bond ratings. As a condition of providing funds to cover rising relief costs, the banks forbade the city from increasing real-estate and bank taxes. Labeling the agreement a dictatorship by Wall Street, La Guardia nevertheless buckled under, taking unprecedented control of municipal finances in order to trim payrolls and extraneous budgets, the legacy of years of Tammany patronage. Until 1938, when it finally paid the banks off after several years of brutal economizing and retooling, the city could not qualify to issue its own bonds at market rates, a constant drain on its treasury.[23]

By late winter 1940, however, the main fiscal problem for New York City and its educational institutions came from the state legislature, which had been mandated since 1928 to finance a substantial part of local school budgets and which, by the terms of the new city charter (passed by referendum in 1936), controlled a great deal of New York City's fiscal infrastructure. As soon as the legislative session opened in January 1939, the new Republican majority imposed a severe regime of fiscal austerity. That included cuts in state aid to education of roughly $10 million for the 1939–40 fiscal year, with $5.3 million sliced from the state appropriation for New York City.[24]

The Republican budget cuts devastated the city schools. During the fall of 1939, as the nation began pulling itself out of the Depression, the school board had to apply yet another in a series of "economy programs" that included a hiring freeze, the elimination of kindergarten and adult-education classes, and the consolidation of more than eight hundred day classes throughout the system. Even with declining enrollments, overcrowding in city high schools (already a problem before the 1939 budget) became so severe that nearly two-thirds of students attended classes over the maximum class size. Hundreds of classes recorded more than fifty pupils in attendance. Teachers told of being forced to falsify their rosters to hide the level of overcrowding, while having students from teacherless classrooms added in as phantom students. One substitute reported that a Manhattan kindergarten class was being taught by a sixth-grader. Students were sent into the streets during recess at another school that lacked personnel for proper schoolyard supervision. School Superintendent Harold G. Campbell estimated that at any given time, ten percent of high school students, lacking chairs and desks, took their instruction standing.[25]

The school system, in the midst of a construction program, had no shortage of classrooms; empty ones stood next to many that were overcrowded. What the city needed were teachers to put in front of them. By January 1940, at least one thousand positions had been left open, and several hundred more were filled by substitute teachers who were paid insubstantial hourly wages. The "no appointment policy" provoked lawsuits by Local 5 and its rival, the Teachers Guild, demanding, on the grounds of court decisions made five years earlier, that the state commissioner of education force the city to fill all vacant teaching positions from the still-growing ranks of unemployed teachers.[26] Tempers were also wearing thin among the teaching staff; evidence that their patience was exhausted began to appear in the press. One substitute, working full time and outraged that the board still had not converted her position after eight years, attacked an associate superintendent in his office, smashing inkwells, a lamp, and the administrator's "favorite family picture." As she was being carted off for psychiatric observation, she screamed, "No matter how long I have to wait I will get you!"[27]

The teachers unions spent most of 1939 battling with the legislature and city government over that year's budget cuts. Then, anticipating another round of cuts when the new legislative session opened in January 1940, Local 5 and its allied unions pulled out all stops, mobilizing a coalition of parent, civic, and labor organizations in blanketing towns and cities across the state with two million pieces of literature, a million matchboxes, and five million envelope seals that called on the public to "Save Our Schools." Teachers and their supporters canvassed, broadcast dozens of radio programs, and set up school defense committees in every assembly district. In mid-January, their efforts seemed to pay off: Governor Lehman and the GOP reportedly cut a deal that would restore educational and highway funds (the latter of which were dear to upstate Republicans) by changing income tax exemptions.[28]

That truce, however, began to break down within a few days under the withering fire of "taxpayer organizations" that objected to the prospect of a "new tax" on wealthy New Yorkers. Conservative activists instead proposed giving cities authority to cut teacher salaries (at the time reserved by law for the legislature), which of course was what the cities were expected to do.²⁹ By late January, GOP legislative leaders were following suit, insisting that fiscal resources were not available to restore funding and returning to their demand for deeper budget cuts, including a cut in teachers' pay that was sponsored by liberal Republican Assemblyman Abbott Low Moffatt of New York City.³⁰

Charging that Republicans were balancing budgets at the expense of teachers and education, the union mobilized yet another successful drive to defend the budget. In mid-February, Local 5, the city's United Parents Association, and unions from around the state descended on Albany for a day of joint legislative hearings on the budget. Expecting as many as eight thousand participants, the state moved the event to an armory a few blocks west of the Capitol that could seat over six thousand people. At that time, it was the largest hearing mounted in Albany's history, with attendees overflowing into neighboring assembly halls.³¹

At the end of February, the Republicans devised a "balanced" budget plan that cut programs a bit less severely but largely made up for expected deficits by a series of sleights of hand, a proposal that Governor Lehman rejected as "dishonest" and "hocus pocus."³² The teachers union and their supporters focused on Moffat's salary cut bill, which merely shifted the power to cut salaries to New York City's Board of Estimate, returned in the 1939 election to the control of Tammany Hall, which would have used that power to re-establish its grip on city schools. The joint organization of teachers unions in the city emphasized that the proposed bill would "return us to conditions prevalent prior to 1900, when political administrations toyed with teachers' salaries and school expenditures, using them to promote their political ends regardless of the effect on the school system."³³ Within a few days, La Guardia withdrew his hastily given support for the Moffat plan, effectively killing it in the legislature.³⁴ Moffat tried one more time to push a pay cut through, only to be thwarted when the teachers pulled out all stops to kill the bill, which like an improperly dispatched vampire kept popping up on the legislative agenda. As he finally withdrew his last pay-cut resolution that March 30, Moffat denounced "the teachers' lobby" for defeating economizing measures.³⁵

The *New York Times* explained the new budget as a straightforward product of conventional fiscal horse trading: A deal had been struck that allowed New York City to use $4.5 million in surplus relief taxes to cover specified items in its general budget (as originally proposed by Mayor La Guardia). Governor Lehman was allowed to apply the surplus from an earlier appropriation for improving rail crossings to needed road development, presumably placating upstate Republicans.[36] What the *Times* left out can be readily inferred—another kind of deal had been struck as well, involving political and ideological control of New York City's schools. By implication (though the payoff had occurred the day before, when the bill authorizing the Rapp-Coudert investigation passed), both budget-conscious upstate Republicans (who wanted a financial probe in order to justify cuts and who strongly opposed teachers unions) and downstate Democrats (many of whom resented Local 5 for successfully breaking Tammany control of school and college appointments) were brought together over the desire to retaliate against the union.

The Rapp-Coudert investigation also appears to have brought upstate Republicans and downstate Democrats together on the need to exercise a moral authority over the city schools. As the budget controversy raged in Albany that spring, the Bertrand Russell case hit the news.[37] Several historians trace the Rapp-Coudert investigations back to the Russell controversy, but the flare-up over Russell's appointment gave only the final nudge to the legislature's drive toward a witch hunt. And focusing on it as the main motive muddies the picture of the ideological alignments at the end of the 1930s.[38] At the end of February, Russell, then perhaps the best-known living philosopher in the English-speaking world, was offered a two-year appointment in the City College of New York (CCNY) philosophy department, which was approved by the department, the faculty, the president of the college, and the Board of Higher Education (BHE). That should have settled the matter. However, the philosopher, widely respected for his work in logic and foundations of mathematics but even more widely known for his popular writings advocating open marriage and condemning religious and moral authority, attracted the indignation of churches and moralists across the state who mounted a campaign to annul the appointment. The BHE reconsidered but reaffirmed its original decision, so Russell's opponents filed suit requesting court action in the middle of March. The Russell controversy reached the floor of the state senate on Monday, March 25, when the legislature voted to protest the philosopher's appointment. It was only a few minutes later that Senator John J. Dunnigan, a Democrat from the Bronx, introduced an initial resolution calling for the investigation of subversive activities in the New York City municipal colleges and public schools.[39] Dunnigan's proposal stoked the ire of his colleagues and constituents, but it was parked in committee.

It was at this point, on Tuesday, March 26, that Herbert Rapp, an upstate Republican, introduced the bill authorizing a legislative investigation of school finances across the state, an idea that was originally floated by

68   The Hearings

Republicans in late February.[40] Lehman had commissioned a similar study from the Regents in 1937. And before that, the Friedsam Commission, initiated by then-Governor Al Smith as an independent investigation of statewide school funding, had produced the current system by which local expenditures for education were equalized by state contributions. The Friedsam Law of 1928 also raised the level of state aid substantially relative to local contributions.[41] La Guardia jumped on Rapp's proposal as part of a compromise resolution of the teacher pay issue. La Guardia wanted an independent commission rather than a Republican-controlled legislative committee to conduct the probe "of educational costs and problems," as La Guardia put it. But the idea was essentially the same as Rapp's. On March 28, the substance of the Dunnigan anticommunist measure was incorporated with its sponsor's approval into Rapp's original financial investigation bill, on the argument that because the Rapp proposal called for studying school administration, an investigation into subversion was allowed for in this bill. And so the Rapp-Coudert investigation was born.[42]

Clearly the passage of the Rapp bill reflected the upstate GOP's conveniently provincial perception of New York City as a sump of moral decay and fiscal liability—the two notions combined in a general sense that city government exercised insufficient restraint on municipal schools and the people who worked and learned in them. Yet, in statements to the press after passage of the Republican Rapp bill, it was Democrat Dunnigan who made it clear that all of the legislature's political and fiscal concerns were closely related: the investigation of subversion was made necessary by the "evidences of scholastic decadence" in the city's educational system, especially the appointment of Russell, which Dunnigan declared was typical of "ungodly and un-American traditions which those in control of the school system in New York City are attempting to instill in the hearts and minds of the children and youth of the schools of the city."[43] In the nearly hysterical language of his resolution that had been proposed the previous Monday, however, Dunnigan revealed that Russell was only one of several nonfiscal concerns: included in his list of complaints were the forced retirements of "prominent educators who have rendered loyal and capable services to the schools and colleges of the City of New York" and who "have been compelled to retire, solely for the reason that their philosophy has not been in accord with the godless, materialistic theories of those now governing the New York City school system." Russell's appointment appears to have been no more important to Democrats than the BHE's recent decisions to get rid of the Tammany-appointed presidents of City and Hunter Colleges (the "prominent educators" referred to by Dunnigan), controversial retirements that were slated to take place later that year.[44]

Eventually the investigation of subversion authorized by the Rapp bill was taken on by a subcommittee headed by first-term Republican State Senator Frederic Coudert, Jr., while Rapp dropped out of the picture. So except for the desultory and largely ignored fiscal study, the witch hunt that swept the New York City colleges over the next year and a half came to be viewed as Coudert's project, while journalists and critics routinely called the subcommittee the "Coudert committee" and its guiding ideology "Coudertism."

4
Vichy's Lawyer?

Simon Gerson later explained in the *New Masses* that with the passage of the Rapp bill, a "new unholy alliance has been created between the budget-cutters, the brass-hat leaders of the American Legion, the Hearst press, and the Coughlin-influenced wing of the Catholic hierarchy." Looking as always for an explanation that could be digested on the pages of the *Daily Worker*, the Communist Party simplistically overstated the role of fiscally conservative, antilabor Republicans in crafting and promoting Rapp-Coudert's enabling legislation, conveniently forgetting the enthusiastic support given by liberal Republicans like Moffat and downstate Democrats like Dunnigan.[1]

As the events of the next two years unfolded, the left came to regard Frederic Rene Coudert, Jr., as the right's perfect candidate for leading an attack on public education. They were right, but for the wrong reasons. Bella Dodd, the Communist Party, and the Committee for the Defense of Public Education (CDPE) asserted that Coudert represented right-wing and even fascist forces in American society and politics. Charles Hendley, addressing the teachers at a rally the month after the public hearings, similarly made opposition to Coudertism part of the antifascist movement: "The real issue is the defense of a free public school system. We are living in a period when we have to fight a fascist advance every inch of the way and there's no getting away from it."[2] In these assertions, the accused teachers and their supporters were seriously mistaken, and the mistake was not just in their perception of Coudert's motives, but also in their understanding of Coudertism's ideological and political origins.

Fritz Coudert

Gerson described Coudert as "tall, patrician-featured, suave" as befit the president of the silk-stocking Upper East Side Republican Club.[3] Indeed, Coudert, known as "Fritz" to his friends and colleagues, came from a family of prominent and powerful lawyers who left an impressive record of public service in the courts and the halls of local, state, and national politics. His grandfather, Frederic Rene Coudert, Sr. (1832–1903), the son of a French refugee, built with his two brothers one of New York's leading international law firms, the first in the United States to open an overseas office in Paris, in 1879. Coudert Brothers, founded in 1852, represented European clients in the United States and abroad but specialized in those from France, where the family still maintained close personal as well as business ties. Frederic, Sr., established himself as one of the leading authorities on international trade law and law of the sea, helping craft the legal framework for ocean salvage and navigation. A strong anti-Tammany Democrat, his close connections with that party's reform wing earned him two informal invitations from President Grover Cleveland to join the United States Supreme Court, both of which he declined.[4]

Fritz Coudert's father, born in 1871 as Frederic Rene Coudert, Jr., took over the family firm in 1899, strengthening its involvement in international affairs. By the turn of the century, the firm—one of the largest in the United States—represented the governments of France, Belgium, Russia, Turkey, Venezuela, and Italy.[5] Under the second generation's direction, Coudert Brothers argued before the Supreme Court key cases in international law and helped shape America's emerging role as an international power. An outspoken anti-imperialist, Fritz's father served before the Supreme Court as senior counsel in the Insular Cases that determined the constitutional status of overseas possessions (an issue that was raised when Puerto Rico and the Philippines were taken from Spain in 1898) and extending some constitutional rights to the inhabitants of new territories.[6] The Couderts established strong ties as well to emerging corporate dynasties such as the Jay Gould family and the House of Morgan, and represented industrial clients such as Renault and Michelin in their American dealings, and General Motors, Western Electric, and Du Pont in France. During World War I, the firm negotiated loans and transfers of money and war materiel for the French, Russian, and Italian governments.[7]

Although the first two generations of American Couderts were anti-Tammany Democrats, young Fritz Coudert slipped into the Republican

Party. Born in 1898, the youngest Frederic Coudert graduated from Columbia in 1918 and then joined the United States Infantry as a first lieutenant and was deployed overseas during World War I. After graduating from Columbia Law School in 1922, he entered the family firm. Young Coudert, however, quickly moved into public affairs, serving as assistant United States attorney before making an unsuccessful run on the GOP ticket for Manhattan district attorney in 1929 (when Fiorello La Guardia made his first and disastrous bid for mayor as a Republican). After a decade of local and unelected service to the party, Coudert finally won election to the state senate in 1938 for the 17th district, stretching along Fifth, Madison, and Park Avenues, the heart of the prestigious Upper East Side. He would remain there until gaining election for New York's 17th Congressional district (a larger piece of the East Side) to the Eightieth Congress in 1946. He served six terms in Washington, D.C.[8]

In their unflattering view, Communist Party publicists aligned Coudert and his family with protofascists in New York's Catholic hierarchy. This particular claim was not entirely far-fetched, as Coudert Brothers represented the Catholic church and as the family had strong ties to Catholic conservatives through New York City's archbishop, Michael A. Corrigan, who was an old friend and associate of Fritz's grandfather, and through powerful Catholic families who were heavily invested in New York and New Jersey real estate. Fritz, who marked out a strongly conservative position in local and national politics after World War II, also counted himself a "good friend" of the notoriously anticommunist archbishop of New York, Francis Cardinal Spellman.[9] Critics less plausibly linked the family law firm to monarchists and fascists in Europe during Fritz Coudert's hotly contested race for Congress in 1942.

Indeed, in a story of banking intrigue suitable for Hollywood, Coudert Brothers represented the Bank of France (then under control of occupying Nazi forces) in a dispute over the disposition of $250 million worth of gold bullion left in France by the Belgian government for safekeeping before the Blitzkrieg broke the Maginot Line. The gold ended up in the physical possession of the Nazis after a brief sojourn under French protection outside Dakar, Senegal. Liberated France paid the Belgians back in 1944, but Coudert's firm evidently helped protect Vichy France's collaborationist government from liability until then, essentially allowing the gold to be used by the Nazis to finance the war.[10] Coudert Brothers also represented Vichy when it purchased the mansion on Fifth Avenue that France still uses as a consulate. And they continued as late as 1942 to argue cases in American court on behalf of French manufacturers who were producing armaments for the Nazi war effort.[11] Some years later, Coudert's father confessed to his friend Henry Simpson relative sympathy for the fascists, preferring them to the Communists, who he believed presented a more serious threat against France.[12] Some parts of his son Fritz's legislative record reinforced this picture: The month before the Rapp-Coudert legislation passed, Fritz had ushered a conservative bill into law that tested the separation of church and state by letting New York public-school students attend religious worship classes on school time.[13] And on the question of political dissent, Coudert already had shown himself to be not especially fair-minded, having supported with his fellow Republicans a virulent anti-red bill in the debates leading up to the passage in 1939 of the "compromise" Devany Law requiring the removal of any public employee in the state who "willfully and deliberately advocates, advises or teaches the doctrine that the government of the United States or any state or of any subdivision thereof should be overthrown or overturned by force, violence or any unlawful means."[14]

But it is unlikely that Vichy sympathies motivated Coudert Brothers to represent French bankers: Fritz Coudert, who ran the firm at the time and litigated the bullion case, remained, like his influential father, a critic of isolationism and a strong proponent of United States intervention on the Allied side in the first two years of the European war.[15] The firm probably took the Belgian gold case as part of its routine business with international clients of all sorts, including prominent Jews and Jewish-owned businesses in France and elsewhere. Moreover Coudert did not quite fit the role of anticommunist crusader that had been established by predecessors like Dies. He supported higher education and sponsored during his first term in the state senate a new law officially extending tenure rights to municipal college faculty.[16]

As a downstate Republican with a reputation for being, at that time, relatively liberal compared to other members of his party, Coudert then was a good choice to run a controversial committee that could disrupt the state's educational system and raise criticism from the left. And, at least at the start, Coudert seemed judicious and evenhanded in setting the committee's agenda. Although he had many conservative ties through the state Republican Party and as a corporate lawyer, Coudert avoided association with antitax extremists like Merwin Hart or Christian Front–supporters like Milo MacDonald. He did not jump at their offers of counsel and advice, even putting Hart off for several months when the right-wing activist pushed for a meeting at which Hart hoped to shape the course of the investigation.[17] Certainly, Coudert's friends on Wall Street had his ear, demanding aggressive action against subversion, probably with budget cuts in mind, but their influence was limited by the fact that the Coudert committee's chief counsel, Paul Windels, exercised strict control over the investigation. As we shall see, other, more insidious right-wing influences affected the probe, but those were largely indirect, mainly operating by default. Moreover, it is unlikely that Coudert believed in destroying public education, like Hart or the state Chamber of Commerce, any more than did Windels or the rest of the Coudert staff, many if not most of whom were liberals.

The List Fight

With one of its first acts, however, the Coudert committee reinforced Dodd's perception that upstate Republicans used the investigation to break city unions: Several weeks before the December public hearings, it subpoenaed the membership lists of Locals 5 and 537 of the American Federation of Teachers (AFT), unions representing public-school and municipal-college teachers and staff in the city. That warrant for evidence—called a *duces tecum* subpoena—opened a series of events that culminated with the spectacle of Charles Hendley hiding out from the police to avoid being jailed for legislative contempt. The union willingly provided all of its minutes, financial records, and other organizational files when Coudert committee staffers pulled up to union headquarters in a taxi with the subpoena in mid-October. It drew the line, however, at handing Coudert its membership lists, which looked to many New Yorkers like an attempt to build an anti-union blacklist.[18]

PM called the membership list subpoena a "new legal weapon against labor unions," noting that "no union member will be safe from the prying eyes of employer groups, manufacturers' associations, chambers of commerce, boards of trade and others who would just love to know who [is], and who is not, a believer in the organization of labor."[19] The union had good reason, moreover, to believe that state legislators or their staff might very well allow school officials who were hostile to the union to use the lists to penalize union members. Superintendents and principals had on many occasions punished teachers who were bold or careless enough to let it be known they belonged to the union or supported union positions on salaries and school conditions. Union records attest to many such reprisals in the city school system, including summary firings of probationary employees, punitive transfers, and denials of promotion. The case of two popular teachers who were transferred out of a district in 1933 for involvement with a local parents organization illustrates how readily the school district punished activist employees. Helen Weinstein and Ralph Fagin taught on a substitute basis at P.S. 225 in Brighton Beach. Appalled by overcrowding in the school, they joined parents in a peaceful protest. For their efforts, they were exiled to hardship posts, Weinstein to Staten Island and Fagin to the Navy Yard. Confronted by a large group of parents who were unhappy about the transfers, Superintendent William J. O'Shea retorted, "they should not have gone out parading through the street and arousing the ire of the people against their employers." One parent pointed out that parades had been a legitimate part of American civic life since the Revolution. To that, O'Shea responded, "Not for teachers."[20]

Concerned about the precedent being set by the Coudert subpoena, unions across the country issued strong protests, with the AFT, declaring, "The opening of the membership lists will introduce into America the very totalitarian methods and spirit which the committee proposes to eradicate."[21] Supported by much of the labor movement, Hendley refused to hand them over, even though Coudert ordered him arrested for contempt in late November as the public hearings approached.[22] But Hendley's resistance, his willingness to risk jail, and the union's devotion of its resources to defending the privacy of union membership were of no avail. The federal courts decided in favor of unions in a similar case in California, but New York state's judges found otherwise. In late January 1941, Hendley finally turned the lists over to Windels's staffers, though it is clear from the Coudert files and from public testimony that they already had a copy anyway.[23]

At the very least, Coudert and Windels were careless about the consequences of their subpoena and probably indifferent to its far-reaching violation of rights. They learned from dealing with school officials that at least one high-level administrator wanted to use the rosters to blacklist union teachers. And while Windels didn't oblige him, he did offer "where it is indicated to us from those lists that there is an undue concentration of union members in any particular school, that if we send for the principal of that school, we may find the existence of organized disorderly and subversive activity." Associate Superintendent John E. Wade understood Windels's proposal generously: "when you give us the list we can have it as a confidential list, but we can easily identify the names as belonging to a particular school organization."[24]

The committee also used union records to cast a wide net for suspects in a manner that was clearly chilling for trade unionism, not to mention First Amendment rights. A very few membership entries specified connections with Communist-affiliated organizations such as the International Workers Order and the Workers School. Of course, those notations proved nothing about party membership, but that didn't stop the committee from publicizing some of those names in the December hearings.[25] Even more chilling was the use to which the committee put data about sponsorship and recruitment. Windels assumed that someone sponsored for union membership by a known Communist was more likely to be a Communist than someone who was not. Such inferences were made from the records of faculty recruited to the College Teachers Union (CTU or Local 537) by BC philosophy professor Howard Selsam, a key CTU activist widely assumed to be a Communist. College staff brought into the union by Selsam automatically went onto a suspects list in the Coudert files and most of them were subpoenaed for questioning by the staff, potentially casting them under suspicion with school authorities as well.[26]

Coudert, who supported the budget cuts that his party rammed through the legislature in 1939 and 1940, further contributed to the view that he was an anti-union zealot by unscrupulously attacking the union and its representatives. Shortly after the lists were subpoenaed, he accused the union of passing them freely to other organizations to use for mailing publicity, including organizations commonly considered fronts for the Communist Party, and "to facilitate the indoctrinating of members of the teaching staff of the New York City school system with the ideas and propaganda of the Soviet Union." But, as Hendley pointed out, Coudert knew full well (because Hendley had showed him) that rather than having handed those organizations the lists, the union had arranged to do the mailings for them or to fold their leaflets into the local's monthly newsletter.[27] In fact, the only organization outside of the New York locals that had ever had access to the New York membership lists was the AFT national office, which used them to send out its monthly magazine.[28]

Yet it is not at all clear that Coudert and the committee's main objective in demanding the lists was union busting, or that they aimed to "smear the schools... and smear the concept of education itself," as the CTU declared.[29] Instead, evidence suggests that their main purpose was the one stated in the subpoena: the rooting out of Communists, toward whom Coudert was palpably hostile. In a speech at a meeting of the Women's National Republican Club later in 1941, Coudert called Communists and Nazis a "different kind of animal" that "cannot be talked to or reasoned with." If anyone had doubts about Coudert's anticommunism, his inflammatory and hyperbolic rhetoric put them to rest: "Now if your dog had rabies you wouldn't clap him into jail after he had bitten a number of persons—you'd put a bullet into his head, if you had that kind of iron in your soul." Coudert warned that it was "going to require brutal treatment to handle these teachers who have been for so long doing precisely what they are told, imbuing students with their communistic and Nazi policies, and sitting for years on the payroll of New York State while they were about it." For this purpose, the lists and other membership records probably were of some limited use. Only around a fifth of teachers were in the union in 1940, so it was reasonable for the Coudert staffers to assume that all Communists at any given school were bound to be on the union membership lists. What is more, with the exception of protests concerning the union's membership lists, Coudert appears to have had the support of many of the state's liberals and trade unionists, including leaders of the American Federation of Labor (AFL), the national leadership of the AFT, and the former and anticommunist leadership of Local 5, who either publicly endorsed the inquiry or cooperated with it privately. AFT President George Counts and his executive council, already campaigning to expel Locals 5 and 537 from the national union, publicly maligned the New York locals for being led by a "totalitarian political faction" that advocated teaching "undemocratic doctrines in the public schools." Many of the leaders of the progressive education movement, including Counts and philosopher John Dewey, openly promoted the expulsion of the two New York locals from the national union, agreeing with the Coudert investigation that "the two New York locals ... have evidently been brought under the domination of Communist forces which have worked under cover to fashion these organizations into tools for their party purposes."[30] Yet, contrary to Dodd and the CDPE's claim that the supporters of Rapp-Coudert aimed at destroying the teachers union and defunding public education, most of these liberals and social democrats strongly supported trade unions as well as educational budgets and other social expenditures that conservatives and right-wingers attacked.

Generally, the union and its defenders misunderstood and ignored the role of these liberals in the unfolding witch hunt, and the consequences of that failure were grave. As Dodd and the Defense Committee attacked Coudertism's conservative motives, they missed the liberal ones. And in doing so, they allowed liberal anticommunists to frame the issues of classroom subversion, union factionalism, and revolutionary violence, which were used to justify outlawing communism and throwing suspected Communists out of the classroom. Unfortunately, the union's and the Communist Party's effort to deflect a frontal attack on the communist left followed from a misunderstanding of the early dynamics of anticommunism, its origins, and its motives. That failure to take the full measure of prewar anticommunism, especially liberal countersubversion, seriously undermined the ability of the teachers union and the party to put up an effective front against "Coudertism" or, as we would eventually call it, "McCarthyism." It was true, as the union's supporters relentlessly and almost desperately insisted, that the hearings contributed to "an attempt to slash State-aid to education and undermine the free public schools" and "an attempt to smash the Teachers Union, the most militant defender of education."[31] But Coudertism was also much more than that.

A Liberal Staff

In setting up the Rapp-Coudert investigation, Republican and Democratic leaders wrangled over who would best promote the alleged interests of the legislature. Senate Majority Leader Joe Hanley and Minority Leader Dunnigan put together the main committee to reflect the balance of legislative power at the time, observing the proper distribution of both parties as well as upstate and downstate members of both houses.[32] But in the end, the composition of the committee was purely cosmetic, as Rapp and eleven members of the larger body "took no part" in the New York City investigations, which were assigned to Coudert's subcommittee. It was that subcommittee that erroneously became known in later years as the "Rapp-Coudert Committee." The four legislative members of that smaller body other than Coudert—Senators John L. Buckley and Peter T. Farrell, and Assemblymen John D. Bennett and Sheldon Wicks—only occasionally showed up for meetings and reportedly never looked at any exhibits or even read the subcommittee's final report. That left Coudert to run the show.[33]

Coudert's reputation and the reputation of the staff of lawyers and investigators whom he had selected that summer were a crucial part of the public campaign they conducted under the auspices of an "investigation." Above all, they struggled to maintain the aura of impartiality and professional responsibility that Dies and other forebears had discarded readily or been unable to sustain. In the first weeks of its existence, the project was already receiving flack in the press and public forums. Perhaps that is why members of the Coudert staff insisted implausibly that the exact point of the investigation was not decided until late summer 1940, under the pressure of "compelling evidence" that a study of subversion was needed, and that Coudert initially (that is, in the spring) expected to concentrate merely on school finances. In fact, while a statewide investigation of school finances did indeed take place, it was far overshadowed by the Coudert subcommittee's inquiry.[34] Coudert and his staff continued this rather disingenuous publicity game over the intentions of the committee long after the investigations had closed down, maintaining the fiction that its ultimate goal was a complete evaluation of the school system's administrative efficiency.

Once one eliminates the role of the larger Rapp committee and the significant participation of the other members of Coudert's subversion subcommittee, it becomes evident that the direction of the subversion probe came down to the work of Coudert and his staff. It is in that relationship and in the relationship of that staff to key informants that one sees the extent to which the committee's work was shaped by a liberal sensibility. Several historians have noted that the staff whom Coudert ended up picking were all "respectable attorneys" like Coudert himself. As Ellen Schrecker put it, "There were no rednecks, but sober and responsible men who realized that the credibility and effectiveness of their enterprise required that they expose genuine Communists and not Popular Front liberals that the Wisconsin and Illinois committees [local investigations similar to Rapp-Coudert] had mistakenly attacked."[35] Regardless of whom the committee actually did expose, there is no question that, in terms of their collective public image, Coudert's staff took the high road. The chief counsel for the New York City investigation, Coudert and Hanley agreed, had to be a downstate Republican, if only to fend off accusations from city liberals that the committee would just be doing hatchet work for upstate conservatives or, worse, Tammany Hall. So they chose Windels, a reformer from Brooklyn who could with some justice consider himself one of the people who ended Tammany's reign over New York, a man who had swept corruption out of the dingy, smoke-filled rooms of city government.[36]

To maintain the hoped-for aura of impartiality in the investigation but also to exclude the inevitable meddling of Albany politicos, Windels demanded virtual independence from the legislature, appointing his own staff, including stenographers. Consequently, though his associate and assistant counsels belonged to both parties, they came from the city rather than the dispersed assembly and senate districts that also had to be served by legislative patronage. Windels additionally demanded full control over the disposition of the investigation records. Freedom from legislative interference extended to the hearings as well, requiring "appropriate rules to insure among other things orderly procedure at the public hearings and the decorum which attaches to trials in courts of justice." Those rules included restrictions on the legislators themselves. Windels reserved the right to "conduct private hearings before any member of the Committee acting as a subcommittee and other members of the Committee shall not attend such examinations except upon the invitation or with the consent of counsel." In theory, Windels's strict ground rules allowed that only he would run the questioning: committee members were supposed to wait until he or his assistants were finished to ask any questions, and they had to apply beforehand to call witnesses.[37]

Windels brought on board several associates from the La Guardia administration, two of them key veterans of Seabury's anti-Tammany investigations. Attorney Phillip W. Haberman, Jr., was added as the chief associate counsel on August 2. As one of "Seabury's boys"—young lawyers just out of law school who had been chosen for their reformist enthusiasm as much as for their knowledge of the law—and a dogged investigator, Haberman had helped track down the letters of credit from Chase Bank that indisputably tied Mayor Jimmy Walker to the bribes for exclusive bus franchises that caused him to be thrown out of office.[38] Later, Haberman served as the city's assistant corporate counsel under Windels. It was Haberman who would write the final report on the subversion inquiry that was released in April 1942.[39] In November, Haberman was joined as associate counsel by J. G. Louis Molloy, another of Seabury's boys. After the Seabury investigations, Molloy went on to head the anti-Tammany Knickerbocker Democratic Club and remained a close adviser to Seabury, who died in 1958. Molloy also drafted some of La Guardia's key campaign speeches in his first successful bid for the mayor's office in 1933, and went on to become La Guardia's law secretary.[40] For the rest of his associates, Windels mainly chose recent graduates of Ivy League Law schools—among them, a preponderance of Yale and Columbia degrees with Fordham and New York University thrown in. All told, four had passed through the corporation counsel's office and two had served as prosecutors, one in the United States Attorney's Office and another for the New York county district attorney. One was the daughter of a well-known suffragette. By August 19, the entire staff was organized and work had begun.[41]

By early September, Windels had begun seeking out informants and collecting testimony. One of the first people to whom he turned was Henry Linville, who was the former president of Local 5 and current leader of the New York Teachers Guild, the rival union formed in 1935 when liberals and conservative socialists resigned en masse in protest of what they considered to be communist control of their union. Linville gladly cooperated with Windels and his staff. In fact, he had been anticipating an investigation of this sort for several years as he lobbied the AFT and the AFL to deal harshly and urgently with his former union and the communists in it. He had also testified along with several far more conservative faculty and staff from the municipal colleges and public schools before the Dies committee two years earlier. Linville directed Windels to other liberals, socialists, social democrats, and former communists who could help them investigate the influence of communists in the schools and the union, most of whom Linville knew would gladly cooperate with Coudert's committee.

Linville also suggested to Windels's staff that they look into the history of factional conflicts in Local 5—the ones that led to Linville's resignation as its president. And the ideal place to start, he told them, would be an obscure episode in the history of teacher unionism, the so-called Dewey Trial of 1933.[42]

PART II
Class War

5
The Dewey Trial

It was an unseasonably warm Saturday at the end of April 1933, two months into Franklin Delano Roosevelt's first term. Tens of thousands of New Yorkers flocked to Coney Island and other nearby beaches to enjoy the warmest April 29 in almost half a century.[1] The mercury peaked in the midseventies early that afternoon, as hundreds of Local 5 members filed through the massive neoclassical portal of New York's High School of Commerce into the vast auditorium at the center of the building. While they might have preferred strolling along boardwalks and sunning themselves on city beaches, the teachers understood the gravity of the meeting, a special general assembly that had been planned since the previous October. Not only would the gathering decide the fate of six colleagues; it would determine the role of radical political dissent in their ranks. Still, they could not possibly have foreseen the way this event would be used against the union and left-wing teachers in just a few short years.

The setting suited the event. In spring 1933, the High School of Commerce stood between Sixty-Fifth and Sixty-Sixth Streets right off Lincoln Square. It has long since been torn down to make room for the performance halls, conservatories, and libraries of Lincoln Center and the Julliard School of Music, which are now showpieces of New York's prosperous Upper West side. Eighty years ago, in contrast, the "Central Park West" district stretched across a more economically uneven landscape. At its eastern edge rose some of the city's grandest apartment buildings, including the Dakota and the Majestic, still familiar parts of Central Park's western skyline. On the far western side of the district, grand hotels and posh apartments lined Riverside Drive, affording priceless views of the Hudson. But just one block west of the park, an elevated rail line clattered above Columbus Avenue, which was described by the 1939 *WPA Guide to New York City* as "a shabby backstreet." The guide judged the area between Broadway and the Hudson north from Fifty-Ninth Street to Seventieth to be "a plebian district" that was "encroached upon" by "run-down" areas to the south and north. Eighteen years later, it would be made the setting of gang warfare in the Broadway hit *West Side Story*.[2]

Like the neighborhoods that surrounded it, Commerce reflected the aspirations and educational failures of the city as a whole. The board of education opened it in 1903 to meet the needs of an emerging financial capital, which only a few years earlier still had no self-standing public high schools. Optimistically built to train graduates for the foreign service and international banking, Commerce was one of five new high schools designed by the school system's official architect, C. B. J. Snyder, who perfected the "H" layout to accommodate thousands of pupils on relatively small footprints, which was no mean achievement at the turn of the century in a city with a huge influx of students and skyrocketing land values. In size and style, Commerce epitomized both the grandeur of New York's educational expectations and the real problems of schooling a diverse and growing population in the midst of a depression. Already overcrowded—enrollments reached two thousand by World War I—and badly maintained, the massive structure of the school also embodied the inertia and corruption of the city's school bureaucracy. An investigation by the city's Public Education Association in 1919 found Commerce to be "filthy" and unsanitary, a source of "much of the wanton destructiveness, thievery and general carelessness of the student body." It was grand but also oppressively weighty and grandiose, the kind of inflexible school building that municipalities around the country would abandon after World War II.[3]

Those very same economic stresses and political inertias led most of the union membership to pack Commerce's warm auditorium on a sunny Saturday afternoon. Suffering cutbacks by city banks and Tammany Hall, teachers were already at odds with the business community in a political contest that would last the decade. Local 5, the city's main teachers union, affiliated with the American Federation of Teachers (AFT), had represented the teachers' side in that struggle for almost twenty years. But the union was not unified. For two years, members had locked horns over how to address deteriorating teaching conditions, pitting liberals and socialists who controlled the union on one side against communists of various stripes on the other. Union leaders had demanded the April 29 meeting for a "trial" of six communist members to determine whether they should be expelled or suspended for fomenting factionalism in the union's ranks. Over the previous five months, a "grievance committee" had conducted an investigation led by the venerable educational reformer and philosopher John Dewey, who would present the committee's findings at the gathering. For that reason, the deliberations that afternoon and evening came to be known as "The Dewey Trial."

The Dewey Trial would enjoy a strange career over the next decade. It failed to resolve the union's internal conflicts, which continued until fall 1935, when liberals, including Dewey, quit the local to form an explicitly anticommunist rival union, the Teachers Guild, whose leaders forced Local 5's expulsion in 1941 from the mainstream of the labor movement. Those liberal anticommunists pointed back to the 1933 dispute as evidence of inherent sectarianism and bad faith on the part of communists and communist-led unions, to justify rendering them pariahs. But the Dewey Trial's most consequential historical role would come when the Coudert committee employed it as a political and ideological touchstone for its investigation. Windels and his staff declared the grievance committee's final report, authored by Dewey, to be full of "penetrating observations" on the rift in the union—it was "a succinct and compelling statement of the basic reasons why Communism is incompatible with democracy." In this manner, the "famous Dewey trial," as the Coudert committee referred to it, figured prominently in the committee's public and private interrogations, as well as in the case that it would make for criminalizing communism.[4]

Henry Linville's Union

Dewey's Special Grievance Committee came into existence because of real problems in Local 5 and other unions in the early days of the Depression. On the surface, the main issue seemed to be an unwarranted "factionalism" that was disrupting union business. In some sense, that factionalism was inevitable. Just below that surface ran a conflict between an entrenched union leadership and dissident members over the meaning and practice of democracy.

On one side of the divide stood the union's elected officials, who had been in power since its founding in 1913 by Henry Linville, who in 1932 still served as the local's president and who the year before had been voted president of the national union. In news photos, Linville looked less like the high school biology teacher he once was than a conservatively dressed

88 Class War

Henry Linville (*right*), testifying before the Dies Committee, U.S. House of Representatives, Washington, D.C. *New York Times*, 28 November 1939. (Times Wide World Photos. Reproduced with permission of the *New York Times* and Redux Pictures.)

insurance agent, with bags under his eyes, his thinning, gray hair parted over a bald spot—a grey man in a grey world, respectable, determined, and realistic.[5] Teachers who were more radically left-wing detested him. Brooklyn College's Howard Selsam called him a "die-hard bureaucrat" and a "little czar." But others praised Linville for his "fairness, decency and kindness," as well as his courage and tact.[6] It was his persistence and resourcefulness, and his tenacious campaign against communists in his union that eventually brought him to the attention of Coudert's staff, who found in Linville a guide and counselor. They credited him above all others in their 1942 report for his "unselfish and devoted service" in supporting and guiding their witch hunt.[7]

Well before Coudertism or the Communist Party appeared on the scene, Linville built a reputation as a progressive trade-union leader and educational reformer, much like his friend Dewey, who offered guidance and support to Local 5 as one of its charter members. In 1916, Linville invited controversy by leading the unaffiliated Teachers League into the newly organized AFT, forming New York City's first teachers local. Critics at the time held that since the interests of teachers were the same as those of the public they served, they could not form adversarial unions that would engage in collective bargaining or might even strike. Instead, many liberals as well as conservatives believed teachers should be limited to professional organizations aimed solely at credentialing members and improving teaching and schools through training and legislative lobbying.[8] To his credit Linville, a socialist who served for many years as editor of the AFT's national monthly, the *American Teacher,* convincingly argued that professionalism did not conflict with the interests of teachers as employees and union members. He and his closest associate, Abraham Lefkowitz, built the New York local on that principle in the hostile climate of the First World War and the red scare that followed, attracting radical activists to its ranks from the social and political movements of the 1910s, including future Socialist Party leader Norman Thomas and founding members of the Communist Party of the United States, including Alexander Trachtenberg and Bertram Wolfe.[9]

In the early years of the union, Linville took uncompromising and even radical positions on many issues, opposing American entry into World War I and supporting women's struggle for equity in the schools.[10] Linville also earned a reputation as a defender of academic freedom, going to bat for fellow teachers persecuted during and after the war by a quick succession of repressive laws and loyalty campaigns, the most notorious of which were New York's Lusk Laws, named for State Senator Clayton Lusk, whose Legislative Committee on Seditious Activities forced their passage in 1920.[11] Among the measures imposed by Lusk and his investigators was the requirement that "every teacher in the state shall be examined as to his character and loyalty" before receiving a certificate. Lusk forced teachers accused of disloyalty into closed hearings in Albany that the teachers union accurately called "star chambers."[12] Thirty were disciplined by New York City's Board of Education and three dismissed, including Communist Party official and teachers-union activist Benjamin Gitlow. Despite the potential liability of doing so, Linville defended them publicly, noting the anti-Semitism that was in league with prejudice against socialism: "If a teacher happens to be a Jew, and a Socialist, and to be personally disliked by an official, the technique of 'indirection' takes care of it all through the euphemism 'conduct unbecoming a teacher.'" Linville continued to defend his colleagues against such witch hunts through the 1920s.[13]

The Left Wing

On the other side of the divide in the teachers union stood two dissident groups, comprising members of several minor left-wing parties that were increasingly popular among faculty, staff, and students in the New York public schools and universities after the 1929 stock market crash. Most of these groups were part of the Communist Party in the late 1920s, before internal power struggles in the Soviet Union and the United States led to the expulsion of several American party leaders and their followers. The tiny contingent of communists that had been active in the teachers union since 1922 fragmented into Stalinists, loyalists to exiled Bolshevik leader Leon Trotsky, and followers of former party secretary Jay Lovestone, whom the Soviets ousted for doctrinal deviations. Each group had at most a handful of adherents in the union in 1932. A few nonaligned parties and political organizations were also represented among the teachers that Linville, Lefkowitz, and their allies derisively called the "left wing," including "militant" Socialists and followers of the anarcho-syndicalist A. J. Muste, whose Brookwood Labor College was an important site for New York progressives to discuss labor and reform issues in the late 1920s and early 1930s.[14]

Political disagreements among the Communist, Lovestoneite, and Trotskyist teachers were almost as rancorous as their disputes with the existing union administration. Nonetheless, left-wing teachers found many points on which to agree, mainly involving objections to Linville's direction of the union and its relationship to the rest of the labor movement. Already in the early 1930s, cracks were appearing in the American Federation of Labor (AFL) that within a couple of years would break apart the national labor organization. Remnants of AFL founder Samuel Gompers's old "machine" remained in charge of the federation, which was still dominated in 1932 by the skilled trades and led from the wings by Vice President Matthew Woll, a rabidly anticommunist lawyer who ran the photoengravers union and helped found the AFL's enormously successful insurance fund.[15] Although the main issue in this unfolding conflict in the AFL is often posed as a contest between craft and industrial unionism, it also had political and ideological dimensions: Like Gompers, Woll and conservative craft unionists believed unions should exclusively focus on economic gains for their members. Labor's left wing argued that in order even to represent the economic interests of employees, unions also must act on behalf of workers as a class in a broader political and ideological struggle with industrial leaders.

Liberals and socialists like Linville and Lefkowitz detested Woll, who indiscriminately attacked and red-baited them along with communists; however, they found an ally in William Green, who replaced Gompers as AFL president in 1924. The teachers' relations with Gompers had been turbulent at best, declining steadily once he lost interest in public sector unionism after the disastrous Boston Police Strike in fall 1919.[16] Through the late 1920s, Green antagonized unionized teachers in much the same vein as his predecessor, supporting professional organizations like the National Education Association (NEA), even failing for several years to appoint an AFT representative to the AFL education committee, run by Woll in Washington, D.C. And Green increasingly directed his own strident anticommunism at teachers, insisting that Brookwood staff be thrown out of the teachers union for their radicalism and their criticism of AFL craft unionism. According to historian Marjorie Murphy, AFT disillusionment with the AFL led to a "revolt of women teachers" against earlier domination of the union by men who sided with Gompers. The substantially female membership in 1926 elected socialist Florence Hanson and progressive Mary Barker to run the AFT until 1931. During that period, relations with the AFL, which Barker called "that Woll-ridden machine," deteriorated even further.[17]

In the early 1930s, however, partly because he was concerned about rising dissent in the ranks of the federation, partly because a declining NEA was failing to deliver on national policy, Green changed course to court the AFT. Green granted access and positions to AFT representatives like Selma Borchardt, a Washington, D.C. public-school teacher, and a friend and ally of Linville, making her secretary of the federation's education committee.[18] For his part, Linville increasingly defended Green's reign over the federation, embracing as well the business model of union organizing that Green inherited from Gompers. In allying himself with Green, Linville followed conservative members of his own Socialist Party, which in 1934 divided along ideological and political lines between an anticommunist "Old Guard" that was aligned with labor conservatives and younger militants who allied with other left parties, including the Communists, to build industrial unions in an explicitly political "class struggle."[19]

At the start of the Depression, Linville and his allies regarded the union to be an organization of skilled professionals with leverage sufficient to negotiate salaries and working conditions through existing channels of communication. And they wanted to keep it that way. Because of New York's idiosyncratic school politics, in which the state legislature substantially funded local school budgets and determined the base rates of compensation for teachers and staff, much of that negotiation went on in Albany, managed by a joint committee of teacher organizations that included Local 5 and other professional groups representing various parts of the public-school teaching staff. Additional lobbying occurred at the city level. Since shortly after World War I, Linville and Lefkowitz, who served as the union's legislative representative, had worked out what they considered an effective system of promoting teachers' interests and improving the quality of public education by cultivating allegiances with other established trade unions, professional organizations, representatives of other public employees, and political leaders, using the resulting leverage to pressure assemblymen and senators, the city's board of estimate, and the mayor's office to raise state and city educational budgets.

Until the Depression, such negotiations seldom if ever became rancorous or openly confrontational. Then Linville's strategy began to fail as austerity budgets froze salaries and hiring, class sizes grew, and buildings deteriorated.[20] In addition, the city employed measures that rank and file teachers found especially deplorable, such as hiring substitute teachers for full-time work at reduced salaries to permit greater flexibility at lower cost. In fall 1931, Tammany, through its appointed board and loyal administrators, also began deducting a "voluntary levy" from teacher paychecks, ostensibly for unemployed teachers on relief, though many school employees believed they just were being forced to kick back a percentage of their salaries into a slush fund for corrupt school officials.[21] By 1933, the city proposed a $6.5 million reduction in the school budget, to be achieved by increasing class size by roughly ten percent across the board. The union estimated that enrollments in ten to fifteen thousand classes would swell to as many as fifty-five students as a result of the cuts.[22]

Although the schools and their teaching staffs were treated with growing contempt by bankers, the board, city officials, and state legislators, Linville, Lefkowitz, and the union's executive board opposed more confrontational mobilizing strategies. "Social sanity is the need of the hour," they declared in response to unilateral salary reductions in 1932. Proposing financial and tax reforms to salvage programs on the chopping block, Lefkowitz argued that "money for necessary, constructive, social purposes can be secured." And it was the teachers union's job, its leaders insisted, to "help the public to a more intelligent and impartial approach to the solution of this problem." Reluctant to unleash what Linville believed would be the uncontrolled wrath of rank-and-file teachers, he and Lefkowitz counseled members to petition the board and organized weak telegram protests through school principals.²³ Moreover, Linville and Lefkowitz accepted budget cuts, provided that "if cutting must be done in Education, then . . . it should be done by educational experts," like themselves, "who can cut intelligently."²⁴

By 1931, many teachers had lost patience with Linville's efforts to negotiate relief from an already intolerable situation. Younger teachers, who gained their credentials in the late 1920s and early 1930s from the municipal college system and had suffered bouts of unemployment or been hired in initially as substitutes disagreed with the emphasis on lobbying and negotiation as the means of achieving even the simplest goals. The pay levy was an especially hot issue, to which Linville responded without energy or incisiveness.²⁵ Meanwhile, Tammany and the board evaded the negotiation and lobbying that Linville and Lefkowitz claimed was the intelligent and effective way of promoting the interests of teachers and public education. The left advocated a boycott of the fund.²⁶

These disputes had deeper philosophical and political roots. In contrast to the Linville administration's emphasis on the common interests of teachers and school boards, the more militant younger teachers believed their interests as teachers, like those of other workers, were opposed to those of the "ruling class," by which they meant not only bankers and other economic elites, but also their servants in city governments and school systems, as well as the venial "sachems" of Tammany Hall. This was the position promoted by Isidore Begun, a Columbia University graduate student who had begun teaching in the city schools just a few years earlier. Born in Russia in 1903 and orphaned as a teenager, Begun graduated City College of New York (CCNY) in 1924; he then studied educational philosophy with Dewey at Teachers College, earning a master's degree while teaching. Initially a Socialist, Begun drifted into the communist movement near the end of the 1920s. By 1933, he was running on the Communist Party ticket for city office, though he claimed that he had joined the party just that year. Eventually he became the party's education director for New York state.²⁷

For militants like Begun, the proper response to Tammany recalcitrance was "mass action," the basis of which, explained the Unemployed Teachers Association (UTA), a small group aligned with the Communist Party and led by Begun, was "the idea that the government is controlled by organized groups motivated by self-interest," like Tammany, and that the bankers and real estate speculators who stood behind them were not going to change "because of tender feelings toward the children or the teachers." To Linville's aversion for mass mobilization, the UTA contended, "polite requests will be answered by most polite refusals. Only the insistent demands of a large group will bring anything more." Left-wing teachers wanted to shift the ground of negotiation away from rational persuasion, arguing that the union must mobilize dormant elements of the public in order to demand democratic control over fiscal and other resources by bringing grievances en masse to board of education meetings: "This large group is the 'mass' that must act. Only a large group will carry meaning to those who run our government." They proposed "emphatic, demonstrative, determined action" such as "mass-meetings, delegations, publicity, more mass-meetings, more delegations," and board meetings "so flooded with teachers and parents that the Board will be 'virtually forced' to hear us." That, the UTA concluded, "is mass-action." While some sort of threat stood behind this strategy, Begun and his allies did not advocate using violence or fomenting revolution.[28] Their goals were as practical and constitutional as Linville's, though perhaps not quite as civil.

The dispute between the communist left and the Linville administration also involved disagreement over the properly democratic conduct of union business. Linville based his charge of factionalism on the claim that radicals disrupted union meetings as part of a strategy to hijack the union. The communists, for their part, found to their frustration that union leaders rigidly refused to address their concerns through the union's existing channels of deliberation and debate. Among other things, Linville ignored the expanding number of substitute teachers, excluding them from membership in the union on the technical grounds that they still lacked certification by the board of examiners. As a result, union membership remained frozen at around fifteen hundred, even as discontent mounted among the city's roughly thirty thousand public-school teachers.[29] Linville wanted to pressure the city into certifying substitutes for full-time work, but he also feared opening the union to younger, marginally employed teachers who were intellectually and politically hostile to his kind of leadership and who were already disrupting the union's carefully constructed system of negotiation. And Linville had no problem subjecting prospective members to political tests. As he explained to Florence Hanson, the AFT's secretary-treasurer, "Without the power of refusing membership to undesirable persons, a Union would be helpless. It would be obliged to accept anyone who applied."[30] Nor were Linville and his allies above outright political retaliation and red-baiting, as veterans of Local 5 knew from experience. In 1925, Linville exposed communists to the press and thus to certain dismissal, erasing the union's tiny communist presence through the end of the 1920s.[31]

Faction Fight

The conflict between militants and union leaders festered until spring 1932, flaring up mainly in general membership meetings when the two opposition factions, the Communist Party–oriented Rank and File group and the coalition of Lovestoneites and militant Socialists called the Progressive Group, forced an issue. Begun regularly offered membership resolutions supporting controversial Communist campaigns such as the Scotsboro defense. These interventions, which had been introduced in some fashion by the tiny left wing of the union in the early 1920s, barely disrupted union business until 1931. That year, however, militants and their supporters began to outnumber moderates at poorly attended assemblies. As in all such forums governed by simple majority votes, the group with the greatest cohesiveness and staying power would win the day. Unable to mobilize his own supporters in sufficient numbers to outweigh the left, Linville resorted to parliamentary maneuvers to close meetings down or invalidate votes.[32]

The opposition, not unreasonably, believed that such measures protected the entrenched power of an administration out of touch not only with its members, but also with the much larger population of unorganized and unemployed teachers. Acting with growing pettiness and belligerence, Linville did little to dissuade his critics of this view. He and his supporters on the union's executive board restricted the number of yearly business meetings at which members could voice concerns about union policy. They refused requests for special business meetings to discuss the deepening economic crisis and the growing army of unemployed teachers. Linville soon opposed public meetings altogether out of "fear that the purpose of those proposing the meeting was mainly political, and not chiefly for the promotion of the welfare of the Teachers Union."[33]

When for the first time since 1925 a small number of opposition candidates began to gain election to the union's executive board, the Linville group took action. After an aggressive election campaign in late spring 1932, Progressive and Rank and File candidates took four seats on the executive board despite Linville's tight control of the nomination process.[34] Even before the elections, however, more belligerent members of the Linville faction lost what little patience they had with the opposition. Abe Lefkowitz was overheard at a Brookwood gathering declaring his and Linville's intention to throw the opposition caucuses out of the local. "There's two hundred of them who do nothing but disrupt, and they've all got to be expelled," Lefkowitz blustered.[35] The left's relative success in the May elections and their growing domination of general membership meetings in early June evidently were the last straw. In mid-June, Lefkowitz introduced a motion to the executive board to expel the entire Communist-affiliated Rank and File, whom the Linville leadership regarded the more seditious of the two factions. This was the same executive board meeting at which newly elected opposition members were added to the board, including Begun and Lovestoneite Ben Davidson.[36]

When the new school year started that September, Linville set up a committee of loyalists to "investigate" left-wing activity and bring charges against specific members.[37] That this investigation would be steered by Linville himself was evident from the start. The committee was given little more than a week to produce its own report. In fact, Linville simply fed them the content of the final document from his own files and writings, which contained a litany of complaints about "Communist subversion" going as far back as 1925, including that some members had "defied the chairman" and "charged officers with neglect."[38] Much of the discussion of the report's contents took place in rump sessions, excluding opposition board members and others who might have had doubts about the course that Linville and Lefkowitz had plotted for the local.[39]

In early October, the charges committee officially indicted twelve left-wing members for "objectionable activities" punishable by expulsion, including "attempts to discredit officers of the Union," "misrepresentations," attempts at "minority control" of general meetings, disruption, and "refusal to respect the commonly understood standards of decency in debate." According to the committee report the communists displayed an "attitude of contemptuousness toward the conditions that would make cooperation possible." The report also blamed the left for resignations and declining recruitment. Most of the specific complaints were petty. According to the committee, for example, the Rank and File defamed the Linville leadership by stating that it "did not arouse the teachers on the threatening salary cuts" and that it "defeated a motion to advise members not to pay the [obligatory] 1% contribution [to Tammany's unemployment fund]." In both cases, the Rank and File was actually right—that was what Linville's administration did (or failed to do).[40] Clearly, the committee was reflecting Linville's growing defensiveness. Elsewhere, the union president waxed into almost apoplectic rage, hyperbolically accusing the left of an "attitude of dishonesty and lawlessness" over a simple procedural dispute. He tagged even reasonable grievances against his administration concerning inadequate action on budget cuts as "sabotage" and "union-wrecking."[41]

At a general membership meeting on October 27, five hundred union teachers heard charges brought against Isidore Begun, Alice Citron, Abraham Zitron, Joseph Leboit, Clara Rieber, and Bertram Wolfe, the six most outspoken opposition members of those who were originally charged. The first five were associated with the Rank and File; Wolfe, a Lovestoneite, was considered the leader of the Progressive faction. The assembly then voted to establish a grievance committee to investigate the charges and bring recommendations before the union as a whole.[42] In addition to union regulars, all of them Linville loyalists, one more was voted onto the grievance committee. Earlier that month, Linville had asked his old friend and supporter John Dewey if he would join the investigation. Although he was not active in the affairs of the union and had not attended a membership meeting in many years, he agreed.[43] He was probably the local's best-known member, an internationally celebrated philosopher whom most of the teachers present looked to as a guiding light of educational reform. They believed that he would be a fair and impartial judge who could help them resolve the crisis in the union. They were wrong.

Dewey

Unlike most academic philosophers, Dewey led a politically engaged life. As a young professor at the University of Chicago, he counted himself a good friend and supporter of several social justice pioneers, among them Jane Addams, the founder of Chicago's best-known settlement, Hull House. After moving to Columbia University in 1904, and in the wake of his disastrous support for Woodrow Wilson during World War I, he branched out into the world of international politics, helping start the movement to outlaw war in the 1920s. But the greater part of Dewey's political reputation was built on his innovative school reforms. A founder of the progressive education movement in the mid-1890s, Dewey by 1932 was considered the nation's leading advocate of a "child-centered" pedagogy based on the cultivation of student interests rather than the inculcation of a rigidly prescribed curriculum. At the time of the crisis in Local 5, his work was widely popular among New York's liberal and left-wing teachers, who promoted a Deweyan "activity program" in the city schools against strong resistance from conservatives. In contrast to many of his generation's educational reformers, Dewey also unequivocally endorsed union representation for public-school teachers, convinced by Chicago's bitter school wars that the professional interests of teachers could only be served if teachers could bargain collectively. So when Henry Linville established Local 5 in 1916, Dewey was on board as a founding member.[44]

John Dewey, date unknown. (Original in Library of Congress.)

Through the 1920s, Dewey and Linville maintained a sporadic professional and political relationship. Linville counted on Dewey's support when the union was under attack during and after the war.[45] Later in the decade, Dewey spoke occasionally at union meetings and dependably came to Local 5's aid at critical moments, such as when conservatives in the AFL attacked the local for its connection to Brookwood Labor College. For his efforts on behalf of Brookwood, Dewey found himself smeared by Woll as a "propagandist" for "communist interests."[46] In spring 1931, Linville and Dewey renewed their political relationship in an abortive anti-Tammany reform project that grew out of the Seabury investigation. By the time Linville resigned from Local 5, in 1935, he considered Dewey a good if not close friend, with whom he consulted regularly. Linville helped organize Dewey's seventieth birthday celebration, in 1929, and his eightieth as well. Dewey in turn served as the keynote speaker at a 1936 testimonial to raise money for Linville's retirement.[47]

Union members venerated Dewey, and most thought that as a defender of academic freedom he would conduct a thorough and dispassionate investigation. Instead the Dewey Trial would test the philosopher's understanding of democracy and his and the union's openness to conflict and dissent. To be fair, Dewey did worry initially over the grievance committee's impartiality.[48] Moreover, the inquiry appeared comprehensive, convening twenty-four meetings of roughly two or three hours each, hearing a hundred and nine witnesses, and producing over seven hundred pages of testimony. And, at least on the surface, it also appeared to be fair: of those witnesses, forty-six spoke on behalf of the "defendants."[49] Yet Dewey's willingness to accept Linville's version of events was evident from the start. "I should be at the T.U. to give you my hearty support," Dewey wrote his friend when asked to head the investigation.[50] Linville had no reason to doubt that Dewey would come through on that promise. They shared a prior understanding about communist manipulation and duplicity, which Dewey expressed to others as well. "I get a little tired of American communists who do the baby act," he confessed to Sidney Hook the previous summer, "standing up for extreme action against counter revolutionists in Russia and then whining when a communist revolutionary is caught somewhere else. And some of them just laugh when they catch a boob of a 'liberal' to help them out."[51]

After several months of investigation, Dewey delivered to the union's executive board a report barely deviating from the Linville administration's version of the previous two years' conflict.[52] The "major cause" of Local 5's factionalism, Dewey argued, was the left's persistent attacks on Linville's leadership. Tracing opposition complaints to ulterior motives, Dewey dismissed them as "integral parts of a deliberately adopted procedure of so discrediting the Administration as to bring about a thorough change in the basic policies, aims and methods of the Union."[53] Meanwhile, Dewey and the committee took the good faith of the Linville administration for granted, never seriously considering the role of political dealmaking, arbitrary authority, defensive retaliation against dissent, or, for that matter, anticommunism in the history of the dispute. And despite a promise from Linville to keep politics out of the discussion, the committee traced the left's factionalism back to one source: communism, whether of the Communist Party of the United States or its Lovestoneite and Trotskyist split-offs. The goals and tactics of the opposition, Dewey insisted, "cannot be understood or put in their proper context without frank discussion of this topic."[54]

Bad Faith

If it were not for this, the report's central conclusion, Dewey's document would be nothing more than the record of a minor union dispute. Instead, it distilled what would become a key premise in the anticommunist argument at the core of liberal countersubversion—that communists habitually practice bad faith. Liberals often referred to communist bad faith without explaining it. Here Dewey's report meant more than just the sort of duplicity found in campaign promises or contracts signed by crooks. It lent the term additional ethical and political connotations: One practiced bad faith not only by deliberately failing to uphold one's side of an agreement, but also by refusing to disclose one's true motives or desires—by "misrepresenting" oneself more generally. And, unlike any other, communist misrepresentation undermined the open deliberation and decision-making at the core of democracy as Dewey envisioned it.

As the most important term in Dewey's political vocabulary, democracy went beyond the right to vote or the rules of governance: Democracy defined human interaction at the most basic levels, marking the modern world's evolution from "formalist" authoritarianism to a social order based on collective deliberation. Democracy, for Dewey, was at once pluralistic and communitarian. At the social and political level, it depended on the maintenance of voluntary organizations representing the interests of specific social groups: unions representing labor, for instance, or business councils representing industries. A modern nonauthoritarian, pluralistic society functioned democratically through the negotiation by those organizations of their interests—the more interests it accommodated, the more democratic a society would be. At the level of the voluntary organization, however, Dewey perceived a communal dynamic. To qualify as democratic, an organization had to be grounded in a community of values, for which openness and honesty were prerequisites. "The principle of democracy," Dewey wrote of Local 5, "demands that within our own ranks we speak openly of all that vitally concerns the Union."[55] At both social and organizational levels, deliberation and negotiation had to be practiced in good faith, which, according to Dewey, is possible only when one understands oneself and one's own "acts, beliefs, and purposes." This, and the democracy that depends on it, can only happen if there is "a community of experiences with others" that "frees and deepens one's further understanding of himself."[56]

As Dewey explained it several years earlier, bad faith erodes this communal and pluralistic democracy and is in turn fostered by its decline. It follows from the "bitterness of misunderstanding" that emerges with the breakdown of common experience and the "reciprocal engagements" at the foundation of shared meanings and mutually understood intentions. The difficulty of creating such community leads men "who so crave the expansion and reinforcement which comes from the agreements of understanding" to "tolerate and invent all kinds of substitute semblances" of such communities that are based on "the repetition of formulae of religious creeds and political platforms" and the "fanatic imposition of fidelity to the same phrases and symbols" that substitute "for real understandings." Bad faith for Dewey, then, involved not just lying to another party, but also systematically misrepresenting oneself to others, and doing so in destructive ways that had become familiar over several centuries of European and American history—from the promotion of religious enthusiasms to the spreading of political ideology. "At bottom" he argued, such false community, achieving no real understanding, "rests on force, on the hope of personal gain, on the fear of private loss."[57]

Dewey concluded that the left-wing factions in the teachers union practiced at least two forms of bad faith. The first was a "concealment" of their true identities as communists. That simple duplicity made it possible for them to hide their intentions, which constituted the second form of bad faith, the refusal of communists known and unknown to own up to the ulterior motives of communism itself, which, according to Dewey, involved taking over the union and making it serve party interests. The left-wing opposition was a "wrecking crew" sent into the teachers union by the Communist Party and other communist groups to "exploit the weaknesses of any union that is not pursuing what is considered the 'correct line,' not for the purpose of correcting the weaknesses, but for the purpose of confusing and dividing the membership."[58] And a divided union was a more easily manipulated one. Dewey insisted on this interpretation despite the protestations of teachers in the opposition factions, whom Dewey considered to be the dupes of communist leaders. The "ultimate aims" of the communist parties "have been so concealed from the sight of many individuals, that even many members of the minority groups are not themselves aware of them."⁵⁹ By "ultimate aims," Dewey did not here mean merely taking over Local 5, but rather "the ultimate desire to convert the Union into an organization for carrying on the class war" based on the notion that "the proper purpose of the Union is to join the class war in order to promote the cause of workers against employers" and to "use the Union as an instrument in militant war to overthrow the existing economic system." This "class war view" lay at the heart of communist bad faith.⁶⁰

Even though the report traced the union's internal conflicts to communism, Dewey and his committee recommended that the accused teachers be suspended only for specific actions that disrupted union business. Among those violations were raising what Linville and others considered irrelevant issues, harping on the limitations of administrative policy, and speaking ill of union leadership in public. The report also accused the Rank and File of "dual unionism"—creating separate labor organizations to compete with a union duly authorized by the AFL—a common charge against communist trade unionists by liberals and conservative Socialists. But the accusations of bad faith and class war lurked beneath the petty charges: communists needed to be disciplined, Dewey and Linville argued, for being communists.⁶¹

The Trial

Under the union's constitution, a general membership meeting had to consider the charges in a cumbersome, semipublic procedure resembling a trial. That was the April 29 meeting at the High School of Commerce. A week earlier, Dewey's committee sent its report to the union's executive committee, which distributed it throughout the local.

Over the previous several months, Linville struck a conciliatory note in public; in private, he was preparing his troops for battle. Against the better judgment of others on the union's executive committee, Linville used Dewey's report to launch an all-out assault: the minority groups were "Communist led," he told his "advisers," and had "accepted the Communist tactic and dual union program," as "proved" in the Dewey Report.⁶² Linville then organized an unapologetic "propaganda campaign" in favor of suspending the opposition, run by a committee of Linville loyalists using union resources.⁶³ Linville egged his supporters on: "If we deal with them [the left wing] with too great tenderness we shall probably live to regret it."⁶⁴ Dewey tried to rein his friend in, having been tipped off that the Linville faction hoped for a rout on April 29. He told Linville that he wanted it made clear that "to their political philosophy apart from tactics we made no objection," even though he did just that in his report. He was "sure the alternative to action we recommended [i.e., suspension of the six opposition leaders] was splitting the Union, and that the radicals outside the Union would be left without influence, and that I preferred to have them inside if they would use the proper methods."[65] But that would change.

Linville carefully planned for a meeting of roughly four and a half hours —two hours for a report from the grievance committee on each of the six cases with fifteen minute rebuttals from each "defendant," an hour-long report by Dewey with a thirty-minute discussion afterward to allow for three speakers in favor and three against.[66] Like any practiced parliamentarian, Linville stationed his most trusted allies on the floor to shape debate, thinking that he easily could move the meeting through his agenda.[67] Instead, chaos reigned. Over eight hundred members showed up, of whom more than three hundred belonged to or sympathized with one of the left-wing factions.[68] Opposition supporters in the audience demanded an extended discussion of the charges, on the grounds that while the Dewey report had been distributed to members the week before, the "defendants" had not been given a similar opportunity to respond except by leaflets and handouts.[69] Meanwhile, by the time Dewey reached the rostrum, he had abandoned a conciliatory approach for one that condemned the Rank and File and Progressives on ideological grounds. Dewey also spent a good deal of time responding angrily to left-wing criticisms, which he interpreted as personal attacks.[70]

For its part, the left not only questioned the investigation's good intentions, but also its professed idea of democracy.[71] To Dewey's assertion that the communists sought conflict for conflict's sake, his critics countered that the factional dispute and the "disorderly character and inefficiency" of union meetings arose from substantive differences exaggerated by Linville's authoritarianism and inflexibility. "The fact of the matter," wrote opposition leaders,

> is that the oppositions have been accused of "delaying" the work of the Union, and of "disrupting" the activities of the Union because they have insisted that the Union take up vital questions affecting the teachers. Criticism of the administration and its policies means bringing in "personalities." Fighting against mechanical, arbitrary rulings of the chair means being "obnoxious" and "obstreperous."[72]

To be sure, the communists viewed labor disputes differently than liberals and conservative Socialists did, perceiving class conflict where Dewey and

Linville did not, and believing that it would lead to revolution. Yet, in questioning the communists' good faith, Dewey ascribed motives to the opposition that were simply not there, insisting that "any let-up in this struggle [for struggle's sake], to say nothing of cooperation with supervisors even for educational purposes, is 'betrayal' of the workers' cause."[73] This was not true—all communist union activity was not, as Dewey contended, "means of carrying on the class struggle"; most communist teachers cooperated effectively with their principals and other administrators.[74]

And if the left emphasized class differences over professional collaboration, it was because they perceived the extent to which class relations shaped all professional and trade-union concerns, not because they wanted to foster class warfare. "What is 'class war' in the life of a union," communist teachers asked, "other than the defense of the interests of the organized workers and other workers in the industry in question, together with relations of solidarity with the rest of the labor movement?"[75] For Begun, class conflict was not an ulterior motive, but the essence of union activism inseparable from specific workplace and professional demands. "What were those ultimate desires? My ulterior, sinister motives?" he asked. "We wanted classroom teacher control in the Joint Salary Committee [JSC].... We contend our interests are not similar to the interests of the superintendents. I pointed out we are a trade union—our interests are not identical with the bosses'—Is that a crime in our union?"[76] Later, Begun aptly observed, "Now, participating in class struggle, my own notion is that you participate in it whether you like it or not. Life settles that for you."[77]

Beneath the issues of factionalism and communism, at stake was the question of how a democratic organization should handle substantive dissent, especially differences over the conduct of the democracy itself. In this case, dissenters attacked the practice over the previous two decades of negotiating salaries and budgets through legislative committee (the JSC), maintaining alliances with conservative trade unionists in the AFL, excluding from membership substitutes and other marginalized teachers, and, above all, avoiding discussion of economic and social questions not directly pertinent to professional school issues. Motions ruled out of order by Linville covered everything from the composition of the school board and its corruption by Tammany to the stranglehold that banks had imposed on city budgets, to the racism and anti-Semitism that coursed through the city's neighborhoods. It was not as if the liberals did not care about these matters—Dewey, Linville, and others just did not think the union, whose main concerns were salaries, working conditions, and teaching, should address Tammany corruption and unemployment.

In part, the difference was a matter of political style and temperament that regularly divide generations: the left proposed moving out of the established channels of negotiation that had worked for the union in the past and onto to the streets, so to speak, to engage in mass protests that would disrupt the façade of neutrality and legitimacy on which the board of education and other city institutions depended. Neither the liberal Dewey nor the conservative Socialist Linville, shared the left's view that embarrassing confrontations were useful means of exposing that corruption and turning the public against it.[78]

As the meeting became more acrimonious, Dewey in his anger became less and less coherent.[79] When Begun entered the docket, Dewey red-baited him without restraint, contending that Begun's disloyalty followed from his "political beliefs and affiliations," which "necessarily color and direct one's activities in the Teachers Union." Begun's animosity toward Linville, Dewey insisted, was driven by ideology and was thus unrelenting.[80] Yet as he blamed communism for the union's problems, Dewey snidely attacked the left for even raising the issue of red-baiting, repeating what he had written earlier to Hook, that Local 5's left wing, "applied what in all honesty and simplicity can only be called the 'baby act,'—they whined, they complained."[81] For Dewey, it was not red-baiting because the charges were true. But what were the charges? Being a communist, or being a communist of the sort Dewey caricatured, to whom he ascribed convictions and intentions that almost all of the accused denied having?

When the time came for discussion, an even more rancorous chaos took over. Begun defended himself adeptly, while attacking the committee. Confusion immediately followed during an evidently staged dispute over the number of votes necessary for suspension. Linville, in an apparently conciliatory gesture, interpreted the rules to require a two-thirds majority. Lefkowitz, from the floor, moved that a simple majority was sufficient, and officially appealed Linville's decision. According to the rules, that appeal would be decided by a simple majority vote. Lefkowitz probably expected to win the appeal and that the suspension would go through on a simple majority. But he lost both votes. And so Begun was not suspended. Since everyone considered Begun the most contentious and the least liked of the opposition activists, they assumed that all the other suspension votes would be lost. Thus, the suspension of left-wing opposition members for factionalism, the entire purpose of the hours-long meeting, was tabled.[82]

At this point, the audience was melting. By 6:00 p.m., it was down to around five hundred. Determined to salvage something from six months of rancorous dispute, investigation, report writing, and meetings, Linville pushed through the adoption of Dewey's report and then muscled through a "debate" on a constitutional amendment replacing general membership meetings with a delegate assembly. Then, he closed that discussion after only giving one of his confederates a chance to speak. As the crowd became restless, the gathering collapsed into pandemonium with pushing and shoving. After trying, and failing, to call in the police, Linville forced a vote on the constitutional revisions, despite the fact that many of the teachers present did not know what the motion was. Then, tossing Robert's Rules to the wind, Linville as chair motioned to adjourn. The meeting closed, its exhausted remnants drifting out into the unseasonably warm night.[83]

Upshot

For all its failures, Linville thought it "a great meeting" that achieved "a complete demonstration of unscrupulous policies" on the part of the left. Dewey gave "the strongest speech that I ever heard him make," as his philosopher friend helped the union "solve" its "tangled left-wing problem." Linville measured Dewey's success in terms that would become commonplaces of liberal anticommunism: the philosopher's presentation of the facts and his reasoned judgments drove "a wedge" between the left "and their 'Romantic Liberal' supporters," leading the romantic yet disillusioned fellow travelers back toward tough-minded liberals and pragmatic socialists like himself, who had no illusions about communist bad faith. "We have been fighting organized misrepresentation masquerading as a mistreated minority," Linville wrote. But "the 'wedge' has been driven in, and ... we may now give our efforts toward the destruction of the spirit of dishonesty and duplicity in our midst."[84]

To drive that wedge deeper, Linville did what he could to expose communist teachers to punishment. Dewey had insisted disingenuously that "whatever discipline the Union may impose on its members does not affect their rights as teachers."[85] And none of the documents from the Dewey Trial were to be circulated outside of the local nor the names of the accused publicized. However, within a few days, Linville sent copies of Dewey's report, with names expunged, to the AFL and AFT "so that they may have the benefit of our findings and experience."[86] And within a few months, he leaked the names of the accused teachers to the press. Lefkowitz also exposed some of his opponents in JSC meetings, against whom the board of supervisors then retaliated.[87] Eventually, all of the documents found their way into the hands of the Rapp-Coudert staff (names included), with Linville's help.

Local 5's factional dispute did bring some benefits to the union. The delegate assembly created in 1933 served the union much more effectively than had the open general membership meetings, operating on the basis of proportional representation and thus enabling the regular expression of minority views.[88] Meanwhile, the left did well in the 1933 elections, keeping four seats on the executive board and adding one more.[89] Increasingly, the approach of the Rank and File and the Progressives to both the employment concerns of teachers and the broader problems of fiscal austerity gained traction. And as the union relaxed its restrictive membership requirements, younger teachers joined, shifting Local 5's political and trade-union perspective increasingly toward the left. This was a situation that Linville and his allies, including Dewey, could not tolerate for long.

6
The Educational Front

The way Americans tell the story, the history of the 1930s was defined by a struggle between progress and reaction, between social forces moving modern society "forward" and those pushing back, between the light of reason and dark attachments to irrational customs and privileges. The rise of fascism and the war partly can be blamed for framing the historical narrative this way, giving real substance to the perception that human progress had met an opposition rooted in ancient prejudices and rigidly institutionalized traditions, a paroxysmal expression of bizarre and atavistic violence against enlightened impulses toward liberty and democracy. Similarly, the Popular Front united in the antifascist movement not only those "progressives" who defended what they believed were the foundational creeds of the American republic against the barbarism of "Hitler, Mussolini and Tojo," but also those who hoped to advance American democracy toward its fuller realization in a modernized economy.[1]

Like other intellectuals and cultural figures who at the time considered themselves progressive, John Dewey sympathized with the antifascist and labor militancy of the poor and dispossessed who fed the front of artists, writers, and activists whom historian Michael Denning argues "labored" American culture leftward before the war, uniting communists, socialists, and liberals around a social-democratic "renaissance" that included the New Deal, the establishment of mass production unions, and the building of a national cultural identity around the figure of the "common man."[2] In this version of the progressive narrative, McCarthyism broke that "cultural front" apart in the late 1940s, pitting former allies against each other in a poisoned atmosphere of suspicion and recrimination. One can imagine social democrats and liberals such as Dewey occupying such a big tent, especially one devoted to arts and literature; however, to depict, as Denning and others do, liberals, socialists, and the communist left standing on such resolutely common political ground obscures the ideological and political differences that also deeply divided them. As we can see in the backstory of the Coudert investigation, the experience of McCarthyism did not just break apart a progressive front that was united on social-democratic principles of the sort that we associate with the New Deal and other regulatory reform. Unfolding long before McCarthyism became a household word, inquests like Coudert's instead made apparent already-existing cleavages, especially those dividing the labor movement between liberals and social democrats on the one hand and communists and militant socialists on the other, cutting through the rhetorical "progressivism" that superficially unified Denning's cultural renaissance.[3]

Both Dewey and his former student Isidore Begun, for instance, would have called themselves "progressive," but they hardly meant the same thing by that term. And nothing in the experience of New York City's unionized teachers made that difference more evident than the anticommunism that gelled after the 1933 Dewey Trial. Literary historian Alan Wald is perhaps justified in accusing Popular Front Communists like Begun of employing the term as protective coloration, a "coyly useful subterfuge ... for deflecting red-baiters and unifying forces without too many questions asked." According to Wald, "Outside of the eighteen months of the Hitler-Stalin Pact ... a Communist identifying himself or herself as a Progressive was telling the truth and lying at the same time." And once McCarthyism had begun herding unrepentant communists into what *Nation* editor Freda Kirchwey called "outer totalitarian darkness," this use of "progressive" as a "weasel word," as Wald put it, made good self-protective sense. Yet the word's ambiguity did not merely serve self-defense. Back in 1939, Kirchwey was more generous about the "double mental bookkeeping" by which Communists "account jointly for their love of Stalin and their adherence to the New Deal." It enabled them to "perform necessary functions in the confused struggle of our time," building front organizations that "clearly serve the cause not of 'totalitarian doctrine' but of a more workable democracy."[4]

The "weasel word" worked for liberals like Dewey and Linville as well, similarly allowing them to double their mental bookkeeping to account for their attachments to liberal institutions while relying on antifascist organizations sustained by the energy and commitment of communists, including Trotskyists and Lovestoneites, to do what liberals and social democrats could not or would not do themselves—for instance, to confront the uglier kinds of authority entrenched in the corporate boardrooms and political clubs of the city. Yet, unlike communists, Dewey and *his* "progressive" allies did not need to seek protection behind the false unity of the term, as they neither came under the same kind of attack nor risked exile from American culture and society, as suspected communists did. Instead, "progressive liberals" like Dewey and Linville used the word in a different kind of subterfuge, offering the philosophical and pedagogical basis for a cultural politics that competed with and soon enough attacked the People's Front, establishing an intellectual, cultural, and even institutional vantage point from which anticommunist "progressives" could and would banish their communist counterparts.

Histories of education enjoy a small but important part in the telling of this story, depicting pedagogical progressives and "radicals" united against a rigidly conservative traditionalism. Like the antifascist movement, "progressive education" claimed to bring Americans of many political affiliations together against the institutional inertia of corrupt school systems, the moral authoritarianism of the conservative churches, and an entrenched ideology of racial inequality. It also seemed to unite them around a pedagogical program written, for the most part, by Dewey.

For communists as well as liberals, Dewey represented the promise of collective enlightenment guided by such watchwords as "the open classroom," "democracy in education," and "a child-centered curriculum." Like Dewey, they thought the school had to be consciously and systematically integrated into its social context, actively involving students in projects that addressed problems facing their communities. Only by cultivating a real interest in the world about them could students digest what they learned, including fundamentals like reading and mathematics. That attention to interest marked Deweyan pedagogy as "child centered," opposing it to educational techniques that were focused on predigested content and guided by the demands of educational authorities. It was in its attention to student interest, its emphasis on participation rather than rote learning, and its insistence that ultimately the teachers themselves (not administrators or boards of education) could build that bridge between what had to be taught and the child's interest in it that Deweyan education could be considered radically "democratic."[5]

In general, progressive education was uncontroversial on the left, and while the Communist Party criticized Dewey's philosophy on political grounds—mainly for conflating educational reform with political action—even the party's educational theorist, Richard Frank, pled a child-centered education that sounded like Dewey's own. Writing in the official party political journal, Frank called for democratizing educational authority by "stimulating and encouraging curiosity" and motivating students through interest rather than "rigorous discipline."[6] In New York City, liberal and communist teachers consistently endorsed Deweyan methods, lining up behind such projects as the "activity program," derived from the "project method" that had been popularized in the 1920s by William Heard Kilpatrick, a disciple who taught with Dewey at Columbia Teachers College.[7] Started in 1935 in seventy select grammar schools with roughly fifty thousand students, by 1940 the activity program was applied in about one fourth of the city's schools, whose pupils were given more latitude in choosing subjects of study and whose learning was structured around series of graded activities such as planning a trip to California, furnishing a home, or building a post office. Children were consulted about lesson plans and organized into committees for collective decisions in an effort to bring "democracy into the classroom."[8] After left-wing teachers took over Local 5 in 1935, the union still promoted Deweyan pedagogy, claiming by 1939 to have become "established as the authority on the activity program in New York City."[9]

Yet, although communists and radicals in the union endorsed and promoted "progressive" educational reforms, they aligned politics and schooling quite differently than liberals like Dewey did. While their ideas about schools were democratic, the Deweyans' idea of democracy was largely about schooling—that is, about rational deliberation and collective learning as rejecting ideological and class division. Built in part around the need to defend existing democratic institutions against fascism, the Popular Front in contrast understood democratic politics agonistically, as a contentious engagement fed by mass social movements based in the historically persistent struggles among social classes. The liberals' inclination to think that modern social problems could bend readily to the force of progressive education strongly biased them against communist class analysis and their penchant for "mass action," which Dewey and Linville derided as "the class war view," including and especially the sort that was gaining popularity among unionized teachers. By the middle of the 1930s, the Deweyans had made their anticommunist position quite clear, and in this way were already ideologically and politically helping give birth to "Coudertism."

Alice Citron

An excellent example of how the communist meaning of "progressive" and "progressive education" diverged from the liberals' can be seen in Local 5 activist Alice Citron's deployment of Deweyan pedagogy on the educational front. A Local 5 member since 1931, Citron could be found at the center of most Popular Front school reform in Harlem, where she taught through the 1930s and 1940s. Born in 1908 to immigrant Jewish garment workers living in Omaha, Nebraska, Citron was raised in Harlem and the Bronx.[10] Sometime in the late 1910s, Citron's mother took in fifteen-year-old Isidore Begun after his parents died, and thereafter Begun considered the Citron household a home base, staying there whenever he returned to town from Albany, where he served as the Communist Party's legislative representative. Eventually, he and Alice were married.[11]

Following the path of many first-generation, working-class women, Citron graduated Hunter College in 1928.[12] In 1931, she joined the teaching staff at P.S. 184, a grammar school on One Hundred Sixteenth Street between Lenox and Fifth Avenues, and remained there for her entire eighteen years in the system, until she was forced out in 1950 by the board of education's first wave of postwar purges. She recalled being "shocked at the hunger and despair in the eyes of the boys and girls" when standing for the first time before her second-grade class. A "transient hotel" through which teachers passed on temporary and often punitive assignment, P.S. 184 like many schools in the district was in deplorable condition: No new grammar school was built in Harlem between 1909 and 1938, and the ones in operation were so overcrowded that many ran on two or even three sessions, some only four hours in duration. In 1935, most Harlem schools lacked adequate toilets and washrooms; two still provided only unheated outdoor facilities with no place for children to wash up. The fire commissioner rated four school buildings as "firetraps." When one principal arrived in spring 1935 for his new position at P.S. 5, he found "the building in such condition that it was a disgrace. The halls and stairs were used as urinals and as worse. We could hardly walk without stepping upon somebody's defecation all over the place. The whole building stunk. You opened the front door and you entered a charnel house."[13]

These conditions led Citron to join Harlem parents in organizing their first Parents Association in 1932. With residents backing her, and with help from fellow members of Local 5, Citron began to force the issue of school conditions before the board of education. In fall 1935, Citron joined with high-school teacher Lucile Spence and several other members to set up the union's Harlem Schools Committee to address the social and pedagogical concerns plaguing the district's educational system. The committee acted in the wake of a riot that tore across Harlem in March that left stores looted and burned, scores injured and wounded, and at least three dead, all of them blacks shot by the police. While the unrest was triggered by a minor incident, a commission of inquiry that was set up by the Mayor that April found the anger and violence of the rioters followed from long-brewing discontent over the declining conditions in the district's hospitals, schools, and apartment buildings; over discrimination in its places of employment and commerce; and over police brutality on its streets. Left-wing union members led in pressing for more decisive and permanent solutions to Harlem's deteriorating and understaffed schools, bringing close to a hundred teachers to testify in closed session before the commission's subcommittee on schooling.[14] From that swell of indignation, Spence, Citron, and the union's Harlem committee organized the Permanent Committee for Better Schools in Harlem in spring 1936, representing dozens of community groups, parents organizations, and churches.[15]

Citron and other teachers active in Local 5 entered the Harlem schools as the Communist Party met unprecedented success at building a multiethnic coalition around the pursuit of racial equality. By 1934, its internal education projects, public antilynching and Scotsboro campaigns, and practical efforts to increase city relief to Harlem's disproportionately unemployed and poor African-American population had put the party at the head of an interracial united front that cut across the district's working and middle classes. More effectively than any other of the left-wing parties, the Communists mobilized whites on behalf of racial justice. Emerging from that united front, the Permanent Committee promoted community-based teaching, integrating parents and community leaders into the management of schools and the development of curriculum, while relentlessly pressing the city for more resources. By 1938, Harlem residents, the union, and Communist teachers had secured the building of two new primary schools and the renovation of several others.[16]

Historian Mark Naison writes that for Communists, "black participation in American institutions represented the acid test of democratic values." On that score, Harlem schools failed miserably.[17] Citron and her colleagues at P.S. 184 found themselves repeatedly obstructed by an institutional and cultural heritage of racism in the curriculum and administration that degraded and tracked their students into menial occupations and social subservience. Ann Matlin, Citron's colleague and friend, recalled having to teach African-American kids with bigoted textbooks, some of them written by New York's public-school administrators.

> There was a picture of slaves dancing in front of their cabins with the notation below stating that you can see that the slaves were very well off: Look how happy they are—they are dancing. It angered me, it really angered me to stand in front of 48 black kids and teach them that slavery was good. How can you stand that? But that's what was going on.[18]

Another textbook, also by New York public-school administrators, defended the Ku Klux Klan for giving "some relief from their suffering" and "protection of their families" to whites "terrorized" after the Civil War "by the Negroes and Carpetbaggers."[19] Citron, Matlin, and other teachers made changing textbook content one of their primary goals, coordinating their efforts with historian Carter Woodson's recently established Negro History Week and opening up the curriculum to the scrutiny of community leaders. This project, which entailed training teachers to revise the content of their classes, providing students with copies of Woodson's *Negro History Bulletin*, writing new texts for use in class, and encouraging students to write their own narratives of American, African, and European history, transformed the public-school curriculum. In keeping with the party's emphasis on community teaching, Citron and the union's Harlem Committee also worked closely with parents' organizations and the Permanent Committee teaching African-American history and culture through lecture series and classes in schools and YMCA's across Harlem.[20]

Community involvement took over Citron's life as a teacher, as she shouldered unusual responsibility for the welfare of her students, regularly conferring with their families and helping them participate in the education of their children. She was "known for her integrity" throughout Harlem, one parent testified at Citron's 1950 trial, and could not walk down Lenox Avenue without being approached by local residents about school and community issues. Always available to parents for children in crisis, Citron dug into her own pockets to cover schoolbooks, lunches, and bus fare. "She is everything to our neighborhood," said a parent whose daughter learned poetry from Citron; she was "a real, true friend of the people in Harlem, especially the parents in Harlem," said another.[21] When Coudert investigators called Citron into their Wall Street office for a private interrogation, Harlemites turned out in force at a rally on her behalf, and many of them traveled downtown a few days later to pack the hallway outside the hearing room in a show of public solidarity.[22]

Pedagogically, there was nothing in the party's Harlem schools program at odds with liberal versions of progressive education. Besides its campaign against overt racism and less explicit forms of prejudice in textbooks and the curriculum, perhaps the most important features of Citron's work in Harlem, or the similar work of union and party activist Mildred Flacks in the Bedford-Stuyvesant section of Brooklyn, were directed against what the Deweyans had long called "isolation in the school," the insulation of teaching from the social and cultural concerns of the surrounding community and the investment of absolute authority over curriculum and pedagogy in the school administration. Such a Deweyan focus is evident in the Communist shop paper for Harlem teachers, *Harlem Lesson Plan*, which began publication in spring 1937 and was probably at least in part written and edited by Citron. *Harlem Lesson Plan* had many of the excesses typical of party publications, including turgid essays on the virtues of Soviet planning, the promotion of Communist electoral campaigns, and occasional *ad hominem* attacks against especially abusive principals and superintendents. But it also promoted community-based curricular projects, the tailoring of lessons to the experiences and needs of African-American children, the incorporation into lessons of practical activities, and, finally, the decentralization of curricular authority and its placement in the hands of teachers, parents, and principals who, according to Deweyan principles, were best able to judge the progress of children in the classroom.[23] It emphasized the need for small classes, after-school activities, using the schools as community centers, treating the student as a member of a community, and incorporating her social interests into the curriculum, which adhered to a very Deweyan principle enunciated by party chair Earl Browder that "the basic struggle for progress in education is . . . a struggle to break the isolation of the school from everyday life." In contrast to other city schools, democratic community-based schooling in Harlem meant incorporating the problems of racism and urban decline into daily lesson plans, but the principle was the same. As was much of the practice: in 1938, the union, the party, and the Permanent Committee successfully pressed the city to create an in-service course with local community participation focused on a single primary school in order to determine how it could be possible for "this particular school [to] create a more effective education for its pupils by relating the school more closely to its community."[24]

Meanwhile, local right-wing opponents of progressive education also lumped its left and liberal proponents together in simplified notions of progressivism. In a formula aligning liberals and communists on curricular reform, New York's conservative educators attacked the activity program with special vehemence for contributing to moral decline. Milo MacDonald, the principal of DeWitt Clinton High School and president of the extreme right-wing American Educational Association, warned that the activity program would foster social degeneration by diluting a traditional curriculum of basic skills and moral instruction. MacDonald, who considered himself an unappreciated historian of philosophy and culture, wrote that Dewey and the progressives set education on a "false atheistic base," aided by "the philosopher Hegel, that philosophical forerunner of both Stalin and Hitler."[25] Progressive advocates of the activity program know that "if they can break down the standards, if they can educate the young upon the principle of activity, upon the thought that there are no eternal truths except as your own activity, your own originality, suggest them to you, the stage has been properly set for the communistic tragedy upon which they wish to raise the curtain."[26]

On the Educational Front

But even if the left and liberal teachers joined in "progressive" opposition to educational "reaction," and even if they agreed on some basic pedagogical methods and principles, several issues deeply divided them throughout the decade, as activists and union members. Although Harlem's Communist teachers framed their pedagogical requirements in democratic terms, they did so with a distinctly non-Deweyan, antifascist edge, aggressively targeting the "Tammany idea of education," whose "reactionary, unprogressive teaching methods" created "starved and stunted beings easy prey in the street and poolroom of gangsterism and its twin, Fascist violence and demagogy."[27]

Above all, by immersing the teacher, the child, and the school in the problems of a real community such as Harlem, the party's sort of democratic schooling brought with it enduring challenges that education by itself could not address. At one of the union's yearly "Education for Democracy" conferences, this was how Citron reframed the Deweyan agenda for communities like Harlem:

> Enunciations like "prepare the child for living" must force the teacher in Harlem and other sections of the city where Negro chil-

dren are the majority in the school, to ask herself, "Am I preparing my pupils for a life of continuous segregation and discrimination?" She must also ask herself, "What do I know of the struggles of the Negro people for social, political, and economic equality? What do I know of the emotional life of children whose people are a favorite subject for comic expression in literature, cartoons and the movies?" The honest answer is little or nothing.[28]

Citron believed that such ignorance could only be dispelled by joining community efforts to challenge the prevailing racism and poverty that defined life for many of her students' families. That meant joining in and leading protests against bigoted principals and racist textbooks, thereby incorporating mass mobilization and social protest into the community schooling process. When in 1936 Gustav Schoenchen, the recently installed principal of P.S. 5, reportedly beat a teenager with a stick for challenging his authority, Harlem turned out in strength to demand his ouster, with union teachers at the front of demonstrations on the school's steps. They were able to force the board to investigate and hold hearings, and while the courts acquitted Schoenchen of beating the boy, school authorities transferred him to another, primarily white district where he remained until retirement. Schoenchen, a white, liberal advocate of Deweyan school reform, may not have harmed the teenager to the extent claimed by protesters, but he unquestionably roughed him up, and as even his supporters conceded, he "did not like Negroes and, although he tried to hide it, the colored people all knew it."[29] Much of the dispute with P.S. 5's parents came from Schoenchen's efforts to improve "discipline" in the halls and classrooms, forbidding parents and family members from accompanying children into the school at the opening of each session, out of concern for their safety in the unsupervised schoolyard and halls. Partly on the recommendation of Henry Linville—whose recently formed rival union, the Teachers Guild, supported Schoenchen—Coudert investigators made the Schoenchen incident central to their case that Local 5 propagandized and agitated in the schools, "promoting," as the Guild put it, "race riots and class war." Like the Guild, the Coudert committee ignored the freely expressed racism of their main witnesses. Schoenchen declared the "negro blood" of one of his otherwise apparently white teachers a "disability." He derided the "ignorance" and "loose mores" of Harlem blacks, as well as the excesses of their "negro imagination."[30]

An even wider schism between liberals and the communist left, however, concerned the communist tactic of mobilizing teachers, students, and parents en masse to force restoration of school funding, wage increases, and improvement in teaching and learning conditions, or as in the case of P.S. 5 in Harlem, the removal of a racist principal. This break was ideological and political, reflecting deeply divergent views on the meaning of democracy. Liberals argued for a democracy that was deliberative and procedural, grounded in shared values and practiced according to plainly enunciated rules of debate and compromise. Communist teachers, in contrast, and this included Lovestoneites, Musteites, Trotskyists, and militant Socialists as well as members of the Communist Party, tended to view democracy as agonistic and rule violating, with procedural and deliberative considerations often secondary.[31] No substantive democracy was possible in a society divided along class lines, they insisted. The rules of deliberation for any supposedly democratic institution, like the law more generally, favored those with class and other privileges, biasing apparently neutral procedures by which democratic decisions were made.

At the time, liberals such as Dewey and conservative socialists such as Linville blamed this schism on a "far left" that sacrificed actual but imperfect democratic practices for authoritarian measures that promoted "class war" for the sake of the distant and perfectionist goals of a postrevolutionary society, or worse, disrupted democratic organizations on directives from fickle authorities in distant Moscow, without regard for the unique characteristics of American democracy. This refrain reappeared in standard narratives of the great struggle between progress and reaction in the 1930s, in which communists who were contemptuous of democratic traditions and employing democratic rhetoric in bad faith merely to enlist support from well-meaning liberals disrupted the labor movement generally and the teachers union in particular, thereby undermining progress toward a more democratic future for the American people and sowing the seeds of an antidemocratic, "totalitarian" politics.

Communists certainly did not shy away from confrontation, yet it is not at all clear that they *intended* to create chaos or that they had any more contempt for American democracy than did the liberals who employed the term as a banal slogan. If anything, by muscling the class struggle into an alignment with the American democratic tradition under Browder's motto "Communism is twentieth-century Americanism," Communists during the Popular Front sold short their commitments to revolution, pledging instead to support electoral campaigns and many of the reform goals of the New Deal. In the teachers union, moreover, the left hardly bore sole responsibility for political divisiveness, which was equally the fault of Linville, Lefkowitz, and their followers, who defended their grip on the union's reins, in the name of a democracy that itself was a matter of dispute. The intensity of this conflict grew in the aftermath of the Dewey Trial, as the left continued to gain traction in the union when younger, uncertified, and substitute teachers began filling the local's ranks, and as the communist practice of "mass action" increasingly alienated the union's liberal leadership. That tension came to a head barely a month after the Dewey Trial in a "riot" involving rank-and-file teachers and the board of education. Then, in summer 1935, relations deteriorated to an even more decisive rift over mass politics and the meaning of democracy, leading the union to split in two.

The Riot in Education Hall

In May of 1933, a "riot" broke out in Education Hall. According to some, it all started when Isidore Blumberg made the wrong prediction.

As chair of the Teachers' Committee to Protect Salaries, Blumberg led the growing movement against fiscal retrenchment in the city schools. In October 1932, he announced that he had information that then-Governor Franklin Delano Roosevelt, who at the time was running for president, would call a special session to allow the state legislature to cut teachers' salaries, a power that it had under New York's statewide system of school funding. It was an intentionally inflammatory statement, and Roosevelt emphatically denied the charge. In substance, though, Blumberg was right: the legislature made the cuts in November. That did not stop the Superintendent of Schools, Edward Mandel, from calling Blumberg on the carpet for "show[ing] a lack of responsibility in a teacher" and demanding that he name others on the committee. Blumberg refused.[32]

Incensed that Blumberg would dare to be "evasive," Mandel then did what New York school administrators often did with recalcitrant teachers, especially probationary ones like Blumberg. He transferred him, from the school where he had been receiving superlative evaluations to one with severe disciplinary problems that was run by a notoriously authoritarian and arbitrary principal. No one was surprised when Blumberg received failing grades from his new supervisor, which Mandel then used as the pretext for bringing disciplinary charges. The disciplinary proceedings led to his dismissal.[33] But before that happened, his friends and associates on the Teachers Committee to Protect Salaries, whom he had shielded under Mandel's third degree, came to his defense. Among the leaders of the Blumberg Defense Committee was Isidore Begun.

On May 25 of the following year, roughly halfway through the "first 100 days" of Roosevelt's New Deal, Blumberg's dismissal motion finally appeared on the agenda for the board's monthly public meeting at its Education Hall at 500 Fifth Avenue. Blumberg had already had a closed hearing with the board, but the recommendation had to be acted on in public, even if the substantive proceedings remained secret. Begun and other supporters showed up in force to call upon the board to hold fully public hearings on Blumberg's pending dismissal.

What happened next was a matter of some dispute, revealing the extent to which the situation in the union was deteriorating under the conflict between a growing communist movement and its liberal anticommunist opponents.[34] The *New York Times* initially reported the incident as a "free-for-all fight with police" started by three hundred teachers who tried to prevent the board from doing its job. "Dozens of young men and women leaped to their feet as the voting progressed, accusing the board of autocracy, fascism and prejudice." Police who had been asked by the board to stand by entered the room at that point "striving to restore order." Board President George P. Ryan then demanded the room be cleared. The police, according to the *Times*, homed in on Begun, who "had led in the denunciation of the board," dragging him from the hall. "Several women assaulted the patrol men with umbrellas, pocketbooks and rolled copies of the board's calendar. Many of them became hysterical," the *Times* reported. More police were called. "Tables and chairs were overturned, eyeglasses were knocked off and clothing was torn in the scuffle." The teachers were forced out of the room and herded down Fifty-Ninth Street.[35]

The board considered the teachers' behavior in the meeting the sort of "conduct unbecoming" that required the severest punishment. They singled out for dismissal the two people they believed had instigated the disturbance, Begun and another member of Local 5's Rank and File, Williana Burroughs, who served on the union's executive board. Raised in the city's Colored Orphan Asylum, Burroughs graduated from Hunter College in 1902 and immediately began teaching in the city's public schools. Although she was dismissed a few years later under rules denying employment to married women, Burroughs returned to the classroom in 1925, at which point she joined Local 5. Initially attracted to the Socialist Party, Burroughs joined the Workers Party (the Communist Party's predecessor) in 1927, becoming active in the party's highly successful Harlem Tenants League. The following year, Burroughs traveled to the Soviet Union as a delegate to the Sixth Comintern Congress, the first of four long trips to the communist "homeland," where like fellow African-American Communists Grace Campbell and Hermina Huiswoud, she was cultivated for leadership in the international workers' movement. This transformative experience established her credentials in the party and enabled her to play a significant role in gaining it a foothold in Harlem while steering the party's position on American race issues.[36]

Both Begun and Burroughs had excellent teaching records, and Burroughs a great deal of experience as well. So it was solely on the grounds of their "conduct prejudicial to good order and discipline" at the board meeting that she and Begun were suspended, pending dismissal. Eventually they lost their jobs.[37] In the course of Begun and Burroughs's public disciplinary hearing, though, a very different account of the events at Education Hall unfolded from the one initially reported in the press.[38] According to their supporters, the board applied the kind of crude political repression for which it and the Tammany regime that it represented were notorious. Hundreds of teachers, parents, and supporters had indeed turned out to petition for an open hearing on Blumberg's dismissal, but did so peacefully. Their request was summarily denied by Ryan, who immediately called on the police to clear the room. Only then did the violence start. Others told similar stories. According to Blumberg's attorney George Friou, when the president of a parents' organization insisted on the right to speak, a policeman dragged him from the room. An American Civil Liberties Union (ACLU) representative and Burroughs also asked to speak.

> These people were manhandled by policemen and shoved about the room. They did nothing to resist.... The police then commenced shoving and manhandling spectators. They tried to rush groups of spectators out of the room, football fashion. I saw one policeman (he weighed close to 200 pounds). He was holding the dress of a young woman who weighed less than a hundred pounds. Her arm and shoulder were fully exposed. She struggled to get out of his grasp.

As Friou, who claimed that the police provoked the confrontation, put it, "the only people in the room who were disorderly were the police themselves."[39] Even the *New York Times* had to admit that there were many different versions of the "Riot in Education Hall." ACLU lawyer Osmond Fraenkel remarked that Ryan, the board, and the police had quite possibly violated the constitutional right of citizens to be heard at open meetings, "even over the ruling of the chairman that he will hear no one."[40]

Linville, detesting "mass actions," agreed in substance with Ryan that the teachers, parents, and other petitioners and spectators had violated "good order and discipline" in Education Hall. This was one of the key examples of "class war" politics that the union president returned to over and over again as evidence of the disruptive "Communist tactics" undermining his authority. He was not entirely wrong. Begun took the confrontation for yet another episode in the class struggle: "Have not the protests and revolts of the hungry always been condemned by the well-fed as 'riots' and injurious to law and order?"[41] He had in mind the businessmen and lawyers on the board, including Ryan, the president of the Long Island City Bank (one of the largest in Queens) and a well-known advocate of conservative Catholic causes.[42] Linville made sure the union's new delegate assembly voted "not to condone the conduct" of the accused teachers, even as the union mildly protested the severity of their punishment. Effectively, he lent the union's tacit support to the dismissals, and the targeted teachers knew it. "We were branded as guilty of the charges pending before the Board," Burroughs complained bitterly, even as the union pretended to support them on technical grounds.[43]

Worse, Linville and Lefkowitz let school officials know of Blumberg, Begun, and Burroughs's links to the Communist Party. In fact, such red-baiting likely precipitated the whole incident. Shortly before Mandel found his pretext for firing Blumberg, the *New York Times* quoted Lefkowitz quite bluntly identifying Blumberg and all of his associates as Communist Party members at a public meeting of the Joint Salary Committee (JSC), which included several school administrators, who Lefkowitz knew full well would not hesitate to fire teachers whom they even suspected of being red.[44]

The board of education fracas and similar confrontations over the next two years further tainted the already-poisonous atmosphere in the union, as relations between the Linville administration and the growing opposition deteriorated rapidly. To an outsider, this persistent conflict might have appeared petty, a sectarian fight over fine distinctions rather than over substantive differences, or even just a matter of political rivalries taken too personally.[45] But real political issues were at stake that were central to the history of liberal anticommunism in general and in Rapp-Coudert particularly.

The "Investigation"

By fall 1934, liberals and social democrats would no longer countenance the approach of left-wing teachers to democratic action. Drawing support from the national trade-union movement, Linville joined the unfolding campaign by American Federation of Labor (AFL) President William Green to purge the labor movement of communists, decisively launched in September 1934 with a letter to all AFL affiliates, accusing Communist Party members of "complying with instructions from the Russian Third Internationale [sic] to 'bore from within' the organizations of labor." Communists, Green insisted, "are engaged in planting 'cells' in our affiliated organizations" in order to "gain control of the American Federation of Labor as the primary requisite to world revolution." He called on member unions "to ferret out all communistic members, all communistic 'cells,' and to expel all such members or groups from the association when it has been clearly established that such members and such groups are engaged in carrying on communistic propaganda."[46]

Green's attack had deep and tangled roots in the history of American trade unionism. He inherited his anticommunism in part from his predecessor, AFL founder Samuel Gompers, whose hostility to socialists, anarchists, and communists shaped the ideological and political terrain of the American labor movement during and after World War I. For Gompers as for Green, unions only functioned effectively when negotiating the terms of employment directly with employers and industry representatives, eschewing broader social and political mobilization or the regulatory intervention of the state. According to historian Jennifer Luff, to defeat communism in the AFL, Gompers and other federation officials collaborated with federal and local authorities by policing the ranks of the trade-union movement through the 1920s, spying on left-wing and antiwar labor activism and reporting it to federal authorities, including the FBI. Until World War II, however, AFL leaders drew the line at supporting espionage and sedition legislation, refusing to back restrictions on civil liberties or measures authorizing direct surveillance of left-wing activists and organizations, fearing that such repressive measures would be turned on more mainstream trade unionists such as themselves. That didn't stop Green or other leaders of AFL unions from using the federation's power through the 1930s to force the expulsion of communists or even eventually to expose them to full-fledged federal repression, first by testifying before the Dies committee and then by using newly minted laws like the Smith Act, as was the case in 1940 for Trotskyists in the Minneapolis teamsters union and the following year in the Seattle machinists union.[47]

Green targeted communists, but progressives were another matter, which indicates the extent to which the labor movement also practiced a version of Kirchwey's "double mental bookkeeping." Luff grounds Green's anticommunism in an antiprogressive, market-oriented "labor conservativism" that was suspicious of state regulation of labor relations, including the Wagner Act. Historian Markku Ruotsila, in contrast, finds in Green's attack strong traces as well of a social-democratic "progressivism" active in the craft unions from the start of World War I. Of special note was the Social Democratic Federation, which exercised an influence on AFL affairs through the 1930s and 1940s that was "by no means negligible." Many of the "socialist anticommunists" who founded the Social Democratic Federation in 1936 descended from the Old Guard that bolted from the Socialist Party when "militants" pushed the party to cooperate with Communists and other radicals in AFL unions. Ruotsila considers these well-placed social democrats, some of them in the leadership of key unions such as the International Ladies' Garment Workers Union, a primary basis for AFL anticommunism. Among these social-democratic anticommunists, whose politics closely resembled the regulatory progressivism of liberals such as Dewey, one can count Henry Linville, who effectively marched out of the Socialist Party with the Old Guard and then joined AFL officials in testifying about the communist scourge in House Committee on Un-American Activities hearings. From their efforts to expel communists and other left-wing organizations, a "prolonged, bitter struggle" emerged for the control of American trade unions, first in the AFL and then even in the Congress of Industrial Organizations, despite strong Communist influence in newly formed industrial unions like the United Auto Workers.[48]

Green's letter also came on the heels of the extraordinary events of the spring and summer of 1934, as workers in the Toledo Auto-Lite strike, the San Francisco general strike, the Minneapolis Teamsters strike and elsewhere launched the kinds of mass action that Local 5's left wing had advocated for several years, expanding the scope of union mobilization to include the entire working-class populations of some industrial cities. Many of the more militant participants in those strikes belonged to the same left-wing parties as Local 5 members, including the Trotskyist Workers Party in Minneapolis and A. J. Muste's syndicalist American Workers Party, at the forefront in the "Battle of Toledo," both of which Green included under the rubric "communist." Green also was reacting against the recriminations over the disastrous strike that fall that essentially killed textile organizing in the south for a generation.[49] Linville supported Green's campaign tacitly and, when confronted by resistance in his own union, explicitly, leading to renewed conflict with the opposition, which at this point included militant Socialists such as Charles Hendley, who, sensing the shifting historical tide as the AFL started to break up over growing working-class militancy, had split with Green.⁵⁰ Complaining that "the world has been changing and Local 5 has not changed with it," Hendley noted "a general radical trend in the A.F. of L. that has no relation to the Communists or the Socialists," of which Local 5's opposition groups were a part. "The radicalism that the [Linville] Administration complains of rises from the conditions of the times, and is not due to the cussedness of left-wingers."⁵¹

Most of the histories of New York teachers' unionism, as well as of the history of anticommunism, treat what happened next as an unremarkable and justified response to the disruptive behavior of the union's left wing. As communist influence grew, Linville, it is assumed, simply had enough and so persuaded liberal-minded supporters to form another union that would be free of communist machinations and interference. But nothing could have been further from the truth. The real cause of Linville's frustration was that he was losing control of "his" union. And what he did next is best described as the use of anticommunist bullying in an attempt to take it back. Still supported by a majority of the local's executive board, Linville pushed through a request to the national American Federation of Teachers (AFT) to investigate his own union for "communist domination" and to consider revoking its charter while handing a new one to a local that had been purged of communists that Linville and his allies planned to establish.⁵² Then, he arranged for the national office in Chicago to send a committee to New York City to conduct an "investigation." Three national officers, President Raymond Lowry, Secretary-Treasurer Florence Hanson, and Linville's friend and ally Selma Borchardt, showed up for a weekend of hearings in early June 1935, with barely a few days' notice given to opposition factions, to hear Linville and his supporters rant from notes and documents that Linville had been preparing for years on how communists and their allies were sabotaging his union.⁵³

Anticipating the psychologically fragile Captain Queeg from Herman Wouk's 1951 bestseller, *The Caine Mutiny*, Linville seemed to recognize that he was losing his grip on the reins of power, interpreting minor slights and legitimate criticisms as attacks on an organization that he identified with his own leadership. Submitting a mind-boggling list of particular charges and dozens of documents in evidence, including the Dewey report, Linville bitterly complained that "the officers [of the local] have been subjected to vituperative and uncalled for attacks for many years," and that factionalism "amounting to civil war ... hindered the effectiveness of the Union." Linville turned every disagreement over policy into an attack on the union itself that was borne of outside political groups' infiltration and subversion, which included collusion that Linville and his supporters perceived to have been carried out by former allies such as Hendley.[54] Lefkowitz mirrored Linville's Queeg-like performance, grandiosely touting his own accomplishments in the third person. He bragged of being offered an administrative position by the superintendent of schools, an offer which the "representative of the union" (referring to himself) turned down even though he was "worth fifty of those who might have been selected. And he says this quite frankly without any attempt at feeling that he is exaggerating the situation." At best, Linville and the supporters who lined up behind him at the inquest confirmed the opposition's complaints about the "rigidity of attitude on the part of the Administration," as Hendley put it, "its fear of [the] least criticism and a demand that we all stand by the Administration 100 per cent."[55]

The teachers being charged by Linville not only sounded reasonable by comparison; they turned what would otherwise have been a kangaroo court into a discussion of the meaning of union democracy. Hendley, who up to this point had sided with Linville and Lefkowitz in the union's internal disputes, endorsed the sort of contentious dispute that had developed among the union members, and between radical teachers and school administrators. "If our organization can make a demonstration of how these differences can be used to develop greater power, it will make a most valuable contribution to the history of organized labor."[56] Lovestoneite Ben Davidson agreed, noting that "differences of opinion" are natural to "human society and human institutions." He asked: "Do you expect everybody to think alike?" He went on to emphasize the "collective" character of social difference and dispute.

> In modern society differences assert themselves in collective form, mind you, not through individuals, through tendencies, through blocs, caucuses, groups. In national conventions of our organization there have been caucuses, not just individuals getting up to speak. There are Farm Blocs in Congress, there are caucuses at conventions, just as there are tendencies in Unions. There are groups in parties, and you cannot stifle this difference of opinion except that you want mechanically to impose your opinion upon those who disagree with you.

"We do not want a graveyard peace," Davidson continued, "that is not going to do any good to our Union even though the Administration would like that very much."[57] Eve Davidson, also a Lovestoneite, concurred: "The whole question of expulsion is inseparably tied up with the question of democratic procedure, discussion and winning adherence on the basis of conviction and better policies and activity. The Administration . . . has chosen the path of expulsions, mechanical, arbitrary suppression of minority opinion instead of the method of democratic procedure, free discussion and the possibility of the best group winning."[58]

Hendley took issue with Linville's claim to nonpartisanship. If factionalism based on political affiliation was going to be an issue, he argued, then the party memberships and alliances of the more conservative side of the union should be addressed as well: "What are we to say as to the enthusiasm of a great many of our members on the right for the Fusion campaign? This Union was not committed to an endorsement of Mr. La Guardia, but it came dangerously near it, it seemed to me." Hendley also noted the strong ties to Tammany of the Central Labor Council, which represented AFL interests in New York City, despite its pretense of having a "non-partisan policy." There is, he warned presciently, "great toleration for the behavior of the people on the right" and not enough for the growing left.[59] Some opposition members merely wanted the most basic electoral safeguards: election rules publicized in advance, closed ballots, supervised vote counting, and supervision of ballot mailings. One asked, "What has the Administration to lose by giving these elementary guarantees of a fair election?"[60] The absence of such guarantees suggested that Local 5 was indeed Lefkowitz and Linville's "vest pocket union," as Eve Davidson put it.

Moreover, the perceptions of teacher interests were changing in a manner consistent with the radical shifts in labor activism across the nation. Lena Tulchen, who ran the Socialist Teachers group and who with Hendley joined the "militants" in 1935, echoed Begun on class struggle: "This idea that [radical teachers] believe in class struggle, and expressions of that type, it isn't something that you believe in. It is here and it has been going on. I, for one, in my own small way, have been in it, and I hope to live and die in such a way that when I am gone they can say about me, as Valentine says of Faust, 'he died a good soldier.' I am not afraid of being associated with the class war."[61]

However compelling in retrospect, at the time such arguments had little effect. An offer of compromise was made in August by the opposition groups, mediated by theologian Reinhold Niebuhr and school reformer George S. Counts, both of whom were union members. Linville rejected it with what Niebuhr called an "uncompromising attitude." Linville probably expected full support in the upcoming AFT convention in addition to the backing that Green and anticommunists in the AFL already were giving him.[62] Green sent a telegram demanding Local 5 be dissolved, persuading the executive council to throw its support behind Linville at the national convention in September. However, the majority of convention delegates, offended by Green's intervention, reversed the decision. Furious that he could not get what he wanted, Linville walked out of the convention and eventually the national union, taking with him roughly eight hundred members of AFT Local 5, including John Dewey.[63] After an abortive attempt to have the entire AFT thrown out of the AFL, Linville and his colleagues proceeded to build their own nonaffiliated organization, the Teachers Guild, to work Linville and Lefkowitz's contacts among liberal educational reformers and anticommunist trade unionists, and to bide their time. They would not have long to wait.

7
Far from the Ivory Tower

Americans passed the third weekend of August 1939 under the cloud of war. Amassing troops along the Polish border, Germany made clear its contempt for Great Britain and France's efforts in the Munich Accords to prop up Europe's teetering balance of power. As the prospects for peace dissolved abroad, delegates converged on Buffalo, New York, that Monday August 21, for the annual convention of the American Federation of Teachers (AFT). On Tuesday, convention-goers opened their morning papers to learn that the governments of Germany and the Soviet Union had reached a nonaggression pact, freeing Russia from immediate threat but allowing Hitler even more latitude than he already had in Eastern and, more ominously, Western Europe.[1]

The Hitler-Stalin Pact plunged teachers in Buffalo that week into profound uncertainty. Like most Americans, AFT members were divided about United States involvement in the European conflict. Even after the fall of Holland and France in summer 1940, Local 5 members split roughly down the middle on the question.[2] At the same time, while a reasonable strategy might be discerned or, at some point in the future, revealed behind the Soviet decision, its damage to left-wing politics in the United States was unmistakable: the pact terminated by fiat from abroad the Popular Front against fascism, to which many of the convention-goers, Communists or not, were loyal adherents. If the Hitler-Stalin Pact showed anything, it was that Communists did not shape the larger contours of their own movement—not even national party leaders appeared to know what was going on or how to justify the Soviet decision.[3] Whatever party members did on the ground in their own countries, party units, and front organizations, or in their daily work shaping the course of the class struggle, and however important those factors were in setting the character of American or any other nationally-based Communism, they and others could clearly see that the core project of defeating fascism was steered from abroad. For many Americans in the Popular Front, that project had been everything; suddenly, it appeared to be nothing. Yet at the same time, the war overshadowed all else, and foreign affairs paradoxically came to dominate party concerns, putting successful trade-union projects and work for racial equality on the back burner. As literary critic Granville Hicks, who quit that September, observed, the party "revealed the likelihood that its domestic policy may be drastically altered" without warning as it scrambled to defend the pact.[4]

The full impact of the Soviet shift in policy would not be felt on this side of the Atlantic for a couple of months, and its immediate effect was limited at Buffalo. The convention supported almost all of the candidates associated with the union's left-wing leadership and passed Popular Front-oriented resolutions—all of them having to do with race relations, education, or trade-union policy—that had been crafted well before the events of August. But the Hitler-Stalin Pact does appear to have tilted one convention vote in a historically decisive direction. Jerome Davis, the sociologist and theologian who had led the AFT for the previous three years and who was widely viewed as a spokesman for the Popular Front, was narrowly defeated for president by an insurgent anticommunist candidate whose prospects did not look especially good at the beginning of the week. That insurgent was George S. Counts.[5]

Counts's election was fateful for the union and for Communist teachers. It drove a wedge into the AFT leadership that Counts and fellow liberals had widened relentlessly, using Counts's position to campaign successfully against the left-wing coalition that led the union since 1935. On that basis, and with help from the anticommunist leadership of the American Federation of Labor (AFL), Counts and his followers achieved what amounted to a coup against the New York locals and the increasingly isolated Communists and supporters that still led them. By January 1941, just a month after the Coudert committee's first public hearings, the expulsion of those locals from the national union was virtually a *fait accompli*. Coudert's staff understood this perfectly well, as Henry Linville and others kept them apprised of the situation.[6] And while there was no *official* collaboration between the investigation and the Counts administration, there is little doubt that each effort served the other. Counts pointed to Coudert's allegations as justification for ousting Locals 5 and 537, including the entirely unsubstantiated claims that Communist teachers indoctrinated their students. The Coudert committee, for its part, cited the AFT expulsion edict as confirmation of their allegations that Communists controlled the New York AFT locals.[7]

Counts's success reflected changing sentiments among unionized teachers who had lost confidence in the Communist-led "democratic front" and the political culture associated with it. So the Hitler-Stalin Pact must be treated as a factor in the liberal anticommunist takeover. But to attribute the expulsion of Communists to a foreign intrigue or even to flaws in the Communist outlook on the Soviet experiment is to miss a crucial part of the story, one which began in 1935 as liberal and social-democratic educators intensified their criticism of the Popular Front's representatives in the teachers union. As those attacks mounted, they fed into the Coudert inquisition, which Counts and his allies tacitly and in some cases explicitly endorsed.

George S. Counts and Educational "Reconstruction"

In February 1932, as towns and cities across the United States went into fiscal meltdown, closing schools, laying off teachers, and in some cases suspending payment of salaries altogether, George Counts delivered a speech to the Progressive Education Association (PEA) that stunned the assembled audience of already-shell-shocked teachers and school administrators with its audacity and vision. Published with two related speeches, Counts's *Dare the School Build a New Social Order* is remembered by many, even those who disagreed with it, as the key text guiding the national discourse on school reform into the postwar period.[8]

In 1932, Counts still enjoyed a reputation as an avid spokesman for the left wing of progressive school reform. Raised on a subsistence farm in eastern Kansas, Counts recalled the enthusiasms for populism and the social gospel sweeping through his heavily Methodist community of Baldwin in the 1890s. After studying classics at local Baker University, Counts taught for several years before moving on to graduate work at the University of Chicago. By the time he was hired on at Columbia's Teachers College (TC) in 1927, at the age of thirty-eight, Counts had made the grand circuit of higher learning, teaching at institutions as diverse and far-flung as Harris Teachers College in St. Louis, the University of Washington, the University of Chicago, and Yale.[9]

At TC, Counts found like-minded "progressive" educators, most of them disciples of John Dewey, who as professor emeritus continued to shape curricular and philosophical discussion well into the 1940s. Based in part on this progressive reputation, by 1930, TC had achieved substantial influence in the world of educational reform. A new kind of institution in an expanding educational economy, a training center for the teachers of teachers, it supplied the nation not only public-school instructors but also normal-school professors to produce educators for the burgeoning population of American elementary and secondary students. Its faculty led a remarkable academically-centered reform movement, organizing a growing number of schoolmen and -women into an archipelago of educational associations, professional groups, and the occasional union that advanced an increasingly central role for schools in a modernizing economy. TC professors saw themselves as forging a national and even international educational policy, a project they invested with enormous importance and self-importance. Counts's colleague William Heard Kilpatrick spoke for many of them when he described education as "society at work consciously remaking itself," or, metaphysically, "life directing itself."[10]

Though urgent in tone, *Dare the School* extended arguments that Counts and others at TC and elsewhere had made over the previous decade. Counts's main premise was that scientific discovery and the new technologies of mass production brought a seismic shift in the foundations of economic life since the Civil War by accelerating productivity and putting "within our hands the power to usher in an age of plenty, to make secure the lives of all, and to banish poverty forever from the land."[11] In 1932, however, that potential for "abundance" was obviously not being realized, certainly not for the vast majority of Americans. There was "starvation in the midst of plenty," even during the supposedly prosperous 1920s. Counts traced such incapacities to the perverse use to which our technical power was put by business enterprise. So long as technology was applied primarily to the pursuit of profit, in an economy unregulated by state institutions, there would always be overproduction crises leading to depression.[12] Americans "stand confused and irresolute" before the current economic emergency, he warned in another manifesto, penned in 1933, also for the PEA. Although they are on the brink of "an economy of plenty," Americans "tolerate an economic system that in the best of times is wasteful, inefficient, and brutal, and at more or less regular intervals is visited by devastating paralysis." To Counts, the solution seemed obvious: Americans must face "the task of reconstructing our economic institutions and of reformulating our social ideals so that they may be in harmony with the underlying facts of life." And at the heart of that "reconstruction," Counts argued, stood the public school.[13]

Such rhetoric led many to consider Counts a socialist and TC a bastion of Marxism. William Randolph Hearst, who sent undercover reporters to snoop out TC reds, forbade his newspapers any mention of Counts or of institutions that invited him to speak. Accusing Counts of engineering a "unification of Leftist ranks," Harold Lord Varney in the conservative weekly *The American Mercury* placed him at the head of "the growing group of Left-wingers at Teachers College," who intended to "take the whole American teaching profession into the camp of social revolution."[14] And there was much about the public lives of these schoolmen that bore out accusations of at least sympathy for a communist perspective. For one thing, Counts and several of his TC colleagues, including Dewey and Kilpatrick, initially expressed support for the Soviet Union, which they visited in the late 1920s and early 1930s. Counts's two books on Soviet planning and educational policies made clear his agreement with a significant part of the Soviet experiment, including the first Five-Year Plan, which he endorsed enthusiastically and uncritically.[15]

It is fairly safe to say that Counts and the "reconstructionists," as he and his colleagues at TC came to be known, did advocate something resembling a "social revolution," certainly from the point of view of Wall Street and its supporters, but also for many residents of Main Street, who had little interest in progressive school reform or in reconstructing American society. So it should not have been surprising that such political views opened several of them to scrutiny during wartime internal security sweeps or, later, when McCarthyism went into full bloom after the war.[16] Starting in 1934, the reconstructionists made plain their position on the pages of *The Social Frontier*, a journal of politics and educational reform founded by TC professors, initially edited by Counts and with a board headed by Kilpatrick. And because it promoted social reconstruction so prominently on its pages, some historians consider *The Social Frontier* sympathetic to a Marxist or communist politics and therefore a part of the emerging Popular Front.[17]

But philosophically and historically speaking, the relationship between these school reformers and the socialist and communist movements of their day was quite a bit more complicated than might appear to an ideologue like Hearst. While some such as Counts were defiantly anticapitalist, at least in the middle of the Depression, their understanding of historical change had a distinctively non-Marxist character that was inherently averse to a communist approach to politics and social movements. Dewey, hostile to Marxism as a philosophy and intentionally ignorant of its tenets, set the tone for his followers, who emphatically considered themselves "pragmatists," philosophically and politically speaking, and who established *The Social Frontier* as an alternative not only to conservative reaction but to the communist left as well. Indeed, far from introducing Marx and Lenin into American school reform, reconstructionists drew on indigenous critiques of free-market capitalism, which argued on historical and evolutionary grounds for a "planning" society but not a socialist one, and which rejected the "class war view," as Dewey and Linville put it, of the communist left. The fact that reconstructionist critiques were drawn from Americans such as economist Thorstein Veblen and historian Charles Beard was relatively little comfort to the defenders of a free market and "business culture," as Veblen acidly called American capitalism. But the reconstructionists were not Marxists, and that is important for understanding the visceral objections they expressed to communists and communism after 1933.

One key point of disagreement with the Marxist left was the reconstructionist emphasis on technology as the motive force behind social evolution, which contrary to the many misinterpretations of the Marxist tradition is a very un-Marxist premise.[18] Reconstructionists borrowed this technological determinism from Veblen through the "institutionalists," a group of academic economists centered at Columbia, Amherst College, and the University of Wisconsin.[19] Institutionalists argued that scientific and technological advances brought modern industry to the point where the capacity to create goods and services exceeded the ability of social and political institutions, including the market and the negligible regulatory apparatus of the state, to distribute them effectively. There was a "fault line," as Amherst College's Walton Hamilton encapsulated this view, "between the industrial arts with which we carry on and the antiquated social organization with which we attempt to harness them."[20] Counts and other reconstructionist educational reformers used institutionalism freely to explain the crisis facing American society in general and American education in particular. While we stood on the eve of an era of abundance, they argued, we limited our ability to plan and organize our economic activity because we believed we still lived in an era of scarcity that was governed by rules of a competitive market and individual achievement appropriate to an earlier "agrarian" stage in American history.[21]

What separated "agrarianism" and "industrialism" for Counts was the "fault line" perceived by Hamilton and the institutional economists, or something like it: Agrarianism as the reconstructionists understood it naturally followed an "individualizing" approach to the world. Isolated by distance and lack of communication, rural Americans of necessity were self-sufficient. But the new technologies of industrialism undermined the world of isolated farm and home production and drew Americans from rural regions of the nation and the globe to work and consume in highly integrated and economically interdependent factories and urban markets. "Already we live in an economy which in its functions is fundamentally cooperative," Counts maintained. "The day of individualism in the production and distribution of goods is gone." It had been replaced by a "collectivist reality," that Counts insisted, citing Hamilton, was a "fait accompli."[22] The public, however, clung to an individualistic, antiregulatory frame of mind, anachronistically and culturally resistant to technologically driven historical progress. That "cultural lag," as the reconstructionists called it, contributed significantly to the economic failures behind the Depression.

By interpreting the Depression as a cultural crisis, reconstructionists such as Counts dramatically increased the stakes for teachers, who as keepers of the national culture could train Americans to a new point of view, especially at that moment in the nation's history. A shift in educational philosophy and practice was needed, Counts insisted, in which Americans "accept industrial society as an established fact" and "cease casting nostalgic eyes towards the agrarian past." And the urgency of the moment required political mobilization. The economic crisis, now interpreted as at root a cultural and educational one, was so pressing that teachers "cannot remain silent" on social and economic issues and must help "reorganize the procedures of the school in the light of the deepest needs of the age."[23] How far should teachers go in training students to a new frame of mind that would be appropriate to the evolving world around them? Should they teach "collectivism?" Counts believed that they should, even if that meant "indoctrination" or the "imposition" of a point of view. Schooling is never neutral, he argued, thinking not only of the traditional role of schools in promoting American democracy, but also of the businessmen controlling boards of education and who put a conservative and individualistic slant on those traditions: "My thesis is that complete impartiality is utterly impossible, that the school must shape attitudes, develop tastes, and even impose ideas."[24] Teachers could no longer "educate the youth for life in a world that does not exist." They "cannot evade the responsibility of participating actively in the task of reconstituting the democratic tradition and of thus working positively toward a new society. The simple discharge of their professional duties leaves to them no alternative."[25]

The reconstructionists likewise repudiated Marxist class analysis as an anachronistic throwback to the days of laissez-faire capitalism and agrarian individualism. Like those industrialists who resisted the regulatory reforms of the New Deal, communists and other advocates of the "class war view" remained, as Dewey put it, "still pathetically held in the clutch of old habits and haunted by old memories" that were associated with the old economy.[26] Class privilege and, even more generally, the class identity of the wealthy in this interpretation of America's pressing social conflicts could then be understood as a culturally determined misinterpretation of the world rather than a structurally determined maldistribution of power and privilege. Dewey's friend Henry Linville underscored that difference: anyone who was attracted to the "class struggle concept" should instead consider the "Capitalist enemy" as "an anti-social aggregation, existing as the by-product of the industrial age rather than as a participant in an inevitable conflict."[27] For Dewey, then, the mounting of machine guns at Ford plants, the hiring of thugs to break up picket lines, and all the other forms of violence enlisted by capitalists to protect their interests during the Depression were matters of choice, encouraged and tolerated by bad habits of mind and *misperceptions* of the actual conditions of modern life *rather than products of it*.

For a while, Counts and several of the younger TC faculty disagreed with Dewey, insisting instead that class identity reflected structural inequalities in economic relations that could not be changed by a simple adjustment of attitude and perspective. The dispute over that issue unfolded on the pages of *The Social Frontier* through 1935 into 1936. By spring 1936, however, liberals under Dewey's tutelage won. Kilpatrick produced the final word on the subject in a June article attacking "high Marxism," the strict adherence to Marxist doctrine that Kilpatrick likened to a religious enthusiasm overseen by authoritarian clerics. Whatever his colleagues left unclear, Kilpatrick plainly enumerated in a declaration comprising all the elements in later liberal demonization of communist ideology: First, Communists advocate class struggle as a choice that necessarily leads to class war, "violent change and overthrow" and a workers dictatorship. Second, teachers who believe in class struggle "must" actively participate by indoctrinating their students. Third, Communists lack morality because all decisions serve their interest in class war; consistent with that "customary war morality" they practice "deceit" and bad faith. They join organizations to disrupt and destroy them if that suits their purpose of bringing about the class war. They "fish in troubled waters, rub salt into old sores, sow seeds of further discord in all conflicts." Fourth, they subject themselves to the authoritarian discipline of a "party with its headquarters in a distant country." And their loyalty is driven and sustained by a "religious fervor" that "pervades" the theory of "high Marxism" and the practice of communism. Like other religious enthusiasts, high Marxists were indifferent to logic and reasonable persuasion. Finally, notwithstanding the Popular Front claims to the contrary, "high Marxism," according to Kilpatrick, "rejects democracy, rejects education as a process of social change, and rejects ... the ethical regard for the personality of others."[28]

Democratization

Meanwhile, Local 5 not only survived but also flourished after Linville, Lefkowitz, Dewey, and fellow liberals jumped ship in September 1935. Between then and 1940, the union and its two subsidiary locals—the College Teachers Union (CTU) and a local that represented Works Progress Administration-paid school employees—grew by around six hundred percent to a total membership of over ten thousand, contributing a significant portion of the national union's growth during the decade. While by no means as dramatic as the rise of the steel or auto unions, for publicly employed professionals this was a major accomplishment. Charles Hendley, who became local president after the split and remained in office through the Coudert investigation, attributed this growth to the politically diverse character of the rank and file, who were encouraged to actively participate in union affairs.[29]

Ironically, some of the democratic features of union governance had been put in place during the Linville administration, including provisions like minority representation on the executive board and major committees that had been demanded by left-wing teachers. Local 5 also instituted proportional representation for electing officers and representatives as well as delegates to send to the national AFT conventions. So, unlike other AFT affiliates, the New York locals often supplied to those conventions vocal opponents to their own leaders and referendum proposals. Additionally, such robust participation was encouraged by a system of school representation and a functional and diverse committee structure. As a change from the Linville period, the union under Hendley also regularly engaged in mass organizing campaigns, some of them impressive in the scope of achievement, especially when promoting expanded school budgets. Hendley ran quarterly general membership meetings that often brought in over a thousand members, including dissenting factions, to address policy and strategy.[30]

Of the two new unions spun off by Local 5, one—CTU Local 537 of the AFT—left an especially impressive record of accomplishment. College faculty and staff who had loosely organized themselves into associations at the various municipal colleges first set up the college section of the main local in March 1935. It addressed salary, appointment and promotion procedures, and the extension of tenure rights at public institutions. It attracted interest from faculty and staff at private colleges as well, promoting tenure and academic freedom where state and municipal legislation could not easily reach. In their initial organizing drive, the college section attracted nearly three hundred members within a year at both private and public schools. The core of the new union, however, was in the municipal system: by early 1936, seventy had signed on at City College of New York (CCNY) alone.[31]

Such enthusiasm for union representation reflected the precarious conditions of college teaching in the mid-1930s, a situation bad enough for professors but even worse for staff and the many underpaid instructors and tutors who took on the bulk of the teaching at public institutions. Bernard Grebanier estimated that they did eighty percent of the teaching at Brooklyn. Pay cuts imposed in 1934 under La Guardia's austerity budgets were not restored when the fiscal emergency ended in 1936. Most instructional staff could be fired at will—usually this just meant not being rehired for a new term—and while tenure supposedly applied to the state's colleges and universities under the 1935 Feld-McGrath tenure law, it was only tenuously in place and, some argued, there in its present form only to protect patronage appointments by Tammany's presidents at Brooklyn, Hunter, and City. Those presidents continued to exercise almost absolute authority over the composition of the faculty, appointing loyal department chairs yet overriding them to hire or fire department members when it suited them.[32]

At private colleges and universities, to which the state's fragile tenure law did not extend, faculty and staff labored under even greater uncertainty. In a confidential 1938 survey of Columbia faculty, the union found an enormous disparity in pay and rank with no tenure protection at all. Even full professors considered themselves employed "at the pleasure of the trustees." At TC, Dean William F. Russell acted with almost monarchical authority—he inherited the position from his father, the two of them serving a total of fifty-six years—and did not hesitate to demand resignations from professors who displeased him. Such capriciousness eroded the quality of education as much as it compromised academic freedom. The union's Columbia chapter described a situation in which "the quiet incompetent who does nothing to antagonize the administration remains, while the able teacher whose teaching, research or outside activity do not meet with the approval of conservative interests in the administration is in constant danger of dismissal."[33]

There was nothing especially new about this situation, except that the Depression made it worse. Until well after World War II, the rights of faculty and students to hold and express personal political, social, or even religious views were always under threat. While the First Amendment supposedly protected political speech and association, its umbrella had not yet been extended to teachers, who were obliged to serve the public good by teaching conventional civic values and by setting an example for their students of proper behavior, both in and outside the classroom. Until the 1960s, when the Supreme Court finally grounded academic rights of speech and conscience in the Constitution, the right of public-school teachers and college faculty to dissent stopped at the schoolhouse door. Moreover, school boards were not obliged to hire teachers whose public statements and behavior they considered out of step with community values. As Justice Oliver Wendell Holmes pithily intoned in an 1892 Massachusetts case upholding a police officer's dismissal for political activism that was often cited as precedent, "the petitioner may have a constitutional right to talk politics, but he has no constitutional right to be a policeman."[34] This principle applied to college faculty as well and remained in place until the Supreme Court finally recognized, as Holmes did not, that the threat of dismissal did in fact compromise First Amendment rights. Meanwhile, organizations like the American Association of University Professors (AAUP), founded in 1915, supported higher education institutions in warding off interference from the state, but did very little to protect individual professors from reprisal by conservative administrators and trustees, whose cooperation the association needed in order to conduct its ostensibly impartial investigation of complaints. Universities and colleges, in other words, enjoyed freedom from outside interference, but individual members of their faculty did not enjoy true academic freedom. Many university presidents and trustees believed the rights of university professors were trumped by "university freedom," which Columbia's Nicholas Murray Butler defined as "the right and obligation of the university itself to pursue its high ideals unhampered and unembarrassed by the conduct on the part of any of its members."[35]

When New York state targeted academics for opposing World War I, and professors at private and public institutions were fired for disloyalty (by Butler, among others), the AAUP just advised faculty to refrain from public criticism of the war effort. Generally, like Holmes, it qualified faculty academic freedom by the professor's duties and contractual obligations to his or her institution and the community it served. Students were yet another matter, and few faculty or administrators thought they enjoyed a freedom of expression comparable to that of their professors, however limited that was. One had a right to express one's views but only within the limits and powers of one's professional competence, of which students, it was assumed, had none.[36]

So, on the eve of the war, teachers and college professors not only needed union representation for improving salaries and working conditions, but also to secure real academic freedom. Local 5 already had earned a reputation for the consistent defense of free speech for public-school teachers, thanks in part to Linville's interventions in World War I loyalty cases. Through the 1930s, the union continued to come to the aid of dozens more teachers who were penalized by principals and superintendents, the board of education, and even the American Legion for their suspected membership in left-wing organizations or their overly zealous engagement in union affairs. The local's college-teachers section extended this commitment to the public and private colleges, largely focusing on beefing up the weak codification of tenure in state law. Then, in 1938, shortly after it split off to become an independent local, the CTU succeeded in setting tenure for municipal college faculty on firmer ground by convincing the Board of Higher Education (BHE) to write it into its bylaws. The new terms were generous even by today's standards: Tenure would be automatic for all full-time faculty, including instructors, after three years of "competent service" as a probationary teacher. Faculty could only be dismissed for "teaching incompetency" or "conduct unbecoming," provided that the latter was not "interpreted so as to constitute interference with academic freedom."[37]

The CTU did not stop there, however; it argued that neither academic freedom nor educational integrity could be adequately secured until colleges and universities had been turned into more-reliably democratic institutions. Along with tenure, the union pressed for additional bylaws expanding the role of teachers and staff in the daily and long-term management of the municipal colleges, thereby building on more-traditional forms of faculty governance and on gains that had already been made in key departments at CCNY in 1937.[38] This "democratization," as the union called it, became a precedent for the modern faculty governance system, which normally is centered at each institution on a governing council with faculty and administrative representatives and includes joint faculty-administration committees to deliberate over the budget, conduct faculty reviews, and hold disciplinary hearings. Under the new bylaws, passed by recently appointed reform members of the BHE in June 1938 on a wave of union agitation, each department would control "its own educational policies" by electing its own chairs, meeting regularly, voting on courses of study, and collectively making the initial recommendations for tenure and promotion up to but not including full professor. In a system that, up to that point, had been under the control of the city's political machine, presidents now had to cooperate with elected faculty and staff committees on major institutional decisions.[39]

Expectations among left-wing faculty and unionists for democratization ran extremely high. Brooklyn College's Howard Selsam epitomized their extravagance, declaring the new bylaws "the most sweeping reform in the history of American colleges and universities." Some of the CTU's notions were naive, including the idea that the faculty "should be the supreme governing body," with presidents serving as "executive agents and far-sighted initiators in the service of education, not autocratic business managers of educational department-stores."[40] Otherwise, the CTU more realistically framed democratization as "an effective instrument for minimizing grievances; establishing professional standards; [and] encouraging constant attention to curriculum revision and student needs," and it was "necessary in order that we may effectively educate for democracy." Similar predictions filtered down from the BHE: democratization would invest faculty with "a sense of responsibility about the educational process" and, in the words of BHE President Ordway Tead, "keep the common interest in educational improvement always to the fore." The positive effects of the reforms were immediately apparent to CTU Secretary Arnold Shukotoff, who reported in early 1939 that the presidents of City and Hunter had begun to cooperate with faculty on personnel issues while opening up the campus for political meetings and protests that their administrations had previously blocked. Faculty meetings had been transformed from "irregular lectures by administrators" into "regularly-meeting deliberative bodies." The "free exchange of opinion and collaborative effort at mutual understanding," had already boosted morale and efficiency.[41]

The new bylaws, however, stoked considerable hostility on the right and among faculty who stood to lose positions and power as their institutions were reorganized. The *Brooklyn Eagle*, on whose pages the American Legion and other right-wing groups for years had been raising alarms about radicalism in the schools, branded the reforms a "red plot" to gain control of BC, featuring virulent opponents of the new bylaws, including the chair of BC's biology department, Earl A. Martin, with whom the union had come to blows over appointments and curriculum and whom the Brooklyn Communists considered a Tammany loyalist. Warning of the "insidious activities of the communist group," Martin called on faculty to "take a stand against the subversive doctrines and propaganda which are flooding the campus" with notions of a phony democracy that Martin predicted would erode academic standards and put the union and its Communist directors in control. Yet he also expressed reasonable fears that the new bylaws would undermine administrative authority and politicize the campus while bogging them down with an excess of committee work.[42] It would bring, as Teachers College liberal John Childs remarked in a different context, a "form of democratic administration that I couldn't quite accept." Martin's role spearheading the backlash against the new rules soon led him to repeat his charges before the Dies committee in Washington, where he was joined by two other right-wing opponents of democratization, one of them a supporter of the Christian Front.[43]

Extremist opposition encouraged CTU activists to regard municipal college democratization as part of the broader antifascist campaign to rebuild American democracy from the bottom up. Writing in *New Masses*, Selsam optimistically gushed that the reforms brought the nation "one step nearer the realization of President Roosevelt's plan ... to make 'our schools and colleges a genuine fortress of democracy.'" Selsam envisioned the CTU as a bastion in that fortress, a living part of its structure. Moreover, contrary to the reputation with which it was saddled during later political inquisitions, in its short history as a representative body for New York faculty, the union remained open to diverse views and factions, electing, like its parent local, governing bodies by proportional representation and urging convention delegates, also chosen proportionally, to vote "according to the their own convictions" rather than by unit rule, the conventional trade-union practice.[44] The impressive number of women in its leadership positions despite the widespread persistence of sexual discrimination in higher education was more evidence of the union's egalitarianism. Although from 1938 through the early 1940s, the CTU elected only male presidents, of its eight governing committees four were headed by women, including the critically important grievance committee, at whose helm sat Helen Adams of Hunter College, and the organizing committee, run by Nelle Lederman of CCNY. Additionally, as legislative director for all the New York locals, Bella Dodd effectively ran the college union's political organization through its legislative committee, shaping overall strategy for dealing with the state legislature and municipal government.[45]

Such open egalitarianism, among other qualities, apparently boosted the CTU's appeal to faculty and staff throughout the metropolitan area. In January 1938, the CTU's ranks stood at seven hundred thirty six, the major part of which (225) worked at CCNY. Brooklyn had 115 members, Columbia (including TC, Barnard, and subsidiary campuses) 123, NYU 107, Hunter 36, Sarah Lawrence 30, and Long Island University 22, with the remaining 39 spread across other institutions.[46] That month, the union, which had planned to reach one thousand members by mid-March, launched a recruiting drive covering all colleges in the metropolitan area. By the beginning of March, the union had successfully added three hundred members, making it by far the largest college teachers union in the country. Moreover, they could claim that roughly one out of four municipal college teachers held a union card.[47]

Yet at the same time, John Childs's unease with the CTU's "form of democratic administration" reflected a growing alienation from the union and its parent, the AFT, among a significant group of college faculty. Such sentiments had been brewing in the AAUP, the AFT's main collegiate rival, since 1936 when AAUP members started joining the AFT's college branches (simultaneous membership was permitted by both organizations). Much of the hostility among AAUP leaders concerned perceived threats to academic professionalism by the AFT's trade unionism, especially the militancy promoted in Local 5 by left-wing teachers. The rivalry between the two organizations came to a head over the firing of Jerome Davis by Yale Divinity School in 1936, right before Davis was elected president of the AFT. In May, Yale informed Davis, who played a leading role in several Popular Front organizations and had long-standing ties to the Soviet Union, that his position would end the following June. An outspoken labor supporter who had worked for decades in the trade-union movement and who had joined the Yale faculty in 1924 on rotating three-year contracts, Davis had raised the ire of Yale trustees and alumni for criticizing capitalism in classes and public addresses. The selective and summary character of the dismissal, which Yale President James Angell claimed had been no more than a routine denial of tenure made on financial grounds, and the length of time Davis had already served on the Yale faculty, raised alarms throughout the American academy. The AFT made the firing a national *cause célèbre*, hammering away at the political motives behind the dismissal. The AAUP, in contrast, hesitated to appoint a committee to consider the case. When the association did end up investigating, it enjoyed privileged access to Yale administrators, who refused to meet with or provide statements to the AFT's investigating committee. And while it held the firing a "violation of the principles of academic tenure," the AAUP did not discern any political motives or accuse Yale of directly infringing Davis's academic freedom, leaving an opening for the university to claim that the association had "upheld" the Davis dismissal.[48] The AFT also violated the AAUP's sense of professional decorum by launching a public mass protest at the annual meeting of the Yale Corporation, bringing several hundred faculty and other supporters from around the country to challenge the university's directors to reinstate Davis. In the end, Davis was given an additional year's salary with a leave, an achievement for which the AFT took public credit, much to the resentment of AAUP leaders, who convinced themselves that if such confrontational tactics had not been used Davis would have been kept on permanently.[49]

Anticommunist undertones resonate throughout the archival record of the AAUP-AFT conflict, as AAUP officers traced the association's problems to the perceived control of the union by the left. AAUP President Ralph Himstead and the association's governing council engaged in ongoing skirmishes from 1937 through 1940 with the CTU's Shukotoff over efforts to establish a cooperation agreement between the association and the union, an agreement that the AFT wanted but the AAUP resisted. Shukotoff's communications with Himstead were consistently cordial, yet despite moments when the two organizations fruitfully collaborated, the AAUP officers grew increasingly hostile to any sort of *modus vivendi* with the growing college-union movement. Sounding very much like Henry Linville in his campaign against "Communist tactics," AAUP officers complained of the class terms used by the AFT to frame issues of academic employment. Most professors, Himstead wrote to his fellow officers, "have no desire to be advocates and are too intelligent not to realize the futility of labor union tactics as applied to institutions of higher education today"; they "prefer to have the faculty-administrative relation not an employer-employee relation."[50] Such ideological differences stoked in the AAUP a strong sense of urgency. "Firmly convinced" that cooperation with the AFT would be impossible "if we expect to survive as an association definitely interested in objective scholarship," Himstead urged his organization to preserve its "professional integrity." Believing that the AFT resorted to "the methods of devious infiltration" to gain more college and university members, Himstead warned that "if the ultimate objectives of the American Federation of Teachers should ever be achieved, the kind of education that makes democracy possible will soon be destroyed."[51]

In 1937, the conflict between liberals and the left still lurked below the surface, invisible to the public eye except as disputes on the pages of academic and political journals, or recorded in correspondence like Himstead's. That changed in early 1938, as the CTU democratization campaign heightened tensions between liberals and the left in the municipal colleges. Such differences, however, still came down to a matter of emphasis. As long as the union kept to the public sector, where the terms of employment and instruction had so precipitously declined through the Depression, the dispute would remain relatively placid.

Then the CTU leadership decided that the upcoming recruitment drive should target New York City's private colleges. That campaign deepened the gulf between liberals and the communist left, and as it did, a wave of anticommunist hysteria spilled out onto the pages of the city's major newspapers.

PART III
The Mortal Storm

> When Barcelona fell, the cry on the roads
> assembled horizons, and the circle of eyes
> looked with a lifetime look upon that image,
> defeat among us, and war, and prophecy,
> *I meet it in all the faces that I see.*
>
> —*Muriel Rukeyser, "1/26/39"*

8
Bad Faith

The College Teachers Union (CTU)'s recruitment campaign in private colleges and universities that year addressed a real need for union representation and tenure rights. But the reaction it triggered led directly to a leadership coup and expulsion drive in the AFT, which fed anticommunist sentiment among liberals and social democrats, promoted the notion that Communists uniquely acted in bad faith, and primed the conditions for an investigation like the Coudert committee's to take root.

At the start of 1938, Columbia University and New York University together employed more than half the college teaching staff in the metropolitan area. With one of the largest student bodies in the city composed almost entirely of future teachers, Columbia's Teachers College (TC) also had tremendous intellectual and political influence throughout higher education. On the basis of membership statistics showing low subscription from Columbia and NYU, in early January CTU President Arnold Shukotoff proposed "greater attention" be given to the problems of private higher education, initiating an organizing drive at private campuses throughout the New York area, where they also pushed more assertively for tenure.[1]

At Columbia, where George Counts and reform-minded colleagues had long before joined the union, Shukotoff expected a positive response. Twenty-five "recruitment squads" were set up to distribute literature and organize informational meetings. A gathering was planned for early May to present a "union program for Columbia" that addressed "insufficient democracy in the administration," the school's lack of tenure, discrimination against women faculty, and the absence of a "satisfactory procedure" for dismissal or grievances. Meanwhile, noting that grievances already filed at Columbia College "have been a means of interesting prospective members," the union began to involve itself in campus disputes, including internal departmental complaints and controversial faculty dismissals, some of them related to the restructuring of TC by its dean, William F. Russell.[2] Such outside interference and public exposure did not sit well with more-established professors at the Morningside Heights campus. It is quite certain, moreover, that other forms of perceived meddling by the CTU provoked a backlash not only from Columbia administration, but also among the union's adherents and allies, especially on the TC staff.

Twilight at Teachers College

The dispute began in fall 1937, when Russell forced Speech Department Chair Elizabeth McDowell, in her seventeenth year at the institution, to take a leave of absence for health reasons and then summarily dismissed her on grounds of teaching and administrative incompetence. Other TC professors supported Russell's action, notably reconstructionist Jesse Newlon, who bluntly told McDowell that she was inept and pressured her to resign. Though not a CTU member, McDowell asked the union's grievance committee for help. In response, the union set up an investigating committee under NYU's Helen S. Adams in early 1938. The committee agreed that McDowell had been a poor administrator, but it was a responsibility that she did not want, and she had proven herself an excellent teacher and scholar. Moreover, Russell and Newlon, the committee concluded, followed "irresponsible and tortuous methods of procedure" in terminating McDowell.[3]

The CTU's support of McDowell infuriated powerful members of the faculty, including liberals such as Newlon who considered the matter none of the union's business; for them, it was a personnel issue involving McDowell's psychological health, which they insisted had made her behavior with her colleagues erratic. "Mrs. McDowell has been suffering from a mild state of paranoia for some years," psychologist George Hartmann, who was active in the AFT but unhappy about the union's interference, had "reason to believe."[4] After trying to smooth the ruffled feathers of TC liberals, the CTU Executive Board sent the Adams committee's findings out for review by the general union membership anyway, overruling efforts by the Columbia chapter to table the embarrassing report.[5] In flagrantly disregarding the objections of chapter members the union may have had in mind a much larger issue: there was evidence that women at Columbia had been regularly mistreated by the administration and senior male faculty. The American Association of University Women seemed to share this concern, expressing to Himstead, of the American Association of University Professors (AAUP), "an interest in this case from the standpoint of women."[6]

Ignoring the warning signs from Morningside Heights, the union unwisely forged ahead, taking increasingly outspoken stands on Columbia affairs, challenging President Nicholas Murray Butler's habitual flouting of student rights, and coming to the defense of the pedagogically progressive and politically radical New College, a subdivision of TC, when Russell decided to close it down.[7] Relations between the union and liberal TC faculty began to deteriorate in earnest in February 1938, when the newspaper of the Communist Party's Teachers College unit, the *Educational Vanguard*, published an article that incensed professors for its apparent impropriety. There was nothing especially surprising or inflammatory in the article, which was about a staff and faculty meeting a month earlier when Russell presented his "reorganization" of the college, which the *Vanguard* predicted would lead to layoffs and program cutbacks. Charging Russell with flouting democracy, the paper named Newlon as one of the dean's "trusted advisors" who was enlisted to help sell the plan to resistant faculty and staff.[8] Even though Newlon's role was common knowledge, TC liberals regarded the appearance of his name on the *Vanguard's* pages as a "vicious, malicious" violation of professional decorum. The Columbia CTU chapter then tabled a resolution condemning the *Vanguard* and the Communists for the article, confirming the liberals' suspicions that Communists controlled the union.[9]

A union rally in May did little to help, as speakers attacked the university administration while egging faculty on to do the same. Former TC student James Wechsler warned the gathering of "the atmosphere of fear" and "the coercion brooding in the background of the campus."[10] That November, Wechsler filled in the details in a scathing article for *The Nation* magazine on the decline of progressive activism at TC. He painted a picture of liberal faculty cowed by an aggressively conservative, business-minded dean, who had no qualms about firing disobedient professors. He traced Russell's "high-handed disregard for democratic procedure" back to 1935, when he had tried to break a newly formed cafeteria-workers union by firing four alleged sympathizers on the cafeteria staff. Their supporters "forced a faculty probe" by a committee whose final report condemned the college's labor policies. Russell retaliated, closing down a student paper for siding with unionizing staff, and turned on faculty who questioned his treatment of college employees, inviting several who remained unnamed in Wechsler's article to submit their resignations.[11]

Meanwhile, late in 1936 at a party for conservative administrators and students, Russell swore that he would purge progressives such as William Kilpatrick and Counts. That January, Kilpatrick was forced to retire. Wechsler recounted yet another incident in which Russell disciplined and silenced Counts for taking the side of graduate student William Gellerman, whom the American Legion had attacked for a dissertation documenting the Legion's influence on educational institutions. Wechsler noted "increasing reticence" among faculty and "a pronounced decline in progressive activity." Wechsler carefully directed the bulk of his criticism at the Columbia administration and trustees, apparently hoping to rally support for a faculty and staff caught in "a tug-of-war between those who want to maintain the institution's integrity and those who favor a discreet Anschluss with Wall Street."[12] Moreover, everything that Wechsler included in the article was substantially true, as Kilpatrick recorded in his diary, from his own forced retirement to the silencing of Counts, right down to Russell's demand (made twice to Kilpatrick as intermediary and finally withdrawn) for the resignations of the two faculty members, John Childs and Goodwin Watson, who had been involved in the earlier labor conflicts.[13] Counts later admitted that he bent to Russell's pressure, claiming that it was for reasons of good administrative practice better understood at the time by the dean than by a member the faculty, let alone a recent graduate such as Wechsler.[14]

"Professors Quit: Union Called Red"

If Wechsler hoped his article would goad TC faculty to stick to their guns, however, he grossly miscalculated. Instead, the exposé only provoked Counts and his colleagues to close ranks in front of Columbia's ivy walls. Worse, it gave them an occasion to air long-simmering political and ideological grievances against the union and its Popular Front leadership. At the vanguard of this reaction stood John Childs. Born in 1889, Childs was a latecomer to progressive educational reform. After graduating in 1911 from the University of Wisconsin, where he first became involved in the labor movement, Childs went to work as the Intercollegiate Secretary of the YMCA. In 1916, he took the position of Foreign Secretary of the YMCA's International Committee in Beijing, China, where he experienced one of the most politically tumultuous decades of China's modern history. Encouraged by John Dewey, whom he met during the philosopher's 1921 tour of the Far East, Childs returned to the United States in his late thirties to take a PhD under Kilpatrick. He wrote his 1931 dissertation on Dewey's educational philosophy and began teaching at TC in his graduate school years, joining the Kilpatrick circle and eventually coauthoring Dewey's two chapters in the reconstructionist manifesto, *The Educational Frontier* (1934). TC officially added him to the faculty in 1931. Later, Childs became the first chairman of New York state's ardently anticommunist Liberal Party, founded in 1944 by disaffected former members of the American Labor Party, including several TC liberals.[15]

Wechsler's only mention of Childs was to praise him for being "a thorn in Russell's flesh" during campus labor disputes. Yet, in garbled and paranoid indignation, Childs interpreted the article as an attack that "insinuat[ed]" he had caved under administrative pressure to resign from the union. Wechsler's perceived offense made it "necessary" to publicize, he complained in a letter to the *Nation*, his real reasons for resigning, though in Childs's confused and confusing chronology of events it was not clear when or even whether that resignation took place.[16] Making no mention of Russell's threats against him and Watson, Childs wanted it known that he withdrew from the AFT "for one reason and one reason only—the present domination of the New York locals by left-wing political sects." As if that were not enough, in a separate letter, he and ten colleagues also discerned behind Wechsler's writing, with its "insinuation and misrepresentation," the same "hand of a political sect in American life which operates on the principle that it will destroy whatever it cannot rule."[17]

Childs's declarations attracted the attention of the press, which flocked to the Columbia professor for interviews about, to use the *Jewish Daily Forward*'s credulous prose, the "sensational news that three leading liberal professors were driven to resign from the Teachers Union because of communist control of that organization."[18] With each interview he repeated the charges freely, adding others as he went along. The newspapers cooperated enthusiastically: "Professors Quit: Union Called Red," the *New York Times*'s front-page headline blared over a story that paid scant attention to the underlying problems at the Columbia campus. All "important decisions" in the union, Childs insisted to the *Times*, "were taken in sectarian caucuses, not in the [union] assembly."[19] To the New York *Post* he added that general membership meetings passed "wholly irrelevant resolutions" that served "the favored interests of the Stalinist group." Echoing articles in *The Social Frontier*, he alleged growing alienation in the union ranks owing to the leadership's "class war" rhetoric, its inclination to characterize college administrators as "bosses" pitted against teachers as "workers," its "tendency to advance the union at the expense of the college," and its undemocratic decision-making.[20]

At first, the union lashed out in response to Childs's denunciation, deriding him as a "defender of academic autocracy" and a fair-weather labor advocate whose "interest in the labor movement ceases when educational problems on his own campus are concerned."[21] Such attacks bordered on the sort of character assassination for which the Communist Party was famous, though Childs and other TC liberals had indeed caved to administration pressure. Nevertheless, in early January 1939, the union changed its tone, inviting Childs to one of their interminable membership meetings to discuss the case. He refused, sending Counts and other colleagues in his place. The union backpedaled in *The Nation* later that month, perhaps recognizing that they had unfairly treated a dedicated labor activist whose contributions they once officially recognized, and that Childs's "resignation" signaled a much broader disaffection in the Columbia faculty. But the lines had already been drawn.[22]

Meanwhile, other Columbia faculty took the opportunity to give voice to a wide range of grievances against the CTU. Two TC colleagues, Bruce Raup and Ernest Johnson, publicly renounced union membership, with Raup explaining that his resignation followed from "my rejection of class struggle and class war as the method of working toward social justice in America." Louis Hacker and George Hartmann, who had recently been elected president of the Columbia CTU chapter, followed soon after, supplying the press with a steady stream of increasingly shrill complaints. Still others renewed earlier denunciations, evidently prompted by reporters eager to milk the story.[23] Counts, in a move that in retrospect looks calculated, threatened to quit the union and red-baited Wechsler and the CTU in the press and on the pages of *The Social Frontier*, yet he refused to renounce his membership. Twisting the facts to minimize Russell's capricious authoritarianism, Counts simply repeated Childs's unsubstantiated accusations against the union. As the Communist Party gained sway on campus and in the union there appeared, Counts contended, "a political faction in the College that ... was irresponsible and operated under the cloak of anonymity. Again and again it made difficult the rational adjustment of differences." Always "malicious, provocative, and irresponsible," campus communists "sabotaged our efforts to advance democratic values and practices at the College" while ruining the faculty relationship with the union.[24]

At some point that spring, the swell of indignation in Morningside Heights turned into an organized effort to wrest control of the union from the left wing. While Childs, Counts, and their colleagues denounced Communist teachers on the pages of liberal journals, seasoned anticommunists in the American Federation of Labor (AFL) renewed threats to push the AFT out of the federation if they did not "clean house." In a maneuver that many in the union condemned as duplicitous and transparently political, the New York City Central Trade and Labor Council, the AFL's local governing body that was loyal to Tammany Hall, suspended the left-wing teachers locals for sending representatives to the convention of a Popular Front organization that other AFL locals also attended.[25] One hand washed the other in this mounting campaign as the Childs "resignation" precipitated the suspension of the CTU and its sister locals from the Central Trade and Labor Council, and this suspension served Childs and his allies as a justification for having attacked the CTU in the first place. In April, Counts, Hartmann, and several other TC liberals announced that they would be running an opposition slate against the "Communist dominated" union leadership in upcoming CTU elections. Although a marginal and unpopular campaign in a relatively small local, the liberals enjoyed a surprising amount of newspaper coverage as the May vote approached. Despite the favorable press, the insurgency was crushed by roughly a five-to-one margin. Only Counts and Clinton Keyes, another Columbia liberal, won seats on the national executive board.[26]

The Mortal Storm

The TC liberals did not let their failure at the polls dampen their spirit of attack. As the summer approached, they prepared for a fight on the floor of the annual national convention in Buffalo, for which they had secured four delegate seats thanks to the local's system of proportional representation. The liberals made up for their lack of electoral support with a rhetorical edge, supplied by the extraordinary literary output of Counts, who published several books and pamphlets justifing the anticommunist position as a "defense of democracy" that caught union leaders and party activists unawares.

The previous fall, Counts brought out his well-received tract, *The Prospects of American Democracy*. In a vein mined by many Popular Front writers, Counts argued that a corporate "aristocracy" of "paper and patronage" had accumulated so much power from the burgeoning factories and mills of the industrial revolution and the counting houses of Wall Street that it put American democracy in "the deepest crisis in its history." Full of inconsistencies and poorly defined terms, the book at first appears to embrace the communist "class war view" that Counts and his colleagues had rejected, as it noted the escalating violence of industrialists and the unprecedented corporate influence in politics and government. However, in a remarkably optimistic about-face that was unsupported by his own historical evidence, Counts proposed that American political institutions instead had evolved in a contrary direction: as industrial and financial aristocrats exercised greater control over the economy, their grip on the national political culture had miraculously weakened, allowing democratic participation in the electoral process to flourish, as evidenced by FDR's survival at the polls in 1936.[27]

Counts offered the book less as a persuasive historical argument and more as an invitation to share his faith in American democracy—a faith that he believed was warranted by the nation's uniquely and innately egalitarian, meritocratic, and even neighborly inclinations. For those who did not embrace that exceptionalist perspective, including the "extreme elements of the left" who slavishly followed party doctrine, Counts had a dire warning: they would reap the same consequences that their Communist brethren did in Germany, who "having sung, with the monotony of a Greek chorus, of the inevitability of violence, ... closed every door to the peaceful solution of the social problem," thereby creating the conditions for "a counter-revolutionary movement" as the corporate aristocracy drew the nation toward fascism.[28]

Then, in spring 1939, Counts turned the accusation of subversion against communists on its head. In the widely circulated pamphlet *The Schools Can Teach Democracy*, he argued that the impending war made it even more urgent, as a matter of national defense, to make public schools into centers for indoctrinating the next generation in the principles and customs of our democratic culture. Communism's attachment to confrontation, its bad faith as Counts understood it, thwarted this "defense and strengthening of the democratic tradition and way of life."[29] People should be schooled for democracy by "rais[ing] to the level of consciousness" the "great ideals of a free society," including "a deep loyalty to the process of free discussion, criticism, and group decision" and a recognition that to "employ discussion for the purpose of delaying and sabotaging action, to refuse to abide by the decisions of the majority, to engage in the methods of conspiracy under the cloak of democracy, or to nourish secretly the ideas of violence and dictatorship is to threaten the moral foundations of popular government."[30] Other liberal reconstructionists at TC chimed in on the pages of *The Social Frontier* and elsewhere. According to Counts's close friend and colleague Jesse Newlon, liberals who condemn "indoctrination" play into the hands of extremists who, under the cloak of neutrality, manipulate the schools and the unions to promote a politics alien to American culture—a politics of "class struggle," dictatorship, "the rigid party line," and economic determinism. On the contrary, "the solution to our problems can be worked out only in the American way and in the American tradition."[31] The problem was not that Communists indoctrinated students to a "party line," but that they officially rejected indoctrinating students altogether, certainly as long as schools were controlled by ruling classes and certainly not according to Counts's demands. Invited in 1935 by *The Social Frontier* to participate in a forum on the question, Earl Browder expressed "scepticism toward any program of social change which relies upon the school system as an important instrument in bringing that change about." The only "revolutionary proletarian system of education" the party cared to undertake could be found in the network of Communist "workers' schools."[32]

Communists hardly could have recognized themselves in Counts's and Newlon's patently distorted portraits of them as militant agitators for "bullets over ballots," covertly propagandizing against democracy in the schools—or, more accurately, failing to propagandize for it. Reviewing *Prospects* in the *New Masses*, Bruce Minton protested that "who has ever contended that Socialism in the United States must experience every difficulty or must mimic every form that the Soviet Union passed through? Certainly not the Communists." It was, after all, the basic principle of the Popular Front after 1934 that communism was just a twentieth-century version of Jeffersonian democracy and that the Communist Party should adjust policies to local and national conditions.[33] Minton made light of Counts's straw-man argument in his otherwise warmly favorable review. Yet if we recognize that these publications served as a preface to what followed, we can see how mistaken Minton was.[34] For as the 1939 AFT convention approached, Counts and his liberal colleagues attacked their straw man with a vengeance, driving home the case that Communists, having no faith in democratic institutions or procedures and being more loyal to Moscow than to the Constitution of the United States, preferred violence over "education for democracy." Beneath the scrim of national-defense rhetoric, an ominous message rose slowly to the surface of public consciousness: that such undemocratic beliefs had no place in a union like the AFT or in the nation's public schools.[35]

The Behavioral Test

The AFT coup raises some obvious questions that historians are in only a slightly better position to answer than were investigators of the era. Let's start with perhaps the most obvious: were Counts and his supporters right about the influence of the Communist Party in the national teachers union and its locals? For all the press they received, the liberals' sensationalist declarations of Communist control and sinister motives were hardly supported by substantive evidence. Though they insisted that Communists dominated the union, the liberals could neither identify individual Communists with any certainty nor adequately explain how they knew that Communists, who did not make their affiliation public, gripped the reins of power. Instead they relied on what Hartmann called "behavioral inferences" or the "test" of "operational logic." Perceiving "a perfect one-to-one correlation" between the "party line" and the words and deeds of union leaders and activists, liberals like Hartmann concluded with absolute certainty that the party controlled the union. Childs similarly invoked the behavioral test when asked by Coudert's staff whether he had come "across any information that would lead you to the conclusion that Local 5 was dominated by the so-called Stalinist group of the Communist Party." Childs replied that he had no "specific documentary evidence," but that "the overwhelming impression made on my mind" after a year in the delegate assembly was that they were. He "began to notice" at chapter meetings that "resolutions would be introduced that I happened to know the Communist Party were favoring." On that basis, he became "convinced that there was a very important group in the Teachers Union that were members of the Communist Party, and to make it very definite, of the official Communist Party of which Browder is head. I have no doubt about that." But he knew of no actual party members other than Howard Langford, a Julliard instructor whom he had exposed in the press. Rather, he had been "interested [only] in the union and in the behaviors of the union. Applying the behavioral test, I reached the conclusion that the group that was in control was the Stalinist group."[36]

Such testimony, however, did not meet the standards of even the liberals' own "operational logic." Neither Childs nor Hartmann considered that they might have mistaken for Communists other radical teachers who took no "orders from Moscow," simply sharing the party's point of view without the influence of party doctrine. Remarkably, few of the aggrieved liberals had much opportunity to observe, let alone test, the behavior of the union or any of its members. When he insisted in *The New Republic* that the CTU Executive Board "vote[d] in accordance with what both sides understand is the omnipresent 'party line,'" Hartmann neglected to mention that he only attended one of the thirteen board meetings since being elected in early 1938. Both Childs and Counts similarly based judgments on little or no empirical observation. Childs never actually joined the CTU and, by his own admission, attended very few meetings of Local 5. Like many of the Columbia liberals, Counts complained that the political excesses of the union had undermined its organizing efforts. Yet when asked in a meeting to give examples, Counts replied that "he wished it known that he regarded himself as not having been as active in the local as he could have been."[37]

The appeal to flimsy evidence, of course, did not mean that Childs and Hartmann were wrong. There were Communists in the union, but they seldom identified themselves as such, certainly not to noncommunists. Former party members like Grebanier, Columbia's Mark Graubard, and CCNY's William Canning, while often mistaken about specific individuals, were not that far off concerning the disproportion of communists in general and Communist Party members in particular among union leaders and activists. We can also assume that a number of the cooperative witnesses, not wanting to ruin the careers of individual colleagues, even if they hoped to purge Communists from the union, refrained from naming people whom they knew in fact to be party members.[38] As for who controlled the union, there is little doubt that a coalition of left-wing activists led Local 5 after the liberals and social democrats quit in 1935. The same was true of the CTU upon its founding in 1938. Who among them were Communists is less clear, since other witness testimony, even when corroborated, often relied on Hartmann's "behavioral test," which resulted in false accusations. In a few cases, accused faculty and teachers made their affiliations public, as did Isidore Begun and Morris Schappes, of the City College of New York (CCNY), whose perjury case resulted in the only instance of someone going to jail as an immediate consequence of the Coudert inquiry. Others such as Hunter philosophy professor V. J. McGill and Bella Dodd acknowledged membership to later investigators. We can surmise as well, though without definitive evidence, that a few others such as NYU's Margaret Schlauch and Edwin Berry Burgum, and BC's Howard Selsam, all of whom were pivotal to the running of the CTU, were in the party.

But did the presence of those Communists in union office add up to "control"? Local 5 President Charles Hendley, who kept his Socialist Party membership until he was expelled in 1938 for an excess of tolerance and openmindedness, didn't think so. As he pointed out, people of all sorts of political affiliations ran the New York locals with general agreement and without apparent outside direction. Moreover, democratic rules enabled just about anyone to occupy offices, especially at the district level. As Jerome Davis noted, the Columbia chapter that Hartmann insisted was controlled by Communists allowed open discussion and voting on resolutions that were hostile to Communist policy. That same chapter tried to recruit Childs, who had long made clear his animosity toward the party and even the union, to serve as an officer, and it elected Hartmann, a conservative Socialist, to chapter president just a couple of months before the Childs affair. While such acts were later explained away by stories of Communist subterfuge and manipulation, they effectively put the chapter in the hands of noncommunists.[39]

Nor does the historical evidence bear out related accusations that the union pursued irrelevant political positions in membership and executive board meetings, whose minutes disclose hardly any time spent on political issues, let alone a preference for the "party line." The CTU membership meetings that Counts, Childs, and Hartmann alleged were dominated by causes of interest only to Communists mainly addressed those matters that one would expect a teachers union to address: legislation governing tenure rules and terms of employment at municipal colleges, Board of Higher Education (BHE) budgets, and the politics of the national labor movement, primarily the ongoing conflict between the AFL and the Congress of Industrial Organizations. The occasional "political" resolution that appeared in the CTU minutes likewise addressed matters that were relevant to the labor movement though no doubt controversial as well: racial discrimination by southern AFT locals, whether to support American Labor Party candidates in New York state elections, the hiring of African-American teachers in the public schools, and the inclusion of black history in the curriculum. Discussion of foreign affairs was a relatively rare occurrence.[40]

What was true of the New York locals was even more evident at the national level. As the largest and most active locals in the union, the New York chapters exerted substantial influence in the AFT under Linville's direction as well as after 1935. As the politics of the era shifted left, so did the union, though not to any greater degree than it did for other trade unions. As they did in the local chapters, the liberals supplied their own counterargument: Counts's election to head the national union in 1939 after so aggressively attacking the New York locals seems to be fairly clear evidence that no one at Communist Party headquarters in New York was pulling strings at AFT headquarters in Chicago, or at least not very effectively.

The New Regime

Amid all of the other convention activities and speeches, the August 1939 contest for president of the American Federation of Teachers (AFT) seemed no more than a sideshow, as the main preoccupations of members appear to have been the impending war and the need to push back nationally against fiscal retrenchment. When the voting in Buffalo was over, Counts defeated incumbent, Jerome Davis, by a very small margin.[41] Confronted with an executive council dominated by left-wing opponents, Counts immediately struck a conciliatory note, promising to be the president "of the entire Federation of Teachers," in which "critical analyses and evaluations of all political programs" would be encouraged. Everyone expressed high expectations of the new president, whom Local 5's monthly magazine, overlooking the contentious disputes of earlier in the year, recalled as standing "in the vanguard of progressive thinking" for the previous two decades.[42] Despite the experience at Columbia, they knew Counts as a trade unionist who was disinclined to sacrifice collective bargaining for a professionalizing ethic. To show his continued commitment to the labor movement, in one of his first acts, Counts brought the teachers union back together with AFL President Green, though this gesture should have been an ominous sign for left-wing teachers and the New York locals. Meanwhile, Counts's anticommunist supporters treated the vote as a mandate. They insisted that the convention had drafted the new president to represent those "who are opposed to using the Union as a 'political' organization," as the liberals complained the Communist Party had done since 1932. Counts's leadership, they predicted, would keep the AFT "concentrate[d] on the educational task."[43]

Barely two months into his administration, however, Counts dropped the apolitical pretense, calling on teachers to take a position on international affairs and join in defending democracy against "totalitarianism."[44] Then, in the December issue of the federation's national magazine, he raised unattributed accusations that the union was "controlled by Communists" under the disingenuous guise of denying those charges. Never mentioning that he had made the very same accusation barely a year earlier, Counts slyly used the question to give implicit grounds for expelling Communists from the union. Communist teachers "constitute but the smallest fraction" of AFT membership, Counts assured his readers, and any control they exercise over the organization is merely an illusion. Yet what he gave with one hand, he took back with the other: "Because of their solidarity, their loyalty to the 'Party line,' their tenacity of purpose, their unflagging zeal, their practice of anonymity and their methods of work generally, coupled with the indifference of many noncommunist teachers, their influence always greatly exceeds their numbers." The Communist Party "has split locals by methods of manipulation, achieved a precarious temporary control in some communities, hampered the work of the national organization and driven teachers from the Federation."[45]

It was a rhetorical tour de force, opening a campaign to wrest control of the executive council at the next national convention. Key to that hijacking was the refashioning of the Popular Front's antifascist rhetoric for a "defense" of freedom and democracy against *all* forms of "totalitarianism," Communism included. Americans are entitled, wrote Counts, "to know not only whether the Communists control the Federation but also where the Federation stands on the entire question of totalitarianism."[46] Other liberal anticommunists involved in the AFT conflict chimed in. That fall, Linville and Hartmann testified before the Dies committee with mounting hysteria. Hartmann declared, contrary to the evidence of Counts's recent election, that the union was "controlled in whole or in part through underground manipulation." Communist teachers and their supporters "pose[d] as defenders of 'progressive education' and 'democracy' while doing GPU espionage and other service for Stalin's regime." The union, he intoned, "is a mysterious riddle to an observer until he grasps the fact of Stalin's machinations."[47]

In spring 1940, as the next national convention approached, liberals who earlier had complained of political issue-mongering in union meetings made plans to force a test of delegates' loyalty to American democracy. The convention opened in late August with a keynote by the AFL's Bill Green, who not only reiterated his demand that the teachers union "put its house in order" and make clear that "you are an American institution" by denouncing "any 'ism' other than Americanism," but also pressed for a program of national defense that would include labor conscription into strategic industries.[48] Green promised that if the teachers expelled Communists, the AFL and its local affiliates would renew their financial and political support for the AFT.[49] Though delegates booed the AFL leader, Counts followed the speech with his own promise to clean house for the sake of national defense. Then, running on a platform that "strongly condemn[ed] and oppose[d]" any "manipulation" by Communists, Counts and his personally chosen slate of candidates swept the executive council. The anticommunists had taken over the union.[50] They were not done, however. Using proxy votes from anticommunist locals that, unlike the New York unions, excluded dissenters from among their delegates, Counts forced through a resolution modeled on one that the American Civil Liberties Union (ACLU) passed the previous February condemning "all dictatorships, whether of Nazi, fascist or Communist origin, whether in Germany, Italy or Russia." Establishing a litmus test of national as well as union loyalty, the liberal anticommunists had laid the final bit of legalistic groundwork that would allow them to purge teachers from the union on political grounds.[51]

The liberal anticommunists who triumphed in the 1940 convention were not just reacting to Stalinist treachery abroad. They shared a common set of principles that had disposed them against the communist movement since its inception in the early 1920s and continued to share them through the Popular Front period, despite the brief romance that some had with the Soviet Union and the willingness of others to collaborate with the party in the antifascist, student, racial-justice, and trade-union movements. Conservatives such as the American Legion and the Christian Front had their own reasons for targeting communists that, for the most part, were the same as their reasons for attacking socialists and New Dealers—as enemies of unregulated capitalism, advocates of higher taxation, proponents of redistributive reform, and opponents of nationalist projects at home and abroad. The main issue for liberals and social democrats, in contrast, concerned the inability of communists to participate in democratic institutions that liberals led, including institutions, such as unions and schools, that enabled precisely the sorts of reforms conservatives hated and opposed.

The Trojan Horse

The liberal anticommunist demonology behind the AFT coup held that the main threat from Communists in unions and schools was that they acted in bad faith: their alleged commitment to "class war" and their advocacy of "force and violence" led them as a matter of principle to join democratic projects without the requisite commitment to core democratic values as liberals understood them. Claiming to believe in democracy, Communists concealed their party memberships, denying their loyalty to party policy, and misrepresented their own motives in order to hijack democratic institutions using democratic rules and procedures undemocratically, as "parliamentary maneuvers" and subterfuge. In public forums, they slandered their opponents, misrepresenting the actions and motives of others in order to manipulate open deliberations. This had been a standard response on the part of liberals and social democrats, including people such as Henry Linville, Abe Lefkowitz, and their supporters in the teachers union and the school reform movement since the 1920s. Communists acted without, to use another expression favorite among liberal anticommunists, "intellectual integrity."[52]

As liberal anticommunists mounted their coup in the AFT, the campaign against Communist bad faith intensified, spurred on by news from the Soviet Union. By 1938, the purges, the disappearances of friends and colleagues into Stalin's prisons and labor camps, and the increasingly irrational and brutal character of Soviet policy in Russia and abroad began to take their toll on the ranks of American radicals, communists, and fellow travelers. For many New York intellectuals, the watershed event was another "trial" run by John Dewey, the so-called "Dewey Commission" that investigated Soviet treason charges against former Bolshevik Leon Trotsky, who had been exiled since 1928 and found refuge just a few steps ahead of Stalin's secret police, in Coyoacan, Mexico. The verdict of not guilty and Dewey's summary of the commission findings, sensationally delivered in December 1937 to a mass meeting of two thousand, galvanized disillusionment among liberals and radicals alike. Certainly, it reinforced anti-Stalinist sentiments among aficionados of Soviet affairs, the Trotskyists, Lovestoneites, Old Guard Socialists, and Progressives who had harbored doubts all along about the course of the Russian regime.[53]

The best-known exposition of the bad-faith argument came in late October 1939 from Dewey's student Sidney Hook, in his essay "Academic Freedom and 'The Trojan Horse' in American Education," which was delivered as a speech at a forum on "The Challenge to Civilization" in New York City. Its primary metaphor, of Communists hiding in a Trojan Horse wheeled into an unsuspecting academy, would figure prominently in American countersubversive demonology for the next half century. Hook shared the dais with Eleanor Roosevelt, who warned against violating democratic traditions in rooting out perceived enemies, and famously declared that she was "not afraid of meeting and talking with a Communist," provided that the conversation was about democracy. But she was the exception that afternoon in a group that included FBI director J. Edgar Hoover, Harvard president and Nazi sympathizer James Conant, professional anticommunist Ben Stolberg, and the AFL's Matthew Woll. The tone of the event was set by poet Edna St. Vincent Millay, who proposed that Communist "termites" were undermining American democracy. Presidential speechwriter Stanley High followed up by praising the Dies Committee for its effective use of "insecticide" to root the vermin out.[54]

Warning that "the Trojan Horse has already been drawn into our temples of learning," Hook conceded to Communists the constitutional right to support the Soviet cause, but insisted that they did not have a right to act with ulterior motives behind a pretense of democracy. Their First Amendment right to free speech and unrestricted political affiliation, he argued, was nullified by their bad faith: they do not have the right to act dishonestly, to conceal their Communist affiliation or to misrepresent their own and their party's views as "democratic" when in fact they are not. "One has a right to represent or defend any cause, provided he honestly declares what that cause is, provided that he does not masquerade under false labels, provided he does not have a secret program that he plans to substitute for the public program on which he solicits confidence." Such "tactics of duplicity" disabled the democratic process, Hook insisted, contradicting its "basic assumption" that citizens would be able to choose between "honest bills of goods."[55]

No court has ever so narrowly interpreted the First Amendment as only protecting *sincere* political speech, nor does anything in the Constitution require the honest disclosure of one's political views (as if that were possible). But, for Hook, as for Paul Windels and other liberals who later would echo this argument, the application of the Bill of Rights to the academy was a special case.[56] And the notion that teachers do not enjoy the same constitutional protection as their fellow citizens had grounds in legal precedent, a view that was gaining support especially among university administrators and boards of education. A professor has a right to his views "correct or incorrect, popular or unpopular," Hook intoned, but he must "declare them openly, submit them to the court of critical inquiry and not cook his conclusions in advance according to some political recipe...." What sort of "political recipe" Hook had in mind was clear, though what relationship one's political affiliation might have to one's scholarship much less so. Ignoring a long history of other sorts of ideological influence on the academy, Hook insisted that Communists were especially inclined to scholarly distortions, even in 1939, after decades of right-wing attacks on the academy and the public schools had forced out dozens of liberal and left-wing teachers. Without any evidence to support his claim, Hook contended that in contrast to Communist subversion, the threat of German propagandizing had diminished since the start of the war the month before. "Much more numerous, and even more devious in their methods of penetration, are the partisans of the Stalin regime on the American educational and cultural front."[57]

Cultural Freedom

It is very difficult to recount the history of anticommunism in general or the emergence of Coudertism in particular without considering the role of philosopher Sidney Hook. Although his part in the Coudert investigation was not as public as Henry Linville's or Bernard Grebanier's, his private testimony did provide Windels's staff useful if misleading (or perhaps usefully misleading) guidance through the thicket of Marxist and Communist doctrine. Hook's influence is evident in the committee's final report, which in its survey of the literature loosely if crudely followed his interpretation of Stalinist orthodoxy. Hook also directed the investigation to specific suspects like Howard Selsam, whom Hook detested and to whose philosophical writing he pointed the committee for evidence that orthodox Marxism posed an ideological threat. It was at this time as well that the vehemence of Hook's anticommunism became legendary, as did the divisive and vituperative tactics he used, seemingly without rest, to unmask Communists. As historian Christopher Phelps quite convincingly argues, as a young man Hook contributed a uniquely American perspective to the Marxist tradition, full of insight and creative reinterpretation of the classic texts, yet by 1939, he had become so consumed by the crusade against Stalinism that he could no longer properly be classified as a Marxist or even a socialist. Within a surprisingly short span of time, he moved from acting as an incisive critic of left-wing and liberal hypocrisies, to behaving as the self-appointed guardian of the nation's political integrity—the "moral hygiene and political responsibility" that he asserted were "presuppositions of the Bill of Rights"—against the bad faith of Communists and their apologists.[58]

Significant though Hook's personal ideological transformation may have been in its own right, more important was his ability in 1939 to mobilize others to join him in his crusade. With their support, he made himself a key spokesman for the anticommunist discontent that was building among New York's liberal academics and intellectuals. That May, Hook, Dewey, and their allies, among them several of Dewey's TC colleagues, founded the short-lived but influential Committee for Cultural Freedom (CCF), ostensibly to protect free expression and the "democratic way of life."[59] The CCF grew partly out of Dewey's work on the Trotsky commission and partly out of anticommunist ferment after 1936. But it also was largely dedicated to rooting out bad faith on the left, especially among academics, and in this capacity it would contribute some of the momentum behind the creation of the Coudert committee the following year. Hook conceived of the organization in reaction to efforts the previous year by Columbia anthropologist Franz Boas and his chemist colleague Harold Urey to unite campus organizations into a national antifascist front.[60] That December, after leading local protests against right-wing activism in New York City schools and universities, Boas and Urey circulated a manifesto denouncing the publication of official Nazi pseudoscience in the journal *Nature*, while at the same time attacking the "ruthless political censorship," the persecution of scientists, and the promotion of unscientific racial ideology by the German regime. Scientists have a "moral obligation," the Boas document declared, to "educate the people against the acceptance of all false and unscientific doctrines which appear before them in the guise of science, regardless of their origin."[61]

Incensed that Boas and Urey failed to denounce the Soviets and the Nazis equally, Hook began circulating a competing declaration written by journalist Eugene Lyons that not only filled in that gap, but made an issue of it as well. Those sorts of failures to draw requisite moral equivalences between Nazi and Soviet totalitarianism came to define the work of the CCF until its demise, in 1942. Lyons's initial statement evolved the following spring into the CCF's founding document, which was signed by hundreds of academics, writers, and artists across the country and which "pledged to expose repression of intellectual freedom under whatever pretext."[62] Effectively demanding a litmus test, the CCF insinuated that someone's willingness to sign revealed whether he or she could be counted among the "genuine friends of cultural freedom." Underscoring the gravity of the choice, the committee warned that "totalitarian states succeed in infecting other countries with their false doctrines" while "spreading panic among intellectuals" who "hasten to exalt one brand of intellectual servitude over another; to make fine distinctions between various methods of humiliating the human spirit and outlawing intellectual integrity." Manifestos like Boas and Urey's did not meet that CCF standard of intellectual integrity: "Instead of resisting and denouncing all attempts to straitjacket the human mind, they clarify, under deceptive slogans and names, the color or the cut of one straitjacket rather than another." The "lines are clearly drawn," the committee concluded, "between those who have declared their hostility 'against every form of tyranny over the mind of man' and the open and disguised apologists for totalitarianism."[63]

The CCF's founding meeting at Columbia's Seth Low Hall on May 16, 1939, brought together roughly two dozen notables who signed Hook's manifesto, including Socialists Frank Trager and Ferdinand Lundberg; philosophers Horace Kallen, David Davidson, and Arthur Lovejoy; poet Babette Deutsch; civil liberties lawyer Morris Ernst; and journalists Victor Riesel, Dorothy Dunbar Bromley, Henry Hazlitt, and James Rorty. Several of the TC liberals were also present, including Childs, Hartmann, Newlon, and Frederick Redefer. Hartmann and Newlon sat on one or another of the executive committees that were formed over the next two years. Counts participated sporadically, and by the spring of 1940, he was signing open letters under the CCF letterhead. Even Kilpatrick showed up at a meeting.[64] Several of Dewey's collaborators in the Trotsky Commission such as Suzanne La Follette, Lyons, and Ben Stolberg also helped run the project, which led to the unfounded Communist Party accusation that the CCF was a "Trotskyite" organization.[65] And later, in fall 1939, after he had publicly broken with the party, Bernard Grebanier began showing up at meetings with his wife, author Frances Winwar, volunteering briefly at one point to run the membership committee. At that first May meeting, Dewey was elected chair, a position that he continued to hold in some form through 1940.[66]

As *The Nation*'s Freda Kirchwey pointed out, the CCF statement was meant to incite—"to drop a bomb into the ranks of the liberal and left groups in the United States." Its "emphasis on Russian totalitarianism," she continued, "reveals the special purpose of the new committee, which is obviously to separate the sheep from the goats" and to "create a clear division on the left by relegating members of the Communist Party and the vague ranks of its sympathizers to outer totalitarian darkness." Anyone who criticized the CCF on the logic of its moral equivalencies was pronounced by Lundberg, the committee's secretary, to be "rank apologist[s] for Stalin" who "gave aid and comfort to the agents of Stalinism in this Country."[67] Unlike its later Cold War reincarnation, which led international campaigns, the prewar CCF focused on perceived domestic threats, not just from organizations like the Communist Party or the German-American Bund, but also from those "panicked intellectuals" who defended Stalinism.[68] Through most of 1939, they primarily targeted intellectuals and academics on the left whom they considered deceitful champions of democracy and cultural freedom, including liberals such as Boas. The purpose of such accusations was to force such "romantic" liberals, as Linville termed them years earlier, to repudiate communism and abandon any association with it. Thus, the committee saw in the Soviet diplomatic reversal that August an opportunity for a "good splitting action" between the party and fellow travelers. Certainly, many liberals and radicals signed the CCF document in the spirit, enunciated by John Dewey in *The New Republic*, that "it is not enough just to be antifascist, but . . . a positive and aggressive campaign is required against every sort of totalitarian influence in this country." The question was exactly how "aggressive" the CCF activists thought that campaign should be. As it turned out, the committee spent most of its time and energy alleging acts of duplicity by Communists and their supporters in order to "get a wedge in," as Dewey privately put it, between "the out-and-out CPs" and the liberals or fellow travelers who allowed Communists to occupy positions of real power in front organizations or trade unions.[69]

A meanness and intolerance was evident in the way the CCF exposed Communists and fellow travelers that spring, as the newly founded committee attacked Boas. In April, the anthropologist officially established the American Committee for Democracy and Intellectual Freedom (ACDIF) to turn the favorable response to his and Urey's initial manifesto toward the task of publicizing the persecution of liberal and left-wing academics at home and abroad. Eventually, as other organizations such as the AAUP abandoned accused Communists or were neutralized like the ACLU by internal disputes, Boas's committee would become the main champion of academic freedom and constitutional rights against the onslaught of Coudertism. Hook and his collaborators well knew that the ACDIF was doing something useful and necessary—right-wing attacks on liberals and the left had accelerated over the previous three years, warranting the creation of such organizations as Boas', even if they did neglect Soviet repression. Hook himself had been the target of such attacks several years earlier. Hook and Dewey could have, without additional controversy, simply complemented Boas's work by independently publicizing the plight of Stalin's victims, as Boas at one point proposed.[70]

But the CCF was not satisfied with letting Boas continue. Instead, the committee wanted to expose his and other alleged front organizations as "one-sided" and hypocritical. And while their attack predated the creation of the Coudert committee, it effectively undermined the ACDIF's ability to mobilize public support in favor of those targeted by Coudert. Hook achieved that effect in a passive-aggressive manner, using precisely the sort of dissembling for which he condemned Communists. In announcing the founding of the CCF to the press, Hook declared his organization to be "independent of control, whether open or secret, by any political group," insinuating, as Boas immediately pointed out, that other groups, such as the ACDIF, were not independent.[71] A flurry of letters followed between Boas, on the one hand, and Hook and Dewey, on the other, over what Boas considered an inflammatory accusation. While Dewey, an old friend of the anthropologist, seemed to mediate in the exchange, he shared Hook's provocative attitude. When the CCF tendered the ACDIF an offer of "formal unification," both Hook and Dewey merely wanted to draw Boas out, to "correct him" and to expose the ACDIF's hypocrisy about "the use actually made of his organization & its name" by the Communist Party. They knew that Boas could not possibly join with the CCF on the terms it set, which required condemning the Soviet Union as "totalitarian." If the ACDIF accepted Hook's and the CCF's moral equivalences, it would no longer be effective in defending Communists and suspected Communists—including, eventually, those targeted by the Coudert committee. By conceding to Hook, the ACDIF would have admitted their guilt—if not in a juridical sense, then in a political one.[72] Months later, in a report on "Stalinist Outposts in the United States," the CCF further insinuated that the ACDIF was "under outright C. P. control." Eventually, the CCF targeted ACDIF contributors, as Frank Trager persuaded the American Jewish Committee (on whose board he sat) to cut its substantial annual contribution to Boas's organization.[73]

Then, in mid-August 1939, the Communist Party and its supporters launched what had to be one of the worst-timed public appeals of the era. What came to be known as "The Open Letter of 400" appeared on the pages of *Soviet Russia Today* and the *Daily Worker* the week before the Hitler-Stalin Pact. Signed by four hundred prominent writers, artists, and academics, it defended the Soviet record on cultural freedom while attacking the CCF. Calling for unity among antifascist forces, the letter warned of international efforts by "the fascists and their friends" to break up the Popular Front "by sowing suspicion between the Soviet Union and other nations interested in maintaining peace." Domestically it pointed to "reactionaries" who were "attempting to split the democratic front by similar tactics" and "encouraging the fantastic falsehood that the USSR and the totalitarian states are basically alike." At this point, the letter's prose became fatefully ambiguous. It clearly stated that some "sincere American liberals," beguiled by the notion that the Soviet dictatorship and fascism are alike, have "unwittingly aided a cause to which they are essentially opposed" and "lent their signatures to the recent manifesto issued by the so-called Committee for Cultural Freedom." And while the Open Letter never directly identified the CCF with "fascists and their friends," it suggested a likeness of mind between the CCF's organizers,

American "reactionaries," and the international fascist movement as being unified under the antitotalitarian banner that the CCF had in fact methodically unfolded.⁷⁴

In response, Hook lashed out with a vehemence and ruthlessness that should have troubled even his least judicious allies. Conveniently misreading the Open Letter and overlooking the CCF's own hyperbolic, false equivalence between Communists and Nazis, Hook accused the Open Letter's signers of the unpardonable defamation of calling "great Americans like John Dewey and Norman Thomas," both CCF founding members, "Fascists and allies of Fascists." Hook then spent the next several months milking his and others' indignation over the apparent offense for whatever it was worth, while easily linking it to the collective embarrassment of the Hitler-Stalin pact. He was still at it in October, when he delivered his "Trojan Horse" speech, citing the *Daily Worker* letter as an example of the "devious" Communist methods that "desert the plane of honest discussion and become the instruments of totalitarian reaction." Overcome with his own drama and indifferent to the ethical and political implications of such an act, Hook then threatened to name academics "who lent themselves to this dishonorable tactic" as being under the influence of the Communist Party, a sure ticket in some cases to administrative sanction if not dismissal.⁷⁵

Thereafter, Hook engaged in an ongoing letter-writing campaign using the "duplicity and dishonorable stooging" of the Open Letter to impugn the credibility of specific signers, claiming defamation and trying to force them off various committees, editorial boards, and boards of nonpartisan organizations such as the ACLU. Hook delivered the most consequential of these attacks against Harry Ward, professor of Christian Ethics at Union Theological Seminary, national chair of the ACLU, and a longtime member of the teachers union. As someone who worked closely with Communists and who defended them against their detractors in the union and elsewhere, Ward had acquired a reputation as a fellow traveler. He did not hesitate to sign the Open Letter, mainly, he told Hook, because he objected to "the fallacy which equates Fascism and Communism" that he "found permeating" the CCF Manifesto. Like others, Ward thought the Open Letter did not characterize the CCF as "Fascists and allies of Fascists," but rather as merely "liberals who are victims of a fallacy" about the moral equivalence between the Soviet Union and Nazi Germany. Feigning righteous indignation at the indecency of Ward's "slanderous attacks," Hook grew increasingly intemperate as he pressed for Ward's removal as ACLU chair. Claiming that he had "evidence in my possession" that Ward "works consistently with the Communist Party to discredit and besmirch by the foulest means individuals who have spoken up in criticism of Russian terrorism," he told ACLU founder and director Roger Baldwin that Ward "has neither the emotional balance nor the judicious mind which seem to be necessary for the post he holds." To Ward, he issued a threat: "Make no mistake about it. We are not going to let anyone slander us with impunity."[76]

And Hook made good on that threat. While the ACLU board initially refused to take Hook's charges seriously, his attack on Ward amounted to merely the first phase in a concerted and ultimately successful effort by ACLU liberals to purge its board of Communists and their supporters. As the purge approached, in January 1940, and as it became clear that he would not be reelected chair, Ward submitted his resignation.[77] While some Communist sympathizers remained in office (Hook could not dislodge Corliss Lamont, who circulated the Open Letter), the ACLU officially accepted the moral equivalence prescribed by Hook and the CCF, effectively neutralizing it just a couple of months before New York authorized the Rapp-Coudert investigation. Politically and philosophically, its support for the accused teachers would be half-hearted.

Making accusations of bad faith to draw out and discredit opponents well suited Hook's aggressively combative style of argument, which was born of a personality prone to suspicion and honed by many years in the give-and-take of left-wing polemicizing.[78] And certainly his style of political extortion and intimidation added significantly to the excesses of the emerging wave of anticommunism. Yet it would be a mistake to place too much emphasis on Hook's contentiousness or on its supposed origins in Marxist sectarianism, as liberals, including Dewey, Hartmann, Childs, and Counts, as well as Socialists such as Trager, Lundberg, and Norman Thomas openly and consistently supported his attacks, while in some cases carrying on similar ones of their own.[79] Writing to Hook in the wake of the Hitler-Stalin Pact, Lundberg, for instance, even proposed using the event to deliver "smashing attacks" on the Popular Front in language that prefigured later witch hunts; he gleefully anticipated "public recantation," confession, and the CCF's acquisition of a power to "rehabilitate."[80] All these CCF devotees accepted Hook's equivalence between the Soviets and the Nazis—one of several hinges on which they hung their accusations of bad faith against Popular Front supporters, ignoring the common sense that the signers of open letters do not necessarily agree with all of the letter's assertions and implications. As his close friend and former student Joseph Ratner pointed out to Dewey, the philosopher's own intellectual integrity could be considered compromised by his leadership of the CCF, which associated him with "unscrupulous, irresponsible so-called anti-Stalinists" who deflected public attention away from growing reactionary threats against liberals and radicals in the academy.[81]

One senses the weight of Hook's machinations when one considers what was happening elsewhere in New York City's political and intellectual universe. As the CCF mobilized public opinion against the Popular Front, George Counts and his supporters prepared to purge Communists from the teachers union, citing the same moral equivalences that Hook did and demanding the same demonstrations of intellectual integrity that the CCF did. And as the AFT drew up the procedures for a national vote to withdraw the charters of the New York locals, the Coudert inquiry broadened its scope to target suspected Communists at CCNY.

9
CCNY

> You know what a treacherous thing memory is.
>
> —*William Martin Canning, 28 January 1941*

Founded shortly before the Civil War, City College of New York (CCNY) enjoyed a reputation during the 1930s not only as the most tolerant and diverse institution of higher education in the city, but also as one of the most distinguished public universities in the nation, celebrated for the eminence of its faculty and the quality of its student body. Known by some as "Harvard on the Hudson," by the mid-1950s, CCNY had graduated more Nobel laureates (nine) than any other public institution in the United States and counted among its alumni Supreme Court Justice Felix Frankfurter and Jonas Salk, the virologist who developed the first effective polio vaccine. Commuters almost exclusively and often employed full time, CCNY students had little opportunity for anything more than completing their degrees while making ends meet. They were relatively untouched by the distractions of fraternal organizations, sports (their championship basketball team was a notable exception), campus hijinks, and ritual drinking.[1]

Yet its reputation notwithstanding, CCNY in 1940 was hardly a quiet academic enclave. Like Hunter (founded 1870) and Brooklyn College (founded 1930), CCNY drew its student body from the working- and middle-class neighborhoods of the five boroughs, from families hard-bitten by years of economic privation and unemployment, most of them Jewish and many of them union households with histories of left-wing activism. This demographic earned CCNY the additional sobriquet of the "Proletarian Harvard," a reputation reinforced by a decade of radical student activism. Like their counterparts at Brooklyn College (BC), CCNY students entered the antifascist movement at its earliest stages. Beginning in 1931, a series of conflicts unfolded with the university's Tammany-appointed president, Frederick C. Robinson, whose heavy-handed management of campus dissent met students' worst expectations about the rising threat of fascism at home and abroad. As historian Robert Cohen summarizes the Robinson regime, "no college tried harder than the City College of New York to suppress student protest." Between 1931 and 1934, Robinson's "anti-radical campaign" expelled forty-three students and suspended thirty-eight, while investigating hundreds of others.[2] Antiwar demonstrations and strikes, which centered on the 1933 signing of the pacifist Oxford Pledge by many American college students, regularly broke up the academic calendar. By the time the American Student Union (ASU) was founded in 1935 to bring together various collegiate wings of the Popular Front, CCNY already had a solid history of conflicts between students and administration, involving several strikes, sit-downs, and countless confrontations at the campus flagpole, where protests gathered.

An archconservative with Christian Front and fascist sympathies, Robinson happily waded into the fray, at one point physically attacking a group of students with his umbrella during an antiwar protest. When, in October 1934, students demonstrated outside a ceremony honoring a visiting group of Italian fascists, Robinson, who had invited the Italians, suspended twenty-six protesters. Students understandably pressed for his removal, raising legitimate concerns about his fitness as a college president. Eventually, he was forced to resign by the Board of Higher Education (BHE). CCNY faculty had some part in these events, but before 1935, their engagement was relatively limited, as the teachers generally were more conservative than their students were.[3]

The Problem with Brooklyn

Despite CCNY's history of political turmoil, Coudert committee investigators concentrated first on rooting out subversion across the East River at CCNY's counterpart in Brooklyn. They did this in part because of Brooklyn's reputation and in part because of persistent anticommunist campaigning on the pages of the conservative *Brooklyn Daily Eagle* and the Christian Frontist newspaper of the Brooklyn Archdiocese, *The Tablet*.

The Brooklyn side of the investigation, however, did not produce the results anticipated by Windels and Coudert. The private hearings that first fall and the public hearings in early December generated a series of contempt charges, starting with Charles Hendley's in October for refusing to turn over membership lists. Hendley and Bella Dodd resisted the committee's subpoenas, leading Coudert to have another warrant issued for Hendley's arrest in mid-January.[4] The committee also held in contempt twenty-five Brooklyn faculty and staff who refused to testify in private hearings on constitutional and procedural grounds. Coudert, however, officially cited only five of them.[5] The Brooklyn faculty responded by filing suit in state court. Several professors, including Howard Selsam and Frederic Ewen, refused to testify because they were neither allowed legal representation nor given transcripts of the hearings, key issues in the constitutionality of legislative investigations. Together with English professor Louie May Minor, who filed a separate suit, they challenged private hearings at which only one official member of the committee was present, an issue that was more than just technical since, in the absence of legal representation and without the record of the hearing available for independent review, the only remaining check on inquisitorial excess was the balance of political views and parties among the official members of the committee.[6]

Incensed, Coudert publicly declared these entirely legal and constitutionally warranted lawsuits "obstructive tactics" to "confuse and mislead by introduction of false or irrelevant issues." Not one of these cases was successful, however, and most BC professors eventually were forced to testify and to sign the waivers of immunity that were required of them. The courts, moreover, affirmed the committee's inquisitorial powers as "an essential auxiliary to the legislative function."[7] Eventually, refusal to testify led to the resignations or dismissals of several professors and staff, but the court proceedings and appeals stretched well into the following year, holding up the committee's achievement of demonstrable results, while Coudert and his co-chair, Herbert Rapp, struggled to convince the legislature and Governor Herbert Lehman to maintain the committee's funding.

But the main sticking point for the inquiry came from its own star witness. Until the spring, the Coudert staff could find corroboration for only three of the eight colleagues whom Bernard Grebanier named in the first public hearings in December. And they were unwilling to accuse someone officially of party membership, let alone subversion, without at least two sworn witnesses. Nor could they confirm the dozens more whom Grebanier identified in executive session.[8] By the middle of December, Coudert staffers were beginning to doubt Grebanier's reliability. Soon they were poking holes in his testimony themselves, scaring up evidence that contradicted his assertions about his own relationship to the BC unit of the Communist Party. "We have shown him far too much consideration," staffer George Shea complained after finding a file in the college president's office that exposed one of Grebanier's misrepresentations. The committee, he proposed, should "put him through a very rigorous and merciless examination."[9]

Meanwhile, the BHE only reluctantly assisted Coudert and Windels, who had expected the board to act swiftly on the "conduct unbecoming" of the BC professors. In November, as the investigation was unfolding, the board passed a resolution merely "asking" municipal college faculty and staff to cooperate with the Coudert committee. When Windels cited BC suspects for contempt in early December, BHE chair Ordway Tead, a liberal who was known for treatises on worker self-management and who had backed the College Teachers Union (CTU) democratization efforts two years earlier, hesitated, asking the city's corporation counsel, William C. Chanler, for an independent judgment on the BHE's course of action. Chanler jumped at the chance to tell the press that the BHE had grounds for dismissing teachers who refused to cooperate. Tead, furious, reproached Chanler for going public, averring that "it might be prudent for this board to await the determination of the courts . . . before taking any action."[10] Pressure mounted, meanwhile, from Albany as Democratic Assemblyman John Devany, Jr., urged that the eponymous Devany Law of 1939, which prohibited public employment in the state to those who advocated government overthrow, be explicitly applied to the Communist Party on the basis of evidence collected by Windels and his staff.[11] The BHE did begin dismissal proceedings in mid-December, setting up official investigative committees to determine the status of each accused professor. But it was not until mid-January that Tead and the board ordered employees, on penalty of dismissal, to submit to the Coudert committee subpoenas and interrogations. And it would not be until later that spring that the BHE would explicitly revoke the right of Communists, along with Nazis and Fascists, to teach in the municipal colleges.[12]

In January, the state legislature reauthorized and refunded the Coudert investigation, but Windels still needed demonstrable results. Their break came unexpectedly later in the month, when a history instructor in CCNY's evening division fell into their net.

Canning

If Bernard Grebanier was a reluctant stooge, William Martin Canning served as the Coudert committee's "willing tool," as his critics put it, dutifully testifying against more than three dozen of his colleagues and coworkers at CCNY.[13] A New Yorker by birth, Canning graduated from Babylon High School on Long Island before moving back to the city to qualify for CCNY's free tuition. Clearly a gifted student, he completed his bachelor's degree in June 1934, at the age of nineteen. He then entered graduate school in Columbia University's history department, where he took classes with progressive Merle Curti and archconservative Carlton Hayes.[14] At Columbia, however, his academic progress stalled once he received his master's in 1936; he never finished his doctorate. He began working at CCNY as a grader, then took on classes in the evening division where temporary instructors provided most of the teaching. There, Canning worked long hours with a full load of classes for very little compensation. In 1940 he earned only $800 a year, relative impoverishment even during the Depression. With many of his colleagues, he joined the Instructional Staff Association and then the college unit of the Teachers Union, switching to the CTU when it officially split off from Local 5 in 1938.[15]

A mere twenty-five years old when he first testified before the committee, Canning appeared in news photos callow yet determined, his plump face crimped by steel-rimmed glasses. Subpoenaed at the end of January in the course of the committee's unfolding CCNY investigation, Canning turned for advice to political scientist Hillman Bishop, a mentor to Canning's twenty-year-old wife, Edna, and who certainly knew of the couple's connections to the Communist Party and probably had given the Coudert staff the Cannings' names in the first place. As a student in Bishop's politics classes, Edna had vocally supported the Young Communist League (YCL), which she had joined in 1937. Disillusioned, in part under Bishop's tutelage and in part in reaction to the Hitler-Stalin Pact, Edna slowly drew her husband into Bishop's orbit, inviting the senior colleague for dinner on at least one occasion. A good friend and collaborator with Henry Linville, a member of the avidly anticommunist Teachers Guild, and a likely member of the Socialist Party, Bishop worked actively in the Instructional Staff Association and CCNY's defunct Antifascist Association to thwart the party's influence on campus.[16]

At first, Canning stonewalled, lying to Coudert staffers about his membership and his associations. Within a week of his first private hearing, however, he returned, accompanied by Edna, to Coudert committee headquarters, where Windels sat Canning in a chair and grilled him as the committee did others, with one staffer perched before him at a table reciting suspects from a pile of notecards while another paced behind him

William Canning at public hearings of the Coudert Committee. *New York Times*, 7 March 1941, p. 12. (Times Wide World Photos. Reproduced with permission of the *New York Times* and Redux Pictures.)

barking questions. In all likelihood, Bishop, other faculty, and friends consulted by Canning after his first interview pressed him to "purge himself." And that is what he did. Within a week, Canning had provided over thirty names of alleged Communists on the faculty and staff at CCNY and confirmed a couple of those at BC named by Grebanier. Unlike Grebanier, however, Canning provided the names of two associates who would corroborate much of his account.[17]

There is little reason to doubt most of William Canning's private testimony. It was consistent with what others said, and provided casually and in detail. Later, during the McCarthy period, parts were confirmed by at least one of the people he accused. A member of the party from January 1936 to early fall 1938, Canning claimed to have been signed up under the party name "John Russell" by library assistant David Cohen.[18] From Canning's testimony in the private hearings, we learn some details about how the Communist Party at CCNY worked, which for the most part appears to have been informally and without much in the way of what Canning, under prompting, called "discipline." It certainly did not resemble the secretive, underground organization that Windels and others regularly described to the public. Meetings were neither tightly organized nor strictly compartmentalized: the smaller units changed membership regularly to accommodate the variable teaching schedules of faculty, so that most of the party members on campus knew each other.[19] Organized under the Communist Party's 12th Assembly District, the entire CCNY Communist group, composed (with one exception) of "instructors, tutors, office workers," regularly met in what Canning called a "plenary," at which English instructors Morris U. Schappes, Seymour Copstein, and Arthur Braunlich presided, along with education instructor Nelle Lederman, college registrar Kenneth Ackley, and Townshend Harris High School teacher David Goldway.[20]

Though it addressed noncollegiate political issues, especially those that were part of the broadly conceived antifascist movement, the CCNY party organization mainly occupied itself with union and campus matters, requiring all of its members to participate in Local 5 and then in the CTU. CCNY party members also acted to some extent as a bloc in union deliberations, though Canning was not clear whether that bloc followed CCNY floor leaders or party floor leaders. They were also required to attend May Day marches, though they proceeded under the banners of the CTU along with noncommunist union members, of which there were quite a few.[21] Otherwise, in his initial private testimony Canning did not describe much enforcement of a party line, or of other membership obligations, for that matter, such as the paying of dues or attendance at meetings. "I don't recall anyone being expelled for failing to attend meetings," he recalled. "That was the threat. It was mostly moral pressure. You were called down, you were scolded at the meeting, and asked to give an account of yourself—self-criticism." Even if a member fell "horribly behind" in his dues, the punishment amounted to sending "some people" to "try to cajole him into paying up." At worst, party members were "scolded" for unorthodox views or for failure to commit enough time to party work, but there were enough "shirkers" for Canning to complain about them.[22]

Convenient Untruths

But much that Canning said was untrue, and fatally so, especially after the Coudert staff finished preparing the young historian for his public testimony, delivered at the second set of public hearings in early March. As generally is the case in telling the history of McCarthyism, it is tempting to focus on the false accusations with which Canning ruined the careers of noncommunist colleagues and coworkers. Political scientist Lawrence H. Chamberlain, who published the first critical study of the Rapp-Coudert investigation in 1951, found "at least half a dozen" examples, though he did not name them, and it is difficult to determine whom exactly he had in mind.[23] Samuel Margolis, a library assistant who noted that friendly witness Annette Sherman-Gottsegen misspelled his name just as in the CCNY catalog (suggesting prompting on the part of Coudert staffers, who mistook him for someone else), was probably one.[24] One of Canning's fellow Columbia graduate students, Theodore Geiger, could have been another: Geiger persistently challenged Canning's defamation up through the legislature, on the grounds that Canning's account did not fit with the actual chronology of Geiger's teaching appointments.[25] There is good reason to believe that Canning targeted several of his fellow Columbia students out of resentment over their relative success in the academic world. Academically stalled with no progress on his PhD, Canning blamed the Communist Party for distracting him and burdening him with party tasks while giving others "permission to spend their time in scholarly work," complaining, "I would have my Ph.D. now except that I spent all my time in this business."[26] That does not mean he was entirely wrong about the affiliation of his rivals. Phillip Foner, the most productive of Canning's three Columbia associates, almost certainly was in the party. Moses Finkelstein, who was forced by McCarthyism in 1953 into exile in

England after changing his name to M. I. Finley and becoming a highly-regarded classical historian, might also have been.[27]

More important was the flimsy evidence accepted by Windels as support for Canning's identifications. Pressed on Brooklyn Communists, Canning regularly recycled hearsay, asserting that Frederic Ewen, Harry Slochower, historian Henry Klein, and political scientist Belle Zeller were "generally assumed" to be in the party. That statement alone fixed their names more firmly on the Coudert committee lists. Like other Coudert witnesses, Canning tended to rely on "behavioral evidence," especially when implicating colleagues at other campuses. "It was almost written on a person's face that he was a member of the party," he declared. "At least, if not on his face, the first few words he utters gives him away." You "wouldn't have to be told who the members were," Canning asserted as he named BC instructor Isadore Pomerance. "You could tell them by a glance, by a handshake, perhaps, by a look, by what they said especially, and where they were." Then he went on to finger BC's Alexander Novikoff, Paul Gipfel, and Samual Kaiser on this basis—even after saying, "I had so little to do with [the BC people] that only their names were familiar to me, and now pretty much vanished from my memory." He admitted, "my knowledge of their party membership is what I might describe as intuitive rather than based upon tangible evidence."[28]

While Canning plausibly could attest to working with quite a few suspects in regular party activities, such as the editing and publishing of the *Teacher Worker*, he incriminated many others on the basis of seeing them at meetings and events also open to noncommunists. As Canning struggled to explain in private testimony why he had "an absolute certainty" that Geiger and other Columbia people were Communists, a Coudert staffer asked whether, as in the case of people whom Canning fingered at BC, this was "simply another case of an instinct." Canning insisted it was not, adding, "I mean, it is people who tell me these things." Nonplussed, Canning insisted that Geiger's membership was "a little better substantiated in my mind." He began to grasp at straws: "I think he was present" at a cocktail party after a May Day parade. "Well," he considered, "there must be something more tangible about Geiger that makes me sure he was a party member." Then, as if suddenly recalling something, Canning found the "proof": he was "informed of the discussion of the executive committee" about whether Geiger and Finkelstein should move from the Columbia party unit to CCNY's because they had recently started teaching in the CCNY evening division, but "not as a formal matter," rather "just mentioned in passing as one of the businesses [sic]." Yet at the same time,

May Day, New York City, 1941. (New York State Archives, Albany.)

he admitted that none of the alleged Columbia Communists "ever participated in any party work that I knew of."[29] What Canning thought he had heard at an unspecified meeting was good enough for Windels, however, whose staff helped Canning beef it up for public consumption in the March hearings, sealing Geiger's fate and eventually Finkelstein's as well.

Others similarly were locked into Windels's sights for standing too close to the Popular Front. On the advice of the Dies committee's Ben Mandel and Frank Trager of the Committee for Cultural Freedom (CCF), Windels's staff used attendance at May Day parades as evidence of party affiliation. Trager informed the Coudert staff that although for several years New York City had a unified May Day celebration, as of 1938 the Socialist Party, along with more conservative trade unions, began to organize their own event, in part because of revelations about the Moscow show trials. But he neglected to mention that many nonaligned socialists and communists, and even some liberals, still joined the Communist parade, often with their trade-union contingents. Such was the case for many members of Local 5 and the CTU. That didn't stop Windels from

184   The Mortal Storm

May Day, New York City, 1941. (New York State Archives, Albany.)

interrogating suspects and witnesses about May Day attendance, theirs and others, including CCNY professor Abraham Edel, whose marching was used to impugn his testimony on behalf of Saul Bernstein. Nor did Windels hesitate at poring over May Day surveillance photos and asking informants to annotate the scenes, identifying those present without considering their motives for being there. Some of that evidence found its way into McCarthy-era persecutions, as happened with an annotated shot of the CTU contingent suited up in cap and gown for a May Day march sometime after 1937, at the front of which prominently stood Ephraim

College Teachers Union contingent, May Day, Union Square, New York City, likely 1938. Annotated by Coudert Committee based on testimony from witnesses. (In RC42, New York State Archives, Albany.)

Cross, a liberal CCNY professor of romance languages. That photo was used, its ambiguity notwithstanding, by NYU lawyers as evidence for dismissing Edwin Berry Burgum in 1953. It should not have been surprising, then, that some marchers in the prewar May Day celebrations hid their identities behind masks.[30]

Other evidence of party membership, and thus of "misrepresentation" on the witness stand, was even weaker. One of the pivotal elements in Canning's testimony as in Grebanier's was the "fraction meeting" of roughly one hundred Communist teachers that allegedly took place on the Lower East Side sometime around the end of 1937 or the beginning of 1938. Grebanier was not especially clear on what the meeting was about, its location, its date, or its exact provenance. The BC English professor spoke of a gathering of all Communist municipal college faculty, open only to them. But his recollection of the meeting was so vague that Windels needed someone else to corroborate it. When Canning brought up the same meeting in a private hearing, he had already read the news about it from Grebanier's December testimony. Like memories of memories, his account was even less precise than Grebanier's. Canning could not quite recall where the meeting took place, except that it was somewhere on the East Side. Edna suggested the Windsor Palace "somewhere between 6th and 14th Streets and Second Avenue," where unions and left-wing groups commonly met. "Didn't Grebanier—?" Canning asked, turning to Coudert staffers. "He was just exactly as definite as you are, somewhere on the lower East Side," they replied (he had said Fourth Street). Canning knew even less than Grebanier of what happened at the "big fraction meeting," speculating that it "was to discuss some great turning point in the history of the Communist units." Nor could he remember the date: "It must have coincided with the change, with the development of the College Teachers Union . . . Of course it raised a lot of issues, and procedures . . . mostly a matter of union policies." But he was fishing, hoping Haberman would help him out, asking, "Didn't Mr. Grebanier remember either what the purpose was?" No, Haberman replied, "I don't believe he did," tacitly disclosing that Coudert investigators were not certain it was a meeting of Communist faculty. Canning then admitted, "I think I recall being rather bored by the length of the meeting and the fact that I didn't have anything to contribute at all." Did he actually attend or was he merely pretending to corroborate Grebanier? Was this a real memory or perhaps a "prosthetic" one, created to suit a narrative Canning sensed the committee wanted? And yet, on the basis of this vague recollection, Canning confidently identified colleagues as Communists.[31]

Amazingly, Canning at first hadn't a shred of documentation to support his fingering of colleagues, nor even to substantiate the story of his own membership in the party. Despite having served briefly as the CCNY unit's financial officer and having spent most of his three years in the party working on the newsletter, Canning could not find a leaflet, dues book, a draft of a *Teacher Worker* article, a piece of the "great array of literature" that had been forced on him at unit meetings, a note from a colleague, or anything else that had to do with the Communist Party activities at CCNY. "I looked around the house," Canning explained. "I couldn't find any such papers. I might make another search and see if we have anything." He added, "We just gave a lot of stuff away, things that we had, some time ago—gave it away." To whom? "Mostly to a friend of Edna's." Could he get some of it back? "I don't think so," Canning replied. "It wouldn't be good for us if we asked for it, perhaps.... I don't think there is anything in it that would be valuable. I don't think there would be any names, or anything like that." What of "membership cards or a letter from the chapter of City College?" a staffer asked. "I don't think I ever received any letter, any card," Canning replied, forgetting that he had mentioned receiving a dues book earlier in the interrogation.[32]

Then, the very next day, the Cannings reappeared at Coudert headquarters with a folded scrap of lined paper. "Suppose you tell us, on the record, what that paper is," Phillip W. Haberman, Jr., suggested. "This," Canning proudly informed the committee, "is scribbled notes [*sic*] from a meeting of the Communist Party cell of the City College unit. The date is not certain." Nor was the meaning of the text, most of which "is crossed out with pencil, since I must have regarded this paper as something I should not let others see." Yet Canning did not explain how this particular note survived, or why he did not discard or burn it if he did not want others to see it, and Coudert staffers neglected to ask. Instead, they simply accepted the note as evidence that Canning had in fact attended Communist Party meetings, making his account of what happened at those meetings appear more credible. At the same time, Canning, with Haberman's help, interpreted the note in a way that would be most gratifying to Coudert staffers. One jotting about the "Eisenberger case to be presented to the Board of Education by the Teachers Union," Canning decided, "indicates how the [CCNY Communist] unit directs the union to do certain things" with an "iron fist," as the Coudert committee later put it. It might, however, just as well have been a statement of fact or of the union's official plans that were announced while Canning was scribbling. Interestingly, Canning's remarks were speculative, as if he were interpreting someone else's notes. "Now, I think that indicates" he said of the Eisenberger scribble. Canning similarly conjectured from the line "The YCL [Young Communist League] to send letter to Teachers Union to get speaker for April 2, Weisman" that "this meant that our cell was to tell the YCL that they should write a letter to the Teachers Union for a speaker and that [Max] Weisman's name should be suggested."[33]

At one point, Haberman had Canning declare for the record that these "were notes that were contemporaneously made while the meeting was going on." But that statement, too, was dubious. The case of Sidney Eisenberger, of the chemistry department, occupied Local 5 in spring 1936. Canning mistakenly recalled that it "must have been some time near the summer of 1937."[34] Elsewhere on this torn and soiled sheet of paper, Canning had jotted notes that he said were from a meeting with Alexander Trachtenberg, head of the Communist Party press, International Publishers, as well as several other historians, discussing the production of a Popular Front series on American history. That meeting took place, according to Canning himself, in 1938, which meant that this scrap of paper, if it were genuine, had lasted through most of Canning's life in the party as a record of what happened at two disparate events, surviving miraculously as no other piece of the Cannings' stationery, correspondence, or political library could.[35]

Coudert's Kangaroo Court

It took Windels and his staff only a few weeks to tighten Canning's flimsy recollections into a carefully constructed story of union bosses and classroom subversion, while setting up corroboration for almost all of the people whom Canning identified. On the first day of the hearings, March 6, Canning named thirty-four colleagues, and according to the *New York Times*, on the second day of testimony he named twenty more.[36]

Canning's most sensational public testimony recounted the recruitment and indoctrination of CCNY students by Communist faculty; much of it, however, was fabricated. In private testimony, for instance, he provided little in the way of evidence that Communists recruited on campus, even when pressed aggressively by the Coudert committee staff. Although YCL members attended educational sessions taught by Communist faculty, including one run by Canning on the Popular Front, Canning had no knowledge of any faculty who recruited students: "I think that the unit wanted to be cautious about that, about directly inviting students, I remember." The students, he recalled "had their own organization. They were really distinct from the party unit."³⁷ Edna Canning similarly described a firewall between the students and Communist faculty, confirming not only her husband's vague recollections, but also testimony by other friendly witnesses, including Grebanier and Granville Hicks. Moreover, Edna Canning's description of the YCL, to which she belonged for roughly two years, hardly resembled a secretive organization with aggressive recruiting practices. It was "very loosely conducted as an organization," with open meetings, which were held every Monday afternoon at the party's district headquarters on Twenty-Eighth Street. She experienced very little pressure to join and none from faculty, who did not attend any of the organization's meetings. Her main complaint was that the YCL pressed too much extracurricular work on its members, taking time away from their studies.³⁸

Edna Canning did not testify in public. At the hearings, her husband painted a different picture of a "direct relationship" between the YCL and CCNY's Communist faculty. He recounted a sit-down strike before President Robinson's office protesting the firing of English instructor Morris Schappes in 1936 as Communist-inspired, adding that the Communists on the CCNY faculty were "delighted and elated" by the action.³⁹ In his private testimony, he'd reported that members of the YCL organized the sit-down strike without the approval of faculty Communists. Later, he embellished this story even further, testifying at Kenneth Ackley's dismissal hearing that the party ordered CCNY Communists to recruit students. "Any students who showed promise as a prospect for the Young Communist League," Canning asserted, "had his name noted and the name was turned over to that league."⁴⁰

A comparison of Canning's private and public testimony also suggests that Windels and his staff, as they did with Grebanier, coached Canning to dress up his testimony to confirm the countersubversive myth of classroom indoctrination. In private sessions, Canning recalled Ingram Bander, a colleague in the history department, bragging to other faculty Communists that students complained of his overuse of terms such as "dialectical materialism" and "the class struggle." Several of the comrades rebuked Bander for indoctrinating his students. Canning made Bander's dressing down out to be a lesson "that the Communist philosophy should be so well integrated into the body of the subject that the patent purpose of his propaganda would not be so palpable, that it should be woven into the very texture of a course in history" that was available "in sugar coated pills." Yet, though he claimed that "suggestions" were offered on how better to proselytize, he nonetheless was "at a loss to say exactly what examples were given." Instead, "as a person who knows the Communist line," Canning offered "examples of my own." He had in mind the inclusion of historical episodes that supported the Marxist interpretation of history, such as teaching the insurrectionary Paris Commune of 1871 as "one of the turning points in history." Canning was not exactly clear why the teaching of the Paris Commune necessarily committed one to "pure Communist doctrine," as he put it, or even a Marxist point of view. That a conservative historian might also want to teach the Commune, or the Bolshevik Revolution for that matter, as historical turning points seems not to have occurred to him.[41]

But even more striking than this lapse of logic was the subtle transformation of the Bander story between Canning's private interview and his public testimony: by the time of the public hearings, the Paris Commune had been changed from an example *suggested by Canning himself* of what *might* work as "sugar-coated" Communist indoctrination, into "one of the examples used to set Mr. Bander right" *by his CCNY comrades*. In other words, under Coudert committee guidance, Canning had miraculously discovered an instance of his colleagues *deliberately conspiring to indoctrinate where no such conspiracy had existed before*, simply by turning his own suggestion into theirs.[42]

Certainly, Windels knew how this would play to the press, which ran with the story that Communist historians were manipulating the past in order to produce dutiful acolytes. In a well-scripted public interrogation, unbroken by the objections or cross-examination of opposing attorneys, Windels seamlessly welded the Bander story to Canning's recollections of the meeting of CCNY and other historians, including Philip Foner, Jack Foner, BC's Herbert Morais, and independent author Herbert Aptheker at International Publishers to plan their Popular Front history of the United States. Canning and Windels painted a scene of high conspiracy among a group of writers and editors to craft a "scheme of a program" to "prove the validity of the thesis the Communists then were using, that Communism is Americanism in the Twentieth Century." To lend an air of conspiracy to this otherwise unexceptional meeting, Windels and Canning made sport of the fact that Morais had used a pseudonym, "Richard Enmale," for his recently published book on the Civil War, comprising the first two letters of the last names of each of the "triumvirate of Marxist leaders," Engels, Marx and Lenin. While Morais, Aptheker, and Philip Foner produced histories for this International Publishers "scheme," Canning's biography of Benjamin Franklin never got past the rough draft.[43]

As the Founders themselves would have pointed out, the proposed history series, which revisited themes and arguments raised by such unrevolutionary historians as Charles Beard and Merle Curti, was not only uncontroversial, but protected by the First Amendment. Yet even the otherwise demure *New York Times* took the bait. "Communist Scheme to Rewrite History Bared at Hearing," its front-page headline blared over an article that made a constitutionally protected editorial meeting out to be a conspiracy to subvert the nation by reinterpreting its past. Windels and Canning added more incriminating episodes to this story of academic sedition, reporting a "concentration of communists" in the offices of alleged party member Ackley. This nest of loyal followers supposedly gave the party a "great advantage" as the registrar's office "afforded a birds eye view of the college but also one in which all the news of the things happening would be known."[44] It was, Canning asserted, a "fertile place for propaganda," though again, he had no evidence that anything of the sort had been produced or distributed there.[45]

Meanwhile, under Windels's guidance, Canning layered on stories of strict party discipline and boss-like control of the teachers union that were similarly based on flimsy and inconsistent personal recollections with little to no corroborating evidence. The committee's final report, in 1942, made much of the "hindrance of professional work" by the party's extracurricular obligations, contrary to the interests of the College. Indeed the demand on his time appears to have been Canning's main complaint against the party, though he also bemoaned the fact that "one or two" of his colleagues allegedly were given special dispensation by the "cell or the unit or the chairman" to do their research.[46] The numbers, however, do not add up. Many of Canning's colleagues built enviable research records despite their alleged party commitments. This was true not only of Philip Foner, whom Canning derided as a "valuable asset" who was allowed to write books, but philosopher V. J. McGill, literary critics Harry Slochower and Frederic Ewen, linguist Margaret Schlauch, psychologist Walter Scott Neff, and physicist Lewis Balamuth, to name just a few.[47]

Canning's perceptions of the party's power over its members appear to have been distorted by his own resentments, mainly of fellow graduate students who had advanced further and faster than he had, such as Foner, Geiger, and Finkelstein, as well as by his sense of personal failure. A deeper psychological dynamic is evident in Canning's testimony on this subject, as well as in his fear of being censured by party leaders and his hypersensitivity to the perceived "moral pressure" of peer criticism.[48] "There is a sort of a tyranny there," he proposed. But if it were a tyranny, then it was largely internalized or even personal in origin: "It was regarded a little, a person was regarded as being a little foolish, a little—what was the word?

Infantile, perhaps—infantile if he did not regard his scholarship as merely a little side issue." Perhaps there were some clear agents of such judgment, but Canning could not pin them down. The only taskmaster he could come up with was himself: "One would feel guilty if he didn't observe this proper order, proper order of activities."[49]

Finally, in the public hearings Canning painted Local 5 and the CTU as the "legal apparatus" for the "illegal" work of the Communist Party, telling of obligatory membership in the union and unit meetings that prepped union members to vote *en bloc*. Canning and Grebanier's single "fraction" meeting of Communist college teachers metastasized into "several" that mobilized a bloc of voters powerful enough to "easily control" first the college section of Local 5 and then, after January 1938, the affiliated but independent CTU.[50] The exact mechanics of this relationship, however, were unclear and inconsistent with other testimony, including some of Canning's own. There is little doubt that a more general Communist point of view on union matters prevailed among members of the party, that party leaders guided it in some fashion, and that party members tended to vote along the same lines (as did other noncommunists who might have regularly agreed with them). But Canning's depiction of the meetings and the dynamics of the bloc voting by which this control was engineered just did not make sense. For instance, "it was taken for granted," Canning stated, that "we would never vote contrary to the will of the—people who knew most about the Union's affairs." Yet when asked who those people were, Canning named only alleged members of the CCNY unit—Schappes, Ackley, Arnold Shukotoff, and Arthur Braunlich.[51] What of the BC Communists? Those at NYU? The Columbia unit? Whom did *they* follow? Did they also think that union policy was discussed at *their* "unit meetings?" Besides, which type of union meeting was he talking about? After the 1935 split, Local 5's general assembly was replaced by a delegate assembly that was attended only by elected representatives. Canning must have been speaking of the less frequent general assemblies that, until the CTU was formed in 1938, continued to practice direct democracy. But it was at the delegate assemblies that the important issues were decided.

Conspicuous Corroboration

The week after Canning's public appearance, three witnesses took the stand to corroborate his accusations. The most damaging for the CCNY faculty was the testimony of Annette Sherman-Gottsegen, a secretary-clerk in the history department of the evening school downtown. In 1936, she joined the Communist Party, remaining a member for some months, possibly a full year, since she recalled attending up to fifty unit meetings. The following year, she married Jack Gottsegen, a CCNY economist who evidently convinced her to leave the party, which she did without any controversy or resistance on the part of her former comrades. Much of her work for the party was secretarial, including typing for the *Teacher Worker*.[52]

Sherman-Gottsegen's testimony was more precise and consistent than Canning's. This was true especially in the private hearings, in which she recalled names and party names with less hesitation, and recounted events more concisely and less speculatively. She not only implicated the same people Canning did, but gave nearly the same account that he did in private of how the CCNY unit operated, describing weekly meetings of her group at the apartment of Ackley and Goldway as "informal," with a rotating chair and limited exercise of authority. Like Canning, she recalled "discussions on Teachers Union policies, things like that ... what might be brought up, how we should feel about it." But she had no recollection of a party line being directly enforced: "I felt that they tried to guide policy by the discussion they held beforehand, that is, certainly when I voted I had been given a line on the idea before I went into the union meeting." CCNY instructor and CTU officer Arnold Shukotoff spoke frequently at joint meetings, giving "us the line of thought which we, as Communists, should understand for the union's problem," but did not direct members to act in the union in specific ways. Later, she added, "I don't remember ever having been told, except in the case of [the] Teacher Worker that I was assigned to, any specific thing. We were all, of course, responsible for cooperating in the union, for going to meetings, voting, and things like that." As for classroom indoctrination, as a secretary she did not pay it that much attention, but she remembered no discussions of the content of lectures or classes at any of the CCNY Communist Party meetings.[53] At the public hearings, Sherman-Gottsegen also changed some of her testimony in ways that appear to have been coached by the Coudert staff. Generally, she continued to name most of the same people as Canning; however, she added several suspicious confirmations, including of Ingram Bander. Naming Bander in the public hearings felicitously confirmed not only Canning's allegation of his party membership, but also bolstered Canning's story of Bander's "correction" by fellow Communists and the insidious use of history to indoctrinate students.[54]

In addition, Sherman-Gottsegen mysteriously added confirmation of the so-called intercollegiate "fraction meeting" that had been testified to by Grebanier and then Canning. Though she reported no such gathering in her private testimony, in public she conveniently remembered "one occasion" to "discuss" the organizing of the CTU as a separate local in "a hall, way down on the east side." Like Grebanier and Canning, her recollections were vague: "about a hundred" people were present, including "Communists from other colleges." She "was informed" that it was a "closed meeting of the Communist Party" that included "not only the Communists in City College, but Communists in the various colleges in the city, all of whom, of course, were concerned with the Teachers' Union." Though she couldn't remember any other specifics about the meeting, she could remember seeing Howard Selsam there and "Mr. Berry Burgum," whom she also knew from antifascist and union meetings. She also could identify Henry Klein, Margaret Schlauch, and Helen Adams, none of whom she named in private testimony.[55]

Between Canning, Sherman-Gottsegen, and two additional corroborating witnesses, the Rapp-Coudert inquisition finally bore fruit: Canning publicly named forty-four municipal college employees as Communists (he had fingered sixty-three in private hearings). Sherman-Gottsegen confirmed thirty-seven of those and named a good dozen more at CCNY, BC, and the private colleges.[56] Within a few weeks, on the basis of that testimony, the BHE began suspending faculty and staff.

10
Flirting with the Right

In May, when the Board of Higher Education (BHE) suspended the first wave of accused Communists at City College of New York (CCNY), New Yorkers noticed something alarming: all but four of the more than twenty faculty and staff suspended were Jews.[1] It was hard not to believe that anti-Semitism was the cause, a suspicion that had been growing since the previous December, when the disproportionate number of Jews targeted by the inquiry first became apparent.

Historians have been reluctant to identify anti-Jewish bigotry as a significant motive force behind McCarthyism, even though Jews continued to be overrepresented among its victims. In part, we can trace that hesitation to the very practice of postwar anticommunism, in the careful negotiation of ethnic and racial prejudices by the McCarthyites themselves. When New York City relaunched its investigation of suspected teachers in 1949 under the state's newly minted Feinberg Law that explicitly denied Communists employment in public education, it continued to accuse on a bias: all but one of the teachers charged (and eventually fired) in 1950 in the first wave of cases were Jews. The teachers' defenders blamed the active anti-Semitic motives of school officials. These charges, however, were mitigated by the prominent role given Jews in those proceedings: Assistant corporate counsel Saul Moskoff (who prosecuted) was Jewish, as were trial examiner Arthur Leavitt and board of education President Maximillian Moss. That strategy, of fronting Jews for the prosecution of Jews (novelist Howard Fast intemperately likened these Jewish jurists to the Nazis' *Judenrat*), was repeated for the Rosenberg case a year later.

195

Prosecutor Irving Saypol, his assistant Roy Cohn, and judge Irving Kauffman brought not only the force of the law but also the wrath of Jewish anticommunism down on the heads of Julius and Ethel Rosenberg. The foreman of the Rosenbergs' all-gentile jury unintentionally disclosed that ethnic identity did indeed inform the deliberations: "I felt good that this was strictly a Jewish show. It was Jew against Jew. It wasn't the Christians hanging the Jews."[2]

To such self-assurances were added the weight of official Jewish public opinion, by 1952 firmly in the anticommunist camp: the American Jewish Committee endorsed the Rosenbergs' electrocutions. It and the Anti-Defamation League, as well as Jewish leaders in the American Civil Liberties Union (ACLU), actively cooperated with federal law enforcement, while condemning the Rosenbergs' defenders for even suggesting an ethnic bias in the whole process. Jews, as historian Deborah Dash Moore recently noted, in this fashion achieved a kind of "symbolic atonement" in the couple's trial and execution for espionage, at once dissociating themselves from the taint of communism while absolving the hunters of "Jew-Communists" of their anti-Semitism.[3] So, during the Cold War, with the help of Jewish jurists, politicians, and cultural leaders, anti-Semitism faded from the public perception of McCarthyism. Citing the prominence of Jews among the persecutors of the Rosenbergs and other victims, historians have tended to accept that view.[4]

Anticommunism *before* the war was a different matter, however, fostered as it was by the well-organized Jew-baiting of the German-American Bund and the Christian Front, the most prominent of the many anti-Semitic organizations active in 1940. The horrors of the Final Solution had not yet shamed Americans into the pretense of philosemitism, and the Cohns and Kaufmans had not yet joined professional anticommunists in adeptly deflecting criticism from the left about ulterior motives. Still, official investigations like Coudert's seldom revealed anti-Semitic intentions, even when they had them. Suspicious but lacking direct proof, critics looked instead for circumstantial evidence of bias. As the committee's work became public, the suspicions were confirmed by an apparent absence of balance on the part of investigators, who though charged by the legislature to root out subversion in all its forms, right-wing as well as left-wing, seemed to ignore fascist and Nazi targets. "Wherever you go, wherever you turn, anti-Semitism is spreading," Bella Dodd's committee wrote in a pamphlet distributed in summer 1941. But, the Coudert Committee "dares not and will not investigate the antidemocratic, anti-Semitic, antilabor ideas, activities, and influences operating in our schools."

Coudert "perpetrated a fraud on the public," Dodd argued, by claiming to pursue subversion in the city's classrooms, while seeking "to protect anti-Semites and pro-fascists, instead of exposing them."[5]

Evidence contained in the Coudert committee's own files supports Dodd's charges. The aggressive probe of communist activity in the schools indeed was not balanced by a similar investigation into the influence of fascism and anti-Semitism. Coudert investigators ignored or diminished testimony and other evidence of extremist right-wing influences, including attacks on Jewish students and teachers on city campuses and in the public schools. And they consistently held evidence of fascist subversion to a much higher standard of proof than for Communists. In doing so, the Coudert investigation helped normalize racial prejudice, not only against Jews, but also against other racial minorities represented by the Communist Party.

The Christian Front

Historians consider the 1930s the worst decade in the history of American anti-Semitism. By 1938, sixty percent of Americans polled had negative views of Jews; more than a third thought they had "too much power." And as the violence of the Nazi regime mounted, the vast majority of Americans, seventy-seven percent, objected to allowing German Jews refuge on American shores. Increasingly, public animosity toward Jews took organized political form. As historian Leonard Dinnerstein has told us, between 1933 and 1941 over one hundred explicitly anti-Semitic organizations appeared in the United States, whereas only five had been created up to that point. The rhetoric of these various fascist and quasifascist groups became increasingly violent in late 1938 and early 1939.[6]

In New York City, all varieties of anti-Semitic organization sprouted up: the German-American Bund mobilized Nazi adherents and sympathizers in the South Bronx and the Yorkville section of Manhattan, the black-shirted *squadristi* of the Italian fascist movement laid claim to Italian neighborhoods in East Harlem, and local versions of the Klan operated in the general metropolitan area. But the shift from mere anti-Jewish sentiment to political anti-Semitism was marked most emphatically by popular radio-priest Father Charles Coughlin's call in May of 1938 for the creation of a "Christian Front" to defend Christian institutions and values actively from the combined menace of godless Communism and Jews.[7] Coughlin's distinctly Catholic anti-Semitism stoked resentments of unemployed industrial workers, many of them descendants of Irish,

Italian, and Polish immigrants, against the titans of Wall Street, identified as Jews despite evidence to the contrary, and against the allegedly Jewish architects of the New Deal's "creeping socialism." But the strongest impetus to Catholic anti-Semitism was the Spanish Civil War (1936 to 1939). As American communists, radicals, and liberals backed the Loyalist government of the secular Spanish Republic, many American Catholics supported the Francoist insurgency as a bulwark around Christian civilization. For too long, the increasingly anti-Semitic rhetoric of that confrontation was countenanced and even endorsed by church authority. Thus, the Brooklyn diocese regularly ran Coughlin's sermons in its weekly newspaper, *The Tablet*, which also included blunt attacks on "anti-Christian" trends in American culture and society, and which Jewish defense groups viewed as an organ of local anti-Jewish bigotry.[8]

The Christian Front and its offshoots (such as the Christian Mobilizers, an especially violent parallel organization) vilified Jews and communists from soapboxes and in assembly halls across the Catholic neighborhoods of Brooklyn and the Bronx. Beginning in the late winter and early spring of 1939, New York experienced a rash of violence against Jews that could be traced back to the Front's street-corner mobilizations and to the regular social and political gatherings of Bundists, Silver Shirts, and black-shirts in places like Ebling's Casino, set up at One Hundred Fifty-Sixth Street and St. Ann's Avenue in the Bronx by local brewers, where German-Americans in dirndls and lederhosen flocked for festivals and parties that occasionally mixed into Bund and Christian Front rallies. In February 1939, as support for Hitler grew among German and Irish Americans, the Bund mounted a rally in Madison Square Garden in downtown Manhattan, attended by more than twenty thousand people with many more spilling out on to the streets outside. To this terrifying display of un-American political might, *The Nation's* George Britt linked two stabbing incidents, one of an eighteen-year-old boy who came to the aid of an old man who had been harassed by Brownshirts. Noting the open support given to the Coughlinite forces by Brooklyn's Catholic hierarchy, Britt concluded that "in 1939 anti-Semitism in New York has ceased to be whispered and has become an open instrument of demagoguery, a vast outlet for idle energies."[9] Confrontations provoked by the Christian Front became increasingly vicious, resembling the sorts of Jew-baiting practiced by the Nazis in the streets of German cities: often on the flimsiest pretext (for instance, of an old women or a child claiming that "the Jew spit on me" or "a big Jew hit me"), Christian Front militants incited crowds to beat up Jews as well as non-Jews with stereotypically

Jewish features or those distributing anti-Coughlin literature at Front rallies. Just a few months after the Madison Square rally, James Wechsler reported in *The Nation* an incident in the Washington Heights section of Manhattan a short distance from the recently finished George Washington Bridge, in which a crowd of Coughlinites listening to rants about "non-Christians" trying to steal America, let loose a torrent of abuse on a young girl who dared question the speaker, beating and kicking her until two police officers reluctantly interceded.[10]

The gravity of this threat, to Jews as well as to the city's democratic life, can be measured in simple numbers: Wechsler estimated the Front held close to thirty outdoor meetings in the city every week during the first half of 1939, with some gatherings attracting as many as two thousand people, who listened as speakers ranted against "President Rosenveld" and the "jewocracy." An official study by the City Commissioner of Investigations William Herlands recorded dozens of attacks on Jews in a single precinct in the South Bronx where Front and other anti-Semitic gangs ran street meetings. The Herlands Commission counted well over three hundred gatherings, most of them outdoors, in that precinct alone between 1939 and 1941. Teenage boys and girls who acknowledged being goaded by anti-Semitic hysterics conducted "Jew hunts" along One Hundred Forty-First Street with the goals of clearing Jewish children from nearby Saint Mary's Park and closing down local Jewish shops. Coughlin half-heartedly repudiated his own creation in summer 1939, disavowing the Front's worst extremism. Yet that did not stop eighteen Front activists, most of them from Brooklyn, from stockpiling weapons in a plot to assassinate political leaders and spark a general anti-Semitic uprising. Not only did Coughlinites come to the plotters' defense after their January 1940 arrest by federal agents, but Christian Front sympathizers in Brooklyn and the Bronx continued to attack Jews and vandalize synagogues well into 1941.[11]

The Gompers Case

Given the magnitude of the problem in the years before and during the Coudert investigation, and given the fact that quite a few of the perpetrators of the worst violence were teenagers, it came as a surprise when Coudert's committee claimed in the March 1941 interim report and again in its final report in March 1942 that it "found no substantial evidence to show the existence of a Nazi or Fascist conspiracy against the schools," but still had sufficient cause to hound allegedly Communist professors out of their jobs.¹² Local 5 and other organizations, including Rabbi Stephen Wise's American Jewish Congress (AJC), supplied a list of counterexamples to the board of education and Coudert of anti-Semitic and fascist proselytizing, harassment of Jewish professors at BC and CCNY, regular fights between Jewish and gentile students, and Jew-baiting by teachers. It was especially galling that Jewish and black teachers had been complaining about harassment for years at several problem schools, only to have their concerns diminished or ignored by school officials and now by legislative inquiry.¹³

As its critics saw it, the Coudert committee observed a double standard, rooting out alleged communist subversion in the schools while overlooking the overt promotion of racism, anti-Semitism, and fascism by students and teachers. As the Coudert committee ignored the problem, its critics publicized cases of school-based bigotry. One of these cases involved the South Bronx's Samuel Gompers Vocational High School, just a few blocks from that stretch of One Hundred Forty-First Street, where teenagers, some of them Gompers students, went "Jew hunting" through 1942. According to Dodd's Committee for the Defense of Public Education (CDPE), the persistent complaints by Gompers teachers, students, and parents since 1937 against Timothy Murphy, a mathematics teacher and the school's dean, indicated a concerted and possibly systematic effort to cultivate student support for right-wing extremism. In sworn affidavits, thirteen Gompers teachers, roughly twenty percent of the teaching staff, recalled that Murphy regularly used racial slurs to address Italian, black, and Jewish students, explicitly and often quite punitively discriminated against black students, and physically abused some students while currying favor with others whom Murphy seemed to be grooming for a larger purpose, including spying on other teachers, especially the ones he identified as "Jew Communists."¹⁴

None of these actions in and of themselves linked Murphy to the Christian Front or any other fascist organization, but they raised suspicions among public-school and political watchdogs, especially given Gompers's proximity to Christian Front and Bundist stomping grounds. And some of Murphy's other actions, including interference with an official racial-tolerance campaign, seemed to link him more clearly to fascist organizations.¹⁵ In January 1941, while the Coudert investigation was well underway, Murphy allowed a student, John Hutchinson, to sell the Coughlinite weekly *Social Justice* on school time while paying him from a special fund provided by the National Youth Administration, a federal work-study program Murphy administered in a manner that seemed consistent with his other acts of favoritism. And sometime in 1938, Murphy invited to the school Werner Gruenwald, an unemployed German-American radio repairman suspected by the defense committee and Wise's AJC of ties with the Bund, very possibly to recruit adherents among teachers and students to place them "into certain industrial enterprises throughout the Country [sic] as fingermen or skeleton crew for his un-American activities" and to sabotage expanding war production.[16]

Assuming that Murphy was the tip of the iceberg, the teachers and the AJC accused the board of education of dragging its feet, as Murphy's colleagues and the AJC brought Murphy's racism to the board's attention in June 1939. While the board conducted an internal investigation, they shifted the focus onto the witnesses themselves, impugning their credibility and motives. Murphy meanwhile received unquestioning support from his principal, who instead removed the chair of the English department for submitting the formal complaint.[17] Jewish fraternal organization B'rith Abraham uncovered additional evidence of Front activity during school hours, including the posting of stickers promoting the boycott of Jewish businesses and the distribution of anti-Semitic leaflets targeting the Teachers Union.[18]

Hard Evidence or Hype?

In December 1940, shortly after the Coudert committee held its first public hearings, the New York Coordinating Committee for Democratic Action, a Jewish organization founded to counter the Christian Front, brought the same incidents and others directly to the Coudert staff's attention.[19] Yet despite such public pressure, and even after the board of education reluctantly disciplined Murphy in early 1941 by demoting him, stripping him of most of his positions, and transferring him to a lesser school, the Coudert committee gave no indication that it believed that the Murphy case warranted more serious investigation. But as critics plausibly argued, if amateur probes such as the ones conducted by AJC or the Coordinating Committee for Democratic Action could turn up so much evidence, what would a concerted effort by a legislative committee with subpoena power uncover?[20]

At the time, the circumstantial evidence of an informal, school-based network of Catholic authoritarian and fascist organizations certainly must have been compelling, especially given the increasingly shocking revelations of Front influence in unexpected places, including the city police. In one notorious incident, in Rockaway Park (an outlying area of Queens not far from present-day JFK Airport), a throng of Coughlinite youths brutally beat a man who was selling issues of the anti-Coughlinite journal *Equality* as two policemen stood and watched. Observers testified that while the young man, a Jew, lay on the ground, one of the officers clubbed him in the head, fracturing his skull. In fall 1939, B'rith Abraham pushed La Guardia to investigate rumors that the Front had recruited over two thousand officers. As it turned out, the rumored number of Christian Front police was probably exaggerated, but the results of a simple survey by the city found that over four hundred of them had joined at one time or another.[21]

Yet although they could make a good case that the Front and other right-wing organizations had a presence in the schools, neither Dodd nor the AJC had evidence that such groups directly shaped the course of the Coudert investigation, or that Coudert and his staff harbored fascist sympathies. Thus, one could argue that, hoping to take advantage of public outrage, Dodd and other critics, much like the witch hunters themselves, exaggerated the problem and tended to convict Coudert and the board of education by association, impugning the investigation solely on the basis of the public support it received from reactionary groups that sought "to gain their objectives behind the smokescreen of a legislative witch hunt," as Dodd's defense committee put it.[22]

On the question of a double standard, however, the suspicions of Dodd and the Teachers Union were well founded. Their only serious error involved the fallacious belief that the absence of a public investigation into fascism meant that no investigation at all was being made. In fact, the Coudert staff did look for ties to fascist organizations in the city schools and colleges. They just did not conduct the investigation in the open. While hardly as extensive or intensive as the anticommunist probe, which racked up over four hundred private hearings, the list of private depositions of suspected fascists among public-school teachers and college staff was substantial (sixty-three hearings), representing the commitment of at least some resources to the semblance of an investigation.[23]

Yet the Coudert committee's claim that "all allegations, leads, charges and clues" concerning fascist and Nazi activity in the schools "have been painstakingly followed and all lines of available inquiry have been exhausted" was just not true.[24] Documents from the investigation's nonpublic side reveal fascist subversion throughout the public schools and universities, which the Coudert staff knew about and failed to pursue aggressively. In almost all of the cases, the committee did not take reliable evidence of fascist ties seriously enough to probe further, failing to put suspects on the spot, neglecting obvious leads, dismissing as hearsay allegations that would have been accepted if directed against communists, and dully refusing to pull apart inconsistencies in testimony. In general, the Coudert committee's interview transcripts, suspect lists, and internal memos show a desultory, pro forma process guided by a double standard according to which Coudert and his staff aggressively targeted the left while showing little interest in exposing fascists.

Fascism in the Schools

The Coudert staff first applied this double standard to an aborted investigation of Italian fascism in city schools and colleges, which was announced in the fall of 1940 in response to repeated allegations in the press.[25] The Dies committee's Ben Mandel recommended several witnesses, including anarchist Carlo Tresca and Harvard University's Gaetano Salvemini, who at the time was writing the definitive study of Italian fascist movements in the United States. Tresca and Salvemini provided the committee staff with contacts in the antifascist community, including recent defectors from the fascist cause, several of whom were interviewed and deposed.[26] That a network of fascist activists extended throughout the New York City school system should not have been news to the Coudert committee, as a number of local educators, including some members of the city's boards of education, had since the late 1920s been quite open about their allegiance to the Mussolini regime. Quite a few openly served the Italian government.[27] Witnesses also directed Coudert staffers to Columbia's Casa Italiana, the venerable Dante Alighieri Society that had been founded fifty years earlier to promote Italian culture and language but was openly fascist as of the 1920s, fascist Italian-language newspapers such as Giovanni Trombetta's *Il Grido della Stirpa* (*The Cry of the Race*), and several shadowy figures in the Italian consulate who cultivated local Italian Americans in positions of power and influence.

From these informants, the committee learned that in its cultural programs and through its intimate connections to the Italian consulate, Columbia's Casa Italiana served as a center for the production and distribution of fascist propaganda. Casa's director, a Columbia professor considered a virulent fascist by many informants, promoted the interests of the Mussolini government, regularly honoring Italian dignitaries, and preparing handbooks for American students of the language incorporating encomiums to the Italian dictator and celebrations of authoritarianism.[28] According to one witness, Casa Italiana worked closely with the Dante Alighieri Society "to compel Italo-American children in the public schools to observe the 'externals' of Fascist loyalty—giving the Fascist salute, wearing the Young Balilla uniform, singing the Fascist political anthems and spreading the literature provided by the official propaganda agencies."[29] Goffredo Pantaleoni, who resigned from the Italian Consulate's information bureau in 1940, called the Dante Society a "tool" of fascist agents. From its headquarters in Rome, the society produced and distributed most of the propaganda for consumption in the United States.[30] According to Salvemini, the "real purpose" of the educational bureau at Casa Italiana was "to instill Italian Nationalism into the Italian population of New York" and to foster "adherence to Italian customs and fascist ideals."[31] An Italian instructor at Queens College who testified to the committee explained that positions in public-school Italian departments were "handpicked by [Casa Director, Professor Giuseppi] Prezzolini" to "extend the Fascist organization."[32]

Witnesses identified several public-school teachers and municipal college professors as active leaders of the city's Italian fascist movement. One of them, Leonard Covello, chair of the Italian department at DeWitt Clinton High School, Salvemini described as "the henchman of the Casa Italiana fascist group in the city high school system" who, according to another witness, remained in regular contact with consular staff and appeared to many to be doing their bidding. As vice president of the Italian Teachers Association—described by yet another informant as "entirely Fascist-dominated"—Covello reportedly used his influence to place and promote fascist teachers. He also participated in weekly radio broadcasts defending Italy after its condemnation by the League of Nations for the conquest of Ethiopia. Joining Covello in this work was Mario Cosenza, a romance-language professor who by 1940 was academic dean at Brooklyn College (BC). At Casa Italiana, Cosenza and Covello reportedly served as conduits for money from the Italian Embassy to send American college students to study in Italy, potentially to serve as future cultural emissaries for the fascist regime. According to another witness, the "most active pro-Fascist" in the city was Vitorio Ceroni, a professor of Italian at Hunter College who incorporated fascist proselytizing into his literary criticism.[33] Pantaleoni described Ceroni as the "probable coordinator of the Fascist propaganda pamphlet distribution in the city schools and colleges." Ceroni arranged for huge crates of books and pamphlets to be sent to professors and teachers and then passed on to college and school libraries, where they stayed on the shelves until removed during and, in some cases, after the war.[34] By his own admission, as late as 1939, Ceroni supervised Dante Society ceremonies in various public schools around the city, at which ranks of black-shirted school children who had been assembled by local fascist clubs sang fascist songs and received awards for scholarship and service from the Italian consulate.[35]

While New York's Italian fascists did not disrupt public order to the extent the Bund and the Front did, fascist proselytizing in the public schools should have alarmed Coudert investigators. According to at least three informants, Italian teacher Carolyn Della Chiesa organized the five or six hundred Italian students at Abraham Lincoln High School into "an extremely strong and organized body," teaching them fascist ideas, building "a loyalty to the Mussolini regime." In 1937, she established a fascist club while teaching fascist principles to her classes. Together with the school librarian, Della Chiesa filled the school library with "Fascist tourist pamphlets."[36] Max Lieberman, who devoted much of his career to establishing Italian-language programs in New York schools, expressed dismay at the level of indoctrination he witnessed in students at New Utrecht High School, where he was assigned. On one occasion, hundreds of students enthusiastically stood and returned a fascist salute by a speaker invited to an Italian Club event. On another, when Lieberman tried to silence a rowdy audience by raising his hand, the assembled students, misunderstanding the gesture, stood and saluted back.[37]

The Coudert staff knew of these allegations: The documents in the committee files include not only depositions, which might have been collected and ignored, but also staffers' interview summaries and digests of testimony and documents. The knowledge not only was at hand; it was consumed, evaluated, and rendered usable for the committee's deliberations. Moreover, there was no lack of corroboration; almost all of the accused were identified by more than one witness.[38]

Yet Coudert staffers explained away the allegations on grounds that are hard to reconcile with the consistency and extent of the testimony in the committee's own files. Memos written by staff in charge of the fascism investigation record obtuse and even studied indifference that would have elicited outrage had it been made public at the time, when right-wing violence still convulsed the city. For example, a staffer who reviewed the investigation in August 1942, in response to public criticism of the final Coudert committee report that spring, evaluated only the case of Hunter's Ceroni, of the dozen or so faculty and teachers named as active Italian fascists by witnesses. According to the staff memo, interviews with a selection of Ceroni's former students turned up no complaints of propagandizing. However, the corroborated testimony of Ceroni's work for the

Italian embassy was disregarded. Otherwise, the staffer disposed of the case on the basis of an earlier investigator's "private impression" that Ceroni had "never carried on any propaganda," even though Ceroni himself had admitted as much under oath.[39]

The prevarications of one staffer, Thomas Meehan, which Coudert committee associate counsel Phillip W. Haberman, Jr., incorporated into the committee's 1942 report, are especially worth noting. While Meehan's records show that the Coudert staff dutifully committed some bureaucratic time and energy to following up on leads about fascist activism, especially in the public high schools, they also disclose an astonishing complacency about the highly suggestive evidence that those inquiries turned up. One example of Meehan's credulousness stands out quite starkly in retrospect: since the summer of 1939, Jewish organizations had been pressuring the city to investigate Otto Koischwitz, a Hunter College German professor who reportedly worked closely with German agents in the United States.[40] Koischwitz would soon achieve lasting fame as the Nazi broadcasting Svengali who lured his former Hunter student Mildred Gillars to become Berlin Radio's infamous "Axis Sally," the wartime hostess of seductive broadcasts aimed at undermining the morale of American and British troops. Not only did Meehan miss interrogating Koischwitz himself (the Coudert staff put off any inquiry until early 1941, by which time Koischwitz was already in Germany), but he cast only a weak light on the question of whether Koischwitz's Hunter colleagues collaborated with him in any way. Even when it was clear that Koischwitz was working for the Nazi government, several Hunter College faculty came to his defense, yet Meehan found no occasion to probe more deeply.[41]

The Murphy case shows similar patterns of negligence and political bias: Coudert investigators gave little indication that they wanted to find out whether Murphy was in the Front, or to expose the suspicious relationships among him, his students, his colleagues, and neighborhood Front and Mobilizer activity. Their investigation showed more concern about the teachers—a "small group" of "troublemakers"—who filed complaints against Murphy than about Murphy himself. Coudert staff put the complainants on a suspect list, recording denunciations against them, their level of activity in the teachers union, and their alleged ties to the Communist Party and its front organizations. Their very act of filing charges against Murphy cast them under collective suspicion and suggested an intention on the part of the Coudert committee to impugn evidence of school-based anti-Semitism rather than pursue it.[42]

The Question of Balance

One way of measuring the laxity of the Coudert fascism inquiry is to take as a standard of scrutiny the sorts of investigative techniques—some of them clearly coercive and in violation of rights—that were applied to suspected Communists. The tenacity of the Coudert staff evaporated suddenly when faced with right-wing subversion. The threshold for pursuing leads, calling in suspects and subjecting them to the third degree, or subpoenaing membership lists of right-wing extremist organizations was much higher than the threshold for hounding alleged Communists was. This double standard reflected what appears to have been an implicit sympathy for or tolerance of right-wing extremism.

Moreover, right-wing extremists were never subpoenaed to testify in public, and thus never forced either to deny their activities under oath or to "take the fifth." Nor were antifascists such as Gaetano Salvemini or witnesses such as Goffredo Pantaleoni called to the stand. This absence of public hearings on fascist subversion Windels and Coudert explained away by saying they had insufficient evidence to warrant them. Yet, as was clear from private depositions and interviews conducted through 1941, that was just not true. Windels's official requirement of having at least two independently corroborating witnesses before a suspect would be publicly exposed was regularly met in the case of fascists, Christian Fronters, and other anti-Semites. Yet none of the suspects' names or affiliations were ever disclosed by the committee.

In the private hearings, moreover, one seldom sees aggressive interrogation of right-wing witnesses and suspects, certainly not in comparison with the browbeating of suspected Communists. Carolyn Della Chiesa, to take just one example, is never pressed to explain witness testimony that she propagandized to her students. Instead staffers allowed her denials to stand unchallenged and even let her denounce colleagues whom she believed were Communists, including several of her accusers. One sees a similar picture when comparing the private deposition of Covello, identified by multiple witnesses as a critically important figure in the city's fascist network, with that of Meriwether Stuart, a suspected Communist. Stuart was grilled by no fewer than three lawyers, who pressed him to name people at meetings he attended in the summer of 1935, which he did, and who tried to trip him up on questions concerning allegedly Communist-instigated union factionalism.[43] Covello in contrast, in a hearing that seems like a conversation over a cup of coffee about a topic that both parties find slightly embarrassing, was never pressed on his role in Casa Italiana or his contacts with the Italian embassy. Or, for that matter, anything to do with fascism. As with Della Chiesa, the Coudert investigators were more intent on squeezing Covello for information on Communists and their supporters in the teachers union.[44]

Committee Motives

It would have been hard to find among the Coudert committee and its largely liberal staff any overt personal sympathy for right-wing extremism. They did not ignore school-based fascists because they agreed with them. More likely, the Coudert committee's decision to avoid a thorough investigation of fascism reflected deference to public prejudice and loyalty to Tammany Hall, the Catholic church, and other pillars of New York conservatism. Tammany had its share of extremists, who would have blocked any official campaign against the Front or Italian fascists. Nor did the La Guardia administration want to alienate Italian-American voters, whom it counted on at the polls and whose volatile nationalism could not be readily detached from that of the Mussolini regime.[45] The presence of open fascists on the city's school boards undoubtedly did not help. At least three witnesses identified Alberto Bonaschi, appointed to the board of education by La Guardia in 1935 over protests by liberals, as a pivotal figure in the city's fascist movement. According to Salvemini, Bonaschi served as a judge on the infamous court of discipline for the virulent Fascist League of North America in 1928.[46]

A genteel anti-Semitism pervading academic culture before the war also framed the Coudert committee's double standard. According to historian Stephen Norwood, not only did apologists for authoritarianism inhabit Harvard, Yale, Vassar, and other venerable institutions, but so did overt adherents to Nazism and Italian fascism. While administrators like Harvard's James Conant and Columbia's Nicholas Murray Butler tended to be discreet about their anti-Semitism, other academics openly endorsed the Nazi and fascist regimes, in papers and statements ranging from simple apologetics to anti-Semitic ranting.[47]

While it is unlikely that academic anti-Semitism influenced the committee's investigation directly, it set a standard against which the Coudert committee normalized the views of politically organized extremists and diminished their threat. One can see the effect of such normalization in the interviews that Coudert staff conducted with those several faculty who unabashedly expressed their prejudices against Jews. Such interviewees, who tended to be less guarded than those faculty who were actually connected to the Christian Front or Italian fascist organizations, merely passed on conventional wisdom about Jews in the academy. For instance, CCNY classics professor Edgar Halliday regularly referred to president "Rosenfeld" in his Latin classes, ostensibly to illustrate some point about the etymology of names, but clearly to goad his many Jewish students, whose distinctively "keen sense of humor" and reluctance to take offense were, he genially declared, "characteristic, I think, of all Jews." He considered the Jewish students "naturally racially affectionate," yet "peculiar" in that they are inclined to lie and cheat: "In spite of their affection they will double-cross you. That is peculiarly Jewish, but it is so. And they double-cross each other."[48]

Such views would not be worth dwelling on were they not also assented to by Windels and others on the Coudert staff, who did not press Halliday on his organizational affiliations. Had the interviewees been suspected Communists who let drop some remark about class struggle or supporting the Soviet invasion of Finland, they would have been hounded about the apparent similarity of their statements to the "Communist Party line." The suspicion of membership, the presumption of guilt, hung behind those interviews while background prejudice against Jews was all that hung behind the interviews with right-wingers.

In a couple of depositions, this normalization of racial prejudice verged on more-official forms of anti-Semitism. In one interview with BC President Harry Gideonse, Windels and his staff, including Associate Counsel Phillip W. Haberman, Jr., who was Jewish, accepted the prevailing "wisdom" that too many Jews were entering higher education and graduating to academic professions, which threatened what Windels, Gideonse, and others believed to be democratic education. Windels asked Gideonse whether "it would be helpful to the students who go to the city colleges to have a faculty more generally composed of a cross-section of American background throughout the country as distinguished from a purely local background?" By the beginning of the war, BC graduates were overwhelmingly Jewish; many of the instructors accused in the Coudert investigation were CCNY and BC graduates. Gideonse agreed: "It is the one way in which we can offset the weakness of the system that has to start off with too much localism in its student body." This was indeed a question of hiring fewer Jews, as Windels made evident a bit later when he stated that he found it "disappointing" that faculty and administrators at CCNY gave employment preference to their own graduates because those graduates "could not find employment in other universities quite as readily as they should," apparently referring to widespread anti-Semitic barriers to academic employment.[49] In responding to the same question about collegiate "inbreeding," CCNY President Harry Wright emphatically agreed, adding "that whole question is hot and is directly tied up with the idea of race," of which he sought "the proper mixture."[50]

Such an implicit relationship between anti-Semitism and the Coudert investigation, of course, was not what Bella Dodd, the AJC, and others had in mind when they accused the investigation of acting prejudicially against Jews. And indeed it would seem that Coudert's accusers fundamentally misunderstood the problem of anti-Semitism at this pivotal moment in the nation's history. Rather than serving as an ulterior motive for active agents of anticommunism such as Windels and Coudert, anti-Semitism shaped both sides of the conflict between Communists and their opponents. The indigenous character of American racism and anti-Semitism was part of the fundamental injustice of the investigation. But its origin was more circumstantial than Coudert's critics allowed: one of the key elements in this relationship was the central role Communists had played through the 1930s in challenging normative racism, bringing to the surface prejudices that many Americans did not consider of much consequence. In doing this, especially on college campuses, the party looked far more subversive than the racism it was challenging. Such racism, after all, simply dwelled in the schoolrooms of the city; it did not take much to convince students to believe in it. Thus, the Christian Front could rely on prevailing bigotry, while any effort to promote racial equality had to be come from the outside.

Anti-Semitism at the time was culturally engrained, but its very pervasiveness and invisibility, in large part, motivated the creation of openly antifascist popular-front organizations. This is, in many ways, the nature of subversion, and Communists should not have been surprised when they were accused of it by people who accepted anti-Semitism and racism as the norm. Similarly, much of the evidence by which Dodd and the AJC linked Timothy Murphy to the Front and the Bund could have been explained by something other than membership in either organization—the products of culturally ingrained racism of the kind that emerges spontaneously in periods of economic hardship that anti-Semitic organizations merely exploited. Murphy sounded like a member of the Front, but perhaps the Coudert committee recognized in Murphy the homegrown American racist that he also was and simply treated his sort of racism much as other Americans did—as an integral feature of American culture—not something that had to be cultivated in order for a creature like Murphy to appear at the head of a classroom any more than in a corporate boardroom or a sporting club. Moreover, protected and promoted by a principal who was engaged in payroll padding, indicted in January 1941, and forced to retire, Murphy's generally thuggish attitude toward the students could also be understood as a secondary effect of the system of patronage that had crippled the city's schools since their creation.

But these observations raise obvious questions about how such beliefs took the dangerous political forms that they did at the end of the 1930s. The mere recognition that racism is customary does not diminish the menace of organizations such as the Klan or the Front that defend prevailing customs and the privileges that are attached to those customs. Since that is the case, the Communist Party, as one of the few political parties willing to confront anti-Semitism and racism in customary as well as institutionalized and political forms, deserved credit rather than vilification for having done so. The Coudert committee's response, so heavily weighted against the party and so apparently in favor or tolerant of fascism and anti-Semitism, must then be viewed as contributing to those customs and their related bigotry and authoritarianism. Thus, critics such as Bella Dodd may have been wrong about the form of the relationship between anti-Semitism and the emerging red scare, but they were absolutely right about its substance.

11
Communism on Trial

The testimony of the Coudert investigation's friendly witnesses in March 1941 severely damaged the already-weakened Popular Front on New York's college campuses. Not only did William Canning and three others identify dozens of faculty and staff as Communists; with the help of Windels and his assistants, they also contrived a history of Communist subversion and classroom indoctrination that fed public anxieties about national security and social order in a time of impending war.

According to its opponents, at this point the Coudert investigation posed two threats to American democracy: Like other countersubversive investigations, it undermined individual civil liberties and rights, especially of dissent and association. Additionally, the inquiry menaced a political party, a union, and a social movement that were valuable parts of the democratic tradition. While these two threats were related, mounting a defense against one did not necessarily serve a defense against the other. Civil libertarians, including many with Popular Front sympathies, tended to focus on the fate of individuals, aiming to strengthen democracy by safeguarding their rights in the courts. While they also took up the constitutional issues, the Communist Party and the people and organizations more directly within its orbit were also occupied with the fate of the party and the movement, as well as with the future of the left in the teachers unions, and it was by no means clear that pursuing constitutional protection of individual rights would effectively help that effort.

Under these circumstances, three courses of action were open to the party and the accused, none of them especially promising. First, they could refuse to cooperate on Fifth Amendment and other grounds, thereby challenging the power of legislative committees to force compliance with their inquiries and pressuring the courts to extend and strengthen constitutional protections. The state and municipal laws that forced public employees to self-incriminate had to be contested—and years later they were, successfully. However, the Board of Higher Education's (BHE) authority to demand full cooperation from its employees under conditions set by Windels and Coudert were bolstered by public perceptions, which were grounded in part in what the Seabury investigations insinuated—namely, that invoking the Fifth was an admission of guilt. Second, the Communist Party could counsel its academic members to lie about their membership, thereby protecting both their jobs and the organized and informal networks on which the party and, to a lesser extent, the antifascist movement, depended. Yet this strategy would make it more difficult for faculty and staff who had disavowed communism to attest to its positive record on campus and in the union. Third, the party alternately could counsel its members to admit they were Communists, challenging the court to protect their jobs by extending the rights of free speech and association to the academy. Though it would almost guarantee the loss of many jobs in the short term and tie up the lives and resources of the accused in court, this course of action also might allow professed Communists to refute the countersubversive myth that faculty were engaged in classroom indoctrination and recruiting hapless students into the Young Communist League (YCL).

The party, Bella Dodd's defense committee, and accused City College of New York (CCNY) faculty and staff initially tried to reconcile the protection of individual liberties with the defense of the party and the movement by splitting the difference between the last two courses of action: they had one faculty member take the fall for the rest, testing the willingness of the public and the BHE to accept party membership among school employees while freeing up a voice to speak directly on behalf of the party, the movement, and the union. That faculty member was Morris U. Schappes. His act, by all appearances noble and self-sacrificing, ended up being a mistake, but it was an understandable one.

Schappes

Born Moise ben Haim Shapshilevich in the Ukraine in 1907, Morris Schappes grew up on the Lower East Side, graduating from Townsend Harris High School then attending CCNY, where he finished with honors in English on the eve of the 1929 stock market crash. Fortunately, his former teachers hired him on as a tutor in the English department, despite a pronounced speech defect that effectively closed him out of the few jobs in the public schools.[1]

When he came before the Rapp-Coudert committee in the fall of 1940, Schappes had a reputation as a trade unionist and leader of the college antifascists. Literary critic Alfred Kazin, who knew him as a fellow CCNY instructor, derided Schappes for his "arrogant stupidity," tagging him in the incongruous fashion of that moment the "college Fuehrer of the Party" who "ground out" orthodox Marxist "literary law" in a "horribly choked out" stammer.[2] Coudert committee friendly witnesses William Canning, Annette Sherman, and Otto Zeichner likewise called him a "dictator," in part because it fit with their story that he threatened them to remain silent.[3] Schappes's students felt differently, however, cherishing him as a teacher and intellectual guide, and inviting him regularly to speak, stammer included, at mass meetings. His union activism and open support for their antifascist and antiwar protests led the college in the spring of 1936 to inform him that his "efficiency as a teacher of English has not been sufficiently notable to justify" his reappointment, though it renewed his contract each of the previous eight years based on his skills in the classroom. Other tutors and instructors were also targeted, reportedly as part of a rotational strategy to hire replacements at lower salaries. The dismissal letter, handed to Schappes two days after he addressed a student antiwar meeting, was composed by a newly appointed department chair, who had served as an official if discredited historian for the American Legion and who justified his decision on the grounds of Schappes's "obvious physical defect of speech," his "disinclination to obey orders or submit to authority," and his tendency to "teach too much sociology and too little English" by, for instance, devoting "his discussion of Shelley mainly to that poet's boyish social theories instead of showing him as earth's greatest lyric poet."[4] Twelve other antifascists were dismissed along with Schappes that week. The board, rocked by the ensuing protests, including yet another student strike, a mock trial of CCNY President Frederick Robinson before an audience of fifteen hundred, and a petition and letter-writing campaign that spilled over onto the editorial pages of the major newspapers, reversed the decision within a couple of months.[5]

Schappes joined the Communist Party around 1934, and by 1941 had become one of its key leaders in the municipal colleges. He made this known in a statement to the press the day before Canning was to testify in the March 1941 public hearings. So on that matter, he was quite honest with the committee and the public. Most of the rest of what he disclosed publicly and revealed to Coudert staffers in private testimony a couple of weeks earlier, however, were half-truths or complete fabrications, including the claims that, until he quit the previous year, he had been the sole remaining member of CCNY's Communist Party unit; that once the three other members departed—two to fight and perish in Spain, the third to serve the party in Boston—he produced and distributed the unit's newsletter, *The Teacher Worker*, on his own; that he knew of no other Communists in the municipal college system; and that the only other members of the party of whom he was aware were those who represented it officially, such as New York party education director Isidore Begun, with whom he shared an office at party headquarters on Twelfth Street. These statements became the bases for the perjury charges that eventually would send him to jail.

Dodd reported years later that for dealing with the Rapp-Coudert probe, the overall "strategy decided on was to defend the teachers by defending the Party." Those party members who had international party contacts that were made in the course of professional travel were instructed to quit rather than submit to interrogation. Others were told first to stonewall—to call in sick if necessary and to refuse to answer questions even under threat of contempt—then to concoct cover stories with the help of Dodd and lawyers hired by her committee. All teachers and staff who actually were Communists were expected to lie about membership. Schappes was the exception, a change in course that was decided on at the last minute, according to Dodd.[6] Clearly Schappes's statement and his public testimony the following day were meant to preempt and discredit Canning, whom the party apparatus and union activists attacked as the real perjurer.[7] In some sense, this was true since Canning misrepresented key elements of his experience, and his lies were of much greater consequence than Schappes'; however, Schappes demonstrably lied to the committee, even if it was about unimportant things. His and the party's main goal appears to have been to let Canning's list of accused CCNY Communists off the hook on the question of membership in the party. For the party, undoubtedly, that was a matter of protecting itself and its members, since witnesses called before the committee could not claim Fifth Amendment protection without losing their jobs. If, however, they told the truth about themselves, then they could be bullied with the threat of legislative contempt into naming names.

In addition to Annette Sherman, two other witnesses backed up Canning the following week, discrediting Schappes on the lie.[8] Before that happened, however, the BHE caved to Coudert committee pressure and started the process of suspending faculty, beginning with Schappes, on charges of "conduct unbecoming a member of the staff." Although Schappes's false testimony ultimately would be the grounds for his dismissal, the board initially built its case around the one statement Schappes made that undoubtedly was true: that he was a Communist. On March 10, two days after Canning's public appearance yet almost a week before he was corroborated by Sherman, the board announced that they would ask acting CCNY President Harry Wright to suspend Schappes pending his hearings before a BHE trial committee.[9] Schappes was not indicted for perjury until eight days later, when District Attorney Thomas Dewey had him arrested at the College Teachers Union (CTU) offices. Eventually, after all the corroborating testimony was in, the board judged Schappes's conduct "unbecoming" on the grounds of his misrepresentations, but it initially charged him as well for his admitted membership in the Communist Party, which they assumed, based on the prejudicial reading of party documents by the Coudert committee, "taught, advocated or advised" that the government be "overthrown by force, violence or unlawful means." The board also accused Schappes of indoctrinating and recruiting students, instructing fellow staff members on "various methods of indoctrinating students," and of "unequivocal adherence" and "unequivocal obedience" to the "party line."[10]

Schappes was able to delay the dismissal proceedings until after his perjury trial, which finished in late June with his conviction on four counts. Although he remained free until the exhaustion of his appeals in late 1943—except for an incarceration of several weeks in the city jail, known as the Tombs, before bail was permitted—he ended up serving just under a year and a half in state prisons at Sing Sing and Walkill. When the BHE heard his dismissal case in September, they reduced the charges to just one, perjury, ignoring all the other accusations and giving the impression, already carried over into the other BHE trials, that he was just fired for lying under oath and other "misrepresentations," not for his political beliefs.[11]

Harry Gideonse, who took on the unofficial role that spring of academic spokesman for the Coudert committee, emphatically promoted the view that Schappes was dismissed only for obstruction, refusal to cooperate, and misrepresentation, insisting that "no one has been dismissed for holding unpopular views or for exercising common rights of freedom of opinion, freedom of speech, or freedom of teaching."[12] While most like Gideonse perceived Schappes's perjury to be the ultimate evidence of Communist bad faith, a few, such as physicist Robert Oppenheimer, countered that "in fail[ing] to adequately implicate others," Schappes acted with greater decency and morality than Coudert, Canning, or the

BHE. "There would be something pretty seriously wrong with the integrity, the loyalty, and the courage of a man who willingly served as an informer," Oppenheimer wrote, adding that "there is something rather less than noble about an investigation which forces a man, either to testify as an informer, to be guilty of contempt, or to be branded a criminal and a coward by sanctimonious administrators."[13]

Yet even the conviction for perjury was not as strongly grounded as Gideonse assumed. On appeal, Schappes's lawyers aptly, though unsuccessfully, argued that the prosecution did not demonstrate the materiality of Schappes's lies—that is, that his misrepresentations were pertinent to a criminal investigation or to the protection of someone in the commission of a crime. At that point, membership in the party still was not illegal, and as the National Lawyers Guild argued in an *amicus* brief, the Coudert committee had not demonstrated that the Communist Party was indeed subversive.[14]

The Setup

The rest of the CCNY people named by Canning, meanwhile, demanded an opportunity to answer his accusations in public testimony before the committee. Legally, Windels was not obliged to open legislative hearings to that kind of forum, but politically he had to appear to be fair to the accused, whom he promised time on the witness stand. Nevertheless, he dragged his feet, postponing the responses until late March and allowing his supporters on the BHE, led by conservative lawyer Charles Tuttle, to force a resolution that explicitly forbade employment in the municipal colleges to Communists based on the "findings of fact" by the Coudert investigation concerning the subversive intentions of the Communist Party. The board of education followed suit for the public schools. Once Canning's testimony was corroborated, the BHE began the dismissals of the dozens of employees whom the young historian had named, starting with physicist Lewis Balamuth, who was summarily fired from his evening-division job on March 17 (for his tenured position at the main uptown campus, Balamuth was entitled to a hearing before he could be dismissed).[15] Effectively, the BHE resolution and the ostentatious launching of the dismissal process closed off the last remaining possibility of acknowledging one's party membership while keeping one's job, thus definitively backing the rest of the CCNY faculty and staff into a corner.

The delay also allowed Windels to release an "interim report" the day before the accused were to tell their side of the story, preempting most of what they had to say. In order to put communism and the entire Popular Front on trial, Windels's release painted a picture of conspiracy and subversion that extended far beyond mere individual misrepresentation. The *New York Times* credulously called the document a "blanket indictment" of the CCNY Communists; Windels, for his part, repeated his December avowal to have proceeded "with complete objectivity," using "only such evidence as would be relevant by legal standards." In fact, the report read like a screed, some of it even comical in its hyperbole. It characterized the party as a minority "especially trained to foment discontent" and to "spread death to democracy," asserting that the testimony revealed an "elaborate organizational system" engaged in activity that "undoubtedly continues to be conspiratorial in nature." As evidence of "the possibility of a financial racket," Windels cited the "great emphasis on money-collecting" through dues and other "expenses" that "constitute a heavy financial burden" on those least able to pay. Yet at the same, time the report concluded that dues were "an income tax," since they were collected on a sliding scale based on salary. On the basis of Canning's implausible assertions about the teaching of history, the report perpetuated the countersubversive myth that the "injection of Communism into teaching ... without detection" was a "Party obligation." It argued, based on "conclusions of fact" derived from "documentary proof," that Communism's "basic creed" is "advocacy of a forcible and violent revolution" to "overthrow the existing form of government," and that the party "seeks to undermine American youth by spreading its alien and subversive principles among them." Finally, despite entirely contrary evidence in their own files, taking Canning's resentments about demands on his time as evidence of an attack on professional ethics, the report asserted, "Teacher-members were not allowed to pursue by postgraduate work the normal path of progress in scholarship and learning for the purpose of preparing themselves for better positions and more effective teaching." Pursuit of research allegedly required the "consent of Party bosses."[16]

By the time the rest of the accused faculty and staff were able to tell their side of the story, in hearings that began on March 24, the verdict had been already delivered. Nearly forty people asked to testify under oath. Coudert limited them to ten minutes each, restricted to just the "facts" of their cases. Almost all denounced the committee's friendly witnesses as "informers and perjurers"; some accused Canning of settling scores, including one secretary who claimed he added her to the list to retaliate for snubbing him romantically.[17] Windels and his staff aggressively interrogated the CCNY witnesses, constantly interrupting their efforts to absolve themselves or to read letters from colleagues, students, and alumni attesting to their characters or skills as teachers. As historian Phillip Foner tried to counter Canning's long-winded allegations of his professional malfeasance, for instance, staffer J. G. L. Molloy broke in repeatedly, incongruously demanding that Foner stick to "whether the testimony about him by other witnesses is true." In another instance, associate counsel Phillip W. Haberman, Jr., snidely insinuated a homosexual relationship between college registrar Kenneth Ackley and Townsend Harris English instructor David Goldway, who for several years shared an apartment behind Carnegie Hall.[18]

William Mulligan and Bella Dodd tried to intercede from the audience, but it only earned Mulligan his second ejection; as in December, he was manhandled by several police officers, this time his arm twisted behind his back.[19] Supporters filled the few seats in the tiny hearing room that they were allowed into, hoping that their presence would rein in Coudert and Windels's excesses. By the last of the four hearings at the end of April, decorum and order had broken down. Goldway refused to sign the required waiver of immunity, yet he testified anyway. Outside, hundreds of students and supporters filled the corridors, shouting denunciations at Coudert, encouraged by several of the suspended teachers. And while the full committee earlier had listened closely to the accusers, no more than two committee members besides Coudert attended while the accused had their chance to respond.[20]

Although the accused tended to dwell on denouncing Canning, they also tried to give alternative accounts of what had been going on at CCNY from the one promoted by Windels in the interim report. Former CTU President Edwin Berry Burgum presented an eloquent defense of a union that "began with all the glow of idealism engendered by the New Deal." Burgum recalled, "We wished to be better teachers. We sought to promote the extension of educational opportunities. We wished to free education from dry rot and political control."[21] Schappes, having admitted party membership, challenged the charge of indoctrination. "My task," he declared, is to help the student "stand on his own feet intellectually, to think for himself scientifically, and to draw his own conclusions on the basis of his own findings and interests."[22] Referring to party policy that was documented in their own files, he reminded Coudert staffers that Communists preferred to run educational and propaganda campaigns through their own schools and organizations.[23]

Yet for the most part, the efforts of accused faculty and staff to acquit the Popular Front and the union of the charges were defensive and flawed, mainly because they could not acknowledge their roles as Communist party activists. Some faculty, especially in the sciences, sounded almost bewildered in their denials. Saul Bernstein, an instructor in biology, said of indoctrination, "I have never been accused of it by anyone, I have never practiced it, and I am fundamentally opposed to it."[24] Canning's fellow historians made a special effort to challenge his assertion that they had "woven" Communist propaganda "into the very texture" of their history lessons. Philip Foner taught in the CCNY history department beginning in 1933, advancing quickly from his appointment as a tutor to become an instructor in 1937 while finishing his dissertation at Columbia. Having befriended Canning, whom he and his family put up in their home one summer, Foner felt personally betrayed by him, declaring, "If I taught propaganda instead of history, as Mr. Canning charges, my students would be the first to realize this. Certainly they are in a much better position to evaluate my teaching than Mr. Canning, who has never been in a single class of mine." History department colleagues, he pointed out, could drop in on his classes at any point during the term or the class hour. Several did, including departmental chair Nelson Mead, who later served as interim president after the firing of Robinson. At one point, Foner taught parts of Mead's classes, without any controversy. Even Robinson, an archconservative, trusted Foner's scholarship enough to hire him as a personal research assistant.[25]

Meanwhile, the BHE moved quickly to charge and suspend the full-time faculty and staff fingered by Canning, pending hearings before administrative trial committees, beginning with English tutor Arthur Braunlich on March 25, followed by Ackley a few days after. The next group of eleven was suspended a month later: Bernstein, Balamuth, David Cohen and Samuel Margolis in the library, Morris U. Cohen and Sidney Eisenberger in chemistry, Jack Foner in history, Walter Scott Neff in psychology, and clerks Jetta Alpert, Jesse Mintus, and Louis Lerman.[26] The BHE removed Goldway on May 12 for his refusal to sign the waiver of immunity. They suspended a second group later that month, including Phillip Foner, Seymour A. Copstein in English, James H. Healey in public speaking, Max L. Hutt in education, and Maxwell N. Weisman in biology. Included in that group were seven staff members: Moe Foner, Murray Smolar, Eugene Stein, Murray Gristle, Hilliard Wolfson, Sylvia Elfenbein, and Nelle Lederman. That brought the total of officially sanctioned CCNY faculty and staff to twenty-six, not including Schappes.[27] Seven BC and public-school teachers were added to that list and suspended in early June for refusing to testify before the committee.[28] CCNY public-speaking instructor Francis J. Thompson was suspended in September. Additional summary dismissals of nontenured faculty and staff never made it into the press or were only mentioned in passing—for instance, CCNY's nonrenewal of Moses Finkelstein in history or the "non-reappointment" of adjunct Max Yergan, the first African American hired to the CCNY faculty, who taught CCNY's first course in African-American history. The BHE treated Yergan's firing, a consequence of Canning's testimony, as a "perfectly routine matter."[29]

The public was given the impression that the suspensions were for false testimony and similarly duplicitous "conduct unbecoming"—that as the BHE put it with regard to Ackley, "he is being discharged, not because of his opinions, but because of his conduct and acts."[30] But the BHE like the Coudert committee did indeed target beliefs. For a start, the board explicitly charged its employees with membership in the Communist Party. If board members believed that in doing so they were suspending faculty and staff merely for the "act" of joining, then they were kidding themselves, for the board quite plainly indicted employees for the beliefs that supposedly came with party membership, such as "the government of the United States should be overthrown by force or unlawful means." The BHE generally assumed that alleged Communists adhered to those doctrines even when they disavowed them. By this logic, membership alone was all that mattered in proving adherence to prohibited beliefs—the beliefs hid, so to speak, behind the shorthand of membership. This was the magic of the "party line" in the emerging anticommunist demonology, according to which the Communist Party, unlike any other party active in the United States, submitted their members to a strictly enforced set of doctrines. To be sure, Communists tended to sound like Communists, parroting the platforms of their party and its leaders. But so did Republicans, and if the Communist Party in principle demanded adherence to a set of doctrines on pain of expulsion, it was very clear from the testimony of former Communists, including the Coudert committee's many friendly witnesses, that members could and did disagree with party policy, privately and even publicly. The BHE followed this logic of the "party line" even for doctrines that the party itself repudiated or explicitly had abandoned, such as the promotion of revolutionary violence.

The BHE, however, took the magic of the party line one step further, and reconverted those alleged beliefs in party doctrine back into equally alleged, one might say fantasized, acts. So, in almost all of the faculty cases, they inferred from membership not just personal endorsement of a policy of classroom indoctrination—disavowed even more categorically than "force and violence"—but also the *act* of indoctrinating *actual* students, *despite the fact that all the substantive evidence*, in the form of student testimonials and departmental teaching evaluations, *said otherwise*. In psychologist Walter Neff's case, the BHE asserted, on the basis of Canning's and Sherman's testimonies, "that indoctrination of students was discussed at Unit meetings" as a "duty" of members. There was no reason to assume that Neff followed such orders, if they were ever given, and plenty of evidence in testimonials from Neff's colleagues and students that the opposite was true. But the BHE convicted Neff of indoctrination, nonetheless, as it did with almost all the other faculty.[31] It was not just Canning and Sherman's word against Neff's, whose classes they never attended, but also their word against other people actually in a position to know something about Neff's teaching, such as his chair and his students. The same rules of inference governed the BHE's judgment generally. History instructor Benjamin Paskoff, who studied with Canning at Columbia, complained that Canning's charges were taken on face value, adding, "This is a splendid example of how this Committee has seen fit to accept the most fantastic statements from Canning without question, although it was obvious he could have no personal knowledge in support of his allegation."[32] In Braunlich's case, the board did come up with student "testimony" of indoctrination, but it was remarkably far-fetched—some unsigned doggerel that appeared in a 1939 issue of a student newspaper, *The Mercury*, titled "Braunlich—English": "Gives his students all prostration / From Marxian interpretation, / Discovers leftist propaganda / In stuff like Ariel and Miranda." It is not surprising that once they had accepted Canning's notion of history as a "sugar coated pill," the board would assert on the basis of this poem that Braunlich's "denial of any effort to indoctrinate students . . . is at variance with student reaction."[33]

Moreover, in addition to being falsely accused of indoctrination and revolutionary violence, CCNY teachers and staff were also persecuted for ideas that they actually held and acted on that were not legally proscribed and had no necessary connection to Communist Party membership, such as about the need for academic democracy and trade union representation, or the recognition of "class struggle" in modern industrial relations. While many on the BHE agreed with the CTU activists who had reformed the municipal college system of governance two years earlier and expanded tenure rights, others, notably Charles Tuttle, who sat on several of the trial committees, did not. Nor did upstate Republican budget cutters and downstate Tammany Democrats who, though they disagreed on most other things, agree on the need to reign in trade union radicals and academic reformers who had challenged Tammany control of the municipal colleges, thereby forcing the ouster of two Tammany-appointed college presidents. Finally, one must not forget the anticommunist liberals such as Linville and Counts who worked behind the scenes in the Coudert investigation and the American Federation of Teachers (AFT) and who violently rejected the Popular Front's version of democracy that was grounded in a confrontational mass movement and guided by a Marxist sociology of class conflict. In this sense, Bella Dodd was absolutely right—there was a strong backlash against the work of Local 5 and the CTU behind the Coudert investigation and the BHE firings—even if she misunderstood the role of liberals in persecuting their Popular Front adversaries for their beliefs.

An Inept Defense

When the BHE hearings opened that summer, union and Committee for the Defense of Public Education (CDPE) lawyers raised procedural and constitutional objections. As administrative hearings conducted before trial committees appointed by the board, the BHE trials followed court procedure, allowing the accused to have legal representation, permitting defense attorneys cross-examination and access to evidence, and observing the right of appeal first to the BHE, then to the state commissioner of education, and finally to the state and federal appellate courts. Mulligan's earlier objections to the legislative hearing process, then, to some extent were answered—finally, lawyers representing the accused were allowed to cross-examine Canning and other friendly witnesses, but for the first time only in early June, and by that time it was too late. For these hearings, Mulligan was replaced by members of the Popular Front's legal network, including Samuel Rosenwein of the National Lawyers Guild (NLG), who handled almost all of the cases, and Herman Rosenfeld, also of the NLG. In Phillip Foner's hearings, Samuel A. Neuberger, of the International Labor Defense assisted.[34]

Severely restricted by the BHE trial committees' evident biases, Rosenwein had relatively few options beyond establishing the grounds for appealing the almost-certain dismissals of his clients. The trial committees thwarted even the most elementary challenges to the trumped-up charges of indoctrination and violent overthrow, cooperating freely with the prosecuting lawyer, Assistant Corporation Counsel Charles W. Weinstein, in excluding all testimony and evidence concerning anything but the most narrowly construed charges. So faculty efforts to bring into the hearings character witnesses and student testimony disproving indoctrination were dismissed as irrelevant to the specific charges of belonging to the party and lying about it.[35] Nevertheless, the charges of indoctrination and fomenting violent revolution remained in place, partly on the assumption that merely establishing membership in the party proved those as well. And disregarding the inconsistency, Weinstein readily brought those and related issues up, even though at one point in Ackley's trial he, too, had trouble with self-contradictions in Canning's testimony.[36] Rosenwein understandably appealed to the full board on grounds of bias, complaining of "the disregard of evidence, the distortion of evidence." But he held out little hope of favorable decisions, as he noted as well the BHE's "unconscionable haste," which he saw as an "attitude of the Board" that "prejudged and predetermined" the outcomes of the cases by running many of them on a fast track over the summer.[37]

Unfortunately, as the BHE hearings unfolded, conditions set by the CDPE, and according to Dodd and others the party as well, also helped box the lawyers into an inept defense based on the notion that "budget cutters" and "reactionaries" stood behind the persecution of municipal college faculty and staff. Stuck with the decision to disclaim party membership, Rosenwein had no choice but to attack Canning and other friendly witnesses as liars who plied their "concocted tale" as part of "a conspiracy, a frame-up, to destroy the Teachers' Union, and all those who took a progressive role in it."[38] Rosenwein promised to show that "forces widely known to be reactionary" caused a bitter and open conflict between all that was progressive on one side, and all that was conservative and antiprogressive on the other side." In this great struggle between progress and reaction, he insisted, the Coudert committee, the anticommunist Teachers Guild, upstate Republicans, and even the BHE, "want to wipe out and eliminate the democratic life of the school and the community."[39] Even without hyperbole, Rosenwein depicted a conspiracy so implausible that it is hard to understand how he thought it would be convincing. To believe the defense, the trial committees would have had to take Canning for an extraordinarily adept and elaborate liar supported by the coordinated lies of three other people. While there might have been some conspiring, and inspiring, on the part of Canning's associates (Hillman Bishop, for instance) and Coudert committee staffers, could there possibly have been a conspiracy to make up the existence of a Communist Party chapter at CCNY out of whole cloth?

Moreover, in lying about membership and in covering the lie with an implausible tale of right-wing conspiracy, Rosenwein and his clients reinforced the public perception that Communists indeed had something to hide and that they served a ruthless organization committed to misrepresentation and vilification, willing to sacrifice any principle for the sake of that organization's survival and success. That they acted, as the liberal anticommunists insisted, in bad faith. In doing so, the accused also missed crucial opportunities to expose the real lie of Canning's testimony, the corroborating witnesses, and the Coudert committee report: that the CCNY Communists actually did something wrong, that they indoctrinated students and fomented revolution, when instead they helped democratize education, challenge administrative and curricular racism, clean up Tammany corruption, and enhance academic freedom in the city's schools and colleges. One can imagine a completely different series of hearings in which openly avowed Communists made a case to the public that what they did at the municipal colleges served the core values of American democracy, especially on questions of economic and racial justice. The disavowal of membership made that impossible. Meanwhile, by spending almost his entire time attacking the characters and veracity of Canning and the corroborating witnesses, Rosenwein squandered the opportunity to cross-examine them to expose their own more material lies about Communists hijacking the teachers union and indoctrinating students.

The Coudert inquiry left the accused, the party, and the union very few options, none of them good. Using the power of the legislative investigation, his control of press and public relations, and the civil-service codes that stripped municipal employees of their constitutional rights, Windels forced accused Communists to lie about the party's organized presence in the city's colleges and universities. At the same time, unable to defend the party's record, the accused and their supporters could not stop the Coudert committee from fabricating a case against the party as a subversive criminal conspiracy to destroy American democracy. The evident lying about membership by many of the suspects, furthermore, lent an air of authenticity to the Coudert committee's case, on the principle that if Communists lied about their membership in the party, then the party must be something to lie about.

And so the apparent act of bad faith came to stand in for a much larger offense in the emerging countersubversive mythology of Communist conspiracy. By the time the cases reached the BHE trial committees in the summer of 1941, the board tribunals could hang their convictions of the accused on that mere act of lying, which they labeled "conduct unbecoming" an employee of the university system, but by which they implied so much more. One has a good sense of the extent of these conflations, and the density of this ideological packaging, in the final judgment of Kenneth Ackley's trial committee, which couched all of Ackley's offenses in terms of "disloyalty": He was disloyal to CCNY by being a member of the Communist Party, "which fostered disloyalty to the Government of the United States." Ackley was "disloyal to the democratic organization of the college" because he gave "his loyalty to an outside organization which sought by clandestine and underground means to influence and control affairs at City College, to inflict its influence upon the students and to destroy that freedom of personal expression which democratic institutions thrive on and need." He was disloyal to the BHE because he refused to cooperate with the Coudert investigation as directed by the BHE. He was "disloyal to his obligations under the law" because he gave misleading testimony to the Coudert committee. And finally he was "disloyal to his obligation as a member of the staff" because he did not turn in fellow Communists. "Any American teacher who joins such an organization, party or group, lends it countenance or works for its aggrandizement," the tribunal concluded, "is guilty of betraying the high trust which the citizens and taxpayers have reposed in him, and merits as the very least punishment, summary dismissal."[40]

Over the next several months, the BHE scheduled tribunals, selected from among the members of the board, for most of the suspended CCNY faculty and staff as well as the few BC suspects named by Grebanier and confirmed by one of the CCNY witnesses. The first took place in early June, resulting in the "conviction" of Ackley. Arthur Braunlich was dismissed in early August. Some of the accused, such as Howard Selsam, Jack Foner, and Lewis Balamuth, resigned before their cases could be decided; however, there was little doubt that they would have been dismissed. Several others, such as Morris Foner and Hilliard Wolfson, refused to cooperate with the trial committees, which fired them in absentia. The regular board of education also fired several public-school teachers targeted by the Coudert investigation, notably Dale Zysman, a Local 5 vice president, and Henry Klein, the former BC instructor whose dismissal in 1937 precipitated a campus strike that fueled right-wing protests against radicalism on that campus. While the war and conscription interrupted the trial and dismissal process, the BHE picked it up again when several untried suspects demobilized in 1946. The last of the Rapp-Coudert dismissals took place in 1948, as library assistant Samuel Margolis was finally fired on the flimsy and inconsistent testimony of Anne Sherman and William Canning.

12
Aftermath

> Come to think of it, you were probably the
> biggest issue in the State, and perhaps even
> the Country, for all I know.
>
> —*Lt. Phillip W. Haberman, Jr., to "Fritz" Coudert, 6 December 1942*

Between the start of Kenneth Ackley's Board of Higher Education (BHE) trial and the decision to dismiss him, which was made and executed on June 24, Germany invaded the Soviet Union. Operation Barbarossa not only changed the course of World War II; it also shifted American public opinion, as first Great Britain and then the United States established alliances with the Soviets against the Nazis. Gallup polls taken in summer 1941 showed American sympathy for the Russians growing, as Germany pushed the Red Army to the suburbs of Moscow. Though still hostile to Communist activism on the home front and still mistrustful of Stalin for signing the nonaggression pact with Hitler, Americans made clear that they did not consider Soviet communism as much of a threat as Nazism. By fall 1941, resistance to American involvement in the war, including FDR's lend-lease aid to the Soviets, ebbed as fears grew that the Germans would win their Eastern-front campaign, opening up the likelihood of an attack on the United States.[1]

Domestic anticommunism lost some of its justification as well, and though the BHE trials and the Coudert investigation were carried through the year by their own momentum, state and city officials began to challenge Rapp-Coudert budget requests. At one point, Governor Herbert Lehman vetoed appropriations to cover the salaries of Windels and his two top aides, Phillip W. Haberman, Jr., and J. G. L. Molloy, which by the standards of some critics were exorbitant: over $20,000 a year for Windels— more than $300,000 in current dollars. Coudert accused Lehman of "playing into the hands of Communists, Nazis and the like," and eventually the salaries were restored, but enthusiasm for the inquiry had clearly waned.[2] When, in early December, Pearl Harbor forced the nation into the war, the hunt for reds in the schoolroom became less relevant to the "defense of democracy" than did mobilizing against the Axis powers.

Inquisitions like Coudert's, however, die slow deaths. In fall 1941, it looked as though the investigation would be wrapped up, and by the first of the year, committee staff were discharged and the offices closed.[3] Morris Schappes rejoiced to his former colleague philosopher Morris R. Cohen "at the good news that the Rapp-Coudert committee is disbanding." Cohen was not so optimistic: "I regret to say that I do not share your joy.... The evil forces which have brought the committee into being are far from defeated and I should be very much surprised as well as gratified if there is no more mischievous legislation at the next session of the legislature."[4]

Cohen of course was right. The following March, when the committee mandate officially ended, Coudert, asserting the continued need to root out domestic subversion in yet more colleges and schools, introduced a bill in the Senate to re-fund the countersubversion probe as well as the dormant study of school efficiency for which the original Rapp-Coudert committee had been formed two years earlier.[5] Complaining that opposition to the committee's work had been "violent, cunning and unscrupulous," Coudert insinuated that failure to restore funding would be an act of cowardice. The bill passed both houses with overwhelming, bipartisan support, and after the brief threat of a gubernatorial veto, it was put into effect.[6] But while Coudert maintained a skeleton staff who were still trying to flush out faculty and student reds, the investigation was a mere shadow of its former self, largely dependent on cranky conservative students and parents informing on left-wing teachers.[7]

In April, meanwhile, the Coudert subcommittee released its final report on school subversion, penned by Haberman, that bolstered Coudert's warnings that Communists still used the city's classrooms to foment insurrection. The document contained the same hyperbole of earlier Coudert committee verdicts, almost all of it based on tendentious readings of Communist Party literature and the embellishments and the fabrications of Canning, Grebanier, and other friendly witnesses.[8] It included a sixty-page treatise on Communist doctrine, arguing that from the principles of class struggle and dialectics the party derived a strategy of searching out opportunities to disrupt democracy. Adherence to "the class view" and the mere employment of dialectical arguments, it concluded, necessarily committed one to a slavish obedience to a "party line" calling for greater social and economic "struggle" leading to "revolutionary upheaval," and from there to the advocacy of "violent overthrow," misrepresentation of professional and scholarly facts and credentials, and subversive teaching. Like Henry Linville and John Dewey, to whose "trial" of Local 5's left wing its final report repeatedly referred, the Coudert committee believed that Communist "tactics" originated in communist ideas: "Advocacy of violence and revolution . . . are, to Communists, not the subject of debate or speculation: they are inherent in the theory of dialectical materialism," which "serves as both a philosophy of life and a guide to action."[9]

Driving home the charge of conspiracy implicit in all of the Coudert committee accusations, the report argued that the Communist Party first "captur[ed] the Teachers Union in the lower schools," and then "organized" the College Teachers Union (CTU), setting in motion "an ambitious scheme to capture control of the colleges themselves." From its tiny following among municipal college faculty and staff, the party built "an elaborate system of conniving, masquerading, interlocking directorates, agitation and propaganda." The committee declared the union's campaign for democratic governance and tenure "a crafty scheme by which the Communists hoped and planned to obtain the actual control of the city colleges, to use them as a feeding ground for Communism and as a precedent for such control in other institutions of learning, thus ultimately subverting the entire educational system to revolutionary ends." The CTU's achievements, the committee concluded, were "a means of ultimate conquest."[10]

The final report also repeated the committee's findings, made public in December, on the "corrupting influence" of communism on student activism, revelations that surely goaded legislators to throw even more funding at Coudert. The Young Communist League (YCL), the December document reported, had engaged in "widespread agitational activity," even encouraging teenagers to threaten their teachers physically. These assertions were informed mainly by the perceptions of administrators, who tended to interpret any student demonstration as a "riot" and whose testimony the Coudert committee privileged over that of students and teachers.[11] Coudert's insistence that the party had "infiltrated" student government and campus newspapers was more credible, as the YCL did have a presence at Brooklyn College (BC) and City College of New York (CCNY), leading strikes that disrupted the campuses through the 1930s. Communist students also enjoyed the support of several student newspapers, though it is uncertain how many editors and writers had any party connection. Whatever the truth of this relationship, it was a rather flimsy basis on which to criticize the BHE for "having played directly into the hands of Communists," in granting campus access to national organizations such as the American Student Union (ASU), a coalition that for much of its existence included Socialists and liberals as well as Communists. On the basis of their accusations, Coudert and his staff pressed the BHE to tighten rules governing campus activism, which the board did that March, restoring the absolute authority of the college presidents to approve student clubs and to demand from those groups lists of members and their political affiliations.[12] The committee's perception of the YCL's sway with students, however, was as overblown as the YCL's own, based in part on the youth group's lax membership qualifications.[13] Still, as the most vocal left-wing political organization in the municipal colleges as well as in many of the communities served by those colleges, the Communist Party filled a leadership vacuum with influence well beyond its own ranks. Once again, behavioral evidence ruled Coudert committee perceptions, lumping in with Communists the many independent students who were influenced by Communist and other left-wing literature and street speakers.[14]

As for the press, it repeated the allegations of the April 1942 report with virtually no independent verification, challenging few of its charges, even after the BHE hearings that permitted the cross-examination of Canning and other friendly witnesses. Parroting the committee's report on student activism, the *New York Times* averred that "communism behind its more or less respectable screen rejects 'bourgeois morality' in its entirety; teaches its adherents to lie and misrepresent; invades individual rights by creating disorder and confusion; and is an avowed enemy of the kind of education that is being offered, at the taxpayers' expense, in the city schools and colleges."[15] The press, to be fair, had little alternative evidence to work with, as almost all of it remained as unavailable to them as to the accused. Even those small concessions made to defense lawyers, such as providing a copy of Canning's scrap of scribbled notes on which so much of Windels and Coudert's case hung, had to be fought for in the courts. Above all, defense lawyers could not access the records of the private hearings, which would have exposed the glaring inconsistencies in the testimony of Windels's friendly witnesses.

That the press and the legislature weighed in so heavily on the side of the Coudert committee's verdict marked the ultimate success of Windels and Coudert's strategy to try the accused teachers and staff in the court of public opinion. Using the weapon of "prescriptive publicity," the committee achieved a kind of political "pedagogy through prosecution," as political scientist Corey Robin recently termed it, which looked very much like the sort of indoctrination that Coudert accused the teachers of practicing—but using the legislative hearing room and the BHE trial committees instead of the classroom.[16] And, though the BHE could fire employees who demonstrably lied under oath, according to the terms of employment set by the city and the state, the investigation's argument that the accused (by lying or by hiding their party affiliations) acted in bad faith was founded on intentional deceit, distortions and manipulations of the evidence, and false claims of judicial objectivity and "courtroom methods."[17] The investigation, in other words, was itself an act of bad faith.

Moreover, Coudert and Windels compounded one deceit—the claim that the teachers and staff were just on trial for lying—with another, namely that they were not on trial for their political beliefs. This misrepresentation, fundamental to the liberal version of the countersubversive tradition, closed off to public discussion the question of whether the committee had proved all those other allegations that Coudert and his staff laid in front of the public but pretended were not the probe's main point: faculty indoctrination of students, use of "force and violence," subversion, the hijacking of the union, and the fomenting of student rebellion. In other words, the committee never showed that anything more had happened than boxing the accused into an untenable position from which they should have been protected by state and federal constitutions. Since the committee had not in fact demonstrated the threat of communism, since they had in fact trumped up the charges and coached testimony and fabricated evidence, the refusal of the accused to cooperate could be considered not "conduct unbecoming" but, as Robert Oppenheimer pointed out, just the opposite. Viewed from this perspective, Windels and Coudert's misrepresentations and manipulations of the public record appear to be far graver threats to democracy than were those committed by communist teachers and their supporters, who were driven to lie mainly by circumstances under the control of anticommunists.

Sadly, the responses of accused teachers and staff, including those by the union, Bella Dodd's defense committee, and the party, tended to serve the Coudert committee's designs, turning the public more decisively against Communist teachers and driving more nails into the Popular Front's coffin. Trading overstatement for overstatement, Dodd called the final Coudert report "the closest approach to a Fascist document that has been printed in this section of the country. It might easily be called 'The Mein Kampf' of Fritz Coudert and Paul Wendels [sic]. It has all the falsehoods and exaggerations of the book written by that Munich Maniac who has plunged the world into this bitter war."[18] Even mild-mannered Charles

Hendley went rhetorically overboard, declaring Coudert and his supporters in the legislature "spokesmen for fascism," who, with the "Counts faction" in the American Federation of Teachers (AFT), were "isolationists, appeasers, Coughlinites" who "fear the advance of democracy more than they fear fascism." The Coudert report, Hendley uncharacteristically fulminated, "is just so much diversionist propaganda" that "breathes the spirit of Hitler's puppets at Vichy."[19]

Meanwhile, some Democrats, led by the left wing of the American Labor Party, viewed by many as a Communist foothold in city politics, mounted a challenge to Coudert in the fall elections. Democratic candidate Jerry Finkelstein made Coudert's countersubversive probe, Coudert Brothers representation of Vichy for real estate purchases, and the firm's transfer of Belgian gold to the Nazis issues in an election in which accusations of fascism and totalitarianism flew across the pages of the city's major newspapers.[20] But the left's negative campaign backfired. The week before the election, prominent Finkelstein backers retracted their support, offended by misrepresentations of Coudert's political record. Recognized for his moderate views on the New Deal and educational funding, and his long-standing interventionist position on the war, Coudert did not fit Finkelstein's caricature of him as "Laval's lawyer," who "fights for the Axis with ... propaganda to divide and divert the people."[21] Real fascist sympathizers were to be found among isolationists and America First adherents, neither of which Coudert was. Antifascist journalist Dorothy Thompson, the first reporter ever thrown out of Germany by the Hitler regime, in 1934, and initially a Finkelstein backer, repudiated the anti-Coudert crusade as a "campaign of smear," after her own "investigation and mature consideration."[22] At the same time, Coudert's camp did their own smearing of Finkelstein as a Communist sympathizer. While Democratic standard-bearers such as Lehman held firm behind their party's candidate, other liberals and antifascists publicly backed Coudert, including the head of the Jewish fraternal organization B'rith Abraham and La Guardia, who called the attacks on Coudert "indecent."[23] Coudert retained his seat in the state senate as voters swept a majority GOP government into state office, including former Manhattan prosecutor Thomas Dewey, who succeeded Lehman as Governor.[24]

The war barely interrupted the pursuit of Communists in New York City schools. As soon as soldiers demobilized, the BHE picked up the Coudert cases that still needed prosecution. In October 1948, the board officially fired its last Coudert suspect, Samuel Margolis, the CCNY library assistant who claimed that Annette Sherman had misidentified him on the

May Day, New York City, 1941. (New York State Archives, Albany.)

prompting of Coudert staffers.²⁵ More significant was the BHE's *failure* to dismiss CCNY public-speaking instructor Francis J. Thompson, whose case lingered even though Thompson, after serving as an army intelligence officer during the war, long since had moved to a job at Johns Hopkins University in Baltimore.²⁶ Thompson successfully appealed his 1946 dismissal to the acting state commissioner of education, who ruled that the BHE not only had failed to prove that Thompson was a Communist, but also that membership in the Communist Party could not serve as grounds for dismissal as long as the party was legal in the state of New York. The Thompson ruling, unsuccessfully appealed by the BHE to the new permanent commissioner, spurred efforts in the state legislature to craft a law explicitly forbidding Communist Party membership to public employees, including teachers. Such a statute, the Feinberg Law, would be passed the following year and used for dismissing teachers through the 1950s.²⁷

Re-funded and reauthorized by the state legislature, in the coming years Coudert worked to guarantee the legacy of his investigation. He and his staffers made the committee's final report available to guide anticommunist legislators and school administrators across the nation in setting up similar investigating committees "with teeth," as one correspondent put it.²⁸ Coudert also made the committee's files available to police agencies and the city boards of education despite earlier assurances from Windels that the files would closed. Well after the Joint Legislative Committee to Investigate the Public Education System of the State of New York finally shut down in 1944, the Coudert files, including extensive lists of suspects and their accusers, were circulated to police, school administrators, and even private colleges for use in cases during the McCarthy period proper.²⁹

Repercussions

The Coudert investigation severely weakened the New York teachers-union locals. It did not, however, break them. That effectively was done by their parent union, the AFT, abetted by the American Federation of Labor (AFL). That fall and the following spring, even before Coudert's first public hearing, AFT President George S. Counts and his executive council methodically set about expelling the New York locals from the national union, using the same "bad faith" arguments that were used by liberals in attempting to purge the local since 1932 and that were passed on to Coudert and Windels. On the pretext of helping Locals 5 and 537 regain membership in the city's AFL-controlled Central Trade and Labor Council, Counts initiated an investigation that did little more than attack the locals for being under "communist control."[30] Having lost half their membership and lacking access to AFT mailing lists, Locals 5 and 537 struggled to mobilize support.[31] Counts mounted an aggressive campaign through the union's press and public relations network, manipulating union rules to call a national referendum in which expulsion would be decided on a simple majority vote, a violation of the union constitution requiring two thirds of the delegates at a national convention. Counts called the referendum more "democratic"; the New York teachers accused him of ending democracy in the AFT "under the guise of extending democracy." The anticommunists handily won the vote, held in June 1941. Although Locals 5 and 537 challenged its legality, Counts immediately chartered the Teachers Guild, still headed by Henry Linville, to replace Local 5. In place of the CTU, Counts set up a college teachers committee that lacked full union status. The New York locals, which had contributed more members to the national teachers union than any other locals and which had forged a union that changed the terms of public school and college employment, were thrown out of the AFT and the AFL. College teacher unionism was dealt a blow from which it would not recover until the 1970s. Though Local 5 hung around in weakened form as Local 555 of the United Public Workers, an affiliate of the Congress of Industrial Organizations, it was dying a slow death.[32]

The replacement of Local 5 with the Teachers Guild, which had been waiting in the wings, sniping at its rival, cooperating with Coudert, and openly conniving with AFL anticommunists, looked suspiciously like something that Counts and his supporters had planned since taking over the national union in the summer of 1940. Communication between Counts and Guild leaders, including Linville, suggests that the liberals in the national leadership did in fact aid the anticommunist union in raiding and undermining Locals 5 and 537, an act of "dual unionism" officially forbidden by the AFL. Counts also met openly with representatives of the Guild as early as the fall of 1940, as the Coudert probe was just unfolding.[33] In this manner, the liberals' anticommunism clearly trumped their liberal values, especially their professed commitment to procedural democracy. Before the expulsion referendum was even decided in June, Counts already negotiated the terms of the Guild's readmission with Linville, who in April set up a semiofficial "provisional committee" to manage the Guild's reentry into the AFT. That provisional committee, ignoring Counts's lip service to democratic values, immediately established a litmus test for joining the new union, interrogating prospective members along lines quite like those used by the Coudert committee. Ultimately Linville demanded the exclusion, along with Communists and unrepentant former Communists, of radical Socialists and Lovestoneites about whom he and others had "misgivings," settling old scores against former opponents such as Lovestoneite Ben Davidson for having cooperated with Linville's Communist rivals after the 1935 split.[34]

Henry Linville did not get to enjoy the full fruits of his labor. He was killed in early October 1941, when the car his brother-in-law was driving ran off a remote mountain road near Blowing Rock, North Carolina. He was seventy-five years old.[35] Most of his associates and friends eulogized him for his greater accomplishments. John Dewey praised his friend for his "fair mindedness" and his "unswerving enthusiastic faith in democracy." He was "a soldier in the ranks of our common humanity." Abe Lefkowitz remembered his "closest associate in many a heroic battle" for being one of only six men to march in the first women's suffrage parade and the first to "advocate and launch a teacher union movement," for whom the AFT "stands as his monument." Few could forget, however, his crusade against communism. It was, they suggested, the test of his "intellectual integrity."[36]

Nationally, the AFT followed the course set by Counts, Green, and Linville into the 1960s. After the war, according to historian Marjorie Murphy, "For the AFT the most important issue was to recover a national image of educational responsibility in the wake of its 'radical' past."[37] Yet, however Counts and his supporters may have justified the expulsion of the left as a *professional* house cleaning, the defeat of communism remained one of the union's principle goals. When in 1948 the House of Representatives opened new investigations of the now-renamed Local 555, Counts did not hesitate to reiterate the liberal countersubversive myth that Communists in the 1930s, still identified according to the behavioral test, ran Local 5 according to the dictates of the Comintern. As he believed they were "under the discipline" of the party, Counts emphatically denied Communists the right to teach in public schools.[38]

The Teachers Guild, now Local 2 of the AFT, continued to support the anticommunist crusade even as McCarthyism expanded in the 1950s to target not just Communists in unions, but also teacher trade unionism in general. Guild leaders found themselves in the increasingly tenuous position of endorsing academic freedom and publicly opposing New York's new anticommunist Feinberg Law on constitutional grounds, while denying fundamental constitutional protections, such as the Fifth Amendment, to teachers who refused to cooperate with local and national inquisitions.³⁹ As before, invoking one's rights under the Fifth Amendment was regarded as an act of concealment, "conduct unbecoming," and evidence of bad faith. Still complaining about the Rank and File faction's advocacy of "mass action" and "class war," Lefkowitz, now the principal of Brooklyn's Samuel Tilden High School though still a Guild member, rehashed before Congress Local 5's entire history, dredging up and embellishing old grievances about the Communists' "dilatory and disruptive tactics," and their "Hitler technique of misrepresentation," as well as their "efforts to enmesh our brilliant, idealistic youngsters, uninformed as to their true objectives, and often not mature enough to realize they were being used."⁴⁰

In 1960, younger militants, among them future AFT leader Albert Shanker, who was a former graduate student of Dewey's at Teachers College, merged Linville's Guild with an ad hoc high-school-teachers group, forming the United Federation of Teachers (UFT). In fall 1961 the UFT struck for collective bargaining rights, along with higher pay, increased benefits, and a voluntary dues checkoff—all the elements of genuine union recognition. The strike forced the city to agree in principle to UFT demands and to hold a union representation election in December 1961, which the UFT won. The former Teachers Guild thus became the sole collective bargaining agent for public-school teachers, closing out rivals, including the old Local 5 (now Local 555), which had shrunk to a fraction of its former size. Ironically, the Guild achieved one of the key goals of the communist left, passing on some of its militant legacy. According to historian Clarence Taylor, however, what the UFT gained in collective bargaining rights and contract achievements, it lost in the broader political mobilization, intense commitment to racial and social justice, and regular community involvement of Local 5's "social unionism linking community concerns."⁴¹ After the establishment of the UFT, Local 555 dissolved, its members absorbed into the new union.⁴²

Dramatis Personae

After the committee's breakup, in 1942, Coudert and his staffers went their own ways. Coudert served six terms as a Republican representative for the 17th Congressional district on Manhattan's Upper East Side, retiring in 1958. He was replaced in Congress by future mayor John Lindsay. In Congress, Coudert cultivated a conventionally conservative voting record on appropriations and foreign policy, while demanding limits on Pentagon spending and presidential war authority. He remained a resolute anticommunist.⁴³ Windels, still a Wall Street lawyer, served on several prominent civic committees, including New York's Regional Plan Association, the Committee of Fifteen, and the Citizen's Transit Committee, through which he pushed the consolidation and modernization of the city's debt-ridden transit system into the publicly owned and operated Metropolitan Transit Authority.[44] Phillip W. Haberman, Jr., after serving as an air force intelligence officer during the war, had a successful career as a corporate lawyer. He represented the Republicans on various state and local commissions until his death in 1971. He continued to pursue Communists in state employment well into the 1960s.[45] J. G. L. Molloy faded from public life until the late 1950s, when as president of the Greenwich Village Association he led efforts to block Robert Moses, New York's czar of urban renewal, from running a highway through Washington Square Park.[46] Robert Morris, one of Coudert's junior staffers, became chief counsel for the Senate Internal Security Subcommittee, otherwise known as the McCarran committee, which had nearly unlimited powers to investigate communist subversion in American life at the height of McCarthyism. He enjoyed the opportunity to revisit the Coudert investigation when former witnesses and suspects, including William Canning, were brought in for questioning. In the late 1950s, Morris unsuccessfully ran as a conservative for United States Senator in the Republican primaries in New Jersey against moderate incumbent Clifford Case.[47]

Like many of his young colleagues at CCNY, Canning served in the armed forces, reaching the rank of sergeant before being discharged in 1945. Then, after brief stints at small colleges in Ohio, he left teaching, eventually landing a job as a technical editor at Grumman Aerospace Corporation in Bethpage, Long Island, not far from Babylon, where he had grown up. In the early 1950s, he reprised the role of informant before the McCarran committee, helping it cast its inquisitorial net more widely by freely elaborating on the history he had already given of alleged Communist infiltration into New York's municipal colleges. His wife, Edna, also served the committee as an investigator.[48] Bernard Grebanier retired in the 1964, after a long career as a popular English professor, poet, dramatist, and highly regarded writer on Shakespeare. As the *New York Times* obliquely put it, he "was not remembered fondly by some of his colleagues" for cooperating with the Coudert committee, but, reluctant witness or not, he never regretted his testimony.[49]

Overall, the colleagues whom Grebanier and Canning fingered did not fare so well. For most, the firings ended their academic careers, as they encountered the first stages of the decades-long academic blacklist against suspected communists and uncooperative witnesses. A handful managed to survive in the academy, including CCNY historian Moses Finkelstein, who taught briefly at Rutgers University in Newark, New Jersey, under a new name, M. I. Finley, only to be fingered again by Canning and another former Columbia graduate student before the McCarran committee in 1951. After searching for academic work throughout the United States, Finley then moved to England, where he found a post at Cambridge University and became one of the leading classical historians in the English language, a reputation he already was beginning to acquire at Rutgers.[50] Other Coudert committee victims worked in Popular Front organizations (for instance, Kenneth Ackley in the International Workers Order), and some, such as Herbert Morais and Nelle Lederman, found positions in left-wing unions such as the United Electrical Workers.[51] Arnold Shukotoff, the first president of the CTU and an English tutor at CCNY, also remained on the left but under a different name and in a radically new occupation. As Arnold Shaw, he became a songwriter, music producer, and author, promoting rock and roll in its early years and turning out histories of jazz, pop, and rock, including a biography of activist calypso singer Harry Belafonte.[52]

Most of the younger men, and even some in their thirties such as Ackley and David Goldway, enlisted, serving the military at all ranks and in a variety of roles, some of them at surprisingly high levels of trust. Clearly, Henry Klein's political affiliations caused the army little concern, as it put him in charge of maintaining morale among fellow soldiers in Paris. He expressed admiration for the army's "far-flung network" of educational activity, "based upon developing in soldiers a democratic understanding of the war through democratic discussions during duty hours." Walter Neff worked as a psychologist in a rehabilitation unit in India, getting battle-scarred soldiers back onto active duty. He received a commission as lieutenant in 1945 without any indication that his history in New York had followed him to Asia. Jack Foner reportedly served in a baking unit until a pamphlet that he wrote on American history found its way to Washington, D.C., at which point he was transferred into a teaching position. Of the many Coudert victims who remained in touch with Morris Schappes, only former CCNY biology instructor Max Weisman, commissioned as a lieutenant in the army field artillery, reported any doubts about his loyalty. In June 1943, he was grilled by a Pentagon representative on his alleged membership in the Communist Party, as well as his participation in the Teachers Union.[53]

While for the most part the Rapp-Coudert casualties were left to their own grim job prospects, the party did not abandon them. Even before

Coudert released the final report, former BC and CCNY faculty found an outlet for their academic talents when Local 555 opened the School for Democracy on Astor Place, in January 1942; the school was soon incorporated into the party's far-flung system of worker education as part of a reinflated Popular Front strategy. Under the direction of Howard Selsam, the school put more than a dozen ousted municipal-college instructors back in the classroom, including Walter Neff, Morris U. Cohen, and Philip Foner. Some were paid for their work. Seymour Copstein and Morris Schappes lectured on poetry, while Lewis Balamuth taught a natural science class. David Cohen set up the school library. Selsam taught his popular treatise *What Is Philosophy?* to hundreds of the many thousands of students of various age groups and occupations who flocked to the school and its successor, the Jefferson School, until the federal government forced the project to close in 1955. Historian Marvin Gettleman estimated that the School for Democracy/Jefferson School, taken with other party schools of the 1940s, constituted "what was probably the most extensive adult education system ever seen up to that time." The School for Democracy even brought some employment opportunities: The president of one engineering company tracked down competent scientists who were fired by CCNY and BC at a school function to ask them to work in military research and development. He recruited Balamuth, Cohen, Iven Hurlinger, and Lloyd Motz for projects developing radar, ultrasonics, optics, and other, sometimes-highly-classified technologies.[54]

Conclusion
The Coudert Legacy

The red scare resumed shortly after the war, in the wake of the largest strike wave in American history and a Republican sweep of both houses in the 1946 midterm elections. As Republicans took over Congressional committees, they passed broadly repressive laws and relaunched legislative inquiries into the political activities and affiliations of liberals and the left. Although it was abetted by the Truman administration, which among other things initiated a loyalty oath for State Department employees in 1947, the emerging witch hunt took on a distinctively conservative character, targeting labor unions aggressively and openly attacking the New Deal. Even explicitly anticommunist unions such as the Teachers Guild (TG) and the American Federation of Teachers (AFT) winced under the full force of the crusade, which reacted feverishly to deteriorating relations between the United States and the Soviet Union, especially after the detonation of the first Soviet atomic bomb in 1949, the Communist ascent to power in China that same year, and the outbreak of the Korean War in 1950.[1]

In New York, the passage of the Feinberg Law, in 1949, reflected this mounting hysteria, as it opened the next chapter in the city's history of school purges. In applying the new law, the state forced teachers to sign oaths pledging loyalty to national and state constitutions while disavowing membership in organizations deemed subversive by the New York State Board of Regents. The year before Feinberg's passage, Sam Tilden High School social studies teacher Louis Jaffe received a punitive transfer for writing an article on academic freedom for a professional social studies newsletter, as well as for teaching about the United Nations and atomic warfare in a manner judged by his principal, the Teachers Guild's Abe Lefkowitz, to "over emphasize a point of view contrary to that of America and the United Nations to favor the Soviet Union and her satellites." His case led to a broader investigation of suspected Communist teachers, including Jaffe, Alice Citron, and six of their colleagues, all of them active in Local 555 (one was the local president), who after signing their Feinberg oaths were brought before Superintendent of Schools William Jansen, the author of racist textbooks that Citron and her colleagues objected to years earlier, to be interrogated about their membership in the Communist Party, not yet even officially designated subversive by the Regents. The teachers refused to answer Jansen's queries, arguing that his right to pose them had not been reviewed in the courts and suggesting that he was motivated by anti-Semitism (all the accused were Jewish). All eight were suspended and then fired in spring 1951.[2]

The following year, in the related case of New York City mathematics teacher Irving Adler, the United States Supreme Court upheld Feinberg and similar loyalty laws limiting the First Amendment rights of public-school teachers to hold unpopular political views.[3] The court reasserted Oliver Wendell Holmes's principle, glibly enunciated half a century earlier, that one's right to a job was not protected by the First Amendment. Effectively the decision authorized boards of education to use the threat of dismissal to control the broader political life of their employees, and to do so according to lists drawn up by political appointees such as New York's regents. Moreover, boards could control teachers' social life as well, since the law and the courts allowed interrogations about groups school employees belonged to, the race of the people with whom they spent their free time, and even the music they listened to, all in the interest of conducting behavioral tests of their political affiliations. Often school boards reached their conclusions on the basis of secret testimony and affidavits supplied by unreliable police informants. As its way was cleared by the courts, New York City's Board of Education proceeded over the next several years to interrogate more than a thousand public-school employees, forcing at least two hundred to resign and firing thirty-three.[4]

Other cases tested the rights of witnesses before legislative inquiries to invoke the Fifth Amendment. Faculty and staff at Brooklyn College (BC), Hunter College, and City College of New York (CCNY) who escaped Coudert's net found it catching up to them as they were called before the McCarran committee in 1952 and pressed on their earlier testimony. Anyone who invoked the Fifth was suspended and then fired, their appeals blocked by state and federal benches, which upheld the requirement in Section 903 of New York City's charter that public employees waive their constitutional protection against self-incrimination. The case of Hunter philosophy professor V. J. McGill, whose criticism of Deweyan psychology earned him the enmity of Sidney Hook, along with a denunciation by Hook to the Coudert staff, was in many ways typical, though unlike others he was given a hearing by the Board of Higher Education (BHE) rather than summarily discharged. McGill tried to testify to his own earlier membership in the party while excusing himself from naming others, a strategy that some call the "diminished Fifth." That approach had already been blocked by the federal judiciary, which ruled that once witnesses testified about themselves they waived their Fifth Amendment protection (called the "waiver rule").[5] McGill confessed to membership before the senate committee, adding that the Communist Party, which he claimed he left in 1941, "hadn't a place in this country—hadn't really ever had any," even though he had been a supporter through the war years. In later proceedings, he offered to help the BHE by persuading two former comrades at Hunter to confess. McGill's cooperation did him little good. He was fired in September 1954 for lying thirteen years earlier in private testimony before the Coudert committee, for "set[ting] himself up as the arbiter to say what questions he shall answer and what questions he shall not answer ," and for his earlier membership in the party, which the BHE investigating committee thought still rendered him unfit to be a teacher. BC English professor Frederic Ewen, publicly named by Grebanier in 1940 but never confirmed under oath by a second witness, found himself similarly entrapped, but he quit, announcing his resignation before the McCarran committee.[6]

The conservative drift of the federal courts prevailed through most of the 1950s, cut crosswise by dissenting opinions such as William O. Douglas's in *Adler*, in which he warned that tests like Feinberg would turn schools into "spying projects" with teachers pressured to prove their loyalty by exposing their colleagues. Eventually, when Earl Warren took over as chief justice, the center of gravity on the bench shifted toward an activist defense of free speech. On June 17, 1957, a day that critics of the Warren court labeled "Red Monday," the dam of anticommunist repression began to crumble, as the majority ruled in favor of First Amendment protections in four cases against loyalty investigations, the two most famous being *Yates versus the United States* and *Sweezy versus New Hampshire*. For veterans of the Coudert inquisition, that dam had already begun to crack the year before. Among the landmark decisions of the new Warren court was the case of BC's Harry Slochower, professor of German literature for twenty-seven years, whose party membership before 1941 was in little doubt. Slochower's evasive testimony during the Coudert inquiry and his invocation of the Fifth before the McCarran committee led to his summary dismissal in 1952 by BC President Harry Gideonse, upheld by the BHE, under article 903. In its 1956 decision, the court held unconstitutional that provision in the New York City charter, as it denied due process to fired employees. Although *Slochower versus the Board of Higher Education* still allowed boards and schools to fire employees for their political views, professors in New York's municipal colleges could no longer so easily be forced to choose between lying and fingering their colleagues. The framework of incrimination employed by the Coudert committee with the connivance of the BHE and others had begun to come down.[7]

The Coudert Logic of Incrimination

Over all of these cases, the Coudert inquisition cast its heavy shadow. Many of them merely picked up where Coudert and Windels left off. Suspects brought before McCarran included people such as Slochower, Ewen, and McGill, whom McCarran's chief of staff Robert Morris and the rest of the Coudert investigators had interrogated in private session, put on their suspect lists, or put before Coudert's public tribunals in 1940 and 1941. Confirmations of membership by second witnesses were now forthcoming from ex-Communists willing to testify to the McCarran committee and the BHE, including Bella Dodd, who had turned to radically conservative Catholicism upon losing faith in the party after the war. While the statute of limitations on perjury had run out, the board could still fire employees for lying. The McCarran investigations and the BHE hearings and judgments afterward followed the same logic of interrogation and incrimination as the Coudert inquiry, though by the 1950s that process had become more routinized and polished—the accused were backed into invoking the Fifth and then summarily fired for "conduct unbecoming" and "untrustworthiness."

As in the earlier Coudert cases, the BHE's charges were equivocal, doubly loading the accusation of bad faith with evidence not just of lying under oath, but also of the assumed deceitfulness and inherent malevolence of communism and the Communist Party. Much of that evidence came directly from the Coudert investigation, including recycled "findings" of the Dewey trial and narrow readings of Communist texts, including Richard Frank's essay on education and the Popular Front, which was selectively requoted through the 1950s.[8] As before, accused teachers were fired for their beliefs, even as defenders of McCarran and the BHE such as Gideonse insisted that beliefs were not at issue and that the cases did not involve First Amendment questions or matters of academic freedom. The accused, Gideonse declared, "chose to appeal to the Fifth Amendment with a smoke-screen of language designed to make their action appear as a defense of freedom and democracy rather than a carefully planned avoidance of perjury charges." As Gideonse claimed he saw it, the teachers' "unprofessional conduct" was nothing more than the act of lying and evading questions. The "basic issue," he insisted, "can be stated in the simple language I used at the time of the Rapp-Coudert investigation, that is to say: Can teachers be trusted in a public and professional capacity if they perjure themselves—irrespective of whether they are Republicans, Democrats, or Communists?"[9]

For teachers who were called before BHE tribunals, it was especially frustrating to run into this insistence that the only issue was that they had lied in response to the "$64 question" about membership, as their "perjury" was used by the board's trial examiner, Irving Kiendl, to rule out of discussion any evidence or testimony about the exemplary records of the accused teachers or about other motivations behind the firings. Yet the "premise that a member of the Communist Party is unfit to teach" because she simply was a communist, whether she lied about it or not, stood at "the very heart" of all of these proceedings, the union's legislative representative Rose Russell argued as she presented the cases for Jaffe, Citron, and their colleagues in 1950. "We want to meet the issue of the right of a teacher," Russell continued, "regardless of what his political views or opinions or associations may be, to be judged by his own character and competence and fitness professionally as a teacher, and that is the heart of the question of academic freedom."[10] Russell understood, as few others did, that Feinberg and Section 903 were conveniences that allowed the board to use the debate over the Fifth Amendment and lying to mask the ideological intent of the purges. Such conveniences helped V. J. McGill's trial committee pretend that firing McGill and two other Hunter faculty "in no way involves any curtailment or invasion of academic freedom," since the dismissals primarily hinged on their "concealment" and perjury. Technically, Gideonse argued, by invoking the Fifth Amendment while under the jurisdiction of the city charter, a faculty member effectively "discharged himself."[11]

After the war, this subterfuge about Communists lying themselves out of jobs wrapped liberal countersubversive mythology in even deeper obscurity. Liberals such as Gideonse were no more hesitant to dismiss suspected Communists after 1945 than they were in the immediate wake of the Coudert investigation. Increasingly, however, they felt the need to distance themselves from conservative inquisitors who made no secret of their contempt for the First Amendment or the principles of academic freedom. Moreover, as political scientist Earl Latham noted, "Anti-New Dealers were not always scrupulously careful to distinguish between liberals and Communists." They "seemed to say that subversion and social reform were the same thing."[12] Gideonse, speaking for liberal anticommunists in general, called these conservative facets of the red scare—which were personified in Senator Joe McCarthy—"vulgar cases of reactionary constraint," arguing that they "should be resisted with all the vigor the academic profession can mobilize." But hunting down and firing reds, which Gideonse took great pride in doing, was another matter, since communists by definition practiced bad faith. Purging Communists was not a repression of ideas and opinions, but rather a front in the *defense* of academic freedom, protection against its insidious corruption by professors and teachers who, Gideonse insisted, had joined an international conspiracy undermining the dispassionate pursuit of the "truth." "It is necessary to stress that this is not a matter of the individual's political *beliefs*," Gideonse declared, "but a question of deliberate *action* through the acceptance of disciplined submission to the dictation of the party." Teachers College Professor John Childs, who after entering the leadership of the purged AFT became the state chairman of New York's newly formed anticommunist Liberal Party, similarly asserted that membership in the Communist Party did not come under the protection of the First Amendment or of academic freedom, as the "definite act" of joining the Communist Party "repudiates both the canons of scholarship and the kind of conduct that is basic in the work of a teacher in a democracy."[13]

But boards and administrators could not help revealing what everyone, liberal anticommunists included, really had in mind. References to the countersubversive myths of force and violence, indoctrination, direction from Moscow, and adherence to the party line ran like red threads through these inquiries, as inquisitors unpacked what they thought the "act" of joining the party entailed. McGill could readily have been fired just for having lied to the Coudert committee. But Charles Tuttle, the conservative BHE member who chaired the hearings, and his prosecutor, Michael Castaldi, who had argued the BHE's case in *Adler* before the United States Supreme Court, held that the real substance of McGill's unfitness lay in his original membership in the Communist Party. It was McGill and his two associates "themselves," the trial committee insisted, "who, on their own confession, abandoned academic freedom and accepted secrecy and [a] clandestine relationship" with the Communist Party. Castaldi drew this lesson largely from the Coudert inquiry, citing the Ackley case for evidence of the international conspiracy of which McGill and his fellow Hunter Communists were "active members," subject to the "rigid iron discipline so inherent in Party obligations," including the propagation of the "party line" to their students and the "forceable [sic] overthrow of our Government."[14] Clearly it was not the case, as Gideonse had vowed, that *anyone* who lied deserved to be fired. Only Communists, according to him, lied by nature, and only Communists really mattered.

The Liberals and McCarthyism

Historian Ellen Schrecker recently asked "why so many liberals consciously abandoned their political principles during the McCarthy era."[15] Schrecker's question inadvertently frames the history of liberal anticommunism much as liberals themselves have done since World War II: seeing themselves as having been collectively sympathetic to the Popular Front in the depths of the Depression, liberal anticommunists date their fall from grace to coincide with the Cold War, blaming their descent into the fervor of McCarthyism on the faults of Communism itself—on Soviet threats to international peace, on revelations of Stalin's brutality, and on the bad faith of rank-and-file communists who allegedly perjured themselves, countenanced spying, indoctrinated others, and fomented conflict in an otherwise functional democracy. The misleading chronology of that story allows liberals to diminish their own role in vilifying and purging communists and in stoking up McCarthyism.

I think the history of the Rapp-Coudert inquisition should lead us to replace Schrecker's question with another one: what were the ideas, attitudes, and interests that led so many liberals to join in the red scare from 1934 on? It is not evident that John Childs or Harry Gideonse abandoned any principles at all as they participated in the mounting anticommunist frenzy. They simply maintained a point of view set during the Depression, a liberal version of the countersubversive tradition that framed communism according to the myths of subversion, indoctrination, class war, and the party line. It was the very same mythology that Henry Linville and John Dewey articulated in the 1933 "Dewey Trial"; that George S. Counts, William Heard Kilpatrick, and the reconstructionists presented on the pages of *The Social Frontier*; that Counts and Bill Green used to justify the expulsion of Locals 5 and 537 from the AFT; and that Windels and Phillip W. Haberman, Jr., incorporated into the Coudert committee's body of reports, interviews, and evidence files that were cited throughout the McCarthy era proper.[16] The notion that Communists are ideologically disposed to acts of bad faith traced back to liberal arguments in the 1930s, echoed across the decades by full-blown liberal anticommunists such as Gideonse, who, warning that "the Reds are after your children," intoned that Communists "have no ethics in our sense of the word; they subordinate morality to the interests of what they call 'the class struggle,'" which they seek to foment on campus.[17] Belief in "class war" automatically leads them to other acts of bad faith, including "demoralizing our youth," which Gideonse, forgetting that the only issue was lying, attributed to Communists, as "instrument[s]" of the Soviets. That cause and effect relation was so automatic that even if a Communist had not yet indoctrinated students or subverted democracy, she inevitably would do so. Morris Schappes underscored the absurdity of this notion when he quipped about the 1950 dismissal proceedings against his friend Alice Citron and her colleagues, "Miss Citron and the other seven teachers are not guilty of misconduct in the classroom, but at some time in the future they might be. So they ought to be fired now before they can be guilty!" Schappes called these "preventive dismissals"; one of the lawyers defending the eight teachers called it guilt "by anticipation."[18]

To be sure, there were Communist Party members who acted in bad faith. We know of a few who misrepresented themselves as patriots and public servants while spying for the Soviets. Other leaders and members of the Communist Party of the United States preached democracy and "communism as twentieth-century Americanism" while conniving with authoritarians or just envisioning a dictatorship of the proletariat after the revolution. But the vast majority of Communists did nothing of the sort; moreover, it should hardly be necessary to point out that such dishonesty and misrepresentation could and can be found in the ranks of any American political party, throughout our history. Where would the Democratic Party be if we held it and its adherents accountable, in the same way that Windels and Coudert did Communists, for the bad faith and corruption of Tammany? Or for the sinister violence of Southern Democrats, who gave lip service to democracy through the 1960s while defending lynching and Jim Crow? Where would the Republican Party be if we held it accountable for the bad faith of Republicans who thought the proper response to the strike waves of 1934 was to hire armed Pinkertons and mount machine guns on the roofs of auto factories and steel plants? Some Americans do condemn Democrats and Republicans for such bad faith, but few would advocate denying them employment as public servants on account of their party affiliations. Moreover, how should we hold liberals accountable for *their* acts of bad faith—the inauthentic endorsements of civil liberties and the false protestations against the methods of McCarthyism, some of which they either invented or supported from the outset, while endorsing the witch hunt's goals? How should we hold them accountable for their misrepresentations of the communist record in purges and probes such as Coudert's, well before the Cold War enveloped the entire nation in the vulgar hysteria of the 1950s? Consider the mere costs in lost jobs and squandered talent of liberal Fusion activist and paragon of bipartisanship Paul Windels's manipulations of William Canning and others to "clean house" at CCNY and BC. Or consider the lasting harm that Counts's AFT purge did to the movement for college teachers unions. What sort of reckoning would they or other liberals and social democrats have called for were it communists playing prosecutor instead of a "progressive" liberal?

The Silence of the Communists

In 1967, the United States Supreme Court finally weighed in on the side of academic freedom in a case involving the refusal to sign Feinberg oaths by five instructors at the State University of New York in Buffalo. Three years after the University of California's free-speech movement that inaugurated the campus upheavals of the 1960s, in *Keyishian versus the Board of Regents of the State of New York,* the Warren court, by explicitly extending the First Amendment to protect teachers' rights of free speech and association, significantly opened up the intellectual life of the American academy, which was already stirring with a new sense that dissenting views had to be valued in their own right. But as Marjorie Heins, the leading expert on that aspect of our nation's legal history, has pointed out, the damage done to the American academy and to American intellectual life in general by the red scare was enormous—the legacy of anticommunist repression was not just an erosion of constitutional rights, but also "an impoverished political discourse that persists in the United States to this day."[19]

This study has underscored the active liberal contribution to an important episode in the history of American anticommunism. It has also exposed some of the costs of anticommunism to our democracy. Not only did Coudert's and similar inquisitions inhibit the free exchange of ideas in the academy, but with the assent of liberals they also augmented a process of excluding valuable perspectives from American politics. It is this need to purify political and cultural landscapes, a liberal as well as conservative compulsion, that Michael Paul Rogin found so dangerous in the countersubversive tradition, the manifold forms of which he recognized in the life of the nation at the end of the twentieth century.[20] That penchant for countersubversion marks a fundamental contradiction in the liberal perspective, which preaches an open society yet silences points of view perceived to be threatening to political stability as liberals understand it. One could argue as well that this particular form of liberal intolerance has been partly responsible for recent attacks on academic freedom, especially those that once again involve punishing faculty for political views expressed off campus. While some of those violations of free speech can be traced to outside pressure, including repressive measures in the "war on terror," much of the motivation for censuring outspoken academics comes from the university itself, in its role as institutional guardian of liberal values.

Additionally, liberal countersubversion has been responsible for purging from American political culture substantive criticism of liberal views, especially of the liberal endorsement of capitalist economic relations. Among the viewpoints abandoned along the path postwar liberals mapped toward the American dream was the Marxist tradition—the "class war view" so ardently attacked by John Dewey and Henry Linville in 1933, on which they and others based the countersubversive myth that communist teachers lie and indoctrinate others because they are communists. While the Marxist understanding of a modern society divided by class and propelled by class conflict did not entirely disappear from the American academy, thanks in part to liberal intellectuals like Linville and Dewey it was decisively removed from the rational discourse of American pluralism, its bipartisan "vital center," as the consummate liberal anticommunist Arthur Schlesinger, Jr., called it. Thereafter, based in large part on liberal arguments similar to those advanced by the Coudert inquisition, believing that class explained anything in American society relegated one to "outer totalitarian darkness" and to exclusion from or silencing in the academy, public schools, labor unions, the book market, Hollywood, and other institutions in which American life is depicted and its terms negotiated. Even after McCarthyism had abated in the 1960s, Marxists still were pushed to the political fringes, to be at best tolerated but not heard—as were frank observations about the reality of "class struggle," like those offered by Isidore Begun or Lena Tulchen in 1935. That national evasion of class, its nearly complete exclusion from the intellectual and political life of the nation, continued with some exceptions (e.g., a few college classrooms and marginal left-wing organizations) into the twenty-first century, until steadily declining standards of living for middle class Americans and malfeasance in the financial sector made attention to economic and class inequality as unavoidable as it was in 1935.

The One Percent

I'm sure readers will ask, Why all this attention to liberal countersubversion? Why does it matter that liberals were so much more entangled in McCarthyism's beginnings than previously thought, especially since the dominant forces behind political repression in the 1950s were so obviously conservative? One reason is that the role of liberals in shaping Coudertism—and, thus McCarthyism—signals the broader significance of communism's absence, as well as the intellectual and political consequences of its erasure from American life. Certainly, as historians, we cannot adequately evaluate McCarthyism without a clearer sense of its origins. Nor can we sufficiently understand the legacy of American liberalism, nationally and internationally, without better understanding its contempt for the left, for Marxism as well as communism, and its role in clearing the postwar world of competing ideologies and points of view. Thus, the emphasis in this study on liberal anticommunism's ideological origins, which liberals have always taken pains to deny.

But there is another, contemporary reason for recovering this original liberal hostility to communism and its "class war view." It is useful to reflect on that history because liberals still shape the discussion of class in ways similar to those employed by forebears such as John Dewey, Henry Linville, and George S. Counts. Only recently has it become acceptable once again to speak openly of class, couched in terms of a conflict of interests between ordinary, working Americans and the "one percent"—the bankers, real estate speculators, hedge-fund managers, and billionaire politicians whose misconduct has made the matter of economic inequality so pressing. Real measures of disparities in wealth, income, and privilege are now easy to find in the American press, thanks in part to widely publicized reports by former Labor Secretary Robert Reich and others that economic inequality has reached levels not seen since just before the 1929 stock market crash. The extremely disproportionate wealth of the top one percent of Americans is now so commonly recognized that it has captured the meaning of the term "one percent." Somewhat less au courant are reports of precipitous declines in standards of living and economic security for the remainder of Americans, including full-time employees, around seventy-five percent of whom live paycheck to paycheck. Author and television personality Neal Gabler stunned readers of the *Atlantic* recently with his account of his own family's "financial impotence." Despite years as a successful journalist and freelance writer, Gabler, like many Americans, found that his bank account could not cover a mere four-hundred-dollar emergency.[21]

Quite a few journalists and politicians even trace the problem of rapidly growing inequality to a "class war," referring to everything from the 2008 banking crisis and bailout to the 2017 Trump tax cut, to the creation by United Airlines of an exclusive and secret eatery for preferred customers. Yet much of the current alarm about class war, as the United Airlines story suggests, is either overstated or confused.[22] Part of the confusion comes, as journalist Thomas Frank regularly reminds us, from the tendency of Tea Party conservatives such as Sarah Palin to intentionally conflate class privilege with the cultural elitism that she and others loathe about the liberal bastions of New York, Washington, D.C., and California—the core antagonism of a "cultural class war" defined by issues of authenticity rather than actual inequalities of wealth and power. Supposedly moderate Republicans and Libertarians have muddied the issue further by attacking even limited forms of progressive taxation, income redistribution, or social welfare as "class warfare" against the real capitalist "job creators" on Wall Street.[23]

But a good deal of the confusion about class still comes from the liberal tradition itself and, more specifically, from the historical commitment of many liberals to anticommunism and to the eradication of the "class war view" from American political life. Much recent liberal attention to impending "class war" has been less a matter of recognizing the reality of systemic and structured exploitation, as is addressed in the Marxist canon, than of lamenting the demise of the middle class as the pillar on which American social stability and moral authority supposedly rested from World War II until the 1980s. Such complaints largely amount to blaming the rich and the greedy for destroying the American dream by inflicting class war on "average Americans" or "against the rest of us," as one writer for Salon recently put it.[24]

Viewed against the history recounted in this book, current liberal discourse on economic inequality appears simply to reverse what liberals such as Counts or Kilpatrick said on the eve of World War II: instead of celebrating and justifying the birth of a new moderate political economy that "solved" the problem of "class warfare" through economic expansion, technological revolution, and the creation of a new middle class, present-day liberals such as Reich just warn about what is going to happen now that the very same middle class is being destroyed. Their main interest is in restoring the vital center, but they also must understand—or at least one hopes they do—that, in the long run, that center probably will not hold. The writer in Salon noted, "one doesn't have to be a socialist to be concerned about the ever-widening gap between the 'haves' and 'have-nots' in our society." Yet one might have to be a socialist, a Marxist, or even a communist to understand why and how such class inequalities and antagonisms came about. For the most part, thanks to the legacy of Coudertism, in the United States few such people have been allowed a public voice in discussions of these problems over the years. We are intellectually and politically impoverished by that silence.

Acknowledgments

> "You think you run an archive," Meadows said. "You don't. It runs you."
>
> —*John le Carré, A Small Town in Germany*

This study began in an archive: the investigation files of the Rapp-Coudert Committee housed at the New York State Archives in Albany. For several years, that extraordinary mass of documents ran my life. My bondage to their collections notwithstanding, I owe great thanks to the staff at the New York State Archives and to many other archivists and librarians for saving, preserving, and organizing the historical documents used in this study. I am especially beholden to Bill Gorman, without whose guidance I would never have made it through the first Rapp-Coudert folder. Additionally, I would like to thank Sidney Van Nort at the CCNY archives for her special help getting me started and the Department of Philosophy at San Francisco State for generously providing several boxes of V. J. McGill's papers.

Other collections that deserve special mention are Tamiment Library and Robert Wagner Labor Archives at NYU, the Kheel Center Archives at Cornell University, the Brooklyn College Archives, the Hunter College Archives, La Guardia/Wagner Archives at La Guardia Community College, the American Jewish Archives in Cincinnati, the Rare Books and Manuscripts Collection at Columbia University, the Columbia Oral History Collection, the Teachers College Archives, the University Archives at SUNY Buffalo, the Hoover Institute Library and Archives at Stanford University, the New York City Municipal Archives, the Franklin Delano Roosevelt Papers in Hyde Park, the National Archives in Washington, D.C., the New York Public Library Special Collections, the NYU Archives, the American Jewish Historical Society in New York City, the

Drawing of Sylvia Wald for *Winter Soldiers: The Story of a Conspiracy Against the Schools* (New York: CDPE, 1941).

American Philosophical Society in Philadelphia, the Union Theological Seminary Archives, Pennsylvania State University's Special Collections, and Duke University's Special Collections. Thanks as well to Union College's superb library staff, who have helped me find sources and publications on the remote shelves and storage facilities of several upstate New York libraries. Union College also deserves some thanks for providing travel money, sabbatical leaves, and student research support, which granted summer stipends to Sarah O'Connor and Adam Koslin for their excellent archival and bibliographic groundwork. Thanks also to Fred Nachbaur, Will Cerbone, Eric Newman, the rest of the Fordham University Press staff, E. A. Williams of Laughing Saint Editorial, and the manuscript's outside readers for their artful guidance and skilled work helping turn an unwieldy manuscript into a streamlined book.

A special thanks to Janet Braga and her staff at the New York State Archives Partnership Trust for providing superb reproductions of photos from the archive's collections. Also, I am grateful to the Sylvia Wald and Po Kim Foundation for preserving the artistic legacy of Sylvia Wald, whose 1941 drawing graces the cover of this book. Wald provided that piece for a fundraising publication of the Committee in Defense of Public Education as part of her enduring commitment to the protection of civil rights and liberties, as well as the pursuit of racial equality. The drawing's appearance here implies nothing further about her or the foundation's political interests or affiliations.

Friends, colleagues, and family who have helped move this project to completion include Jim Collins, Vera Conrad, Blanche Cook, John Cramsie, Lisa Davis, Phillip Deery, Barbara Falk, John Feffer, Jean Finley, Marvin Gettleman, Ben Harris, Ed Johanningsmeier, David Kranz, Steve Leberstein, Lori Marso, Mark Mishler, Ellen Schrecker, Jack Selzer, Carol Smith, Emily Socolov, Dan Tompkins, and Larry Wittner, plus Marge Heins and Mike Slott for their perceptive reviews of the entire manuscript, and especially Michelle Chilcoat, whose impeccable judgment, close reading of many drafts, and constant encouragement and devotion kept me going over the last ten years.

Abbreviations Used in the Endnotes

AAUP Papers: William Thomas Laprade Papers, 1660–1975, Manuscript Department, David M. Rubenstein Rare Book and Manuscript Library, Duke University, Durham, North Carolina. These papers are unprocessed.

Ackley Case Files: Case files of Kenneth Ackley, Board of Higher Education Papers, La Guardia/Wagner Archives, La Guardia Community College (electronic access).

BHE minutes: Minutes of the Board of Higher Education (BHE). Bound copies of the BHE minutes are kept in the office of the trustees at City University of New York headquarters on 535 E. Eightieth St., New York.

Boas Papers: Franz Boas Papers, American Philosophical Association, Philadelphia.

Braunlich Case Files: Case files of Arthur Braunlich, Board of Higher Education Papers, La Guardia/Wagner Archives, La Guardia Community College (electronic access).

CCF Papers: American Committee for Cultural Freedom papers, TAM 23, Tamiment and Robert F. Wagner Labor Archives, Bobst Library, New York University.

CDPE: Committee for the Defense of Public Education.

CDPE Accused: CDPE, "Report on Testimony of Accused Teachers," B7 F10, Schappes Papers (see below). There appears to be no extant copy of the full transcript for these public hearings, which were held at the end of March 1941. This nonpaginated collection of individual statements is one of the few sources of public testimony by CCNY faculty and staff who were accused by history tutor William Canning. Other parts of the testimony were read into the records of several BHE trials.

Citron Papers: Alice B. Citron Papers (SC-2097), American Jewish Archives, Cincinnati.

"Communist Tactics": Henry Linville, "A Study in Communist Tactics," typescript dated June 1936 in B2 F15, Kheel 5279.

Copstein Case Files: Case files of Seymour Copstein, Board of Higher Education Papers, La Guardia/Wagner Archives, La Guardia Community College (electronic access).

Coudert Papers: Frederic R. Coudert, Jr., Papers, Rare Books and Manuscripts, Butler Library, Columbia University, New York.

Coudert, Sr., Papers: Frederic R. Coudert, Sr., Papers, Rare Books and Manuscripts, Butler Library, Columbia University, New York.

Coudert, Sr., Reminiscences: "Reminiscences of Frederic Rene Coudert," transcript of interviews by Allan Nevins, Henry Steele Commager, Owen Bomard, 1949 and 1950 (1972), Columbia Oral History Project, Columbia University, New York. These are the reminiscences of Fritz Coudert's father.

Counts Interview: Interview with Dr. George Counts by Warren Seyfert, Southern Illinois University, 21 September 1964. Typed transcript (copy). George S. Counts Papers, Special Collections, Columbia Teachers College Library, New York. Accessible online though Teachers College's proprietary Pocket Knowledge system (http://pocketknowledge.tc.columbia.edu/home.php).

Dewey Correspondence: *Correspondence of John Dewey*, Barbara Leven, Anne Sharpe, and Harriet Furst Simon, eds., electronic edition (Charlottesville, Va.: InteLex Corp., 1999–).

Dewey Trial Minutes (1939): "Minutes of a Special Meeting of the Teachers Union Held at High School of Commerce, Saturday, April 29, 1933 at 1:30 p.m.," transcript copy in B7 F4A, Kheel 5015.

Dewey Trial Report (1939): Local 5 (AFT), "Report of the Special Grievance Committee of the Teachers Union," 29 April 1933. A copy is in B1, Kheel 5279.

Duces Tecum: "In the Matter of the Application to Vacate a Subpoena Duces Tecum Addressed to the Teachers Union of the City of New York by Charles J. Hendley, President." B6 F2, Kheel 5445.

EW: John Dewey, *the Early Works, 1859–1952* (Carbondale: Southern Illinois University Press, 1967–1972).

Ewen Papers: Frederic Ewen Papers, TAM 277, Tamiment and Robert F. Wagner Labor Archives, Bobst Library, New York University.

Abbreviations Used in the Endnotes 261

Foner Case Files: Case Files of Phillip Foner, Board of Higher Education Papers, La Guardia/Wagner Archives, La Guardia Community College (electronic access).

Grebanier Interview, 1974: Interview with Bernard Grebanier conducted by Marvin Gettleman, 1974, Columbia Oral History Project, Columbia University, New York.

Grievance Report: "Report of the Special Grievance Committee of the Teachers Union," presented 29 April 1933 to special meeting of general membership, copy in B1, Kheel 5279.

Hendley Papers: Charles James Hendley Papers, TAM 109, Tamiment and Robert F. Wagner Labor Archives, Bobst Library, New York University.

Hook Papers: Sidney Hook Papers, Hoover Institution Archives, Palo Alto.

Kheel 5015: Teachers Union of the City of New York Records, 1916–1964, Kheel Center for Labor-Management Documentation and Archives, Catherwood Library, Cornell University, Ithaca.

Kheel 5279: New York Teachers Guild Records, 1923–1957, Kheel Center for Labor-Management Documentation and Archives, Catherwood Library, Cornell University, Ithaca.

Kheel 5445: Teachers Union of the City of New York Records, 1920–1942, Kheel Center for Labor-Management Documentation and Archives, Catherwood Library, Cornell University, Ithaca.

Kilpatrick Diaries: Diaries of William Heard Kilpatrick, William Heard Kilpatrick Papers, Teachers College Archives, Milbank Memorial Library, Teachers College, Columbia University. Accessible online though Teachers College's proprietary Pocket Knowledge system (http://pocketknowledge.tc.columbia.edu/home.php). They are organized most clearly by date, which is how they will be cited here.

La Guardia Papers: Fiorello H. La Guardia Papers, Municipal Archives, New York.

Lazar FOIA: Documents from the FOIA collection of Ernie Lazar, https://archive.org/details/lazarfoia.

LW: John Dewey, *Later Works, 1925–1953* (Carbondale: University of Southern Illinois Press, 1981–1990).

Matthews Papers: J. B. Matthews Papers, Manuscript Department, David M. Rubenstein Rare Book and Manuscript Library, Duke University, Durham, N.C.

McGill Report (1954): "In the Matter of Charges Preferred by the Board of Higher Education's Special Committee on Section 903 of the City Charter, the Feinberg Law and Related Matters against V. Jerauld

McGill, Louis Weisner, and Charles W. Hughes: Report of the Trial Committee to the Board of Higher Education," typescript, 17 September 1954, B2, Board of Higher Education: Academic Freedom Cases, Tam 332, Tamiment and Robert F. Wagner Labor Archives, Bobst Library, New York University.

McGill Trial: "In the Matter of Charges Preferred by the Board of Higher Education's Special Committee on Section 903 of the City Charter, the Feinberg Law and Related Matters against V. Jerauld McGill, Associate Professor in the Department of Psychology and Philosophy, Hunter College," stenographic trial transcript. B2, Board of Higher Education: Academic Freedom Cases, Tam 332, Tamiment and Robert F. Wagner Labor Archives, Bobst Library, New York University.

MW: John Dewey, *Middle Works, 1899–1924* (Carbondale: University of Southern Illinois Press, 1981–1990).

Neff Case Files: Case files of Walter Scott Neff, Board of Higher Education Papers, La Guardia/Wagner Archives, La Guardia Community College (electronic access).

Parry Papers: William T. Parry Papers, ca. 1919–1984, University Archives, Capen Library, State University of New York, Buffalo.

Public Hearings, December 1940: New York (State) Legislature. Joint Committee on the State Education System, *In the Matter of the Investigation of the Public Educational System of the State of New York, Pursuant to Joint Resolution of the Senate and Assembly of the State of New York, Duly Adopted March 29, 1940*, hearings held at New York County Supreme Court, New York City, 4 December 1940. (Albany: State of New York, 1941).

Rapp-Coudert CCNY: Rapp-Coudert Investigation Collection, Record ID: 00210, City College Archives, City College Library, City College, New York.

Rapp-Coudert Interim Report (1941): New York (State) Legislature Joint Committee on the State Education System, *First Report of the Joint Legislative Committee to Investigate Procedures and Methods of Allocating State Moneys for Public School Purposes and Subversive Activities* (Albany: Fort Orange Press, Inc., 1941).

Rapp-Coudert Report (1942): Joint Legislative Committee to Investigate the Public Educational System, *Report of the New York City Subcommittee Relative to the Public Schools and Colleges in the City of New York* (Albany: [New York State Legislature], 1942).

Schappes Case Files: Case files of Morris U. Schappes, Board of Higher Education Papers, La Guardia/Wagner Archives, La Guardia Community College (electronic access 15 June 2016).

Abbreviations Used in the Endnotes 263

Schappes Papers: Morris U. Schappes Papers, P–57, American Jewish Historical Society, New York.

Selsam Papers: Howard Selsam papers, Rare Book and Manuscript Collection, Butler Library, Columbia University, New York.

Selsam, et al. (1941): "The Matter of the Application to punish Howard Selsam, Maurice Ogur, Harry Slochower, Frederic Ewen and Murray Young Severally for Contempt," submitted January 3, 1941, by Paul Windels for the Joint Legislative Committee to Supreme Court (New York County), Hon. Benedict A. Dineen, Justice, presiding, copy in RC521.

SISS Education: *Hearings before the Subcommittee to Investigate the Administration of the Internal Security Act and Other Internal Security Laws of the Committee on the Judiciary,* United States Senate ("McCarran Committee"), on Subversive Influence in the Educational Process.

SISS Pacific Relations: *Hearings before the Subcommittee to Investigate the Administration of the Internal Security Act and Other Internal Security Laws of the Committee on the Judiciary,* United States Senate ("McCarran Committee"), on the Institute for Pacific Relations.

Slochower Papers: Papers of Harry Slochower, Accession Number 88–007, Brooklyn College Archives and Special Collections, Brooklyn College.

UFT Papers: United Federation of Teachers Records WAG 022, Tamiment and Robert F. Wagner Labor Archives, Bobst Library, New York University.

Windels, Jr., Interview: "Interview with Paul Windels," interviewed by Kenneth Durr, Security and Exchange Commission (SEC) Historical Society, 8 September 2007, http://c0403731.cdn.cloudfiles.rackspacecloud.com/collection/oral-histories/windels_091807.pdf.

Windels, Sr., Reminiscences: "Reminiscences of Paul Windels," interviewed by Owen Bombard, 1949/1950, Columbia Oral History Project 1972, Columbia University Archives and Special Collections, New York (microform).

Withrow (1941): "In the Matter of the Application to Vacate Subpoenas Served upon William J. Withrow, Alfred J. Brooks, Herbert M. Morais, Dale Zysman, Howard Selsam, Henry L. Klein and Samuel Kaiser against the Joint Legislative Committee to Investigate the Educational System of the State of New York, Supreme Court of New York State, Appellate Division—First Department, Index No. 12164–1941."

Some explanations of sources:

1. All of the records of the Rapp-Coudert inquiry were given to the New York State Police sometime after World War II. They remained

there until archivists at the New York State Archives in Albany saved them from an incinerator. They are now housed at the state archives as the "Investigation Files of the Rapp-Coudert Committee," Series Number L0260. The entire Rapp-Coudert collection is organized according to numbered folders, by which they are cited here (for example, "RC560"). The records are now accessible in microfilm form (available at several locations, including the Tamiment and Robert F. Wagner Labor Archives at NYU), but the folder organization remains.

2. Over the past few years, the records of the American Federation of Teachers (AFT) and its various New York locals at the Cornell University's Kheel Center have deteriorated significantly, to the point that many of the folders are no longer properly labeled and some have been moved to the wrong boxes. Having accessed those records at several points in the past ten years, I have cited them according to whatever reference points are possible.

3. The archives of the Teachers College at Columbia University are now only accessible online for a fee through the College's proprietary Pocket Knowledge system (http://pocketknowledge.tc.columbia.edu/home.php). The quality of the digital reproduction is undependable. There is no discernable logic to their organization, and researchers are at the mercy of the system's search engine.

4. Copies of *The Staff*, the Communist Party "shop" paper for the Brooklyn College Unit, can be found in RC91. Copies of *Teacher Worker*, its counterpart at City College of New York (CCNY), are at the CCNY Library's Archives and Special Collections.

Notes

Introduction

1. Robert S. McElvaine, *Great Depression* (Random House, 1984), Chapters 13–14; William E. Leuchtenburg, *Franklin D. Roosevelt and the New Deal* (Harper & Row, 1963), Chapter 13; *New York Times*, 5 December 1940, 1.

2. *New York Times*, 7 December 1940, 30; *New York Times*, 1 December 1940, F7; *New York Times*, 5 December 1940, 29.

3. *New York Times*, 30 September 1940, 35; *New York Times*, 15 December 1940, 172; *New York Times*, 6 December 1940, 1, 46.

4. *New York Times*, 3 December 1940, 1; Simon W. Gerson, "Coudert School for Slander," *New Masses*, 37 (17 December 1940), 14–15; *Sun* (New York), 2 December 1940, 1.

5. *PM* 5 December 1940, 9.

6. Public hearings, December 1940, 19; *New York Times*, 1 December 1940, 64.

7. Roughly $8.5 million when adjusted for inflation.

8. Rapp-Coudert Report (1942), 6–12. Most of the 684 names on the list were of suspected Communists but it included some fascists. "Summary of Evidence Secured against Individuals Now in the Educational Systems" (RC560).

9. Justice William O. Douglas (dissenting), *Adler versus Board of Education of the City of New York*, 342 US 485 (1952); Marjorie Heins, *Priests of Our Democracy: The Supreme Court, Academic Freedom, and the Anti-Communist Purge* (New York: New York University Press, 2013), 3.

10. Heins, *Priests*, 202; Paul F. Lazarsfeld and Wagner Thielens. Jr., *Academic Mind: Social Scientists in Time of Crisis* (Glencoe, Ill.: The Free Press, 1958), 79, 80, 192, 218–20; John McCumber, *Time in the Ditch: American Philosophy and the McCarthy Era* (Evanston, Ill.: Northwestern University Press, 2001), xvi, 12.

11. Quoted in Heins, *Priests*, 66. See Elizabeth Casey private testimony, 14 January 1941, 2–5 (RC524).

12. Robert Justin Goldstein, *Little Red Scares: Anti-Communism and Political Repression in the United States, 1921–1946*, ed. by Robert Justin Goldstein (Surrey, England: Ashgate, 2014), Preface; M. J. Heale, "Citizens versus Outsiders: Anti-Communism at State and Local Levels, 1921–1946," in *Little Red Scares*, ed. by Robert Justin Goldstein, 63–68; Ellen Schrecker, *No Ivory Tower: McCarthyism and the Universities* (New York: Oxford University Press, 1986), 69–70.

13. Stephen Leberstein, "Purging the Profs: The Rapp Coudert Committee in New York, 1940–1942" in *New Studies in the Politics and Culture of US Communism* (New York: Monthly Review Press, 1993), 95.

14. There have been many "crimes of the century," beginning with the sensational 1932 kidnapping of Charles and Anne Lindbergh's one-year-old son. J. Edgar Hoover appropriated the term for the sedition case of Communists Julius and Ethel Rosenberg in 1951. See Ellen Schrecker, *Many Are the Crimes: McCarthyism in America* (Princeton, 1998), xviii.

15. Mason B. Williams, *City of Ambition: FDR, La Guardia, and the Making of Modern New York* (New York: W.W. Norton, 2013).

16. Richard Hofstadter, "Pseudo-Conservative Revolt—1955," in *Radical Right*, ed. by Daniel Bell (Garden City: Doubleday & Company, 1963), 64–66, 69–71, 79; Daniel Bell, "Interpretations of American Politics—1955" in *Radical Right*, ed. by Daniel Bell, 39, 46–48, 51.

17. Goldstein, *Little Red Scares*, xiv.

18. Michael Paul Rogin, *Intellectuals and McCarthy: The Radical Specter* (Cambridge, Mass.: MIT Press, 1967). See also Athan Theoharis, "Politics of Scholarship: Liberals, Anti-Communism, and McCarthyism," in *Specter: Original Essays on the Cold War and the Origins of McCarthyism*, ed. by Robert Griffith and Athan Theoharis (New York: New Viewpoints, 1974), 265.

19. Michael Paul Rogin, *Ronald Reagan, the Movie and Other Episodes in Political Demonology* (Berkeley: University of California Press, 1987), 35.

20. With the exception, of course, of Ronald Reagan himself, about whom Rogin weaves his explorations of national anxiety, guilt, and vilification. See Rogin, *Ronald Reagan*, Chapter 1.

21. Rogin, *Ronald Reagan*, Chapter 4.

22. On early anticommunism as primarily conservative in origin, see Goldstein, *Little Red Scares*, xiv.

23. My argument here is odds with the views of most Deweyans, including Robert Westbrook, who traces Dewey's anticommunism to his alliance after the Moscow trials with "anti-Stalinist misfits." See Westbrook, *John Dewey and American Democracy* (Ithaca: Cornell University Press, 1991), 464. Similarly, see also Christopher Phelps, *Young Sidney Hook: Marxist and Pragmatist* (Ann Arbor: University of Michigan Press, 2005), 7, 9, 101, 196; Ellen Schrecker, "Mc-

Carthyism: Political Repression and the Fear of Communism," *Social Research*, 71 (Winter 2004), 1043.

24. Historian Judy Kutulas dates the birth of liberal anticommunism to the expulsion of Elizabeth Gurley Flynn from the ACLU in 1940. See Kutulas, *Long War: The Intellectual People's Front and Anti-Stalinism, 1930–1940* (Durham: Duke University Press, 1995), 197, 200. Political theorist Corey Robin similarly accepts the view that "liberal Democrats" only "reluctantly joined" conservatives in the red scare after World War II. See Robin, *Fear: The History of a Political Idea* (New York: Oxford University Press, 2004), 182.

25. John Dewey, *Liberalism and Social Action* (New York: G. Putnam and Sons, 1935/1963), 55–56.

26. Schrecker dates the liberal academic demand for good faith much later, to the early 1950s, as a "formula" for helping manage external conservative anticommunist attacks on the academy. See Schrecker, "Subversives, Squeaky Wheels, and 'Special Obligations': Threats to Academic Freedom, 1890–1960," *Social Research*, 76 (Summer 2009), 532.

27. Theoharis, "Politics," 267.

28. John Earl Haynes and Harvey Klehr, *VENONA: Decoding Soviet Espionage in America* (New Haven: Yale University Press, 2000).

29. See Maurice Isserman, "Open Archives and Open Minds: 'Traditionalists' versus 'Revisionists' after Venona," *American Communist History*, 4 (2005), 215–23.

30. For example, Robin D. G. Kelley, *Hammer and Hoe: Alabama Communists during the Great Depression* (Chapel Hill: University of North Carolina Press, 1990); Fraser M. Ottanelli, *Communist Party of the United States: From the Depression to World War II* (New Brunswick: Rutgers University Press, 1991); and Daniel Horowitz, *Betty Friedan and the Making of The Feminine Mystique: The American Left, the Cold War, and Modern Feminism* (Amherst: University of Massachusetts Press, 1998).

31. Clarence Taylor, *Reds at the Blackboard: Communism, Civil Rights, and the New York City Teachers Union* (New York: Columbia University Press, 2011), Introduction.

32. Theoharis, "Politics," 268.

1. The Threshold

1. *Brooklyn Eagle*, 3 December 1940, 1.

2. Simon W. Gerson, "Coudert School for Slander," *New Masses*, 37 (17 December 1940), 14–15.

3. Windels, Sr., Reminiscences, 58–61. Windels, Jr., Interview, 1; Alyn Brodsky, *Great Mayor: Fiorello La Guardia and the Making of the City of New York* (New York: Truman Talley Books/St. Martin's Press, 2003), 150.

4. Windels, Jr., Interview, 1–2; Brodsky, *Great Mayor*, 415.

5. Brodsky, *Great Mayor*, 150, 287, 358, 415; Windels, Sr., Reminiscences, 83–84.
6. Windels, Sr., Reminiscences, 22–26, 40, 51–53; *New York Times,* 16 December 1967, 41; Robert A. Caro, *Power Broker: Robert Moses and the Fall of New York* (New York: Vintage Books, 1975), Chapter 27.
7. Public hearings December 1940, 8; Walter Goodman, *The Committee: The Extraordinary Career of the House Committee on Un-American Activities* (New York: Farrar, Strauss and Giroux, 1968); Maurice Isserman, *Which Side Were You On?: The American Communist Party during the Second World War* (Middletown, Conn.: Wesleyan University Press, 1982), 67–72.
8. *Brooklyn Eagle*, 11 August 1940, 10A.
9. Public hearings (December 1940), 8, 14, 19–20.
10. *New York Times,* 3 December 1940, 22.
11. Public hearings (December 1940), 16.
12. William G. Mulligan, Jr., (counsel to the TU Local 5) to the Members of the Investigating Committee, 2 December 1940; B14 Coudert Papers; public hearings (December 1940), 127.
13. Gerson, "Coudert School," 14–15.
14. In the 1920s and 1930s, this broad latitude was supported by liberal reformers such as United States Supreme Court Justice Felix Frankfurter and New Dealer James M. Landis. See Louis B. Boudin, "Congressional and Agency Investigations: Their Uses and Abuses," *Virginia Law Review*, 35 (February 1949), 143–213; and James M. Landis, "Constitutional Limitations on the Congressional Power of Investigation," *Harvard Law Review,* 40 (December 1926), 153–221. Conservatives tended to weigh individual liberties more heavily than the need for "administrative efficiency" (as Landis justified legislative investigatory power). One prominent critic of "inquisitorial activities of Congress" was Frederick Coudert, Sr., father of the New York state senator who presided at the December 1940 hearings. Coudert's alarm appears to have depended on whose liberties were endangered—in this case, corrupt industrialists. See Frederic R. Coudert, [Sr.], "Congressional Inquisition versus Individual Liberty," *Virginia Law Review*, 15 (April 1929), 537–52.
15. Tim Hurley, "Seabury, Samuel," in *Great American Judges: An Encyclopedia*, vol. 2, ed. by John R. Vile (Santa Barbara: ABC-CLIO, 2003), 683–88.
16. Herbert Mitgang. *Man Who Rode the Tiger: The Life and Times of Judge Samuel Seabury* (New York: J. B. Lippincott Company, 1963), 159–60, 266–81; Brodsky, *Great Mayor* 260–70.
17. Mitgang, "Man Who Rode," 167, 180, 203–18.
18. Tammany's popularity and service to New York's diverse population presents a set of problems that cannot be addressed here. See Dennis R. Judd and Todd Swanstrom, *City Politics: Private Power and Public Policy* (New York: Longman Press, 1998), Chapter 3; and Lynne W. Weikart, *Follow the Money: Who Controls New York City Mayors?* (Albany: State University of New York Press, 2009), Chapters 2–3.

19. Mitgang, "Man Who Rode," 159–65.
20. Mitgang, "Man Who Rode," 180, 229, 239.
21. On likening the Communist Party to Tammany, see *New York Times,* 8 December 1940, 96.
22. Brodsky, *Great Mayor,* 402.
23. Paul Windels to Frederic Coudert, Jr., August 2, 1940, B14 Coudert Papers; Minutes of the Executive Session, 2 December 1940 of Rapp-Coudert Committee, B16 Coudert Papers.
24. Mulligan also ran events for La Guardia's 1933 campaign, served under Windels in the office of Corporation Counsel, and spearheaded with Windels, Haberman, and economist Adolph Berle the unification of the city subway system. See Mitgang, "Man Who Rode," 175, 323, 344; and Samuel Seabury, Oren C. Herwitz, and William G. Mulligan, Jr., "Legislative Investigating Committee," *Columbia Law Review,* 33 (January 1933), 1–27.
25. Boudin, "Congressional," 212–13; William G. Mulligan, Jr., "Brief in Support of Petition to Be Heard," in the Matter of Public Hearings before the Joint Legislative Committee to Investigate the Educational System of the State of New York, 2 December 1940 (RC601).
26. Selsam, et al., (1941), 12; Paula M. Coudert, Paul B. Jones, and Lawrence Klep, *Frederic R. Coudert: A Biography* (New York: Paula M. Coudert, 1985), 47.
27. See for example Section 903a of the City Charter. See also *Slochower versus Board of Higher Education of New York City,* 350 US 551 (9 April 1956).
28. "Grand Juries May Inquire into Political Beliefs Only in Narrow Circumstances," *Columbia Law Review,* 73 (April, 1973), 867–81; Lawrence H. Chamberlain, *Loyalty and Legislative Action: A Survey of Activity by the New York State Legislature, 1919–1949.* (Ithaca: Cornell University Press, 1951), 85–86.
29. William G. Mulligan, Jr., to Members of the Investigating Committee, 2 December 1940, B14 Coudert Papers.
30. Mitgang, "Man Who Rode," 176, 309.
31. Windels, Sr., Reminiscences, 159–62.
32. Mulligan to Investigating Committee, 2 December 1940.
33. Windels later claimed this was not his objective, but the public hearing transcripts and other documents tell a different story. See Windels, Sr., Reminiscences, 153.
34. On Mulligan's complaints about lacking access to evidence, see Mulligan to Joint Legislative Committee to Investigate the Educational System of the State of New York, 11 March 1941 (RC601).
35. Jeffrey B. Perry, "Pseudonyms: A Reference Aid for Studying American Communist History," *American Communist History,* 3 (2004), 75; Richard Frank, "Schools and the People's Front," *Communist,* 16 (May 1937), 432–45.
36. Public hearings (December 1940), 137, 225; Frank, "Schools," 440.
37. Frank, "Schools," 435.
38. Public hearings (December 1940), 226; Frank, "Schools," 437.

39. Frank, "Schools," 445.

40. Isidore Begun private hearing, 28 October 1941, 17, 28 (RC523); Selsam, et al., (1941); deposition of William G. Mulligan, Jr., January 2, 1941, 7. Even William Canning, the former party member who served as Windels' prime witness at CCNY, admitted that he was unaware of Frank's article. See William H. Canning private hearing, 28 January 1941, 54 (RC576).

2. The Stooge Grebanier

1. Public hearings (December 1940), 22–24; Simon W. Gerson, "Coudert School for Slander," *New Masses*, 37 (17 December 1940), 14.

2. *New York Times,* 3 December 1940, 1; BC YCL, "General Grebanier, Dies' Stooge," leaflet, n.d. (RC506).

3. Gerson, "Coudert School," 14–15.

4. *New York Times*, 20 March 1977, 40; Dennis Wegman, "Winwar, Frances," *American National Biography Online*, February 2000, http://www.anb.org/articles/16/16-03551.html.

5. *New York Times,* 6 November 1931, 19; Grebanier interview, 1974; Murray Horowitz, *Brooklyn College: The First Half-Century* (Brooklyn College Press, 1981), 18.

6. Educational Investigation, Memorandum: 21 September 1940, No. 9 (RC47). According to the "Brooklyn College Suspect List," also in RC47 and "Grebanier's Private Testimony, January 30, 194—Names Not Mentioned in Public Hearing" (RC153), the informant in memo No. 9 was Harry Gideonse. See *New York Times,* 6 May 1931, 1; *New York Times,* 29 May 1931, 1.

7. Horowitz, *Brooklyn College*, 27, 37–43; *New York Times,* 6 December 1933, 25; Grebanier interview, 1974; Educational Investigation, Memorandum: 21 September 1940, "Interview with Therese Wolfson, Brooklyn College, December 17, 1940," (RC357); BC Unit of the Communist Party, open letter "To the Board of Higher Education," 5 November 1936 (RC91); *Staff* 1 (1 June 1935), 4; *Staff* 2 (December 1935), 1, 8. BC Communists, however, insisted that even the dismissal of an abusive racist required due process. See *Staff* 2 (May 1936), 3.

8. Mario Cosenza to Paul Windels, 15 October 1940 (RC47); BC Citizens League, "Report of the Committee on Higher Education," 14 March 1939 (RC47); Grebanier private hearing, 23 October 1940, 7 (RC551).

9. Maurice Isserman, *Which Side Were You On?: The American Communist Party during the Second World War* (Middletown, Conn.: Wesleyan University Press, 1982), 3–7; Fraser M. Ottanelli, *Communist Party of the United States: From the Depression to World War II* (New Brunswick: Rutgers University Press, 1991), 21–27.

10. Isserman, *Which Side*, 12–13; Robert Cohen, *When the Old Left Was Young: Student Radicals and America's First Mass Student Movement, 1929–1941*

(New York: Oxford University Press, 1993), 137–39, 165. On the early shift to a Popular Front strategy in the United States, see Ottanelli, *Communist Party*, 47–54, 80–87; and Michael Denning, *Cultural Front: The Laboring of American Culture* (New York: Verso, 1998). On the ASU, see Joseph Lash private hearing, 17 June 1941, 18–19 (RC570).

11. Cohen, *When the Old Left*, 80–95, 109–17; Stephen H. Norwood, *Third Reich in the Ivory Tower: Complicity and Conflict on American Campuses* (New York: Cambridge University Press, 2009).

12. Grebanier private hearing, 23 October 1940, 12; Grebanier private hearing, 27 February 1941, 185 (RC551); McGill Trial, 20 November 1953, 17. Collegiate antifascist groups were not especially well organized. See Louie Miner private hearing, 17 June 1941, 4–7 (RC534).

13. Grebanier private hearing, 23 October 1940, 3 (RC551); Grebanier interview, 1974; *New York Times,* 4 December 1940, 1, 30.

14. Grebanier interview, 1974.

15. Grebanier private hearing, 23 October 1940, 24 (RC551).

16. Bernard D. N. Grebanier, "Stalinites Use Slander Machinery to Keep Honest Progressives in Line," *New Leader* (9 September 1939), copy in RC153.

17. Mark Graubard private hearing, 5 February 1941, 5–7 (RC529).

18. BC Branch of the Communist Party to Bernard Grebanier, 18 August 1939 (RC506, Subfolder 4).

19. "Ex-David Arden" [Grebanier] to BC Branch of the Communist Party, 23 August 1939 (RC506, Subfolder 4).

20. Bernard D. N. Grebanier, "An Open Letter to Students," *Vanguard* 6 October 1939, copy in RC506 Subfolder 4. Sidney Hook blamed the party for exposing Grebanier, thus forcing him into a position where he had to testify to the Coudert committee. But Grebanier publicized his own association with the party well before the Coudert inquiry was even authorized. See Sidney Hook, *Out of Step: An Unquiet Life in the Twentieth Century* (New York: Harper & Row, 1987), 253.

21. Grebanier interview 1974. *New York Journal American* (4 January 1940), copy in RC153; CCF, Minutes of General Membership Meeting, 1 October 1939; B2 F8, CCF Papers.

22. Much later, Grebanier insisted that Windels already knew most of those names, having gotten them from CCNY professor William Canning. "Of course, I was staggered," he claimed in 1974. "I did not supply a single name they didn't have." But that was not so: Grebanier testified against his colleagues several weeks ahead of the December hearing, long before Canning was ever interviewed. See Grebanier interview 1974; and Grebanier private hearing, 23 October 1940, 15–18 (RC551).

23. Grebanier private hearing, 23 October 1940, 13–15 (RC551).

24. Grebanier private hearing, 18 November 1940, 76 (RC551). Grebanier named several students as YCL members in later, private interviews. See

272 Notes to pages 43–52

Grebanier interview, 27 February 1941, 168–69. Identifying YCL members should not have been difficult. According to Miriam Marder, a former member of the YCL, YCL activists at BC were open about their affiliation. See Marder private hearing, 11 July 1941, 2–8, 23 (RC570).

25. Grebanier private hearing, 18 November 1940, 75–76, 78–79 (RC551). Klein, who shifted to the public schools, was among the eight Communist teachers named by Grebanier.

26. "Trial Brief—Examination of Grebanier," n.a., n.d., 17–18 (RC153). This document organizes and refines questions and statements from Grebanier's private depositions in October and November. Many of Grebanier's responses in the public hearings follow those in the trial brief verbatim.

27. Public hearing (December 1940), 52–54.

28. Public hearing (December 1940), 54–55; Grebanier private hearing, 18 November 1940, 76–80 (RC551). Although in the private hearing Grebanier assented to the statement quoted by Windels, he had clearly said just the opposite earlier in that interview and did so again a moment later, remarking that the "inspiration" for student demonstrations did not come from the faculty—that if the political agitation was "engineered," it was "not by my unit as such." He was obviously confused by Windels' questioning, thinking that by "unit" his interrogator meant the BC chapter of the YCL. In all other private statements, Grebanier consistently recalled a firewall between the faculty Communists and the BC chapter of the YCL.

29. *Brooklyn Eagle*, 3 December 1940, 1, 2.

30. *Brooklyn Eagle*, 4 December 1940, 14.

31. *New York Sun*, 2 December 1940, 1.

32. *New York Times*, 6 December 1940, 21.

33. Rapp-Coudert Report (1942), 6, 20.

34. Benjamin Gitlow private hearing, 24 April 1941, 4 (RC528).

35. Graubard private hearing, 5 February 1941, 1, 4–7, 33 (RC529).

36. Sidney Hook private hearing, 6 May 1941, 17–18 (RC530).

37. Granville Hicks private hearing, 20 May 1941, 50 (RC530).

38. Grebanier private hearing, 27 February 1941, 163–65, 173–74 (RC551).

39. BC Citizens League, "Report." Miriam Marder, who attended YCL meetings from 1938 to 1940, estimated that the organization had only one hundred members. She also reported virtually no contact between the campus YCL and BC faculty. Marder private hearing, 11 July 1941, 8, 17–18 (RC570).

40. Mario Cosenza to Paul Windels, 15 October 1940 (RC47). See also John E. Wade private hearing, 24 February 1941, 8–10 (RC547).

41. "Students Speak! It's Our Education! We'll Defend It!!!," pamphlet (stapled mimeo), n.a., n.d. [probably late May or early June 1941] (RC47).

42. *Staff*, 2 (January 1936), 3.

43. *New York Post*, June 9, 1943, 3 (clipping in RC144); *Brooklyn Eagle*, 4 December 1940, 14.

44. *New York Times*, 9 June 1939, 22; Mont Pelerin Society, "Inventory of the General Meeting Files (1947–1998)," Mont Pelerin Society, 2004–5. On the Mont Pelerin Society, see Kim Phillips-Fein, *Invisible Hands: The Making of the Conservative Movement from the New Deal to Reagan* (New York: Norton and Company, 2009), Chapter 2.

45. Public hearings, December 1940, 155.

46. Public hearings, 4 December 1940, 165, 172.

3. Coudertism

1. The provision in the city charter prohibiting employees' Fifth Amendment protection was declared unconstitutional by the USSC in *Slochower versus Board of Higher Education*, 350 US 551 (1956).

2. At first, the union retained one party-associated lawyer, Nathan Witt, which strained relations with Mulligan. See William G. Mulligan, Jr., to CDPE, 26 February 1941, B11 F13, Hendley Papers.

3. Many, however, were not able to escape later inquisitions based on the Rapp-Coudert records. These later victims included philosopher V. J. McGill, linguist Margaret Schlauch, historian Moses Finklestein (M. I. Finley), and literary critic Harry Slochower.

4. Charles Hendley, "Autobiographical Sketch" [1961], B1 F1, Hendley Papers.

5. Hendley to Arthur A. Boylan, 30 March 1930, B1 F4, Hendley Papers.

6. *Daily Worker*, 5 December 1940, 1, 4. Hendley joined the Communist Party in 1948. Hendley's "exclusion from the Socialist movement" came for "collaboration" with communists as Local 5 president. See Arthur McDowell to Hendley, 2 June 1938, B1 F13 Hendley Papers.

7. Hendley, "Autobiographical Sketch" [1961].

8. Hendley to Arthur Kallet, 18 March 1937, B1 F1 Hendley Papers; "A Portrait of Charles J. Hendley," [*New York Teacher*], 18–19, B1 F1, Hendley Papers.

9. Page references are to public hearings (December 1940).

10. *New York Times*, 5 December 1940, 1, 2.

11. Hendley to Mike Gold, 2 September 1946 B1 F5, Hendley Papers.

12. *Teacher News*, 9 (20 September 1940), 1, 4; copy in B6 F2, Kheel 5445.

13. Walter Rautenstrauch to Charles Hendley, 30 April 1940; B6 F10 Kheel 5445; "Report of Investigator for the Coudert-Rapp Legislative Committee," 11 November 1940 (RC70). Though not an official member, Dodd worked for the Communist Party as a "nonparty Bolshevik." See SISS Education (1952), 3.

14. CDPE, "It's No Secret," n.d. (RC411); CDPE, "Truth about the Schools," n.d. (RC70).

15. SISS Education (1952), 3.

16. Bella Dodd, *School of Darkness* (New York: P. J. Kenedy and Sons, 1954), 2–3, 16–17, 22, 38–39; "Re: Bella Dodd," 3 January 1940 (RC416); trustees of Columbia University, *Catalogue, 1927–1928* (New York, 1928), 373.

17. Grebanier interview, 1974; Dodd, *School*, 53, 64.
18. Dodd, *School*, 58, 66, 69–70, 78.
19. Dodd, *School*, 62–63; Marion R. Mack private hearing, 4 December 1941 (RC561); *Staff* 2 (February 1936), 3.
20. Dodd, *School*, 74–77.
21. CDPE, "It's No Secret" New York State Economic Council, "Council Letter" (1 April 1940); B14 Coudert Papers.
22. Quoted in CDPE, "Truth about the Schools."
23. Lynne W. Weikart, *Follow the Money: Who Controls New York City Mayors?* (Albany: State University of New York Press, 2009), 23–26; George J. Lankevich, *American Metropolis: A History of New York City* (New York: NYU Press, 1998), 163–64, 176; Alyn Brodsky, *Great Mayor: Fiorello La Guardia and the Making of the City of New York* (New York: Truman Talley Books / St. Martin's Press, 2003), 295–300; Lawrence H. Chamberlain, *Loyalty and Legislative Action: A Survey of Activity by the New York State Legislature, 1919–1949*. (Ithaca: Cornell University Press, 1951), 69.
24. *New York Times,* 14 January 1940, D6.
25. *New York Times,* 10 January 1940, 16; Local 5 (AFT), "Over 1/2 a Million," February 1939 (RC407); Betty Moorsteen, "Teachers Tell First-Hand Stories of Chaotic Conditions in Schools," *PM* [1937]. By comparison, overcrowding stood at thirty-nine percent of classes in 1931. See Inez C. Pollack (Local 5 Auxiliary) to George J. Ryan (President of Board of Education), 12 June 1932; Clipping and letter in B2 F43, UFT Papers.
26. *New York Times*, 11 January 1940, 21; *New York Times*, 3 January 1940, 23.
27. *New York Times*, 1 February 1940, 19.
28. *Teacher News*, 7 (19 April 1939), 1; *New York Times*, 14 January 1940, D6; *New York Times*, 17 January 40, 17.
29. Already one third of localities had reduced teacher wages in response to the previous year's budget cuts. See *New York Times*, 27 January 1940, 1; *New York Times*, 20 January 1940, 1.
30. *New York Times*, 15 January 1940, 1.
31. *New York Times*, 13 February 1940, 1; *New York Times*, 22 February 1940, 24.
32. *New York Times*, 29 February 1940, 1; *New York Times*, 1 March 1940, 1; *New York Times*, 5 March 1940, 1.
33. *New York Times*, 6 March 1940, 3.
34. *New York Times*, 7 March 1940, 1.
35. *New York Times*, 31 March 1940, 1; *College Newsletter* (Local 537, AFT), 1 April 1940, 1.
36. *New York Times,* 31 March 1940, 68.
37. Chamberlain, *Loyalty*, 70.
38. See for instance Brodsky, *Great Mayor*, 409; Ellen Schrecker, *No Ivory Tower: McCarthyism and the Universities* (New York: Oxford University Press, 1986), 76.

39. *New York Times*, 1 March 1940, 19; "Bertrand Russell Litigation," *University of Chicago Law Review*, 8 (Feb 1941), 316. Russell's appointment was reversed by state courts. Chamberlain, *Loyalty*, 71.

40. *New York Times*, 29 February 1940, 1; *New York Times*, 27 March 1940, 1; *New York Times*, 11 March 1940, 8.

41. *New York Times*, 24 January 1940, 17; Prem Lata Sharma, *World Educational Reforms* (New Delhi: Sarup and Sons, 2004), 82–84; New York State Federation of Teachers Unions, "Call to a Conference on Federal and State Aid," 1 April 1939 (RC407).

42. *New York Times*, 28 March 1940, 1. La Guardia supported Rapp's bill on the instigation of Abe Lefkowitz of the Teachers Guild, the anticommunist union.

43. *New York Times*, 30 March 1940, 1, 9, 72.

44. Minutes of Board of Higher Education Meeting 20 November 1939, typescript carbon, (RC177); *New York Times*, 26 March 1940, 15.

4. Vichy's Lawyer?

1. Simon W. Gerson, "Coudert School for Slander," *New Masses*, 37 (17 December 1940), 15; Isidore Begun, "Rapp Investigation: A Letter from the Communist Party," 1 June 1940 (RC506).

2. *New York Times*, 29 January 1941, 1.

3. Gerson, "Coudert School," 14.

4. Frederic also spearheaded the campaign to bring the Statue of Liberty to New York City. See Virginia Kays Veenswijk, *Coudert Brothers: A Legacy in Law—The History of America's First International Law Firm, 1853–1993* (New York: Truman Talley Books/Dutton, 1994), 40, 52, 70–93.

5. Veenswijk, *Coudert Brothers*, 117; Coudert, Sr., Reminiscences, 10–11, 104.

6. Coudert, Sr., Reminiscences, 39–40; Veenswijk, *Coudert Brothers*, 147–51.

7. Similarly, the firm acted as a go-between for the French in the first two years of the Second World War. See Veenswijk, *Coudert Brothers*, 158–59, 173–74, 189, 214, 242–43.

8. Veenswijk, *Coudert Brothers*, 238; Paula M. Coudert, et al., 79.

9. Veenswijk, *Coudert Brothers*, 43–44, 55.

10. Gerson, "Coudert School," 15; *New York Times*, 5 March 1944, 18; *New York Times*, 23 December 1944, 1. Veenswijk argues that the Belgian gold was balanced by Belgian and French assets in American banks; however, the gold in Senegal physically passed through the Banque de France into Nazi hands during the war, and French assets in the United States would have been frozen after 1941 regardless of the disposition of Belgian gold in French possession. Moreover, what happened after 1945 concerned the French liability for the debt and would have had little effect on the gold's use as financial backing for the Nazi war effort. See Veenswijk, *Coudert Brothers*, 257–66; *New York Times*, 18 March 1942, 34.

11. *New York Times*, 26 March 1942, 11; "Case against Coudert," B6 F3, Kheel 5445.

12. Coudert, Sr., Reminiscences, 118–19.

13. *New York Times*, 27 March 1940, 11.

14. The Devany Law was incorporated as Section 12–a of New York State's civil service code, a pivotal part of the legal framework under which suspected teachers and staff were fired in 1941 and during the McCarthy period. See Lawrence H. Chamberlain, *Loyalty and Legislative Action: A Survey of Activity by the New York State Legislature, 1919–1949*. (Ithaca: Cornell University Press, 1951), 64–66. Coudert eventually became a close confidante of archconservative William F. Buckley. See Paula M. Coudert, et al., 83.

15. Paula Coudert, et al., 77; *New York Times*, 19 June 1940, 22; *New York Times*, 31 December 1940, 4.

16. *New York Times*, 23 April 1940, 17. Historian Ellen Schrecker identifies Coudert as a liberal "façade for an upstate legislative crack-down on the city's school budget." See Schrecker, *No Ivory Tower*, 76. Coudert also supported La Guardia in 1941. See *New York Times*, 17 October 1941, 1.

17. See Merwin K. Hart to Frederic Coudert, Jr., 3 April 1940, 1 May 1940, and 9 July 1940. See also Coudert to Hart, 19 April 1940, 2 May 1940, and 12 July 1940, B14 Coudert Papers.

18. "In the Matter of the Joint Legislative Committee to Investigate the Educational System of the City of New York, in the Matter of the Application to Punish Charles J. Hendley, President of the Teachers Union of the City of New York for Contempt, Supreme Court of New York, Justice C. B. McLaughlin," 16 October 1940, B6 F2, Kheel 5445; Hendley, "President's Column," *New York Teacher*, November 1940, typescript draft, B11 F12, Hendley Papers.

19. *PM*, 4 December 1940, 9.

20. See "Cases of Anti-Union Discrimination," a chart apparently composed by the Teachers Union office staff for Mulligan's use in the courts (B6 F10, Kheel 5445). See also New York City Teachers Union (Local 5 AFT), Teachers Union (New York), "You May Be Next! The Teachers Union Fight for Academic Freedom and Teachers' Rights as Citizens," pamphlet (8 June 1934), 12, copy in B11 F14, Hendley Papers; and *Unemployed Teacher* 1 (May 1933), 1. For other cases, see *Porteous Case: A Challenge to Teachers and the Community* (N.Y.: Teachers Union [1935]).

21. Executive Council of AFT, "Statement of Executive Council Regarding Membership List of Local 5," n.d., B6 F1, Kheel 5445.

22. *Duces Tecum*, deposition by Charles Hendley (18 October 1940). Hendley's arrest was attempted and then stayed by a state appellate judge just a few days before the public hearings in early December. See *New York Times*, 1 December 1940, 64.

23. Windels probably received an official copy from AFT Secretary Treasurer Irvin Kuenzli. See Kuenzli to Hendley, 5 November 1940, B6 F1, Kheel 5445;

and Bella Dodd, *School of Darkness* (New York: P. J. Kenedy and Sons, 1954), 121. The US Supreme Court eventually extended constitutional protection to the membership lists of all voluntary organizations, putting limits on such subpoenas in *Bates versus City of Little Rock* 361 US 516 (1960).

24. John E. Wade private hearing, 24 February 1941, 23 (RC547); Paula M. Coudert, et al., 50–51.

25. Public hearings, (December 1940), 257–59.

26. "List of Sponsors for Teachers Union," n.a., n.d., (RC416). The committee's stack of union dues cards for members sponsored by Selsam is in RC506.

27. Supreme Court of the State of New York, County of New York, "In the Matter of the Application to Punish Charles J. Hendley President of the Teachers Union of the City of New York, for Contempt," n.d., attached to documents entered into the courts by Local 5 on 14 October 1940, B6 F2, Kheel 5445; Local 5 (AFT), press release, "Our Answer to Senator Coudert," 29 October 1940, B6 F2, Kheel 5445; *New York Times,* 29 October 1940, 27.

28. Mulligan to Kuenzli, 9 October 1940, copy in B6 F10, Kheel 5445. Coudert also lied to the court to discredit Hendley, whom he claimed withheld all union files when Hendley provided everything but the lists. See *Duces Tecum*, deposition by Frederic Coudert, Jr., (16 October 1940); *New York Times*, 4 June 41, 11.

29. *College Newsletter* (CTU Local 537), 4 (25 November 1940), 2; Stephen Leberstein, "Purging the Profs: The Rapp Coudert Committee in New York, 1940–1942" in *New Studies in the Politics and Culture of US Communism* (New York: Monthly Review Press, 1993), 97.

30. New York Times 4 June 41, 11; Executive Council of AFT, "Statement of Executive Council Regarding Membership List of Local 5," n.d., B6F1 Kheel 5445; John Dewey, et al., "Statement Re: New York Locals by a Number of Prominent Educators," n.d., B1 Kheel 5279.

31. CDPE, "Education Defense Bulletin" (3 December 1940), B17 Coudert Papers.

32. Joseph Hanley to Frederic Coudert, Jr., 25 May 1940, B14 Coudert Papers.

33. Chamberlain, *Loyalty*, 75, 111, B16, Coudert Papers; F[rederic] C[oudert, Jr.], "Memorandum. Re: Education Investigation," 24 April 1940; Coudert Sub-Committee Minutes, 26 September 1940, B16, Coudert Papers.

34. Chamberlain, *Loyalty*, 79–80.

35. Schrecker, *No Ivory Tower*, 76.

36. Windels, Sr., Reminiscences, 22–53, 58–61, 96–106. Dodd attacked Windels as a "smooth, slick Wall Street type of lawyer" and "the attorney for many open shop companies and firms," including the *Brooklyn Eagle*. See "A Meeting of the Teachers Union of the City of New York, Local 5," 13 September 1940, 56–7, (RC411); and George J. Lankevich, *American Metropolis: A History of New York City* (New York: NYU Press, 1998), 174–76.

278   Notes to pages 80–89

37. Paul Windels to Frederic Coudert, Jr., 1 August 1940, B14, Coudert Papers; Joe Hanley to Coudert, 5 August 1940, B14, Coudert Papers; Coudert to Hanley, 27 August 1940. See also Paul Windels to "Fritz" [Coudert, Jr.], 2 August 1940, B14, Coudert Papers. See also Executive Session (of Coudert Sub-Committee) Minutes, 2 December 1940, B16, Coudert Papers.

38. Herbert Mitgang. *Man Who Rode the Tiger: The Life and Times of Judge Samuel Seabury* (New York: J. B. Lippincott Company, 1963), 247–50.

39. Frederic Coudert, Jr., to Mrs. Phillip W. Haberman, Jr., 4 June, 1945, B2 FH, Coudert Papers.

40. Mitgang, "Man Who Rode," 319–43; *New York Times,* 15 June 1972, 44.

41. A list of committee staff with short biographies is in B16 Coudert Papers. The suffragette was Elizabeth Rogers. Her daughter, Elizabeth Rogers Horan, was one of Yale Law School's first female graduates. See memo from Paul Windels to Joint Legislative Committee to Investigate the Educational System of the State of New York, 1 February 1941, B16, Coudert Papers; and "Memorandum to Be Included in Report of Joint Legislative Committee to Investigate the Educational System of the State of New York," B16, Coudert Papers.

42. Linville to Robert Morris, 4 September 1940 (RC599); "Continuation of Interview with Dr. Linville at the Teachers Guild Office," 4 October 1940 (RC407).

5. The Dewey Trial

1. *New York Times*, 30 April 1933, 1.

2. Federal Writers Project, *WPA Guide to New York City* (New York: Pantheon Books, 1983), 271–84.

3. G. W. Wharton, "High School Architecture in the City of New York," *School Review*, 11 (June 1903), 456–85; George Locke, "High School of Commerce, New York City," *School Review*, 9 (September 1903), 555–62; *New York Times*, 1 February 1919, 13.

4. Rapp-Coudert Report (1942), 193–95. See also Public Hearings (December 1940), 134–44; C. J. Hendley, "Memorandum on Hearings before the Coudert Legislative Committee, September 26th, 1940," B11 F12, Hendley Papers; Isidore Begun private hearing, 28 October 1941, 8, 45–47 (RC523).

5. *New York Times*, 28 November 1939, 1, 16.

6. *New York Times*, 27 October 1941, 18; *New York Times*, 29 March 1936, 31; John Herman Randall, Jr., to Howard Selsam, 13 September 1935, Selsam Papers.

7. Rapp-Coudert Report (1942), 179, 185.

8. See for instance William Kilpatrick to Henry Linville, 12 April 1922, B13 F23, UFT Papers.

9. Bertram Wolfe private hearing, 28 January 1941, 52 (RC547); Clarence Taylor, *Reds at the Blackboard: Communism, Civil Rights, and the New York City Teachers Union* (New York: Columbia University Press, 2011), Introduction.

10. Marjorie Murphy, *Blackboard Unions: The AFT and the NEA, 1900–1980* (Ithaca: Cornell University Press, 1990), 104–5.

11. Teachers Union of the City of New York, "Terrorizing Our Public Schools," (New York: 1920), B13 F8, UFT Papers.

12. Teachers Union of New York City, "Press and the Lusk Law," (New York: 1922), 5, 10, B13 F11, UFT Papers. By the midtwenties, two thirds of the states had similar loyalty oaths. See Murphy, *Blackboard Unions*, 122.

13. Linville quoted in Murphy, *Blackboard Unions*, 96–97. See also Teachers Union of the City of New York, "For the Right of Teachers to Think and for the Professional Spirit," (New York: 1926), B13 F11, UFT Papers; Linville to Joseph Miller, Jr., 17 November 1926; "Teachers Union Charges Superintendent Mandel with Unprofessional and Dishonest Conduct," open letter, B13 F8, UFT Papers; *New York Times*, 11 November 1926, 12.

14. Murphy, *Blackboard Unions*, 156–7; "Communist Tactics," 2. Abe Lefkowitz was one of the founders of Brookwood, from which Muste resigned in March 1933 over related political and ideological disputes. See Richard J. Altenbaugh, "'Children and the Instruments of a Militant Labor Progressivism:' Brookwood Labor College and the American Labor College Movement of the 1920s and 1930s," *History of Education Quarterly*, 23 (Winter 1983), 395–411; Eugene M. Tobin, *Organize or Perish: America's Independent Progressives, 1913–1933* (Greenwood Press: New York, 1986), 204–12; and Roy Rosenzweig, "Radicals and the Jobless: The Musteites and the Unemployed Leagues, 1932–1936," *Labor History*, 16, no. 1 (1975), 52–77.

15. Sandra Opdycke, "Woll, Matthew," *American National Biography Online* (Oxford University Press, 2000), http://www.anb.org/articles/15/15-00768.html.

16. Murphy, *Blackboard Unions*, 80–90, 102–9, 113–14.

17. Murphy, *Blackboard Unions*, 117–21.

18. Selma Borchardt to Henry Linville, 18 October 1933, B15 F24, UFT Papers; "Borchardt, Selma Munter" in *Notable American Women: The Modern Period: A Biographical Dictionary*, ed. by Barbara Sicherman and Carol Hurd Green (Cambridge, Mass.: Belknap Press of Harvard University, 1980), 92–93; Linville to William Green, 31 December 1934, B15 F24, UFT Papers.

19. Linville to Norman Thomas, 23 November 1934, B15 F24, UFT Papers. On the Socialist Party split, see Fraser M. Ottanelli, *Communist Party of the United States: From the Depression to World War II* (New Brunswick: Rutgers University Press, 1991), 90–91.

20. Abraham Lefkowitz, *Educational Budget and the Financial Crisis* (New York: Teachers Union [of New York City], 1933), 5.

21. *New York Times*, 3 March 1932, 21; Minutes of General Membership Meeting [Local 5, AFT], 9 June 1932, B1 F14, Kheel 5279.

22. Lefkowitz, *Teachers and the Economic Situation* (New York: Local 5 of the AFT, 1932), flyleaf; Teachers Union Defense Committee, "Teachers Are Challenged," (New York: 1932), B6 F5, Hendley Papers.

23. Lefkowitz, Teachers and the Economic Situation, flyleaf; "Teachers Are Challenged"; "Statement of the Rank and File Committee," [May 1932], B1, Kheel 5279.

24. Lefkowitz, *Cry of the Children or the Demands of the Profiteers* (New York: Teachers Union, n.d.), 5.

25. Minutes of the Executive Board Meeting of Local 5 AFT, 12 March 1932, (RC382); *New York Times,* 28 January 1932, 12; *New York Times,* 4 April 1932, 19; *New York Times,* 3 March 1932, 21.

26. Grievance Report, 3; "Statement of the Rank and File Committee," [May 1932], B1, Kheel 5279.

27. Isidore Begun private hearing, 28 October 1941, 7–8 (RC523); Rapp-Coudert Report (1942), 210–15.

28. "What Is This 'Mass Action'?," *Unemployed Teacher,* 1 (May 1933), copy in Commintern Papers, Russian State Archives of Social-Political History, Fond 515, Reel 258.

29. As late as the early 1930s, new members had to be nominated by someone already in the union. This system disappeared because of its inefficiency, though in 1934 Lefkowitz wanted it reinstated. See Murphy, *Blackboard Unions,* 154. Once rules relaxed, membership climbed to over two thousand one hundred members in the 1935 school year. Union membership statistics are in B13 F53, UFT Papers.

30. Linville to Florence Curtis Hanson, 1 April 1931, B6 F24, Hendley Papers. And, in search of allies, Linville sought from the Socialist Party the names of Socialist teachers. See August Claessens to Linville, 17 March 1932, B15 F5, UFT Papers.

31. Even though in 1925, there were only ten communists in the local. See Benjamin Mandel private hearing, 18 January 1941, 3–4, 13–14, 17–18 (RC534); and Linville, et al., to Union Members, May 1925, reprinted in "Communist Tactics." That year, Linville exposed Mandel and Scott Nearing, forcing Mandel from public-school teaching. Nearing safely taught at the Rand School. See Nearing to Executive Committee of Local 5 (AFT), 28 April 1925, B13 F23, UFT Papers; *New York Times,* 29 May 1925, 18. See also Memo to the Executive Board of the Teachers Union, 30 September 1932, B25 F9, Kheel 5015. See also Nearing to Linville, 19 May 1925, B13 F23, UFT Papers; Nearing to Linville, 3 June 1925, B13 F23, UFT Papers; Helene P. Gans (ACLU) to Benjamin Mandel, 4 May 1934, B691 Matthews Papers; Linville to Florence Hanson, 1 April 1931, B6 F24, Hendley Papers; Linville to Members of the [Local 5] Staff, 1 April 1931, B6 F24, Hendley Papers; and Robert Iversen, *Communists and the Schools* (New York: Harcourt, Brace and Co., 1959), 21–27.

32. Joseph Jablonower, "When Is an Emergency an Emergency," 25 May [1931], B25 F9, Kheel 5015; Minutes of General Meeting, Local 5. 4 December 1931, B1 F14, Kheel 5279; Minutes of the Executive Board Meeting of Local 5 AFT, 9 January 1932 (RC382); Progressive Group, "Call to Action: Our Union Threatened with a Split," June 1932, B6 F24, Hendley Papers.

33. Linville memo to membership, 21 May 1930, B1 F3, Kheel 5279; Florence Gitlin, Ben Davidson, David M. Wittes, and Peter Nunan, "Election Appeal of the Progressive Group in the Teachers Union," leaflet [April 1931], B1 F3, Kheel 5279. See also "Statement of the Rank and File Committee," [May 1932], B1 Kheel 5279; and Progressive Group, "An Appeal," n.d., B42 F2, Kheel 5015.

34. Jablonower, "When Is"; Minutes of the Executive Board Meeting of Local 5 AFT, 9 April 1932 (RC382).

35. Affidavit, County of New York, State of New York, 25 April 1933, by Robert F. Roberts, reprinted in Joint Defense Committee, "A Letter to the Union Membership," n.d., B74 F2, Kheel 5015.

36. Minutes of the General Membership Meeting, 9 June 1932, B1 F14, Kheel 5279; Progressive Group, "Resolution Presented to the Special Meeting of the Teachers Union," 24 May 1932, B6 F24, Hendley Papers; Minutes of the Executive Board Meeting of Local 5 AFT, 16 June 1932 (RC382); Progressive Group, "A Call to Action: Our Union Threatened with a Split."

37. All on the "charges committee" were Linville loyalists. See Memo to Members [of committee to bring charges], 17 September 1932, B8 F1, Kheel 5445.

38. [Linville] to "Members," 12 September 1932, B1 F6, Kheel 5279; Minutes of the Executive Board Meeting of Local 5 AFT, 16 September 1932 (RC382). A comparison of [Linville] to "Members" [of the committee to bring changes], 3 October 1932, with [Charges Committee] Memo to the Executive Board of Local 5, 7 October 1932, shows verbatim transfers of content and language. Both documents are in B8 F1, Kheel 5445.

39. Linville to Members of Staff and Special Committee on Left-Wing Activities, 8 October 1932, B2 F1, Kheel 5279; Memo to the Executive Board, 30 September 1932, B25 F9, Kheel 5015.

40. Report on Left-Wing Activities in Local 5, 20 October, 1932, B6 F24 Hendley Papers.

41. [Linville], Memo to the Executive Board of the TU, 30 September 1932, B25 F9 Kheel 5015.

42. Linville to Hardy, 3 November 1932, B2 F26 Kheel 5279; Florence Gitlin, Ben Davidson, David M. Wittes, and Isidore Begun, "Executive Board Minority Report against Expulsions," B74 F4a Kheel 5015.

43. Linville to Hardy, 3 November 1932.

44. John Dewey, "Why I Am a Member of the Teachers Union," (1927) *LW*3, 269–75; Dewey, "Professional Spirit among Teachers," (1913) *MW*7, 109–12.

45. Dewey, "Democracy and Loyalty in the Schools," (1917) *MW*10, 158–64. See also Dewey's Introduction to the Teachers Union of New York City, "Press and the Lusk Law," (New York, 1922), B13 F11, UFT Papers.

46. For Dewey's defense of Brookwood, see "Freedom in Worker Education," (1928) *LW*5, 331–37. See also Dewey, "Mr. Woll as a Communist-Catcher" [1929] *LW*5, 392.

47. Linville to Horace Kallen, 1 May 1939, B3 F54, UFT Papers; the program for Dewey's eightieth birthday dinner, B3 F54, UFT Papers; Dewey "In Reponse" [1930] *LW*5, 419; Dewey, "Henry Linville Pension Fund" [1936] *LW*11, 380–81.

48. Dewey to Linville, 7 November 1932, B3 F54 UFT Papers.

49. Grievance Report, 7. Officially, the committee called those charged "the defendants" and itself "the prosecution," conveying a false impression of juridical rigor and reinforcing suspicions that the accused were being railroaded by a packed court.

50. Dewey to Linville, 25 October 1932, B13 F20 Kheel 5279.

51. Dewey to Sidney Hook, 22 August 1932, Dewey Correspondence.

52. In the April 29 meeting, Dewey took "personal responsibility" for drafting much of the report. See Dewey Trial Minutes (1933).

53. Grievance Report, 3–4.

54. Grievance Report, 6.

55. Grievance Report, 7.

56. Introductory Note in Joseph Kinmont Hart's *Inside Experience* (1927), *LW*3, 342–46.

57. Introductory Note in Joseph Kinmont Hart's *Inside Experience* (1927), *LW*3, 342–46; Linville, "How Communists Injure Teachers' Unions," *Social Frontier*, 5 (March 1939), 175. Ultimately, the dispute was ideological: "The issue is not whether the New York City teachers' unions are democratically managed, but whether they are Stalinist-controlled." Dewey agreed: Linville's point "gave the whole show away." See Dewey to Linville, 20 February 1939, B3 F54, UFT Papers. In the Grievance Report, Dewey only speaks of the absence of "good faith" on the part of the left-wing opposition. See "On the Grievance Committee Report" (1933), *LW*9 316–17.

58. Grievance Report, 5.

59. Grievance Report, 4.

60. Grievance Report, 4, 7.

61. Grievance Report, 5, 7.

62. [Linville] to "Advisers," 28 April 1933, B2 F17 Kheel 5279; Linville to Harry Ward, 20 April 1933, B2 Kheel 5279.

63. Celia Weiser, "Report. Meeting of Staff and Advisers, Saturday, February 18, 1933" (holograph); "Present Activities of the Union, March 1, 1933," n.a.; Committee of Twenty-Five for Union Defense, "Second Statement of March 17, 1933"; Truda Weil to Local 5 Members, 20 April 1933; Committee of Tewnty-Five to "Fellow Member,"11 April 1933; Committee of Twenty-Five Open Letter to Membership, 8 March 1933. All documents in B1 F16, Kheel 5279.

64. [Linville] to "Advisers," 28 April 1933. That Linville organized the committee is evident from Linville to "members," 21 February 1933, B1 F16, Kheel 5279. Evidence of Linville's continued direction of the committee is in Linville

to Truda Weil, 9 March 1933, B1 F16, Kheel 5279. See also Linville to Weil, 13 March 1933, B1 F16, Kheel 5279. That Linville arranged for the committee to use union resources can be seen in Linville to Weil, 10 March 1933, B1 F16, Kheel 5279. See also Linville to Weil, 17 March 1933, B1 F16, Kheel 5279.

65. Minutes of the Executive Board of Local 5 AFT, 7 April 1933 (RC382); Dewey to Linville, 24 April 1933, B2 F17, Kheel 5279.

66. Dewey Trial Minutes (1939), 1–3.

67. Linville, "Memoranda for Al. Smallheiser," typescript copy, n.d. [27 April 1933], B2 Kheel 5279; "Memoranda for April 29 Meeting: Approved at Staff Meeting April 26," B2 F17, Kheel 5279.

68. Linville to Florence C. Hanson, 1 May 1933, B25 F9, Kheel 5015.

69. The opposition had no access to membership or mailing lists. See Dewey Trial Minutes (1939), 3, 6–14, 9.

70. Dewey Trial Minutes (1939), 40–42. On Dewey's anger over left-wing criticism, see Linville to Florence C. Hanson, 1 May 1933, B25 F9, Kheel 5015. See also Gitlin, et al., "Executive Board Minority Report"; Linville to Dewey, 9 November 1932, B25 F9, Kheel 5015; and Joint Defense Committee, "Reply to the Grievance Committee Report," n.d., B1 F19, Kheel 5279.

71. Grievance Report, 5, 8.

72. Gitlin, et al., "Executive Board Minority Report."

73. Grievance Report, 4.

74. Teachers Union (New York), "You May Be Next! The Teachers Union Fight for Academic Freedom and Teachers' Rights as Citizens," pamphlet (8 June 1934), 12, copy in B11 F14, Hendley Papers; "Begun-Burroughs Case," memorandum, n.d., B1 F17, UFT Papers; Henry Linville, "Statement Submitted by the Academic Freedom Committee of the Teachers Union Relative to the Appeal of Mr. Isidore Begun and Mrs. Williana Burroughs to the State Commissioner of Education," 24 May 1935 (RC396 Subfolder 1).

75. Joint Defense Committee, "Reply to the Grievance Committee Report."

76. Dewey Trial Minutes (1939), 28–29.

77. Begun private hearing, 28 October 1941, 11–12 (RC523).

78. Dewey, "Crisis in Education" (1933), *LW*9, 113.

79. Dewey Trial Minutes (1939), 40–43; see also the castigation of Dewey by Bertram Wolfe on pages 44–45.

80. Dewey Trial Minutes, 21–23.

81. Dewey Trial Minutes, 39–40.

82. Dewey Trial Minutes, 30–35.

83. Dewey Trial Minutes, 58–59; "Memoranda for Staff Conference," 26 April 1933, B2 F17, Kheel 5279; Linville to Florence C. Hanson, 1 May 1933, B25 F9, Kheel 5015.

84. Linville to Hanson, 1 May 1933 (emphasis in original); Linville to Dewey, 1 May 1933, B3 F54, UFT Papers.

85. Dewey Trial Minutes (1939), 20.

86. Minutes of the Executive Board Meeting of Local 5 AFT, 5 May 1933 (RC382).

87. Linville to Lee B. Wood (Executive Editor, *World-Telegram*), 14 October 1933, B42 Linville folder, Kheel 5015; Rank and File, "Undemocratic Rulings and Restrictive Regulations," 9 April 1934, B74 F2, Kheel 5015.

88. *New York Times*, 28 October 1933, 16. Committee of One Hundred, open letter to members, 7 November 1933, B1 F16, Kheel 5279.

89. Minutes of the Executive Board Meeting of Local 5 AFT, 13 October 1933 (RC382).

6. The Educational Front

1. An example of this narrative frame can be found in a recent *New York Times*: Paul Krugman, "Perspective on the Deal," *Conscience of a Liberal* blog, New York Times Online, 1 January 2013, http://krugman.blogs.nytimes.com/2013/01/01/perspective-on-the-deal/. See also Jennifer Luff, *Commonsense Anti-Communism: Labor and Civil Liberties between the World Wars* (Chapel Hill: University of North Carolina Press, 2012), Chapter 8.

2. Michael Denning, *Cultural Front: The Laboring of American Culture* (New York: Verso, 1998), xvixviii.

3. See Markku Ruotsila, "Leftward Ramparts: Labor and Anticommunism between the World Wars," in *Little Red Scares: Anti-Communism and Political Repression in the United States, 1921–1946*, ed. by Robert Justin Goldstein (Surrey, England: Ashgate, 2014), 165–93.

4. Alan Wald, *American Night: The Literary Left in the Era of the Cold War* (Chapel Hill: University of North Carolina Press, 2012), 9–11; Freda Kirchwey, "Red Totalitarianism," *Nation*, 27 May 1939, 605–5.

5. Dewey first enunciated these principles in *School and Society* (1899). He later raised these arguments to a higher philosophical plane in *Democracy and Education* (1916). For a summary of his educational views, see Robert Westbrook, *John Dewey and American Democracy* (Ithaca: Cornell University Press, 1991), Chapter 6.

6. Richard Frank, "Schools and the People's Front," *Communist*, 16 (May 1937), 436.

7. Michael Knoll, "Project Method: Its Vocational Education Origin and International Development," *Journal of Industrial Teacher Education*, 34 (Spring 1997), n.p., http://scholar.lib.vt.edu/ejournals/JITE/v34n3/Knoll.htm on 8/7/2012.

8. *New York Times*, 16 February 1940, 19.

9. Teachers Union, Local 5, Course Announcements (RC407). See also Local 5 (AFT), "Activity Program of Local 5," [September 1937], B6 F1, Hendley Papers; Samuel Wallach, "New York Local Describes Work of Policies Body," *American Teacher*, 24 (September 1939), 9; "Evaluating the Activity

Notes to pages 111–15   285

Program," in *Education for Democracy: Annual Education Conference* (New York: Teachers Union Local 5, 1940), 18–24.

10. United States Census, 1920; Clarence Taylor, *Reds at the Blackboard: Communism, Civil Rights, and the New York City Teachers Union* (New York: Columbia University Press, 2011), 15.

11. Alice B. Citron private hearing, 2 June 1941, 3–4, 8 (RC524); *New York Times*, 23 January 1988, 10; Social Security Administration, "Social Security Death Index," database, Ancestry.com, http://ssdi.rootsweb.ancestry.com/cgi-bin/ssdi.cgi, entry for Isidore A. Begun, 1903–88, no. 088-01-8983.

12. *New York Times*, 14 June 1928, 24.

13. Citron to John Doar, 1 March 1969, Citron Papers; Gustav Schoenchen private testimony, 19 January 1941, 5 (RC542).

14. *New York Times*, 11 April 1935, 16; Lauri Johnson, "Generation of Women Activists: African American Female Educators in Harlem, 1930–1950," *Journal of African American History* 89 (Summer 2004), 225; Robert Oxford, "Harlem Riot, 1935: Urban Colonialism and Early Struggles for Civil Rights," unpublished master's thesis (2014), American Studies, New York University, 5–23.

15. Florina Lacker (ACLU) to Citron, 29 May 1933, Citron Papers; Citron to Doar, 1 March 1969, Citron Papers; Johnson, 227.

16. Mark Naison, "Communist Party in Harlem in the Early Depression Years: A Case Study in the Reinterpretation of American Communism," *Radical History Review* (Fall 1976), 68–95. *New York Times*, 4 September 1938, 23.

17. Mark Naison, *Communists in Harlem during the Depression* (New York: Grove Press, 1985), 225.

18. Ann Matlin video interview, Dreamers and Fighters project, https://www.youtube.com/watch?v=Mwaw5RAHB8Y. The text cited by Matlin was a widely used geography text written by district superintendent William Jansen, who would become superintendent in 1947 and dismiss suspected Communists like Citron and Matlin a couple of years later. He appeared on the 19 October 1953 cover of *Time*. See "Boys & Girls Together," *Time*, 19 October 1953, 74.

19. Taylor, *Reds*, 248.

20. Citron, "Negro History in New York City," *Negro History Bulletin* (April 1942), 152–53; Citron to editors (*Amsterdam News*), draft of letter 22 August 1979, Citron Papers. The textbook campaign began the regular observance of Black History Week in New York Schools.

21. "Citron—'Best of the Best . . . ' to Harlem Mothers" (New York: Teachers Union Local 555 UPW, 1950).

22. Citron private hearing, 6–7.

23. As in other contexts, neither the union nor the party hesitated to work with cooperative administrators, even praising some of the worst of them when they made good decisions. See for instance "Dr. Harthill, Take a Bow!,"

Harlem Lesson Plan, 2 (September–October 1938), 2. Harthill, anti-union and anticommunist, is praised for cleaning up P.S. 5; notes on interview with Rufus M. Harthill, 7 November 1940 (RC160). On Flacks, see Taylor, *Reds*, 291–93.

24. "Teachers Study Harlem Problems," *Harlem Lesson Plan*, 2 (September–October 1938), 1; Earl Browder, "Education—An Ally in the Workers' Struggle," *Social Frontier*, 1 (January 1935), 23; Ella Flagg Young, *Isolation in the School* (Chicago: University of Chicago Press, 1901).

25. *Educational Signpost,* 3 (March 1940), 4. MacDonald was the *Signpost's* editor.

26. *Educational Signpost* 1 (April 1938), 1.

27. The words are Begun's. "Communist Teacher for City Council," *Harlem Lesson Plan* 2 (October 1937), 1; "School Budget 1938," *Harlem Lesson Plan* 1 (June 1937), 1, 2.

28. Citron, "Has the Negro Youth a Chance?," *Education for Democracy, 1939: Annual Educational Conference* (New York: Local 5 of the American Federation of Teachers, 1939), 51–52.

29. Gustav G. Schoenchen, *Activity School: A Basic Philosophy for Teachers* (New York: Longmans, Green and Co., 1940); Harthill interview, 7 November 1940 (RC160); notes on interview with Mrs. Sadie Bassett (principal, P.S. 157), 5 December 1940 (RC160); "Continuation of Interview with Dr. Linville at the Teachers Guild office," 4 October 1940 (RC407). See also Taylor, *Reds*, 289; *New York Age*, 21 November 1936, 1.

30. Charles Hendley, open letter "To the Principals," of New York City Schools, [February 1937] (RC397); Hendley to Jacob Greenberg (Associate Superintendent), 5 February 1937, (RC397); Schoenchen private testimony, 8, 19, 42. Another witness "remarked" that a white teacher had danced with a black teacher at a Central Park restaurant, which either the witness or the investigator took to be part of Communist efforts to "actually fawn over the colored teachers." Harthill interview, 7 November 1940.

31. On deliberative democracy, see Joshua Cohen, "Economic Basis of Deliberative Democracy," *Social Philosophy and Policy*, 6 (Spring 1989), 25–50. On agonistic democracy, see Chantal Mouffe, "Decision, Deliberation and the Democratic Ethos," *Philosophy Today*, 41 (1999), 24–29. See Ian Shapiro, *Democratic Justice* (New Haven, Conn., 1999), 14. See also Wendy Brown, "We Are All Democrats Now . . . ," in *Democracy in What State?* (New York: Columbia University Press, 2009), Chapter 4.

32. Teachers Union (New York), "You May Be Next! The Teachers Union Fight for Academic Freedom and Teachers' Rights as Citizens," pamphlet (8 June 1934), 12, copy in B11 F14, Hendley Papers, 11; *New York Times,* 8 October 1932, 1.

33. "Isidore Blumberg Dismissed, Williana Burroughs Suspended, Isidore Begun Suspended. Why?," n.a., n.d., in B11 F14, Hendley Papers; *New York Times,* 18 November 1933, 34. Blumberg remained active in the American

Labor Party through the 1940s, serving also as a legislative representative for the Transit Workers Union and then the executive secretary of the left-wing Tenant Council. See *New York Times*, 5 December 1946, 31; *New York Times*, 21 December 1949, 34.

34. Celia Zitron, *New York Teachers Union* (New York: Humanities Press, 1968), 178.

35. *New York Times*, 25 May 1933, 3. The official name of the building was Hall of the Board of Education. One of the umbrella-wielding women reportedly was Citron. See "You May Be Next!," 13.

36. On Williana Burroughs, see Erik McDuffie, *Sojourning for Freedom: Black Women, American Communism, and the Making of Black Left Feminism* (Durham: Duke University Press, 2011), Chapter 1.

37. *New York Times*, 1 June 1933, 19; *New York Times*, 29 June 1933, 21. Burroughs ran on the CP-USA ticket for city comptroller in 1933. In 1935, she rejoined two children left in the Soviet Union for their education. Burroughs remained in Moscow, serving as the Soviets' only English-language radio announcer during the war. See McDuffie, Chapter 1; *Chicago Defender*, 6 October 1945, 3.

38. As full-time teachers, Begun and Burroughs had open hearings.

39. Blumberg Defense Committee, "Isidore Blumberg Dismissed."

40. *New York Times*, 14 June 1933, 21.

41. Isidore Begun to [Ruth] Hardy, 20 July 1933 (RC43).

42. *New York Times*, 5 October 1949, 29; *New York Times*, 19 September 1932, 18; *New York Times*, 11 February 1946, 42.

43. "Statement by Mrs. Burroughs on Her Case at the Teachers Union Meeting on Academic Freedom—June 8, 1934," B1 F3, Kheel 5279.

44. *New York Times*, 9 September 1932, 2.

45. See for example John Herman Randall to Selsam, 13 September 1935, B1, Selsam Papers.

46. William Green (open letter), 11 September 1934, B13 F22, UFT Papers.

47. Luff, *Commonsense*, Chapter 10. On Minneapolis, see Donna T. Haverty-Stacke, *Trotskyists on Trial: Free Speech and Political Persecution since the Age of FDR* (New York: NYU Press, 2015).

48. Ruotsila, "Leftward," 172–75.

49. Denning called 1934 "one of the lyric years in American history." See Denning, *Cultural Front*, xiv. See also M. J. Heale, "Citizens versus Outsiders: Anti-Communism at State and Local Levels, 1921–1946," in *Little Red Scares: Anti-Communism and Political Repression in the United States, 1921–1946*, ed. by Robert Justin Goldstein (Surrey, England: Ashgate, 2014), 56–57.

50. Henry Linville, "What Price Factionalism?," 1 February 1935, B1 Kheel 5279; Linville to Borchardt, 8 January 1935, B13 F22, UFT Papers; Abraham Lefkowitz, et al., "Left Wing Groups Again Undermine the Very Foundation of the Union," [n.d.], B6 F10, Hendley Papers. Linville began writing for the

Social Democratic Federation-aligned newspaper *New Leader* shortly after bolting from the local.

51. Charles Hendley to AFT Executive Council Investigating Committee, 22 June 1935, B6 F10, Hendley Papers.

52. *New York Post*, 6 September 1935, reprinted in American Teacher Part III, Supplementary Bulletin, 1, 14 September 1935, B1 F9, Kheel 5279.

53. On Borchardt and Linville, see Marjorie Murphy, *Blackboard Unions: The AFT and the NEA, 1900–1980* (Ithaca: Cornell University Press, 1990), 160. The official and complete transcript of the hearings, including the response from the left, is in the AFT archives at Cornell. See "Meeting of a Special Committee of the Executive Council of the American Federation of Teachers Investigating Differences in Local No. 5 New York City," hearings, 8–9 June 1935, New York City, B1 F1, Kheel 5279. On the railroading of the process, see pages 6, 7, 10, 129, 131, 267.

54. Linville, et al., "Letter on the Union Investigation," 7 June 1935, B6 F10, Hendley Papers; Linville, "In Rebuttal," 21 June 1935, B2 F10, Kheel 5279.

55. "Meeting of a Special Committee," 59, 63, 157.

56. "Meeting of a Special Committee," 148.

57. "Meeting of a Special Committee," 278, 280.

58. "Meeting of a Special Committee," 317.

59. "Meeting of a Special Committee," 152–53; see also [Charles Hendley], "What Shall We Do?," speech at Local 5 Delegate Assembly Meeting, 12 June 1935, B6 F10, Hendley Papers; Hendley to AFT EC Investigating Committee, 22 June 1935, B6 F10, Hendley Papers.

60. "Meeting of a Special Committee," 212–13.

61. "Meeting of a Special Committee," 358–59. On Tulchen's role as whip for Socialist Teachers Committee, see Tulchen to "Dear Comrade," 10 June 1934, mimeo typescript, B6 F24, Hendley Papers.

62. Dale Zysman, et al., to Florence Curtis Hanson, 16 August 1935, B6 F10, Hendley Papers. See Alexander Ostrow, "Linville Balked Union Peace Plan, Says Dr. Neibuhr [sic]," *New York Post*, 5 September 1935; and "Fouling Their Own Nest," editorial, *New York Post*, 6 September 1935, both reprinted in *American Teacher* Part III, Supplementary Bulletin, 1, 14 September 1935, B1 F9, Kheel 5279. See Henry Linville (press release), 14 September 1935, B1 F2, Kheel 5279.

63. George Davis, "New York Situation," *American Teacher* Part III, Supplementary Bulletin, 1 (14 September 1935), printed leaflet, B1 F9, Kheel 5279; D. Benjamin (Ben Davidson), "Reactionaries Threaten Split in New York Teachers Union," *Workers Age*, 14 September 1935, 1–2. Linville and Lefkowitz accused Hanson of colluding with Hendley, Tulchin, and left-wing Socialist Maynard Krueger, an economics professor at the University of Chicago, to stack the convention with illegitimate delegates. Abraham Lefkowitz, "Communists Wreck the Teachers' Union," *New Leader*, 7 September 1935, reprinted as leaflet, B1 F2, Kheel 5279.

7. Far from the Ivory Tower

1. *New York Times,* 20 August 1939, 1; *New York Times,* 22 August 1939, 1.
2. Local 5 member newsletter, 2 July 1940, B6 F7, Hendley Papers.
3. Peggy Dennis, *Autobiography of an American Communist: A Personal View of a Political Life, 1925–1975* (Westport, Conn.: Lawrence Hill & Co., 1977), 135–37.
4. Granville Hicks, "On Leaving the Communist Party (Letter to Editor)," *New Republic,* October 1939, 244–45. Others regarded the pact as a necessary strategic maneuver. See Harry Slochower to Malcolm Cowley 9 December 1983, B13, Slochower Papers. Even forty-four years later, Slochower still thought the pact "a brilliant countering of the treacherous Chamberlain maneuverings to turn Hitler 'eastwards,' but, of course, disturbing to the United Front." Browder reportedly resisted defending the pact. Fraser M. Ottanelli, *Communist Party of the United States: From the Depression to World War II* (New Brunswick: Rutgers University Press, 1991), 191–98.
5. Harry Rothman, "A.F. of T. Convention: 1939," *New York Teacher,* 5, no. 1, 10–11; "Changing Scene," *Frontiers of Democracy,* 6, no. 48, [November] 1939, 35–38; *New York Times,* 22 August 1939, 13; Marjorie Murphy, *Blackboard Unions: The AFT and the NEA, 1900–1980* (Ithaca: Cornell University Press, 1990), 166.
6. "Interview with Mr. & Mrs. U & T X," 16 September 1940 (RC93). The Coudert committee's document codes indicate this interview was conducted with Linville allies Minna and Joseph Colvin, who remained in Local 5 after joining the Teachers Guild. See Linville to Robert Morris, September 4 1940 (RC599); "Continuation of Interview with Dr. Linville at the Teachers Guild office," 4 October 1940 (RC407); memo: Talks with Dr. Linville, May 8 at 3 p.m. and May 12 at 4:45 p.m., 13 May 1941 (RC416); "Memo to Mrs. [Elizabeth] Horan," n.d. (RC124); memo re: Gabriel R. Mason, Principal of Abraham Lincoln High School, Brooklyn (RC2); and memo of Meeting with Ben Mandel, 20 October 1940 (RC600). Mandel directed Coudert investigators to Lefkowitz, Hook, Counts, CCNY's Hilman Bishop, and George Hartmann at Teachers College.
7. Benjamin E. Lippincott to the Coudert Committee, 21 February 1941 (RC610). Lippincott inquired whether the Coudert committee had finished its work so that the AFT could mobilize support for expulsion. See also Henry Linville to Dr. [George S.] Counts, 9 January 1941, B7 F19a, Kheel 5279; Rapp-Coudert Report (1942), 183–85; and Charles Hendley, "Address to Local 192 [Philadelphia]," 10 January 1941, B2 F2, Kheel 5279.
8. Ellen Condliffe Lagemann, "Prophecy or Profession? George S. Counts and the Social Study of Education," *American Journal of Education,* 100 (February 1992), 152–53.
9. Claudia J. Keenan, "Education of an Intellectual," *Kansas History: A Journal of the Central Plains,* 25 (Winter 2002/2003), 262; Gerald L. Gutek, *George S.*

Counts and American Civilization: The Educator as Social Theorist (Macon, Georgia: Mercer University Press, 1984), 5–7; Lagemann, "Prophecy," 142; Counts interview, 34.

10. William Heard Kilpatrick, *Education and the Social Crisis: A Proposed Program* (New York: Liveright Publishing Corporation, 1932), 4; Kilpatrick. *Education for a Changing Civilization* (New York: MacMillan Company, 1929), 124.

11. Counts, *Dare the School Build a New Social Order* (New York: John Day Company, 1932), 31–32, 36; Kilpatrick, *Education and the Social Crisis*, 13.

12. Stuart Chase, *Challenge of Waste* (New York: League for Industrial Democracy, 1922), 22–23.

13. Committee of the Progressive Education Association on Social and Economic Problems, *Call to the Teachers of the Nation* (New York: John Day Company, 1933), 6. Counts was principle author of this tract. See Counts, *Dare*, 44–45, 47–49.

14. "Unmentionable Counts," *Time*, 28 (20 July 1936), 72; Harold Lord Varney, "Class-War on the Campus," *American Mercury*, 40 (1937), 463, 466; Gutek, *Educational Theory of George S. Counts* (Columbus: Ohio State University Press, 1970), 76, 79, 207–10.

15. Counts, *Soviet Challenge to America* (New York: John Day, 1931), 13, 17; Counts, "Education in the USSR," *New Republic*, 13 February 1935, 8–11.

16. John A. Beineke, "Investigation of John Dewey by the FBI," *Educational Theory*, 37 (Winter 1987), 43–52; Bill Cooke, "Kurt Lewin-Goodwin Watson FBI/CIA Files: A 60th Anniversary There-and-Then of the Here-and-Now," *Human Relations*, 60 (March 2007), 440–42.

17. The most tendentious example is C.A. Bowers, *Progressive Educator and the Depression: The Radical Years* (New York: Random House, 1969), 13–14, 28–29, 108–09. But even former Communists misperceived the political alignments. See William T. Parry, "In the Beginning . . . ," *Science & Society*, 50 (Fall 1986), 321.

18. Lewis Corey, "Veblen and Marxism," *Marxist Quarterly*, 1 (January–March 1937), 163–64; Sidney Hook, "Meaning of Marx," in *Meaning of Marx: A Symposium*, ed. by Sherwood Eddy (New York: Farrar & Rinehart, 1934), 56–59.

19. Malcolm Rutherford, *Institutionalist Movement in American Economics, 1918–1947: Science and Social Control* (Cambridge, England: Cambridge University Press, 2011), 4; Rutherford, "Institutional Economics at Columbia University," *History of Political Economy*, 36 (Spring 2004), 38–39, 42, 49, and 57.

20. Hamilton writing to Clarence Ayres, quoted in Rutherford, *Institutionalist Movement*, 36.

21. Counts, *Secondary Education and Industrialism*, 4, 7. See also Kilpatrick, *Education for a Changing Civilization*, 45.

22. Counts, *Dare*, 48–49; *Call to the Teachers*, 17; "Collectivism and Collectivism," editorial, *Social Frontier*, 1 (November 1934), 3; "Orientation," editorial, *Social Frontier*, 1, no. 1 (1934), 3–5; American Historical Association Commission

on the Social Studies, *Conclusions and Recommendations of the Commission* (New York: Charles Scribner's Sons, 1934), 16–18, written by Counts and Charles Beard.

23. *Call to the Teachers*, 6, 21; American Historical Association Commission on the Social Studies, *Conclusions and Recommendations*, 34–35; Goodwin Watson, "Education Is the Social Frontier," *Social Frontier*, 1 (October 1934), 22; Henry R. Linville, "Challenge of the Economic Situation to Organized Teachers," presidential address, 17th Annual Convention of AFT, Milwaukee, Wisconsin, 27 June 1933, B6a F39, UFT Papers; Kilpatrick, "Public Elementary School: Its Status and Problems," *New Republic*, 12 November 1924, 1.

24. Counts, *Dare*, 19.

25. *Call to the Teachers*, 19.

26. Dewey, *Liberalism and Social Action*, 43.

27. Linville to Kilpatrick, 9 June 1936, B13 F22, UFT Papers.

28. Kilpatrick, "High Marxism Defined and Rejected," *Social Frontier*, 2 (June 1936), 272–74.

29. Irvin Kuenzli, AFT's unsympathetic recording secretary, reported that of the two thousand five hundred members added in the 1938–39 school year, one thousand six hundred were recruited in New York City. See "Kuenzli Traces AFT Growth for 1938–39," *American Teacher*, 24 (September 1939), 11; and Hendley, "Address to Local 192." The national AFT grew from about seven thousand five hundred members in 1932 to thirty-two thousand in 1940. See Murphy, *Blackboard Unions*, 150.

30. Hendley, "Address to Local 192"; Bella Dodd private testimony, 26 September 1940, 97, 107 (RC550).

31. *Union Teacher* (CCNY), 1 (February 1936), 1, in B1 F18, Kheel 5279; Abraham Edel, *Struggle for Academic Democracy: Lessons from the 1938 "Revolution" in New York's City Colleges* (Philadelphia: Temple University Press), 40–41.

32. Edel, *Struggle*, 31, 39. According to some estimates, faculty salaries generally declined during the 1930s. See James C. Hearn, "Faculty Salary Structure in Research Universities: Implications for Productivity," unpublished manuscript, 6, http://www.usc.edu/dept/chepa/pdf/Hearn.pdf; Grebanier interview, 1974; Leonard Chalmers, "Crucial Test of La Guardia's First 100 Days: The Emergency Economy Bill," *New-York Historical Society Quarterly*, 57 (July 1973), 246–51; *Union Teacher* (CCNY), 1 (March 1936), 6; *College Newsletter* (CTU), 1 (14 January 1938), 1; Charles Nelson Winslow private hearing, 17 June 1941, 4 (RC547). Winslow applied for his BC job directly through J. P. Turner, chair of philosophy and psychology. No one else was involved in his hiring.

33. *College Newsletter* (CTU), 1 (14 January 1938), 1, 4. On Russell, see Kilpatrick Diaries, 16 March 1936 and 13 April 1936. According to Hook, the entire NYU faculty was on yearly contracts without tenure. See Sidney Hook, *Out of Step: An Unquiet Life in the Twentieth Century* (New York: Harper & Row, 1987), 206.

34. The case was *McAuliffe versus Mayor and Board of Alderman of New Bedford*, 155 New Bedford, Mass. (1892), 216. See Marjorie Heins, *Priests of Our Democracy: The Supreme Court, Academic Freedom, and the Anti-Communist Purge* (New York: New York University Press, 2013), 88.

35. *New York Times*, 4 October 1940, 14; *New York Times*, 5 October 1940, 1.

36. Heins, *Priests*, 25, 49.

37. *College Newsletter* (CTU), 1 (10 February 1938), 3. The tenure bylaw was written and passed as the state courts invalidated the Feld-McGrath law in a case involving a Hunter College mathematics tutor. See *College Newsletter*, 1 (8 March 1938), 1; and *College Newsletter*, 1 (22 June 1938), 1. The union also hoped for faculty representation at BHE meetings. See *College Newsletter*, 1 (10 February 1938), 1, 4; Ordway Tead, "Place and Function of Faculties in College Government," *Bulletin of the American Association of University Professors*, 25 (April 1939), 163.

38. Edel, *Struggle*, 47–49; Carl Wittke, "Place and Function of Faculties in College and University Government: How Budgets and Appointments Are Made at Oberlin," *Bulletin* of the AAUP, 25 (April 1939), 157–63.

39. *College Newsletter* 1 (22 June 1938), 1; Edel, *Struggle*, 48; Larry G. Gerber, *Rise and Decline of Faculty Governance: Professionalization and the Modern American University* (Baltimore: Johns Hopkins University Press, 2014).

40. Howard Selsam, "New Deal on the Campus," *New Masses*, 18 October 1938, 17–19; Edel, *Struggle*, 53.

41. *College Newsletter*, 2 (14 October 1938), 1; Tead, "Place and Function," 163, 167; Arnold Shukotoff, "Democracy in N.Y. City Colleges," *American Teacher*, 23 (February 1939), 15.

42. *Brooklyn Eagle*, 15 May 1938, 1–2; *Brooklyn Eagle*, 17 May 1938, 1–2; *Brooklyn Eagle*, 24 May 1938, 1–2; "Interview with Earl A. Martin," 14 November 1940 (RC246), *Staff*, 1 (1 June 1935), 4.

43. John L. Childs private testimony, 30 January 1941, 11 (RC524).

44. Selsam, "New Deal on Campus," 17. On the union's openness, see Minutes of CTU Executive Council, 14 October 1938 (RC389). Delegates, however, also were given the "power to impose unit rule upon themselves." See Minutes General Membership meeting of CTU 3 June 1938 (RC388).

45. *College Newsletter*, 2 (27 January 1939), 3. The rival Teachers Guild also promoted women to high ranks in the organization. However, it represented only public-school teachers, a much larger percentage of whom were women.

46. Minutes of the Executive Board of the CTU, 4 January 1938 (RC390).

47. *College Newsletter*, 1 (10 February 1938), 1; *College Newsletter*, 2 (10 March 1939), 1; American Federation of Teachers, "Largest College Teachers' Union Formed," press release, n.d., B1, AAUP Papers; *College Newsletter*, 1 (25 February 1938), 1.

48. *New York Times*, 23 May 1937, 21; *New York Times*, 26 May 1937, 21.

49. *New York Times*, 13 June 1937, 2; *New York Times*, 24 August 1937, 23; Ralph Himstead to William Laprade, 30 September 1937. These views are

recorded in memos passed between AAUP President Ralph Himstead and his board in 1937, B1, AFT folder, AAUP Papers.

50. Himstead to William T. Laprade and other members of the AAUP council, 5 March 1937, B1, AAUP Papers.

51. Himstead to A. J. Carlson, 11 March 1938, B1, AAUP Papers; Himstead to Paul V. West (NYU School of Education), 7 April 1938, B1, AAUP Papers.

8. Bad Faith

1. Minutes of the Executive Board of CTU, 4 January 1938 (RC390); *College Newsletter*, 2 (24 March 1939), 3; "Resolutions Submitted to the American Federation of Teachers Convention by the New York College Teachers Union, Local 537, A.F.T. Passed by the General Membership Meeting of 27 May 1938," (RC388).

2. *College Newsletter*, 1 (26 April 1938), 1, 4; *College Newsletter*, 1 (25 February 1938), 1. Although the dean of TC answered to Columbia's president and the university trustees, he acted much as a college president would have. TC also had its own board of trustees.

3. New York College Teachers Union, "Investigation into the Dismissal of Professor Elizabeth McDowell, Teachers College, Columbia University," n.d., B11 F14, Hendley Papers.

4. Kilpatrick Diaries, 13 February 1938; George W. Hartmann to Ralph Himstead, 17 February 1939, B1 AAUP Papers. Hartmann had no clinical basis for that assessment. When McDowell pursued the case in court, Hartmann derided her interest as "litigious paranoia." See Hartmann to Himstead, 9 March 1940, B1, AAUP Papers.

5. Minutes of the Executive Board of the CTU, 19 May 1938 (RC390); Kilpatrick Diaries, 13 February 1938.

6. Kilpatrick records the case of psychologist Lois Meek, whose divorce and quick remarriage led Russell to ask for her resignation, which Kilpatrick thought appropriate. See Kilpatrick Diaries, 27 April 1938; and Kathryn McHale (AAUW) to Ralph Himstead, 24 May 1938, B1, AAUP Papers.

7. *College Newsletter*, 1 (8 March 1938), 3; *College Newsletter*, 2 (16 December 1938), 1. See also Kilpatrick Diaries, 12 November 1938; and Minutes of General Membership Meeting CTU, 2 December 1938 (RC388).

8. *Educational Vanguard*, 3 (17 February 1938), 1–2.

9. John L. Childs private hearing, 30 January 1941 (RC524), 7; "Resolution Tabled by Teachers College Union Members," typescript copy titled as "Exhibit 1" (evidently copied and authorized by the Coudert committee) (RC61); *New York Post*, 30 December 1938, 8 (clipping in RC61).

10. *College Newsletter*, 1 (12 May 1938), 1. The words are the reporter's.

11. James Wechsler, "Twilight at Teachers College," *Nation*, 17 December 1938, 661–63; *Educational Vanguard*, 1 (23 July 1936), 1. Labor tensions in the

Columbia cafeterias three years earlier had led President Butler to expel Reed Harris, editor of the student newspaper, for exposing mistreatment of workers, leading to one of the earliest student strikes of the 1930s. Only one professor, Mark Van Doren, signed a petition for Harris. According to Wechsler, Dewey refused. See Robert Cohen, *When the Old Left Was Young: Student Radicals and America's First Mass Student Movement, 1929–1941* (New York: Oxford University Press, 1993), 63–68.

12. Wechsler, "Twilight," 661–63.

13. Kilpatrick Diaries: 10 March, 16 March, 30 March, 4 April, 7 April, 13 April, 8 May, 21 November, and 24 December 1936; 5 October 1938.

14. *Educational Vanguard*, 1 (10 August 1936), 1; *New York Times*, 24 July 1936, 19; George S. Counts, "Whose Twilight?," *Social Frontier*, 5 (February 1939), 137.

15. Childs private testimony, 1–4; *New York Post*, 31 October 1944, clipping in Childs Faculty File, TC Archive. Contrary to Russell's insinuations, Childs never joined the Communist Party. See Childs to James Mendenhall, 4 October 1935, B1 F2, Kheel 5279.

16. Wechsler, "Twilight," 661, 663; Childs, letter to the editor, *Nation*, 24 December 1938, 703. The union noted that he had never been a member of the CTU. He had simply ceased paying his dues to Local 5, to which he did belong, back in December 1937. See *College Newsletter*, 2 (27 January 1939), 1.

17. Childs, et al., "Teachers College and Mr. Wechsler," *Nation*, 24 December 1938, 703. Though unquestionably red-baiting and very probably untrue, this accusation was not entirely unreasonable: Wechsler had only the year before quit the YCL (he joined in 1935). See Murray Polner, "James Wechsler: The Editor Who Dared Challenge J. Edgar Hoover," History News Network, http://hnn.us/article/2869.

18. L. Hendin, "Communist Intrigues Drive Liberal Professors from Teachers Union," *Jewish Daily Forward*, 3 January 1939, typescript copy, translator unknown, B1, Kheel 5279.

19. *New York Times*, 30 December 1938, 1, 2.

20. *New York Post*, 29 December 1938, 1, 8; Childs private hearing, 16–17. In the process, he also exposed as a Communist Julliard psychology instructor Howard Langford, who had tried to mediate the dispute and who lost his job as a result. See *New York Post* 31 December 1938, 8; letter to the editor, *Nation*, 28 January 1939, 131; *New York Times*, 24 May 1940, 22; and Childs private hearing, 17.

21. "Statement Issued by the Joint Board of Teachers Unions of New York City regarding Professor Childs' Statements in the New York Post of December 29, 1938," signed by Edwin Berry Burgum, Chair; Clifford McAvoy, Vice-Chair; and Helen Lokshin, Secretary; for Teachers Union joint board, B13 F23, Hendley Papers.

22. Minutes of the General Membership meeting of CTU, 5 January 1939 (RC388); letter to the editor, *Nation*, 14 January 1939, 76, signed by Edward Berry Burgum and Arnold Shukotoff, Executive Board of CTU, 3 January 1939.

See also Childs's response, *Nation*, 14 January 1939, 76. Communist Party member and City College instructor Morris Schappes thought the press release unfair and pressed unsuccessfully for its tone to be softened. See *College Newsletter* (27 January 1939), 1; minutes of the Executive Board of CTU, 17 January 1939 (RC391); and *College Newsletter*, 2 (10 February 1939), 1. The composition of the committee might not have been satisfactory to Childs, since it included several people whom he probably suspected were party members. See Shukotoff to Childs, 20 January 1939, typescript copy entered as evidence, RC61. For Childs's refusal, see Childs to Shukotoff, 24 January 1939, typescript copy entered as evidence, RC61.

23. Minutes of the Executive Board of CTU, 3 January 1939 (RC391); *New York Times*, 4 January 1939, 16; *New York Times*, 30 December 1938, 1, 2; *New York Times*, 31 December 1938, 17; *College Newsletter* 2 (14 October 1938), 4. See also Dewey to Henry Linville, 13 February 1939 and 20 February 1939, B3 F54, UFT Papers.

24. Counts, "Whose Twilight?"

25. *College Newsletter* 2 (27 January 1939), 2; *New York Times*, 6 February 1939, 1; *New York Times*; 14 February 1939, 2; New York *Herald Tribune*, 20 January 1939, 1, 4, clipping in RC506.

26. *New York Times*, 28 April 1939, 1. Hunter College's Charles Hughes noted the ease with which Counts and his allies made it onto the ballot. Nominations were made at an open meeting. See also *New York Times*, 3 May 1939, 5; *New York Times*, 24 May 1939, 24.

27. Counts, *Prospects of American Democracy* (New York: John Day Company, 1938), 37, 40, 51, 75, 78, 194–95. Counts wrote the book in 1937. See Counts interview, 32.

28. Counts, *Prospects*, 170; Counts, *Schools Can Teach Democracy* (New York: John Day Company, 1939), 6.

29. Counts, *Schools Can Teach*, 16.

30. Counts, *Schools Can Teach*, 18–19. Dean Russell struck the same theme in a three-day event that brought liberal educators together with bankers, the US Chamber of Commerce, labor leaders, politicians, and international dignitaries. See *New York Times*, 18 August 1939, 9; and "Changing Scene," *Frontiers of Democracy* 6 (1939), 3–7. For the criticism from the teachers union, see *New York Teacher*, 5, no. 1, 5.

31. Jesse Newlon, "Are We Growing Up Politically?," *Social Frontier*, 5 (June 1939), 262–64. On Counts' friendship with Newlon, see Counts interview. See also Goodwin Watson, "Is Progressive Education Progressing?," *American Teacher*, 23 (February 1939), 7–10.

32. Earl Browder, "Education—An Ally in the Workers' Struggle," *Social Frontier*, 1 (January 1935), 22–23. For a misrepresentation of Browder's essay, see C. A. Bowers, *Progressive Educator and the Depression: The Radical Years* (New York: Random House, 1969), 118. On the workers' school movement generally, see Marvin Gettleman, "Lost World of US Labor Education: Curricula at East

and West Coast Community Schools, 1944–1957," paper presented at the 2001 Gotham History Festival, http://www.gothamcenter.org/festival/2001/confpapers/gettleman.pdf. See also Begun private testimony, 28 October 2941, 28–30 (RC523).

33. Bruce Minton, "Program for Democracy," *New Masses*, 11 October 1938, 26–28.

34. Other reviewers recognized the straw-man argument as one of Counts' main points. See Thomas C. Linn, "Books of the Times," *New York Times*, 17 September 1938, 15; John Chamberlain, "Ten Points for Democrats," *New Republic*, 28 September 1938, 219–20; and Kilpatrick Diaries, 27 September 1938.

35. For an example of the liberal invective see G[eorge] H[artmann], "Changing Scene," *Social Frontier* 5 (May 1939), 228.

36. Hartmann, "Union Teachers and Intellectual Integrity (Letter to the Editor)," *New Republic*, 26 April 1939, 337–40; Hartmann, "Hoodwinking Labor-Minded Teachers," B6 F21, Hendley Papers. The latter is a draft of the former. See Childs private testimony, 4–6, 24.

37. Lovestoneite Bertram Wolfe pointed out, "there are many people who accept their [the Communist Party's] views without actually feeling that they are following their line, or without the feeling that they are tied up with them in any way." See Wolfe private hearing, 14 October 1940, 17 (RC547). See also Edwin Berry Burgum and Charles Hendley, "Union Teachers and Intellectual Integrity (Letters to the Editor)," *New Republic*, 26 April 1939, 340. Hartmann's name begins to show up in CTU executive board minutes in mid-1938, but he is always listed as absent. Minutes of the Executive Board of CTU, 1938 (RC390). On Childs, see *College Newsletter*, 27 January 1939, 1; and Childs private testimony, 4. On Counts, see CTU, Minutes of General Membership meeting, 5 January 1939 (RC388).

38. *New Masses*' book review editor Granville Hicks almost certainly knew party members among the accused academics, but pleaded ignorance to Rapp-Coudert interrogators. See Granville Hicks private testimony, 20 May 1941, RC530: 43.

39. Goodwin Watson to Childs, 14 April 1938, typescript copy entered as evidence (RC61); Childs to Watson, 16 April 1938, typescript copy entered as evidence (RC61).

40. Based on a survey of the minutes of CTU General Membership meetings from 1938 through 1941 (RC388). Such was also a matter of open public discussion. See *College Newsletter*, 2 (14 October 1938), 1; minutes of General Membership meeting of CTU, 7 October 1938 (RC388).

41. *New York Times*, 24 August 1939, 17; *New York Times*, 22 August 1939, 13. The vote was 344 to 320. See Hattiesburg (Miss.) *American*, 25 August 1939, 11; and *New York Times*, 20 August 1939, 13.

42. *American Teacher*, 24 (September 1939), 1–2; *New York Teacher*, 5 (October 1939), 5.

43. *American Teacher*, 24, Part II (November 1939), 5–6; H[arold] R[ugg], "Changing Scene," *Frontiers of Democracy*, 6, no. 48 ([November] 1939), 35–38; John Dewey to Henry Linville, 13 February 1939 and 20 February 1939, B3 F54, UFT Papers; Linville, "How Communists Injure Teachers' Unions," *Social Frontier*, 5 (March 1939), 173.

44. *American Teacher*, 24 (October 1939), 5–6. See also *American Teacher*, 24 (March 1940), 5–6.

45. Counts, "Is Our Union Controlled by Communists?," *American Teacher*, 24 (December 1939), 5.

46. Counts, "Is Our Union," 5.

47. "Hearings before a Special Committee on Un-American Activities, House of Representatives, Seventy-Sixth Congress First Session on H. Res. 282," 7, testimony of George Hartmann, 27 November 1939, 6841, 6847; "Editorial: The Dies Committee and True Americanism," *Frontiers of Democracy*, 6, no. 50, ([January] 1940), 102–04.

48. *New York Times*, 20 August 1940, 16.

49. Marjorie Murphy, *Blackboard Unions: The AFT and the NEA, 1900–1980* (Ithaca: Cornell University Press, 1990), 168–69. The payoff came that fall in the form of two full-time organizers and travelling expenses for volunteer recruiters. See *American Teacher*, 25 (November 1940), 5.

50. Allies and members of the rival Teachers Guild openly lobbied and made deals at the convention, a practice that should have been condemned by the AFT leadership. See "A Meeting of the Teachers Union of the City of New York, Local 5," stenographic transcript of meeting at Washington Irving High School, New York City, 13 September 1940, 8–9 (RC411); and *New York Times*, 23 August 1940, 14. See also "Interview with Mr. & Mrs. U & T X," 16 September 1940 (RC93).

51. *American Teacher*, 25 (September 1940), 2; "A Meeting of the Teachers Union," 38–39; *New York Times*, 24 August 1940, 4; J. H. N[ewlon], "Changing Scene: The A.F. of T. Moves Forward," *Frontiers of Democracy*, 7 ([October] 1940), 3–7; Judy Kutulas, *American Civil Liberties Union and the Making of Modern Liberalism, 1930–1960* (Chapel Hill: University of North Carolina Press, 2006), 73.

52. Neil Jumonville, *Critical Crossings: The New York Intellectuals in Postwar America* (Berkeley: University of California Press, 1991), 40–48.

53. *New York Times*, 13 December 1937, 1; David C. Engerman, "John Dewey and the Soviet Union: Pragmatism Meets Revolution," *Modern Intellectual History*, 3, no. 1 (2006), 59; Sidney Hook, *Out of Step: An Unquiet Life in the Twentieth Century* (New York: Harper & Row, 1987), Chapter 17.

54. *New York Times*, 25 October 1939, 1, 12.

55. Hook, "Academic Freedom and 'the Trojan Horse' in American Education," *Bulletin of the American Association of University Professors*, 25 (December 1939), 550–51. Similarly, Coudert declared that "intellectual dishonesty" was "the most serious of crimes against free society." See "Summary of Speech by

Senator Frederic R. Coudert, Jr., at Luncheon of United Kindergarten Mothers Association" at Hotel Pennsylvania, 18 January 1941, B16 F4, Coudert Papers.

56. The Supreme Court would not protect academic free speech until the Keyeshian decision of 1967. See Marjorie Heins, *Priests of Our Democracy: The Supreme Court, Academic Freedom, and the Anti-Communist Purge* (New York: New York University Press, 2013), Introduction.

57. Hook, "Academic Freedom," 552–53. J. B. Matthews, the Dies committee chief of staff, first used the Homeric metaphor of the Trojan horse, adopting it from the 1935 speech by Georgi Dimitrov in which he declared the Popular Front. See Special Committee on Un-American Activities, "Investigation of Un-American Activities and Propaganda," 75th Congress, 3 January 1939 (US Government Printing Office, 1939), 23–24; and Dies, *Trojan Horse in America* (New York: Dodd, Mead and Company, 1940). According to Walter Goodman, Matthews ghostwrote this book for Dies. See Goodman, *The Committee: The Extraordinary Career of the House Committee on Un-American Activities* (New York: Farrar, Strauss and Giroux, 1968), 35.

58. Christopher Phelps, *Young Sidney Hook: Marxist and Pragmatist* (Ann Arbor: University of Michigan Press, 2005); Hook to Ralph Ingersoll, 23 July 1940, B117 F7, Hook Papers.

59. Official Statement of the Committee for Cultural Freedom, CCF *Bulletin*, 1 (15 October 1939), 6–7.

60. Kutulas, *Long War: The Intellectual People's Front and Anti-Stalinism, 1930–1940* (Durham: Duke University Press, 1995), 155.

61. *College Newsletter*, 1 (7 April 1938), 4; *Educational Signpost*, 1 (March 1938), 1–2; *New York Times*, 11 April 1938, 32; *New York Times*, 11 December 1938, 50. Only scientists were asked to sign the document. See "Confidential Press Release" (for publication, 11 December 1938), ACDIF section, F8, Boas Papers.

62. Jumonville, *Critical Crossings*, 50. Hook initially set up an organization called League Against Totalitarianism, sparking the formation of the *Socialist* League Against Totalitarianism by Dwight MacDonald and other anti-Stalinist writers, artists, and academics. Their manifesto avoided Hook's moral equivalences by aligning "reactionary" progressives with "a national-democratic myth conjured out of America's historic infancy." See "Manifesto and Appeal (Letter to the Editor)," *Nation*, 15 July 1939, 83–84; and Eugene Lyons, *Red Decade: The Stalinist Penetration of America* (New York: Bobbs-Merrill, 1941), 343.

63. Phelps, *Young Sidney Hook*, 203; Jumanville, *Critical Crossings*, 50; "Committee Gains Wide Support," *Bulletin* of the Committee for Cultural Freedom, 1 (15 October 1939), 1, 6–7. The quotation is from Thomas Jefferson, B2 F9, CCF Papers. The statement also was republished many times in whole or part, including in *Social Frontier*, 5 (June 1939), 258.

64. Minutes of 16 May [1939] meeting, B2 F8, CCF Papers. Twenty-three people were present at this first meeting. Counts signed an official CCF letter

supporting Bertrand Russell with Dewey, Hook, and Kallen in April 1940. Dewey, et al., to Fiorello H. La Guardia, 2 April 1940, Dewey Correspondence. Counts attended in late November 1939. According to an undated letter from Hook to Franz Boas, a committee for organizing the CCF was active as early as mid-April. See Hook to Franz Boas, n.d, B117 F7, Hook Papers.

65. *Daily Worker*, 19 May 1939, n.p., clipping in B2 F23, Kheel 5279.

66. Hook's correspondence suggests that Grebanier started working with the committee during the summer. See Ferdinand Lundberg to Hook, 14 August 1939, B117 F7, Hook Papers.

67. Freda Kirchwey, "Red Totalitarianism," *Nation*, 27 May 1939, 605; Lundberg, "Committee for Cultural Freedom" (Letter to the Editor) *New Republic*, 28 June 1939, 218.

68. Lundberg, "Committee for Cultural Freedom," 217. The history of the Cold War–era CCF is well chronicled elsewhere. See Frances Stonor Saunders, *Cultural Cold War: The CIA and the World of Arts and Letters* (New York: New Press, 1999). See also Jumonville, *Critical Crossings*, Chapter 1.

69. Dewey, "Committee for Cultural Freedom (Letters to the Editor)," *New Republic*, 14 June 1939, 161–62; Dewey to Hook 13 September 1939, Dewey Correspondence; Dewey to Evelyn Scott, [19] November 1939, Dewey Correspondence.

70. Editorial, "Liberty and Common Sense," *New Republic*, 31 May 1939, 90; Hook, *Out of Step*, 205–7. Boas proposed that the ACDIF continue to focus on academic freedom, while the CCF concentrated on artists, writers, lawyers, and the nonacademic professions. See "Relations with Professor Boas' Organization," CCF *Bulletin*, 1 (October 1939), 11. See also Boas to Dewey, 26 May 1939, Dewey Correspondence.

71. *New York Times*, 15 May 1939, 13; Boas, letter to the editor, *New York Times*, 17 May 1939, 22. See also Hook, letter to the editor, *New York Times*, 17 May 1939, 22.

72. The key letter is Dewey to Hook, 27 May 1939. It is part of a complicated skein of letters that were exchanged among Boas, Hook, and Dewey that May concerning Hook's statement in the *New York Times* and the ability of the CCF and the ACDIF to coexist. See Hook to Boas, [17 May 1939] and Boas to Hook, 20 May 1939, B17 F7, Hook Papers. A few historians will object to this reading of Dewey's intentions, pointing to letters between Dewey and Hook the following September as evidence of a more temperate approach on Dewey's part. See especially Dewey to Hook, 13 September 1939, concerning the CCF response to the notorious Letter of the 400 in August. See Phelps, *Young Sidney Hook*, 210; and Kutulas, *Long War*, 157–59. Hook thought Dewey's draft of that response "very mild," but Dewey's difference with Hook on the tone was tactical, as both he and Hook point out. See Hook's note on Dewey's draft, Dewey to Signers of 14 August 1939 Open Letter on Soviet Union, 13 September 1939, Dewey Correspondence. The conflict with his old friend Boas

led Dewey to try resigning as the CCF's honorary chair, citing to Hook public misrepresentations of Dewey's position that were brought to the old philosopher's attention by Boas. See Boas to Dewey, 12 November 1939; Dewey to Boas, 12 November 1939; Dewey to Hook, 16 November 1939; and Dewey to Frank Trager, 16 November 1939 and 18 November 1939. Yet this resignation does not appear to have stuck. Dewey continued to associate himself publicly with the CCF well into 1940, indicating that his disagreement with Hook was not as serious as it might have seemed. See *New York Times* 6 March 1940, 25; and Dewey, letter to the editor, *New York Times*, 6 May 1940, 12.

73. Fifty years later, Hook even more baldly accused the ACDIF of being a "Communist party front." See Hook, *Out of Step*, 257–59; Committee for Cultural Freedom, "Stalinist Outposts in the United States," April 1940, typescript (RC94); Wesley C. Mitchell to Hook, 30 April 1940, B117 F7, Hook Papers; and Hook to Mitchell, 3 May 1940, B117 F7, Hook Papers. On the American Jewish Committee's funding of ACDIF, see Kutulas, *Long War*, 159. ACDIF financial summaries indicate that they depended on the American Jewish Committee, Corliss Lamont, one of the Rosenwald daughters, and a couple of others for much of their funding. See "Contributors to the Committee since Its Inception," memo to ACDIF members, n.a., n.d., ACDIF F10, Boas Papers.

74. "To All Active Supporters of Democracy and Peace," *Nation*, 26 August 1939, 228; Lundberg to Hook [August 1939], B117 F7, Hook Papers; and Sidney Hook to Max Lerner, 23 August 1939, B117 F7, Hook Papers.

75. Hook, "Academic Freedom," 554–55.

76. Hook to Ward, 29 September 1939. In the case of journalist I. F. Stone, Hook tacitly threatened a CCF boycott if Stone and Maxwell Stewart remained on the *Nation's* editorial board. See Hook to Kirchwey, 23 August 1939, B117 F7, Hook Papers; Ward to Hook, 18 and 28 September 1939, B117 F7, Hook Papers; Hook to Roger Baldwin, 27 September and 18 October 1939, B117 F7, Hook Papers; and Hook to Ward, 2 [Oct] 1939, B117 F7, Hook Papers.

77. Baldwin to Hook, 8 December 1939, B117 F7, Hook Papers; Kutulas, *American Civil Liberties Union*, 65–66, 73–79. ACLU board member Norman Thomas supported Hook's charges against Ward. See Thomas to Hook, 24 October 1939, B28 F45, Hook Papers.

78. On his personality, see Phelps, *Young Sidney Hook*, 227. Evidence of Hook's tendency to "impute ... a capacity for treacherous dealing" dates back to the beginning of his academic career, as NYU philosopher Philip Wheelwright attested in a letter to Hook in late 1929. See Wheelwright to Hook, 23 December 1929, B30 F16, Hook Papers.

79. See Dewey to Signers of 14 August 1939 open letter on Soviet Union, 13 September 1939, Dewey Correspondence.

80. Lundberg, "Committee for Cultural Freedom," 217. Save for its intemperate finish, Lundberg's letter offered a trenchant condemnation of Popular Front excuses for Soviet brutality. See Lundberg to Hook 27 August 1939,

B117 F7, Hook Papers. See also Suzanne LaFollette to Hook, 24 August 1939, B117 F7, Hook Papers.

81. Joseph Ratner to Dewey, 20 November 1939, Dewey Correspondence.

9. CCNY

1. Jeffrey S. Gurock, *Jews in Gotham: New York Jews in a Changing City, 1920–2010* (New York: NYU Press, 2013), 47–49.

2. Robert Cohen, *When the Old Left Was Young: Student Radicals and America's First Mass Student Movement, 1929–1941* (New York: Oxford University Press, 1993), 108.

3. Cohen, *When the Old Left*, 130, 239. See also Sidney Hook, *Out of Step: An Unquiet Life in the Twentieth Century* (New York: Harper & Row, 1987), 209. Robinson left on a sabbatical at full pay ($21,000 a year, a fortune at that time) and full retirement calculated on that final salary. See Charles H. Tuttle private testimony, 5 December 1941, 6–7, 18–19 (RC561); and Nelson Mead to Paul Windels, 30 September 1940 (RC505).

4. *New York Times*, 26 January 1941, 1, 33; *New York Times*, 29 April 1941, 16; *New York Times*, 20 May 1941, 25; William G. Mulligan, Jr., memo [4 March 1941], B11 F13, Hendley Papers.

5. *New York Times*, 1 December 1940, 64; *New York Times*, 20 December 1940, 1.

6. *New York Times*, 11 December 1940, 29; Selsam, et al., (1941).

7. *New York Times*, 24 January 1941, 1.

8. Hunter classics instructor Meriwether Stuart confirmed Selsam; history instructor Henry Klein, who no longer taught at BC; and hygiene instructor Clara Parodnek. Eventually, William Canning and Annette Sherman-Gottsegen confirmed biology instructor Samuel Kaiser and historian Herbert Morais. See "Brooklyn College Teachers on Whom We Have Two or More Witnesses," 21 May 1941 (RC47); and Meriwether Stuart private testimony, 11 December 1940, 1–5 (RC544).

9. "Memorandum of Interview with Prof. Grebanier on December 17, 1940" (RC153); "RE: Brooklyn College, February 3, 1941" (RC153); "Memorandum of Confidential Talk with Dr. Grebanier, November 18, 1940" (RC153).

10. *New York Times*, 19 November 1940, 27; *New York Times*, 7 December 1940, 22; *New York Times*, 12 December 1940, 22; Ordway Tead to William Chanler, reprinted in CPDE, "Education Defense Bulletin" (18 December 1940), B17 F3, "Printed materials," Coudert Papers.

11. *Brooklyn Eagle*, 4 December 1940, 3.

12. *New York Times*, 17 December 1940, 29; *New York Times*, 22 December 1940, 34; *New York Times*, 21 January 1941, 16; *New York Times*, 18 March 1941, 1; Lawrence H. Chamberlain, *Loyalty and Legislative Action: A Survey of Activity by the New York State Legislature, 1919–1949.* (Ithaca: Cornell University Press, 1951), 159–63.

13. "In the Matter of the Charges Preferred against Seymour A. Copstein," trial hearings of the BHE, 11 July 1941, 8, B1 F8, Copstein Case Files.

14. "In the Matter of Charges Preferred against Walter Scott Neff," transcript of hearings before BHE trial committee, 16 July 1941, 64–68, B3 F25, Neff Case Files.

15. Private testimony of William Canning, 23 January 1941, 1 (RC576); catalog of Columbia University, 1936–7 (Morningside Heights: Columbia University, [1937]), 215; 1940 US Census, New York County, New York State, New York City, population schedule, enumeration district 31–251, sheet 3-B, line 68–69, William and Edna Canning, plus supplementary questions, digital image, Archives.gov, http://1940census.archives.gov. Physicist Lloyd Motz, reporting that he earned on average $600 a year as a CCNY instructor with a PhD, called the conditions of employment in the evening division "evil." See CDPE, Report on testimony of accused teachers, B7 F10, Schappes Papers.

16. Edna Moskowitz Canning private hearing, 19 March 1941, 2, 26, 38–39 (RC571); Neff BHE hearings, 31; memo of trip to Washington in October 1940 (RC600); "Interview with Mr. Hillman Bishop," 24 October 1940 (RC79). On Bishop's history, see William Canning private testimony, 10 February 1941, 95 (RC576); Copstein BHE hearings, 51–55; Hillman Bishop to Henry Linville, 21 April 1936, B1 F18, Kheel 5279; Bishop to Linville, 17 August 1937, B2 F22, Kheel 5279; and *Campus*, October 7 1941, 1, 4.

17. Copstein BHE hearings, 55.

18. Copstein BHE hearings, 55; William Canning private hearing, 28 January 1941, 31–33 and 11 February 1941, 204 (RC576).

19. Canning private hearing, 10 February 1941, 93.

20. The one exception was Alexander Lehrman, a professor in the chemistry department. Canning private hearing, 28 January 1941, 35, 37, 42. Townshend Harris High School served as the preparatory school for CCNY and was attached to its uptown campus.

21. Canning private hearing, 28 January1941, 37; Theodore Geiger private hearing, 25 February 1941, 16 (RC528).

22. Canning private hearing, 10 February 1941, 140 and 28 January 1941, 61; Rapp-Coudert Report (1942), 261.

23. Chamberlain, *Loyalty*, 100.

24. Transcript of BHE trial of Samuel Margolis, 10 April 1942, B3, Rapp-Coudert CCNY.

25. Theodore Geiger to Frederic R. Coudert, Jr., 6 March 1941, and 9 April 1941, with "Statement for the Record by Theodore Geiger" attached (RC141); memo dictated by E[rnest] H[ochwald], 7 April 1943 (RC141); Hochwald to the Honorable Irwin Davidson, 7 April 1943 (RC141); Madelyn Brown to William Canning, 31 March 1943, (RC589).

26. Canning private hearing, 28 January 1941, 63, 81. The BHE grudgingly acknowledged that CCNY chemistry instructor William J. Withrow, who

was suspended on grounds that Sherman saw him at a "unit meeting," might also have been wrongly accused. BHE reinstated him, acknowledging that being seen at a meeting was not sufficient grounds for assuming he was in the party. He was punished, however, for refusing to cooperate with the Coudert committee by being denied his back wages. The BHE, however, did not generalize the principle exonerating Withrow to other cases. See *New York Times,* 16 March 1943, 15; *New York Times,* 8 September 1953, 31.

27. On Finley, see Daniel P. Tompkins, "Moses Finkelstein and the American Scene: The Political Formation of Moses Finley, 1932–1955," in *Moses Finley and Politics*, ed. by W.V. Harris (Leiden: Brill, 2013), 6.

28. Canning private hearing, 11 February 1941, 177–78, 226 and 28 January 1941, 65, 69, 73, 77. See lists of suspects in RC221.

29. Canning private hearing, 11 February 1941, 42, 213–15.

30. Ben Mandel to Robert Morris, 8 January 1941 (RC600); Trager private hearing, 2 April 1941 (RC546), 3–5, 7–8; RC public hearings, December 4, 183, 219; *New York Times,* 16 January 1978, 78; Philip Locker private hearing, 20 March 1941 (RC535), 3; memo: "Principle Points in re: Selsam" (RC315); Lewis Feuer private hearing, 20 March 1941 (RC527), 16; George Searle to Arad Riggs, 10 February 1953 (RC42).

31. *New York Times,* 4 December 1940, 1, 30; "Memorandum of Confidential Talk with Dr. Grebanier at His Home, 11/26/40" (RC153); Canning private hearing, 28 January 1941, 42–43, 59–60. On prosthetic memory, see Alison Landsberg, *Prosthetic Memory: The Transformation of American Remembrance in the Age of Mass Culture* (New York: Columbia University Press, 2004).

32. Canning private hearing, 10 February 1941, 103–4.

33. Canning private hearing, 11 February 1941, 166–67, 169.

34. Canning private hearing, 11 February 1941, 168, 171.

35. Documents on the Eisenberger case in B1 F17 of the UFT Papers. *Campus,* 7 October 1941, 1, 4.

36. *New York Times*, 7 March 1941, 1, 12; *New York Times*, 8 March, 1. The full transcript of Canning's public testimony of March 1941 is lost. Parts, however, were reproduced in the committee's final report and in legal documents, including transcripts of BHE trials later that year.

37. Canning private hearing, 10 February 1941, 151.

38. Edna Canning private hearing, 19 March 1941, 17–18, 24–26, 37 (RC571).

39. *New York Times*, 8 March 1941, 8.

40. Canning private hearing, 10 February 1941, 125; *New York Times,* 10 June 1941, 25.

41. Canning private hearing, 11 February 1941, 243–45.

42. Rapp-Coudert Report (1942), 267.

43. Canning private hearing, 28 January, 66–68, 74; RC Report (1942), 270–73; Canning's rough draft eventually fell into the Coudert committee's hands with incriminating marginal scribbles in Bander's handwriting, evidence

that led to his dismissal from the public-school system that fall for lying, not for indoctrination. See *New York Times,* 11 September 1941, 25.

44. New York Times, 8 March 1941, 1.
45. Canning private hearing, 11 February 1941, 221.
46. Canning private hearing, 28 January 1941, 63.
47. He identified Schlauch and McGill as people who were "given permission to spend their time in scholarly work," with no other basis than the fact that they got their scholarly work done. See Canning private hearing, 28 January 1941, 81.
48. Canning private hearing, 10 February 1941, 140–41.
49. Canning private hearing, 28 January 1941, 69–70.
50. Rapp-Coudert Report (1942), 246, 248.
51. Rapp-Coudert Report (1942), 250.
52. Annette Sherman (Gottsegen) private hearing, 15 February 1941, 1–5, 8 (RC576). Regarding her marriage, see *Brooklyn Eagle*, 30 July 1937, 24.
53. Sherman private hearing, 15 February 1941, 24, 26 and 26 February 1941, 63, 67, 78, 85.
54. "Digest of Private Testimony of Annette Sherman" (RC304).
55. Public hearings, December 1940, 607–11; Committee for Defense of Public Education, Report on testimony of accused teachers, B7, F10, Schappes Papers.
56. Compiled from public and private testimony as well as lists in RC560.

10. Flirting with the Right

1. "New York Schools Are Invaded: The Coudert Committee a Spur to Anti-Semitism, a Shield for Pro-Fascists," (New York: Committee for Defense of Public Education, June 1941), 3, copy in B6 F11, Kheel 5445; Louis Lerman, "When Freedom Needs Defending," *New York Teacher* (June 1941), 10–11.
2. Quoted in Nicholas von Hoffman, *Citizen Cohn* (New York: Doubleday, 1988), 109.
3. David Suchoff, "Rosenberg Case and the New York Intellectuals," in *Secret Agents: The Rosenberg Case, McCarthyism, and Fifties America*, ed. by Marjorie Garber and Rebecca L. Walkowitz (New York: Routledge, 1995), 159; Howard Morley Sachar, *History of Jews in America* (New York: Knopf, 1992), 636; Deborah Dash Moore, "Reconsidering the Rosenbergs: Symbol and Substance in Second Generation American Jewish Consciousness," *Journal of American Ethnic History*, 8 (Fall 1988), 26, 33–34.
4. See for instance Lucy S. Dawidowicz, "'Anti-Semitism' and the Rosenberg Case," *Commentary*, 14 (July 1952), 41–45.
5. "New York Schools Are Invaded," 2, 32,
6. Leonard Dinnerstein, *Antisemitism in America* (New York: Oxford University Press, 1994), 105, 121, 127.

7. Girolamo Valenti, "Italian Fascist Propaganda in the US," *Look*, 17 December 1940, 36–37; Alan Block, *Space, Time and Organized Crime* (New Brunswick: Transaction Publishers, 1994), 142–45. The Non-Sectarian Anti-Nazi League reported 183 Klan posts in New York and 184 in New Jersey. See "Ku Klux Klan Rides East," *Jewish Review* 3 (19 December 1940), 7.

8. Dinnerstein, *Antisemitism*, 113, 117. See also Ronald H. Bayor, "Klans, Coughlinites and Aryan Nations: Patterns of American Anti-Semitism in the Twentieth Century," *American Jewish History*, 76 (December 1986), 181–96. The *Tablet* printed Coughlin's radio addresses through 1940, after the radio priest was cut from the local airwaves, and regularly came to his defense. See "Naughty Coughlinites" (editorial rpt. From the *Evangelist* of Albany, N.Y.), *Tablet*, 31 (12 August 1939), 8; *Tablet*, 31 (30 September 1939), 10; and Richard Gid Powers, "American Catholics and Catholic Americans: The Rise and Fall of Catholic Anticommunism," *US Catholic Historian*, 22 (Fall, 2004), 19, 21–23.

9. George Britt, "Poison in the Melting-Pot," *Nation*, 1 April 1939, 374, 376.

10. James Wechsler, "Coughlin Terror," *Nation*, 22 July 1939, 93.

11. Wechsler, "Coughlin Terror," 92, 95. See also "Reply to Coughlin," *Nation*, 12 August 1939, 164–65; New York City Department of Investigation, "Investigation of Anti-American and Anti-Semitic Violence, (New York: City of New York, January 5 1941), 2, 36–43, 48, 128–29; *New York Times,* 15 January 1940, 1; *New York Times,* 3 January 1941, 21; Michael Cleary, "Behind the Christian Front Arrests," *New Masses*, 30 January 1940, 3–6; *Tablet*, 31 (27 January 1940), 1, 6; and Gene Fein, "For Christ and Country: The Anti-Semitic Anticommunism of Christian Front Street Meetings in New York City," *US Catholic Historian,* 22 (Fall, 2004), 43.

12. Rapp-Coudert Report (1942), 6–7; "Coudert Blind to Fascists," *PM*, April 24 1942, clipping in B6 F8, Kheel 5445.

13. "New York Schools Are Invaded," 5, 8–15. See also "Confidential Memorandum: On the Relation between the Coudert Committee and Certain Pro-Fascist and Anti-Semitic Groups and Activities," n.a., n.d., 9–11. AC-DIF F15, Boas Papers; Margaret Schlauch, "Fascist Activities in New York's Schools," in *For Victory over Fascism in Our Schools: Against Coudertism & Defeatism in Education* (Proceedings of a Conference in New York City, 27 July 1942, sponsored by the National Federation for Constitutional Liberties), 3, copy in B11 F10, Hendley Papers; minutes of the Executive Board of CTU, 4 January 1938 (RC390).

14. Bella Dodd, "Race Hatred at Gompers Vocational School," *Equality,* 2 (October–November 1940), 10–12; statement by Louis Solomon, n.d. (RC239 F2A).

15. Dodd, "Race Hatred," 10–12; statement by Harry Rutkoff, 15 September 1939 (RC239); statement by Felice Manzelli, n.d, (RC239).

16. "New York Schools Are Invaded," 8; T[imothy] F. Murphy to Werner Guenwald, n.d. "In the Matter of the Hearing of the Charges against

Timothy F. Murphy," 13 December 1940 hearing before Superintendent. Frederic Ernst. The last quotation comes from a typescript document on Samuel Gompers Vocational High School (n.d.), which is apparently a memo summarizing the case for fellow board of education members by Joanna Lindlof, to whom Murphy's colleagues brought their complaints in fall 1939. All three documents in RC239. The suspicion was not far-fetched. Several German spy operations had already been uncovered in New York City alone. See Thomas Reppetto, *Battleground New York City: Countering Spies, Saboteurs, and Terrorists since 1861* (Washington, D.C.: Potomac Books, 2012), 127–28; and *Jewish Review* 2 (31 October 1940), 1.

17. Dodd, "Race Hatred," 10–12.

18. *B'rith Abraham* 5 (10 March 1940), 1, clipping in RC239.

19. "New York Schools Are Invaded," 5, 10; *City Reporter*, 3 (15 April 1941), 1 (RC477); *City Reporter*, 3, no. 44 (2 December 1941), 2 (RC477); Maurice Rosenblatt to R. E. Herman, 18 December 1940 (RC477); Shelby Scates, *Maurice Rosenblatt and the Fall of Joseph McCarthy* (Seattle: University of Washington Press, 2006), Introduction.

20. "New York Schools Are Invaded," 11; Florina Lasker and Osmond K. Fraenkel to Frederick [sic] R. Coudert, Jr., 26 June 1941 (RC588).

21. Dinnerstein, *Antisemitism*, 121; Wechsler, "Coughlin Terror," 96; *B'rith Abraham* 5, (10 March 1940), 1.

22. "New York Schools Are Invaded," 8, 16. See also Miss Shultz to Judge Perlman, 26 March 1940 (RC239 F2A); and *Jewish Review* 2 (31 October 1940), 1.

23. Rapp-Coudert Report (1942), 6.

24. Rapp-Coudert Report (1942), 7.

25. See "Fascism at Columbia," *Nation*, 7 November 1934, 530–31; and M. B. Schnapper, "Mussolini's American Agents," *Nation*, 15 October 1938, 374–76.

26. "Digest and Extracts of Salvemini Report" (RC438); "Synopsis of Material Picked Up from Benjamin Mandel, Washington, D.C. September 4, 1942" (RC475).

27. Admirers of Mussolini included Board of Education President George Ryan. See Mateo Pretelli, "Culture or Propaganda? Fascism and Italian Culture in the United States," *Studi Emigrazione/Migration Studies*, 43, no. 161 (2006), 171–92.

28. "Digest and Extracts of Salvemini Report."

29. Interview with Remo Fioroni, 25 April 1941 (RC475).

30. Interview with Goffredo Pantaleoni, 6 January 1941 (RC468).

31. "Digest and Extracts of Salvemini Report, Leonard Covello, Additions and Corrections To" (RC425).

32. Interview with Dr. Milano, 10 December 1940 (RC475).

33. Interview with Dr. Milano, 10 December 1940 (RC475); "Digest and

Extracts of Salvemini Report"; interview with Dr. Max Leiberman [sic], 24 June [1941] (RC468). According to Coudert records, however, Covello's political associations were quite eclectic, including a long-standing working relationship with left-wing congressman Vito Marcantonio. See the list of suspects in RC560. After retiring in 1956, Covello promoted racial tolerance in the city's schools. See Salvatore John LaGumina, *Italian American Experience: An Encyclopedia* (New York: Garland, 2000), 149–50; interview with Dr. Gaudens Megaro, 28 January 1941 (RC475); interview with Mrs. Carlo La Porta, 19 December 1940 (RC475); memo on fascist suspects, 4 December 1941, F2C (RC239).

34. Interview with Goffredo Pantaleoni, 6 January 1941 (RC468); Lieberman interview. La Porta saw Ceroni frequently at the Italian Consulate, where she taught classes, meeting with the man in charge of distributing fascist propaganda. See La Porta interview.

35. Vittorio Ceroni private hearing, 12 June 1941, 16, 24–27, 35 (RC564); Vincent Luciani private hearing, 10 February 1941 (RC563).

36. Interview with Benjamin Gerdy, 29 January1941 (RC475); Simon Goldbloom private hearing, 7 February 1941 (RC528); interview with Umberto Gualtieri, 22 November 1940 (RC475).

37. Lieberman interview; Megaro interview.

38. Robert Herman made some effort to extend the investigation by subpoenaing Dante Society membership lists, yet he failed to find teachers among the listed members, which included Covello, Ceroni, Bonaschi, and Cosenza, all of whom were publicly acknowledged officers of the Society. See interview with [Giralamo] Valenti (notes), 18 October 1940 (RC475). Herman recorded his action in a marginal note. See Pantaleoni interview, 6 January 1941.

39. Memo, 20 August 1942 (RC477).

40. *Jewish Review,* 24 August 1939, 1.

41. [Thomas] Meehan, untitled typescript (RC478).

42. T[homas] M[eehan], untitled typescript memo, 18 December 1941 (RC239); handwritten list, n.a., n.d. (RC239). The writing appears to be Coudert staffer George Shea's.

43. Meriwether Stuart private hearing, 30 December 1040, 44 (RC544).

44. Leonard Covello private hearing, 26 September 1941 (RC524); "Hearings of Rapp-Coudert Committee—Private, January 12, 1942" (RC221); interview with Adolf Weil, 31 May 1941 (RC475). Della Chiesa, shows up on the committee's master list of suspects, but much of the testimony against her does not. Instead, what appears are her exculpatory statements (RC560).

45. Schnapper, "Mussolini's American Agents," 374–75; Alyn Brodsky, *Great Mayor: Fiorello La Guardia and the Making of the City of New York* (New York: Truman Talley Books / St. Martin's Press, 2003), 445–46.

46. "Dr. Alberto Bonaschi," n.a., n.d. (RC448); *New York Times,* 19 November 1948, 31; *New York Times,* 27 June 1949, 1; interview with Goffredo Pantaleoni, 12 December 1940 (RC475); "Coudert Blind to Fascists."

47. Stephen H. Norwood, *Third Reich in the Ivory Tower: Complicity and Conflict on American Campuses* (New York: Cambridge University Press, 2009), 61–70, 158–95.

48. Edgar Halliday private hearing, 11 July 1941, 15–20 (RC530); Francis T. Williamson private hearing, 20 February 1941, 18–20 (RC547).

49. Harry Gideonse private hearing, 16 December 1941, 20 (RC561).

50. Harry Wright private hearing, 19 December 1941, 26 (RC561).

11. Communism on Trial

1. *New York Times,* 9 June 2004, C15; transcript of public hearing 24 March 1941; Kenneth Ackley testimony, in Ackley Case Files. See also Morris U. Schappes, *Letters from the Tombs* (New York: Schappes Defense Committee, 1941), 109–15.

2. Alfred Kazin. *Starting Out in the Thirties* (Boston: Little, Brown and Company, 1962), 138.

3. *New York Times,* 15 March 1941, 1, 18.

4. *Campus,* 24 April 1936, 1; *Campus,* 24 April 1936, 1; Charles F. Horne to Morris U. Schappes, 22 April 1936 (RC314); Horne to BHE, 28 April 1936 (RC314). On Horne, see Adam Laats, *Other School Reformers: Conservative Activism in American Education* (Harvard, 2015), 93–94. On the rotational strategy, see CDPE Accused.

5. *Campus,* 19 May 1936, 1; CCNY *Union Teacher,* 6 (11 May 1936), 1; Stephen Leberstein, "Morris U. Schappes at City College," *Jewish Currents*, September–October 2004, 22–26.

6. Bella Dodd, *School of Darkness*, 120–29. Dodd may have been right, but her account has many chronological inaccuracies (e.g., she reports the dates of the investigation incorrectly). Schappes recalls having made the decision himself. See Leberstein, "Morris U. Schappes," 26.

7. Bruce Minton, "Learn from This Teacher," *New Masses,* 8 July 1941, 15.

8. The two were Abraham Goodhartz from the registrar's office and history instructor Oscar Zeichner. See *New York Times,* 15 March 1941, 1, 18.

9. *New York Times,* 11 March 1941, 1; *New York Times,* 18 March 1941, 1, 6.

10. *New York Times,* 19 March 1941, 1; BHE, "Amended Charges, in the Matter of the Charges Preferred against Morris U. Schappes," 24 March 1941, B4 F28, Schappes Case Files.

11. *New York Times,* 29 June 1941, 1.

12. Gideonse to Members of the ACDIF, 8 October 1941 (RC593).

13. Robert J. Oppenheimer to Harry Gideonse, 27 October 1941, copy in ACDIF F17, Boas Papers.

14. "Memorandum of the New York City Chapter of the National Lawyers Guild, Amicus Curiae," B4 F28, Schappes Case Files.

15. *New York Times,* 18 March 1941, 1, 6; *New York Times,* 26 March 1941, 25; *New York Times,* 20 March 1941, 23; *New York Times,* 21 March 1941, 23.

16. The committee released the report to all the major newspapers, belying its claim to "refrain from making charges in the public press." See Rapp-Coudert Interim Report (1941), 60, 62, 65, 67, 71; and *New York Times,* 24 March 1941, 1, 12.

17. Lawrence H. Chamberlain, *Loyalty and Legislative Action: A Survey of Activity by the New York State Legislature, 1919–1949.* (Ithaca: Cornell University Press, 1951), 102, 110–11; CDPE, "Education Defense Bulletin" (26 March 1941), 1, B1 F4, Rapp-Coudert CCNY; *New York Times,* 25 March 1941, 1, 32.

18. Transcript of public hearing 23 April 1941, Philip S. Foner testimony, 3, B2 F14, Foner Case Files; Transcript of Ackley public hearing, 24 March 1941, 8, B1 F4, Ackley Case Files.

19. *Withrow,* 1941, 20; *PM,* 9 April 1941, 11; *New York Times,* 9 April 41, 27; *Brooklyn Eagle* 8 April 1941, 3.

20. CDPE Accused. Senators John L. Buckley and Peter T. Farrell, both of Queens, joined Coudert. See *PM,* 9 April 1941, 11; *Brooklyn Eagle,* 23 April 1941, 1, 10; and *New York Times,* 24 April 1941, 10.

21. CDPE Accused.

22. CDPE, "Education Defense Bulletin" (6 March 1941), B1 F4 Rapp-Coudert CCNY; *New York Times,* 7 March 1941, 1, 12.

23. E. Horton [Morris U. Schappes], "Educational Commission Report," *Proceedings of New York State Communist Party 10th Annual Convention* (New York: New York State Communist Party, 1938), 291–93, copy in RC314.

24. CDPE, "Education Defense Bulletin" (26 March 1941), 2, B1 F4, Rapp-Coudert CCNY. See also "Statement of Educational Principles by Eleven Teachers in the Social Science Studies at the College of the City of New York Whose Teaching Methods Were Attacked before the Rapp-Coudert Committee," 11 March 1941, (RC133). Others tried to put into the record letters and petitions from students. See "Statement of Lewis Balamuth," 24 March 1941, 6, B1 F16, Ewen Papers.

25. Public hearing, 23 April 1941, Philip S. Foner testimony, 1–3, 7–9, 14–16. Jack Foner reported that his family took in Canning, fed him, did his laundry, and cared for him when he was ill so that he could continue his dissertation research and look for a permanent job in the city. See CDPE Accused; and *Brooklyn Eagle,* 23 April 1941, 1, 10.

26. *New York Times,* 27 March 1941, 25; *New York Times,* 22 April 1941, 23.

27. *New York Times,* 20 May 1941, 13. Many on the staff at CCNY were also highly qualified academically. Lederman served as a psychologist at the Educational Clinic. Mintus did graduate work in classical languages. Several of the librarians had advanced library degrees. See CDPE Accused.

28. *New York Times,* 7 June 1941, 32; *New York Times,* 6 June 1941, 1; *New York Times,* 11 June 1941, 23. The BHE identified a total of thirty-three who were suspended by late September, including Goldway and Schappes, in addition to Shukotoff and Withrow, whom the *Times* appears to have missed. The BHE did not count public-school teachers Klein, Bander, and Zysman, all under regular board of education jurisdiction. See Pearl Bernstein to Mayor

Fiorello H. La Guardia, 29 September 1941, B3271 F6 (microfilm reel 545), La Guardia Papers.

29. *New York Times,* 28 September 1941, 25; 16 October 1941, 20; 27 April 1941, 35. David Henry Anthony, *Max Yergan: Race Man, Internationalist, Cold Warrior* (New York: NYU Press, 2006), 184, 201. The total, not including summary dismissals of non-tenured staff and faculty, comes to thirty-six. I have counted James H. Healey and Eugene Stein, who were suspended but whose dismissals I could not confirm, as well as William Withrow, who was dismissed but reinstated later, Francis Thompson, whose dismissal after the war was successfully appealed, and Samuel Margolis, who was suspended in 1941 but whose dismissal did not go through until after the war.

30. *New York Times,* 1 July 1941, 18.

31. "In the Matter of the Charges Preferred against Walter Scott Neff," B4 F27, Neff Case Files.

32. CDPE Accused.

33. *New York Times,* 10 July 1941, 21; "In the Matter of the Charges Preferred against Arthur R. Braunlich," Report of the Trial Committee, 5 August 1941, B1 F6, Braunlich Case Files.

34. Rosenwein, a well-respected civil-liberties lawyer, helped defend the Hollywood 10. Rosenfeld represented the National Maritime Union in many court cases. Neuberger, who ran on the left-wing slate of the American Labor Party, is best known for defending Judith Coplon against espionage charges in 1950. See *Los Angeles Times,* 18 May 1996, 20; Jennifer E Langdon, *Caught in the Crossfire: Adrian Scott and the Politics of Americanism in 1940s Hollywood* (New York City: Columbia University Press, 2008), Chapter 9, ftnt 27; and *New York Times,* 10 March 1950, 1.

35. Neff BHE hearings, 5, 8. Weinstein dismissed written testimony from Neff's chair, Gardner Murphy, that he taught without bias, noting that "with respect to the charge of indoctrination, Dr. Murphy was not in the classroom with Dr. Neff . . . ," forgetting that neither was Canning, on whose testimony the charge was based. See Braunlich BHE hearings, 2.

36. *New York Times,* 10 June 1941, 25.

37. Samuel Rosenwein, "Application for Adjournment, in the Matters of the Charges Preferred against Seymour A. Copstein and Walter Scott Neff," B4 F27, Neff Case Files.

38. Neff BHE hearings, 10.

39. Copstein BHE hearings, 4–5, 8.

40. *New York Times,* 26 June 1941, 1.

12. Aftermath

1. *New York Times,* 13 July 1941, 2; *New York Times,* 31 August 1941, 13; *New York Times,* 5 October 1941, 4.

2. *New York Times,* 6 May 1941, 44; *New York Times,* 24 May 1941, 13; "Estimated Budget for Period from January 1, 1941 to July 1, 1941," B16 Coudert Papers.

3. *New York Times,* 1 January 1942, 27.

4. Morris Schappes to Morris R. Cohen, 27 November 1941, Schappes Papers; Cohen to Schappes, 5 December 1941, B7 F14, Schappes Papers.

5. Rapp-Coudert Interim Report (1941), 3; memo to Herbert A. Rapp from Coudert, et al., 11 February 1942, cover letter for the committee's final report, in B16 F12, Coudert Papers.

6. *New York Times,* 31 March 1942, 24.

7. Madelyn Brown to Detective Stanley Guadzo, Alien Squad, 4 June 1943 (RC593); interview with Dean John L. Bergstesser, City College Uptown Branch, 17 May 1943 (RC94); Mrs. J. H. Birmingham to Coudert, 26 April 1943, (RC582); "Interview with Mrs. Katherine Lynch" 14 June 1943 (RC94).

8. Coudert to Mrs. Phillip W. Haberman, Jr., 4 June 1945, B2 Coudert Papers.

9. The Coudert committee's 1942 report devotes roughly thirty pages to the Dewey trial, which it quotes extensively. See Rapp-Coudert Report (1942), 31, 185–214.

10. Rapp-Coudert Report (1942), 2–3, 20, 173–74, 287, 291.

11. Abraham Lefkowitz private testimony, 16 December 1941 (RC555); *New York Times,* 5 December 1941, 25.

12. *New York Times,* 22 March 1942, 21.

13. See Miriam Marder's account of YCL activism at BC in her private testimony of 11 July 1941 (RC570).

14. *New York Times,* 10 December 1941, 27.

15. *New York Times,* 4 December 1941, 24.

16. Corey Robin, *Fear: The History of a Political Idea* (New York: Oxford University Press, 2004), 182, 187, 202. The term "prescriptive publicity" is Earl Latham's.

17. *New York Times,* 2 October 41, 27.

18. Bella V. Dodd, Press release, NYS Federation of Teachers Unions, 23 April 1942, B16 F4, Coudert Papers.

19. [Hendley], "Sixth Annual . . . "; *New York Times,* 26 April 1942, 26.

20. "The Case against Coudert." B6 F3, Kheel 5445.

21. Allied Voters Against Coudert, "Who's Back of Coudert?," n.d., B7 F1, Schappes Papers.

22. Coudert to Phillip Haberman, Jr., 29 December 1942, B2 Coudert Papers; *New York Times,* 21 October 1942, 15.

23. *New York Times,* 22 October 1942, 17; *New York Times,* 23 October 1942, 14; *New York Times,* 20 October 1942, 15.

24. *New York Times,* 15 December 1942, 30; *New York Times,* 5 December 1942, 17.

25. The BHE, however, did not try to dismiss Margolis for membership in the party, only for failing to cooperate with the committee, for false and evasive testimony, and for participating in publishing the *Teacher Worker*. See *New York Times*, 19 October 1948, 20.

26. *New York Times*, 8 January 1948, 27.

27. *New York Times*, 9 January 1948, 8. On the Thompson case and the Feinberg Law, see Marjorie Heins, *Priests of Our Democracy: The Supreme Court, Academic Freedom, and the Anti-Communist Purge* (New York: New York University Press, 2013), 3–4, 69–70, 75–76.

28. Fred Niendorff to Governor Thomas Dewey, 16 November 1946, B15, Coudert Papers; Niendorff to Coudert, 17 November 1946, B15 Coudert Papers.

29. As early as 1948, Congress revisited the Coudert investigation in hearings before the House Committee on Labor and Education, at which many of the principle actors, including school officials as well as Dodd, George Counts, and Lefkowitz testified on factional disputes in the union among other things. See Marjorie Murphy, *Blackboard Unions: The AFT and the NEA, 1900–1980* (Ithaca: Cornell University Press, 1990), 184–87. On use of the files, see case of Seward High School speech instructor, Abraham Tauber, B15 Coudert Papers; and John J. Bennett ("Jack") to "Fritz," 1 April 1946, B15 Coudert Papers.

30. Celia Lewis Zitron, interview (by Glenn A. Goldstein, 8 May 1976), Tamiment Oral History collection. In a confidential note, Counts stalwart Mark Starr admitted the red-baiting strategy. See Starr to Members of the Executive Council, A. F. of T., 15 November 1940, B2 F2, Kheel 5279.

31. "Report of the Executive Council Acting as a Committee of the Whole on the Investigation of Local 5," n.d., B2 F2, Kheel 5279. [Hendley], "Sixth Annual . . . "; "Mr. Hendley's Address to Local 192, January 10 1941," B2 F2, Kheel 5279. [Hendley], "Sixth Annual . . . "

32. See "No Charter for Totalitarianism!," Committee for Free Teacher Unionism [May 1941], B2 Kheel 5279; *College Newsletter* (CTU), 4 (24 February 1941), 2; *New York Times*, 8 June 1941, 1; and *New York Times*, 19 June 1941, 23. On AFT anticommunism after the war and the later years of the Teachers Union (Local 555), see Murphy, *Blackboard Unions*, Chapter 9.

33. [Henry Linville] to George S. Counts, 19 October 1940, B13 F14 [c], Kheel 5279. Hendley accused the AFT executive council of having "aided and abetted" the Guild in raiding Local 5 on the pretext of arranging a reunification. See "Mr. Hendley's Address to Local 192." See also Charles Hendley, "To the Locals of the American Federation of Teachers," open letter, 7 November 1940, B11 F7, Hendley Papers. CTU President Robert Speer made a similar accusation. See *College Newsletter*, 4 (25 November 1940), 2; Henry Linville to Counts, 9 January 1941, B7 F19a, Kheel 5279; and Benjamin E. Lippincott to the Coudert committee, 21 February 1941 (RC610).

34. [Linville] to Counts, February 3 1941, B2 F8, Kheel 5279; minutes of the Provisional Committee, 23 May 1941, B8 F7, UFT Papers; minutes of

the Investigating Section of the Provisional Committee, 5 June 1941, B2 F8, Kheel 5279.

35. *New York Times*, 3 October 1941, 25.

36. Linville testimonials in B6a F36, UFT Papers.

37. Murphy, *Blackboard Unions*, 175.

38. US Congress, *Hearings before a Special Subcommittee of the Committee on Education and Labor of the House of Representatives Pursuant to H. Res. 111*, 80th Congress, September and October 1948, 103–7.

39. Murphy, *Blackboard Unions*, 192.

40. *Education and Labor Hearings* (1948), 107–19.

41. Clarence Taylor, *Reds at the Blackboard: Communism, Civil Rights, and the New York City Teachers Union* (New York: Columbia University Press, 2011), 298. On Shanker, see Dana Goldstein, *Teacher Wars: A History of America's Most Embattled Profession* (New York: Doubleday, 2014), Chapter 7.

42. Taylor, *Reds*, Chapter 10.

43. *New York Times*, 23 May 1972, 1945; "Congress: Perilous Penny-Pinching," *Time*, 59 (21 April 1952), 27; "Telegram Intercepted," *Time*, 63 (10 May 1954), 27.

44. Windels, Sr., Reminiscences, 112–21; *New York Times*, 16 December 1967, 41.

45. *New York Times*, 19 July 1971, 28.

46. *Village Voice*, 3 (26 February 1958), 1.

47. *New York Times*, 17 November 1959, 29. For Morris's interrogations of current and former municipal college faculty, see SISS Education (May 1953), 951–99.

48. *New York Times*, 10 September 1953, 4. The BHE also hired Edna Canning as an investigator for its Special Committee on Section 903 of the City Charter, which the following year renewed the "prosecutions" of faculty and staff that were left hanging when the Coudert committee folded. See BHE Minutes, 16 February 1954, 63; *New York Times*, 7 August 1988, 49; and SISS Pacific Relations (August 1951), 466–70.

49. *New York Times*, 20 March 1977, 40; Grebanier interview, 1974.

50. Ellen Schrecker, "Moses Finley and the Academic Red Scare," in *Moses Finley and Politics*, ed. by William Harris (Leiden and Boston: Brill, 2013), 61–78.

51. Morris Schappes to Kenneth Ackley, 17 October 1941, B7 F14, Schappes Papers; Schappes to Jack [Green], 2 November 1942, B7 F14, Schappes Papers; Nelle Lederman to Schappes, 3 June 1943, B7 F16 Schappes Papers; Schappes to Elton Gustafson, 1 September 1945, B8 F9, Schappes Papers.

52. Judith E. Smith, *Becoming Belafonte: Black Artist, Public Radical* (Austin: University of Texas Press, 2014), 292. Shukotoff/Shaw also did public relations for Elvis Pressley and Paul Simon. See Ronald Cohen, "Arnold Shaw," *American National Biography Online* (Oxford University Press, 2000), https://doi.org/10.1093/anb/9780198606697.article.1803004; *New York Times*, 7 October 1989, 29.

53. Henry Klein to Schappes, 29 March 1944, B8 F11, Schappes Papers; Walter Neff to Morris Schappes, 11 April 1945, B8 F15, Schappes Papers; Neff to Sonya Schappes, 27 December 1944, B8 F15, Schappes Papers; Schappes to Ingram Bander, 12 October 1943, B8 F3, Schappes Papers; Lt. Maxwell N. Weisman to Captain William A. Consadine (Pentagon), 21 June 1943, B7 F16, Schappes Papers.

54. Marvin Gettleman, "'No Varsity Teams': New York's Jefferson School of Social Science, 1943–1946," *Science & Society*, 66 (Fall 2002), 340–43. Balamuth also consulted for the Manhattan Project and went on to develop the ultra-sonic technology used in modern dental drills. See SSIS Education (September–October 1952), 953–57, 971, 977; "Communist Infiltration and Activities in Public Housing Authority, New York City Government," transcript of hearings in Executive Session of the House Committee on Un-American Activities, 28 February 1958, EBF 3724 of HQ 61–752, Lazar FOIA; and *Life*, 3 November 1952, 97.

Conclusion: The Coudert Legacy

1. Earl Latham, *Meaning of McCarthyism*, ed. by Earl Latham (Boston: D. C. Heath and Company, 1965), Introduction; Ellen Schrecker, "McCarthyism: Political Repression and the Fear of Communism," *Social Research*, 71 (Winter 2004), 1049.

2. *Teachers Fight for Freedom: Eight New York City Teachers on Trial* (New York: Teachers Union, Local 555, U. P. W., 1950); "In the Matter of the Trial of the Charges against Alice B. Citron," 16 October 1950, typescript trial transcript, Anti-Communist Investigations, Published Materials, ca. 1940–1962, Board of Education Records, New York City Municipal Archives. Two years later, the regents and the board explicitly proscribed the Communist Party as a subversive organization, membership in which was held to be prima facie grounds for dismissal. See *New York Times,* 26 September 1953, 16.

3. Marjorie Heins, *Priests of Our Democracy: The Supreme Court, Academic Freedom, and the Anti-Communist Purge* (New York: New York University Press, 2013), 92–96, 120.

4. Heins, *Priests*, 88, 99, 111, 120; Schrecker, "McCarthyism," 1061–64. For the use of confidential witnesses, see the Citron case file (case #9, series 594) in the board of education records at the New York City Municipal Archives. Key information in these files, which are still restricted, is profoundly inaccurate; for example, reports from investigators have Citron married to the wrong Isidore Begun, even though that Isidore Begun, a lawyer, had married a woman named Alice White. Investigators then collected evidence on White, whose voting records they meticulously copied, insisting that her handwriting, found on petitions for Communist candidates, resembled Citron's.

5. Clark Byse, "Teachers and the Fifth Amendment," *University of Pennsylvania Law Review*, vol. 102 (1954), 876; Heins, *Priests*, 139.

6. "In the Matter of the Investigation of the Board of Higher Education into Subversive Activities in the Municipal Colleges," 30 March 1954 hearing, stenographic transcript, 22–50; 8 April 1954 hearing, 123–27, B2, Board of Higher Education: Academic Freedom Cases, Tam 332, Tamiment; McGill Trial (27 May 1954), 18; SISS Education (24 September 1952), 174–76; Heins, *Priests*, 143.

7. *Slochower versus Board of Higher Education of the City of New York*, 350 US 551. Just before the BHE was about to reopen proceedings to fire him on the grounds of his false testimony before the Coudert committee, Slochower resigned. See Heins, *Priests*, 138–43, 152–58.

8. For direct use of Coudert files delivered from state police headquarters, see McGill Trial (27 May 1954), 40–47.

9. SISS, 11 March 1953, 553–54, 574.

10. *Teachers Fight for Freedom*, 40.

11. SISS Education (11 March 1953), 549; McGill Report (1954), 102.

12. Latham, *Meaning of McCarthyism*, v–vi.

13. Harry Gideonse, "Changing Issues in Academic Freedom in the United States Today," *Proceedings of the American Philosophical Society*, 94 (21 April 1950), 92; John L. Childs, "Communists and the Right to Teach," *Nation*, 26 February 1949, 231, 233.

14. McGill Report 1954, 4, 55–58; *New York Times*, 1 October 1954, 1, 12; McGill Trial (23 July 1954), 968–84. See also *Conformists, Informers or Free Teachers* (New York City: Teachers Union, n.d.), 2, 40–41.

15. Schrecker, "McCarthyism," 1071.

16. Gideonse promoted the Coudert committee as "a model of effective and constructive public service" that brought liberals together with conservatives to produce "well-substantiated data." See Harry D. Gideonse, "Reds Are after Your Child," *American Magazine*, July 1948, 130, 134, clipping in B5 F14, Ewen Papers.

17. Gideonse, "Reds Are After,"130.

18. Morris Schappes, "Free Education on Trial," *Jewish Currents* 5 (December 1950), 21; *New York Times*, 18 January 1951, 20.

19. Heins, *Priests*, 13.

20. See Introduction.

21. Neal Gabler, "My Secret Shame," *Atlantic*, 317 (May 2016), 52–63.

22. Tim Forster, "United Airlines' Tacky, Invite-Only Restaurant Is Begging for a Class War," 20 September 2017, https://www.eater.com/2017/9/20/16339554/united-airlines-classified-restaurant-newark-exclusive.

23. Thomas Frank, *What's the Matter with Kansas: How Conservatives Won the Heart of America* (New York: Metropolitan Books, 2004).

24. Donald Jeffries, "Class War Is a One Sided Fight, and the Very Rich Are Winning," *Salon*, https://www.salon.com/2017/07/12/the-class-war-is-a-one-sided-fight-and-the-very-rich-are-winning.

Index

academic blacklists, 238–39
"Academic Freedom and 'The Trojan Horse' in American Education" (Hook), 164–65
academic freedom rights, 3–4, 139, 165, 169–70, 236–37, 241–44, 249–51
Ackley, Kenneth: Coudert investigation of, 180, 191, 192, 193, 219, 247; dismissal hearing of, 189, 220, 221, 226; post-Coudert investigation, 239
activity program, 97, 111, 116
act of concealment, 237. *See also* Fifth Amendment
Adams, Helen S., 142, 150–51, 194
Adler, Irving, 242
Adler vs. Board of Education (1952), 243
agrarianism, 134–36
Alpert, Jetta, 220
American Association of University Professors (AAUP), 51, 139–40, 143–44, 151
American Association of University Women, 151
American Civil Liberties Union (ACLU), 121, 163, 171–72, 196
American Committee for Democracy and Intellectual Freedom (ACDIF), 169, 299n70, 299–300nn72–73

American Federation of Labor (AFL): anticommunist probe support from, 77, 106–7, 123–25, 128, 162, 164–65; expulsion of NY locals from, 3, 25, 155, 234–35; internal issues of, 90–91; Tammany Hall affiliation, 127
American Federation of Teachers (AFT): anticommunist probe of members, 16, 74–78, 81, 106–7, 125–28, 130–31, 157, 223; Child's resignation from, 153–54; Dodd and, 61*f*; expulsion of NY locals from, 3, 10, 25, 234–35; influences on, 155, 160–61; leadership of, 91–92, 129–30, 155–57, 161–63; post-Coudert investigation, 236–37, 241; rivals of, 143–44. *See also* College Teachers Union (CTU); Local 5
American Jewish Committee, 170, 196
American Jewish Congress (AJC), 200–2, 210
American Labor Party, 153, 232
American Legion, 37, 140, 152, 163
The American Mercury (weekly paper), on Counts as social revolutionist, 133
American Student Union (ASU), 39–40, 52, 175, 230
American Workers Party, 124
Amter, Israel, 51

318　Index

Angell, James, 143
Anti-Defamation League, 196
anti-fascist movement: activism of, 142, 162, 167, 170–71, 214; alliances of, 11–12, 39–40, 108–10
anti-Semitism: academic, 208–11, 242; of Christian Front, 196, 197–99; of Coudert committee, 16, 195–97, 200, 208–11; of German-American Bund, 196; Gompers case as example of, 199–201; historical context for, 197; McCarthyism and, 195–96
Aptheker, Herbert, 190
Atlantic, on financial impotence of Americans, 252
"Axis Sally," 206

bad faith: accountability for, 248–49; accusations of, 45–47, 46f, 118, 136–37, 149, 163–66; civil rights and, 23–24, 237; class war view and, 163–64, 248; Committee for Cultural Freedom and, 166–73; Coudert committee and inquiry as, 231; Dewey on, 12, 16, 87, 100–2; Linville on, 106; local unions expulsion from national organization due to, 234–35; perjury and, 14
Balamuth, Lewis, 191, 220, 226, 240
Baldwin, Roger, 172
Bander, Ingram, 189–90, 193
Bankers Agreement (1934–1938), 64
Barker, Mary, 91
Begun, Isidore, 93, 95–97, 105, 109, 119–22, 127, 159
behavioral test, 158–61, 182
Bell, Daniel, 6–7, 10
Bennett, John D., 78
Bernstein, Saul, 184, 220
Bishop, Hillman, 178
bloc voting, 192
Blumberg, Isidore, 119–20, 122
Board of Education, 242
Board of Estimate, 66
Board of Higher Education (BHE): Brooklyn College and, 37–38; cooperation with Coudert committee by, 177; faculty governance system bylaws, 140–41; Fifth Amendment rights interpretation by, 213; hearings, 223–26; on Klein's firing, 43–44; on McGill case, 243; post-Coudert investigation, 244–45; resignations forced by, 175; on Russell's appointment, 67; suspensions and dismissals by, 25, 194, 195, 215–16, 220–22, 232–33; tenure bylaws and, 140
Board of Regents, 241–42
Boas, Franz, 167, 169–70, 299–300n72, 299n70
Bonaschi, Alberto, 208
Borchardt, Selma, 91, 125
Boylan, William A., 37–38, 43
Braunlich, Arthur, 180, 192, 220, 222, 226
B'rith Abraham, 201, 202, 232
Britt, George, 198
Bromley, Dorothy Dunbar, 168
Brooklyn College (BC): accused Communist Party members from, 194; anticommunist probe at, 3–4, 16, 159, 175–77, 182 (*see also* Gideonse, Harry; Grebanier, Bernard); anti-Semitism incidents at, 200, 209; BHE suspensions and dismissals, 220, 226, 244–45; democratization at, 141–42; founding of, 37–38; reputation of, 38; YCL at, 33, 44–45, 49–50, 229, 271–72n24
Brooklyn Daily Eagle (newspaper): anticommunist campaign of, 175; on Communism at Brooklyn College, 45, 46f; on democratization bylaws, 141–42; on Gideonse, 52; on Grebanier's testimony, 45
Brookwood Labor College, 90–91, 98–99, 279n14
Browder, Earl, 39, 48, 115, 118, 157
Brownshirts, 198
Buckley, John L., 78
Burgum, Edwin Berry, 159, 186, 194, 219
Burroughs, Williana, 120–21, 122, 287n37
Butler, Nicholas Murray, 139, 151, 208

Campbell, Harold, 65
Canning, Edna, 178, 186, 189, 238
Canning, William Martin: attempts to discredit, 215, 218–20; on Frank's article, 270n40; as McCarran committee informant, 238; post-Coudert investigation, 238; private testimony

of, 177–81, 186–88, 193–94, 217, 221; public hearing testimony of, 179*f*, 181–83, 188–92, 194, 214, 224
Casa Italiana, 203–4, 207
Castaldi, Michael, 246–47
Catholic church, 70, 72, 198–202, 208, 232
Central Labor Council (of New York City), 127
Ceroni, Vitorio, 204–6
Chamberlain, Lawrence H., 181
Chanler, William, 177
Chiesa, Carolyn Della, 207
child-centered education. *See* progressive education reforms
Childs, John: background, 152–53, 294n16; at CCF's founding meeting, 168; on Communism in unions, 153–55, 160; on Communist behavior testing, 158–59; on democratization reforms, 142, 143; post-Coudert investigation, 246
Christian Front, 163, 196, 197–202, 206, 210
Christian Mobilizers, 198, 206
Citron, Alice, 96–97, 112–17, 242, 245, 248
City College of New York (CCNY): anticommunist probe at, 3–4, 16, 181–89, 222–26 (*see also* Canning, William Martin; Schappes, Morris; Sherman-Gottsegen, Annette); anti-Semitism incidents at, 200, 209–10; BHE suspensions and dismissals, 195, 220–21, 232–34; democratization of, 140; leadership of, 52, 67, 68; reputation of, 174–75; union membership at, 138, 143; YCL at, 189, 229
civil liberties violations, 23–24, 54–56, 74–78, 212–13, 237, 268n14
classroom indoctrination: accusations of, 33–35, 47–51, 76, 136, 157, 188–91, 193, 216, 220–22, 224–25; Communist Party policies on, 51, 219; defined, 14; by fascists, 205–6; by reconstructionists, 135–36, 156–57
class war view: bad faith and, 163–64, 248; of Communists, 118–19, 250, 251–53; rejection of, 11–12, 134–37, 156;

unions and, 102, 104, 111, 122, 127, 144, 153–54
Cohen, David, 180, 220, 240
Cohen, Morris R., 228
Cohen, Morris U., 220, 240
Cohen, Robert, 175
Cohn, Roy, 196
Cold War, 4–5
collectivism, 134–35
College Instructors Association, 62
College Teachers Union (CTU): accomplishments of, 137–43; anticommunist probe of members, 3, 62, 159–60, 178, 180–81, 192–94, 222–23, 229; defense strategy of, 219; expulsion from national union, 234–35; grievances against, 152–55; at May Day parades, 183–86, 185*f*; membership list subpoenas for, 74–78; national elections, 155–57, 161–63; recruitment campaign of, 145, 149–50, 280n29; support for McDowell by, 150–52
Colligan, Eugene, 62
Columbia's Teachers College (TC): anticommunist probe at, 182–83; Childs at, 152–53; leadership of, 138–39; progressive education reforms and, 9–10, 131–33; union presence at, 143, 149–52, 154–55
Columbia University, 4, 143, 149–50
Committee for Cultural Freedom (CCF), 42, 166–73, 299–300n72, 299n70
Committee for the Defense of Public Education (CDPE), 59, 70, 200–1, 223, 224
Communism and Communist Party: Ackley's membership in, 226; bad faith accusations against, 45–47, 46*f*, 118, 136–37, 149, 163–66; Begun's membership in, 93–94; at Brooklyn College, 3, 38–39; Burroughs' membership in, 122; Canning's membership in, 178, 180; CCF's mission against, 167–73; at CCNY, 180; classroom indoctrination accusations against, 33–35, 47–51, 76, 136, 157, 188–91, 193, 216, 220–22, 224–25; classroom indoctrination policies, 51, 219; class war view of, 118–19, 250, 251–53; on Coudert family, 72;

Communism (*continued*)
defined, 17; Dodd's membership in, 60–62, 159; double bind of, 55–56; espionage by, 13–14, 123, 248; evidence of membership (*see* behavioral test; fraction meetings; May Day parades; *specific testimonies*); factionalism and, 90 (*see also* Dewey Trial (1933)); Feinberg Law and, 195, 234, 236–37, 241–42, 245; First Amendment rights and, 246; Grebanier's membership in, 36, 40–41, 271n20; liberals' view of, 136–37; McGill's membership in, 243, 246–47; "The Open Letter of 400," 170–71; party line accusations, 35, 158–60, 183, 209, 221–22, 228–29, 246–47; pluralism and, 58–59, 118–19, 250, 251–53; on progressive education reforms, 34, 110–19; on racial equality, 113–15, 210–11; on Rapp legislation, 70; rebellion fomentation accusations against, 2, 32–35, 47–48, 94, 218, 225, 228–29; resigning and expulsion from, 41–42, 181–82; Schappes membership in, 214–15; Sherman-Gottsegen's membership in, 193; subversion accusations against, 32–35, 45–47, 46f, 118, 136–37, 149, 163–66; Teachers Guild membership exclusion for, 236. *See also* Coudert committee and inquiry; Coudert legacy

The Communist (journal): on communism in the classroom, 33–34; popularity of, 34

communists and communism, defined, 17
Conant, James, 164, 208
Congress of Industrial Organizations, 39
conservatives: Coudert and, 72–74; Coudert inquiry and, 9, 59, 67–69, 77–78; McCarthyism and, 7, 10, 11, 241, 246; Rosenwein on, 224; school budget cuts by, 62–67; on teachers unions, 89. *See also* American Legion; Catholic church; Christian Front; German-American Bund

Coordinating Committee for Democratic Action, 201
Copstein, Seymour, 180, 220, 240
Corrigan, Michael, 72

Cosenza, Mario, 50, 204
Coudert, Frederic "Fritz": background, 69, 71–74; on bad faith, 231; on budget requests, 227–28; election of, 232; member list subpoenas from, 75; post-Coudert investigation, 237–38, 273n3; at public hearings, 2, 219; Rapp-Coudert subversion subcommittee staff decisions, 78–81; reputation of, 76–77. *See also* Coudert committee and inquiry
Coudert, Frederic Rene, Jr., 71, 73
Coudert, Frederic Rene, Sr., 71, 268n14
Coudert Brothers (law firm), 71–73
Coudert committee and inquiry: accused faculty and staff defense strategy, 59, 213–17, 223–26; accused faculty and staff testimony, 217–21; anti-Semitism accusations against, 16, 195–97, 208–11; background, 1–3, 265n8; as bad faith, 231; behavior testing by, 158–61, 182; campaign against, 59 (*see also* Committee for the Defense of Public Education; Dodd, Bella); civil liberties and rights violations, 23–24, 54–56, 74–78, 212–13, 268n14; countersubversion of, 6–13, 32–35, 78; double standards of, 199–206, 208–11; final report of, 80, 166, 191, 199–200, 206, 227–32, 234; formation of, 62–69, 70; as McCarthyism's prelude, 4–6, 247–49; member list subpoenas from, 74–78, 276–77n23; motives of, 77–78, 208–11; private records of, 48–51 (*see also specific testimonies*); public hearings, 2–3, 21–25, 56–59 (*see also specific testimonies*); public opinion on, 26–32, 208, 230–31; on right-wing subversion, 207–8; Schoenchen case and, 117; staffing decisions, 78–81; suspensions and dismissals resulting from, 195, 215–16, 220–22, 232–33, 244–47. *See also* Coudert legacy

Coudertism, 9–10
Coudert legacy: on academic freedom, 3–4, 241–44; BHE suspensions and dismissals, 195, 215–16, 220–22, 232–33, 244–47; on class war concept, 251–53; on McCarran committee,

244–45; as McCarthyism prelude, 4–6, 247–49; repercussions, 234–37; silencing of communism, 249–51; on unions, 241
Coughlin, Charles, 197–99
Coughlinites, 198–202, 232
Counts, George: Committee for Cultural Freedom and, 168; on communist union membership, 154, 155–57, 159, 161–62; on educational reconstruction, 131–36, 156–57; election of, 160–61; leadership of, 77, 130–31, 161–63, 234–36; Russell and, 152
Covello, Leonard, 204, 207–8
Cross, Ephraim, 186
cultural freedom, 166–73

Daily Worker (Communist paper): "The Open Letter of 400," 170–71; on Rapp bill, 70
Dante Alighieri Society, 203–5, 307n38
Dare the School Build a New Social Order (Counts), 131, 132
Davidson, Ben, 96, 126–27, 236
Davidson, David, 168
Davidson, Eve, 126–27
Davis, Jerome, 130, 143–44, 160, 161
Della Chiesa, Carolyn, 205
democratization reforms, 137–45. *See also* tenure rights
Democrats: in Fusion administration, 6; Seabury investigation and, 28; union opposition by, 67, 222–23
Denning, Michael, 108–9
Deutsch, Babette, 168
Devany, John, Jr., 177
Devany Law (1939), 73, 177, 276n14
Dewey, John: on ACDIF, 169–70; advising Childs, 153; background, 97–99, 98*f*, 108–10; CCF and, 166–70, 172–73, 299n70, 299–300n72; on class war view, 12, 136; on Coudert investigation, 77; on Linville, 236; Local 5 grievance committee head, 87; progressive education theories of, 10, 34, 110–11, 115–16, 266n23, 284n5; on reconstructionism, 133–34; Trotsky investigation, 164; union membership change, 128. *See also* Dewey Trial (1933)

Dewey, Thomas, 216, 232
Dewey Commission, 164
Dewey Trial (1933): background, 85–87; factional fighting, 94–97; factionalism investigation and report, 99–102, 282n49; factionalism "trial," 102–6; left wing ideology, 90–94; legacy of, 106–7, 118–19, 125, 229; Linville's role in, 81, 87–89
Dies, Martin, 22–23, 73
Dies committee, 4–5, 22–23, 88*f*, 123, 142, 162, 165
Dinnerstein, Leonard, 197
Dodd, Bella: assumptions about Coudert committee origins, 70, 74, 77–78, 202, 223; background, 59–62, 61*f*, 63, 142; Communist Party membership of, 60–62, 159; on Coudert report, 231; defense strategy against Coudert inquiry, 176, 196–97, 210, 213, 215, 219, 224; post-Coudert investigation, 244; on Windels, 277n36
Douglas, William O., 3, 243
dual unionism, 102, 235
duces tecum subpoena, 74, 276n22
due process rights, 2, 54–55, 244
Dunnigan, John, 67–68, 78

economic inequality. *See* class war view
Edel, Abraham, 184
The Educational Frontier (Dewey), 153
Educational Vanguard (Communist paper), on Russell's reorganization of TC, 151
Education Hall riot, 119–22
education reforms. *See* progressive education reforms
Eisenberger, Sidney, 187–88, 220
Elfenbein, Sylvia, 220
Equality (journal), 202
Ernst, Morris, 168, 180
espionage, 13–14, 123, 196, 248
Ewen, Frederic, 176, 182, 191, 243

factionalism: Local 5 dispute (*see* Dewey Trial (1933)); tolerance and, 127, 142, 154, 207–8; within Communist Party, 90
faculty indoctrination, 48–50
Fagin, Ralph, 75

Farrell, Peter T., 78
fascism, 40, 72–73, 175, 196–208, 231–32, 265n8, 307n38. *See also* anti-fascist movement
Fascist League of North America, 208
Fast, Howard, 195
Feinberg Law (1949), 195, 234, 236–37, 241–42, 245
Feld-McGrath tenure law (1935), 138
Fifth Amendment, 15, 28, 29, 30, 54, 213, 215, 236–37, 242–43, 245, 273n1
Finkelstein, Jerry, 232
Finkelstein, Moses (M. I. Finley), 181–83, 191, 221, 239, 273n3
First Amendment, 23–24, 31, 54, 139, 165, 242–44, 246. *See also* academic freedom rights
Flacks, Mildred, 115
Foner, Jack, 190, 220, 226, 239
Foner, Morris (Moe), 220, 226
Foner, Philip, 181, 190, 191, 219, 220, 223, 240
Fourteenth Amendment, 54
fraction meetings, 186–87, 193–94
Fraenkel, Osmond, 121
Frank, Richard (Francis Franklin), 33–34, 43, 111, 270n40
Frank, Thomas, 252
Friedsam Commission, 68
Friedsam Law (1928), 68
Friou, George, 121
Fusion movement, 22, 26, 28

Gabler, Neal, 252
Geiger, Theodore, 181, 182–83, 191
Gellerman, William, 152
German-American Bund, 196, 197, 198, 201
German Communist Party, 39
Gerson, Simon, 24, 36, 70, 71
Gettleman, Marvin, 240
Gideonse, Harry, 37, 51–53, 58, 209, 216–17, 244, 245–46, 248
Gillars, Mildred ("Axis Sally"), 206
Gipfel, Paul, 182
Gitlow, Benjamin, 48, 89
Gold, Mike, 59
Goldway, David, 180, 193, 219, 220, 239
Gompers, Samuel, 90–91, 123

Gompers case, 90–91, 199–201
Gottsegen, Jack, 193
Graubard, Mark, 48, 159
Great Depression, 8–9, 16, 27, 38–39, 60, 91–92, 135–36
Grebanier, Bernard: background, 36–42, 168, 271n20; post-Coudert investigation, 238; on teaching staff workload, 138; testimony of, 36, 42–50, 176–77, 186, 189, 192, 193–94, 243, 271n22, 272n28
Green, William, 91, 123–25, 128, 161–62
Gristle, Murray, 220
Gruenwald, Werner, 201

Haberman, Phillip W., Jr.: background, 80; Coudert committee final report written by, 80, 206, 228; insinuations against, 219; interrogations by, 43, 186–88; post-Coudert investigation, 238; salary, 227
Hacker, Louis, 154
Halliday, Edgar, 209
Hamilton, Walton, 134–35
Hanley, Joe, 78, 79
Hanson, Florence, 91, 94, 125
Harlem, 112–18
Harlem Lesson Plan (Communist shop paper), 115
Harlem Schools Committee, 113, 114
Hart, Merwin K., 63
Hartmann, George, 150, 154–55, 158–60, 162, 168, 293n4
Harvard University, 49
Hatch Act (1939), 4–5
Hazlitt, Henry, 168
Healey, James H., 220
Hearst, William Randolph, 133
Heins, Marjorie, 249
Hendley, Charles: on AFL, 124–25, 126, 127; contempt charges against, 175–76; on Coudert investigation, 70; on Coudert report (1942), 231–32; leadership of, 74–75, 76, 137, 276n22; on political tolerance, 159–60; public hearing testimony of, 24, 56–59
Herlands, William, 199
Herlands Commission, 199
Herman, Robert, 307n38

Hicks, Granville, 49, 130, 189
High, Stanley, 165
High School of Commerce, 85–86, 102
Himstead, Ralph, 144, 151
Hitler-Stalin Pact (1939), 10, 41, 49, 129–31, 171
Hofstadter, Richard, 6–7
Holmes, Oliver Wendell, 139, 242
Hook, Sidney: Committee for Cultural Freedom and, 166–73, 299n70, 299–300n72; on Communist bad faith, 12, 164–66; on Communist indoctrination, 14, 49; Dewey's correspondence with, 105; on exposing Grebanier, 271n20; on McGill case, 243; on "The Open Letter of 400," 171–73
Hoover, J. Edgar, 164
House Committee on Un-American Activities hearings, 124
Hunter College, 60–63, 143
Hunter College Instructors Association, 62
Hurlinger, Iven, 240
Hutchinson, John, 200–1
Hutt, Max L., 220

individualism, 134–36
indoctrination. *See* classroom indoctrination; faculty indoctrination
industrialism, 134–36
Instructional Staff Association, 178
insurrectionism accusations, 2, 32–35, 47–48, 94, 218, 225, 228–29
intellectual integrity, 167
International Labor Defense, 223
International Ladies' Garment Workers Union, 124
International Workers Order, 239
Italian Embassy, 204–6, 208
Italian Teachers Association, 204

Jaffe, Louis, 241–42, 245
Jansen, William, 242
Jefferson School, 240
Jewish Daily Forward (newspaper), on Communism in unions, 153
Johnson, Ernest, 154
Joint Legislative Committee to Investigate the Public Education System of the State of New York. *See* Coudert committee and inquiry; Coudert legacy
Joint Salary Committee, 104, 106–7, 122

Kaiser, Samuel, 182
Kallen, Horace, 168
Kauffman, Irving, 196
Kazin, Alfred, 214
Keyes, Clinton, 155
Keyishian vs. Board of Regents of State of New York (1967), 249
Kiendl, Irving, 245
Kilpatrick, William Heard, 111, 132, 136–37, 152, 153, 168
Kirchwey, Freda, 109, 168
Klein, Henry, 43–45, 182, 194, 226, 239
Klu Klux Klan, 114, 197
Koischwitz, Otto, 206
Krivitsky, Boris, 41
Kutulas, Judy, 267n24

La Follette, Suzanne, 168
La Guardia, Fiorello, 6, 22, 26, 62, 66, 68, 208, 232
Lamont, Corliss, 172
Latham, Earl, 246
League Against War and Fascism, 39
League of American Writers, 40
Leavitt, Arthur, 195
Leberstein, Stephen, 5
Leboit, Joseph, 97
Lederman, Nelle, 142, 180, 220, 239
Lefkowitz, Abraham: as Brookwood founder, 279n14; on Communism in unions, 122, 126–28; Jaffe Case, 242; on Linville, 236; Local 5 factionalism and, 92–93, 95–96, 105, 106–7, 118–19; as Local 5 founder, 89; post-Coudert investigation, 237; on union recruitment, 280n29
Lehman, Herbert, 63, 65–67, 68, 227, 232
Lerman, Louis, 220
Liberalism and Social Action (Dewey), 128
Liberal Party, 153
liberals: alliances of, 39–40, 57, 108–109; anticommunist ideology of, 16–17, 21, 42, 63, 77–78, 158–61, 163–66, 235–36, 267n24 (*see also* Coudert committee and inquiry; Coudert

liberals (*continued*)
  legacy); bad faith argument of (*see* bad faith); on class war, 136–37; Committee for Cultural Freedom and, 168–73; on Communism in unions, 150–51; countersubversion of, 6–13, 32–35, 78, 100–2, 250–51; defined, 11; election coup (AFT) by, 155–57, 161–63; on evidence of Communist union membership, 158–61; on mass mobilization, 117–19; at May Day parades, 183–86; progressivism and, 109–11, 116; support for Coudert's election, 232
Lieberman, Max, 205
Lindsay, John, 237
Linville, Henry: background, 87–89, 91–93, 95–97, 124–28, 140; on class war view, 136; death of, 236; Dewey and, 98–100; at Dewey Trial proceedings, 102–6; Dewey Trial report circulation by, 106–7; Dies committee testimony of, 88*f*, 162; on Education Hall riot, 121–22; as informant, 80–81; support for Schoenchen, 117; as Teachers Guild leader, 235–36
"Little Red Scares," 4–5. *See also* Coudert committee and inquiry
Local 2 (AFT), 236–37. *See also* Teachers Guild
Local 5 (AFT): activism of, 112–16; Canning's testimony on, 192; CCNY's Communist Party membership in, 180, 192; defense against Coudert investigation by, 58; democratization of, 137; Dodd's membership in, 60–62, 61*f*; expulsion from national union, 128; factionalism dispute, 94–97; factionalism investigation and report, 99–102; factionalism "trial," 102–6; free speech defense by, 140; leadership of, 57; left wing ideology, 90–94, 159; Linville and, 81, 87–89, 106–7; May Day parade attendance, 183; membership list subpoenas, 74–78; on NYC's vacant teaching positions, 65–66; post-Coudert investigation, 234–35, 237; on school-based bigotry, 200; Tammany Hall and, 67

Local 537 (AFT). *See* College Teachers Union (CTU)
Local 555 (CIO), 235, 237, 240. *See also* Local 5
Long Island University, 143
Lovejoy, Arthur, 168
Lovestone, Jay, 90
Lovestoneites, 90–91, 95–97, 164, 236
Luff, Jennifer, 123–24
Lundberg, Ferdinand, 168, 172
Lusk, Clayton, 89
Lusk Laws (1920), 89
Lyons, Eugene, 167, 168

MacDonald, Milo, 63, 116
Madison Square Garden rally, 198
Mandel, Ben, 183, 203
Mandel, Edward, 119, 122
Margolis, Samuel, 181, 220, 226, 232–33
Martin, Earl A., 141–42
mass-organizing campaigns: at CCNY, 175, 189; for Davis case, 144; diverging views on, 111, 137; against Tammany Hall, 93–94
Matlin, Ann, 114
May Day parades, 61*f*, 180, 183–85*f*, 183–86, 233*f*
McCarran committee, 238–39, 242–45
McCarthy, Joseph, 4, 7, 10, 246
McCarthyism, 4–8, 108–9, 195–96, 247–49
McDowell, Elizabeth, 150–51, 293n4
McGill, V. J., 159, 191, 243, 245, 246–47, 273n3
Mead, Nelson, 220
Meehan, Thomas, 206
The Mercury (student paper), Braunlich's poetry in, 222
Michels, Robert, 8
Millay, Edna St. Vincent, 164–65
Minneapolis Teamsters strike, 124
Minor, Louie May, 176
Minton, Bruce, 157
Mintus, Jesse, 220
Moffatt, Abbott Low, 66
Molloy, J. G. Louis, 80, 219, 227–28, 238
Mont Pelerin Institute, 52
Moore, Deborah Dash, 196
Morais, Herbert, 190, 239

Morris, Robert, 238
Moscow Trials (1936), 10
Moskoff, Saul, 195
Moss, Maximillian, 195
Motz, Lloyd, 240
Mulligan, William: background, 269n24; on Coudert investigation, 24, 29–32, 223, 269n34; on fair investigational practices, 47–48, 54; at public hearings, 2, 22, 219
Murphy, Marjorie, 91
Murphy, Timothy, 200–1, 206, 210–11
Mussolini's regime, 60
Muste, A. J., 90, 124, 279n14

Naison, Mark, 113
The Nation (magazine): on anti-Semitic violence, 198; on CCF's mission statement, 168; Child's letters to, 153; CTU response to Child's letters, 154; on progressive activism at TC, 151–52
National Education Association (NEA), 91
National Lawyers Guild (NLG), 217, 223
National Youth Administration, 200–1
Neff, Walter, 191, 220, 222, 239, 240
Negro History Bulletin (Woodson), 114
Negro History Week, 114
Neuberger, Samuel A., 223
New College, 151
New Deal, 118–19
Newlon, Jesse, 150–51, 157, 168
New Masses (Communist-affiliated weekly): on Coudert hearings, 24; on democratization reforms, 142; *The Prospects of American Democracy* review, 157; on Rapp legislation, 70
The New Republic (magazine): on CCF's anti-totalitarianism campaign, 169; on Coudert investigation, 158–59
New Utrecht High School, 205
New York City Central Trade and Labor Council, 155
New York Post, on Communism in unions, 153
New York Sun, on Communism at Brooklyn College, 45–46
New York Teachers Guild, 80–81
New York Times: on Canning's public testimony, 188; on Communism, 46–47, 153; on Communist Party membership, 122; on Coudert report, 230; on education budget, 66–67; on Education Hall riot, 120, 121; on Popular Front history series, 191; on Windels, 23, 218
New York University, 143, 149
Niebuhr, Reinhold, 127–28
Norwood, Stephen, 208
Novikoff, Alexander, 182

Old Guard Socialists, 164
one-percent, 251–53
Oppenheimer, Robert, 216–17, 231
O'Shea, William J., 75
Oxford Pledge, 40, 175

Palin, Sarah, 252
Pantaleoni, Goffredo, 204
Parents Association, 112
Paris Commune (1871), 190
party line accusations, 35, 158–60, 183, 209, 221–22, 228–29, 246–47
Paskoff, Benjamin, 222
People's Front, 110
Permanent Committee for Better Schools in Harlem, 113, 115
Phelps, Christopher, 166
philosemitism, 195–96
PM (progressive weekly): on British and German fighter planes, 21; on Rapp-Coudert committee hearings, 2; on union membership list subpoenas, 74
Pomerance, Isadore, 182
Popular Front: Communists in, 42, 79, 109, 118–19; educational sessions on, 188; historical context for, 11–12, 39–40, 108, 129–30, 170; history curriculum by, 190–91; on mass mobilization, 111–12; mobilizing public opinion against, 162, 172–73; post-Coudert investigation, 239–40; on trial, 212, 218–20, 223, 231, 244–45; union representation by, 130–31, 152, 155–57, 161–63
prescriptive publicity, 230–31
Prezzolini, Giuseppi, 204
private college union recruitment, 149–50
Progressive Education Association (PEA), 131, 132

progressive education reforms: background, 110–11, 129–31; communist view, 34, 111–16; liberal view, 10, 34, 110–11, 115–16, 266n23, 284n5; politics of, 116–19, 133–37; reconstructionism, 131–36, 156–57
progressivism, 95–97, 108–10, 164
The Prospects of American Democracy (Counts), 155–56
P.S. 5, 117–18
P.S. 184, 112–13
Public Education Association, 86
public hearings. *See under* Coudert committee and inquiry; *specific testimony*
public opinion: on anti-Semitism, 208; on Communism subversion, 32–35; on Coudert investigation, 26–32, 230–31; pre-war hysteria, 4–5; on Tammany Hall, 26–28

race and racism: Communist approach to, 113–14, 115, 121, 144, 225; of Coudert committee investigation, 16, 117, 195–97, 200, 208–11; in New York City schools, 113–15. *See also* anti-Semitism
Rank and File group, 95–97, 102, 103, 107, 237
Rapp, Herbert, 67–68
Rapp-Coudert committee and inquiry. *See* Coudert committee and inquiry; Coudert legacy
Ratner, Joseph, 172–73
Raup, Bruce, 154
reconstructionist education reforms, 131–36, 156–57
Redefer, Frederick, 168
Reich, Robert, 251, 253
Rieber, Clara, 97
Riesel, Victor, 168
Robin, Corey, 230
Robinson, Frederick, 175, 189, 214, 220
Rogin, Michael Paul, 7–9, 250
Roosevelt, Eleanor, 164
Roosevelt, Franklin Delano, 26–27, 28, 119
Rorty, James, 168
Rosenberg, Ethel, 196
Rosenberg, Julius, 196

Rosenfeld, Herman, 223–25
Rosenwein, Samuel, 223
Ruotsila, Markku, 124
Russell, Bertrand, 52, 67, 68
Russell, Rose, 245
Russell, William F., 150–52
Ryan, George P., 120–22

Salon, on class war view, 252–253
Salvemini, Gaetano, 203–204, 208
Samuel Gompers Vocational High School (Gompers), 90–91, 199–201
San Francisco general strike, 124
Sarah Lawrence College, 143
Saypol, Irving, 196
Schappes, Morris: background, 213–14; case against, 159, 192, 214–17, 239–40; Communist membership of, 214–15; on Coudert investigation, 228; on "preventive dismissals," 248
Schlauch, Margaret, 62, 159, 191, 194
Schlesinger, Arthur, Jr., 250
Schoenchen, Gustav, 117
School for Democracy, 240
The Schools Can Teach Democracy (Counts), 156–57
Schrecker, Ellen, 10, 79, 247, 267n26
Seabury, Samuel, 26–28, 31
Seabury Commission, 26–28, 31, 42–43, 80
Section 903a, 243, 245
Selsam, Howard: on academic freedom, 4; charges against, 194; Coudert inquiry challenges by, 176; on democratization reforms, 141, 142; Hook on, 166; on Linville, 88; post-Coudert investigation, 240; probable Communist Party member, 159; resignation of, 226; support for, 50–51; union recruitment by, 76
Senate Internal Security Subcommittee, 238
Shanker, Albert, 237
Shea, George, 177
Sherman-Gottsegen, Annette, 181, 192–94, 214, 222, 232–33
Shukotoff, Arnold (Arnold Shaw), 141, 144, 149, 192, 193, 239
Silver Shirts, 198
Simpson, Henry, 73
Sixth Amendment, 54

Slochower, Harry, 182, 191, 244, 273n3, 289n4
Slochower vs. Board of Higher Education (1956), 244, 273n1
Smith, Alfred E., 68
Smith Act (1939), 4–5, 123
Smolar, Murray, 220
Snyder, C. B. J., 86
Social Democratic Federation, 124
social democrats, 10, 11, 77, 109–10, 122–24, 163–64
The Social Frontier (journal): on Communism in unions, 153–54; on indoctrination in schools, 157; reconstructionist platform, 133–34, 136
Socialists: in American Student Union, 230; anticommunist ideology of, 102; at CCF's founding meeting, 168; on democracy, 118; expulsion of Hendley from, 57; faction dispute involvement by, 90, 95; Linville on, 236; Teachers Guild membership exclusion, 236
Soviet Russia Today, publication of "The Open Letter of 400," 170–71
Spanish Civil War (1936–1939), 198
Spellman, Francis Cardinal, 72
Spence, Lucile, 113
The Staff (Communist newsletter), on classroom propagandizing policies, 51
Stalinism, 90, 167–69
star chambers, 89
Stein, Eugene, 220
Stolberg, Ben, 164, 168
Stuart, Meriwether, 207
student indoctrination. *See* classroom indoctrination
subversion accusations, 32–35, 45–47, 46f, 118, 136–37, 149, 163–66
Supreme Court, 139
Sweezy vs. New Hampshire (1957), 243

The Tablet (newspaper): anticommunist campaign of, 175; Coughlin's sermons published in, 198
Tammany Hall: AFL affiliation with, 127; Fusion movement and, 22; influences on colleges, 37–38, 52, 62, 138; public opinion on, 26–28; unions and, 67, 92–94, 155, 222–23

Taylor, Clarence, 237
Teachers College. *See* Columbia's Teachers College (TC)
Teachers' Committee to Protect Salaries, 119
Teachers Guild (TG), 65–66, 87, 128, 235–36, 241
The Teacher Worker (Communist paper), 215
Tead, Ordway, 141, 177
tenure rights, 16, 62, 73, 138–41, 144, 149–50, 229
Theoharis, Athan, 12–13
Thompson, Dorothy, 232
Thompson, Francis J., 221, 234
Toledo Auto-Lite strike, 124
totalitarianism, 42, 118, 161–62, 167–71
Trachtenberg, Alexander, 188
Trager, Frank, 168, 170, 183
Tresca, Carlo, 203
Trojan Horse analogy, 164–65
Trotsky, Leon, 90, 164
Trotskyists, 90–91, 124, 164, 168
Trotskyist Workers Party, 124
Truman, David, 8, 11, 12
Tulchen, Lena, 127
Tuttle, Charles, 222, 246–47

Unemployed Teachers Association (UTA), 93–94
United Electrical Workers, 239
United Federation of Teachers (UFT), 237
United Public Workers, 235
Urey, Harold, 167, 169

Varney, Harold Lord, 133
Veblen, Thorstein, 134
VENONA files, 13–14
Vichy France, 72–73
Visono, Maria Assunta Isabella, 60. *See also* Dodd, Bella
The Vital Center (Schlesinger, Jr.), 12–13

Wade, John E., 75
waiver rule, 243
Wald, Alan, 109
Wald, Sylvia, 256
Walker, Jimmy, 27–28

Ward, Harry, 171–72
Warren, Earl, 243–44
Warren court, 249
Watson, Goodwin, 152
Wechsler, James, 151–52, 153, 154, 199
Weinstein, Charles W., 223–24
Weinstein, Helen, 75
Weisman, Max, 188, 220, 239
Westbrook, Robert, 266n23
Wicks, Sheldon, 78
Windels, Paul: on academic anti-Semitism, 209–10; background, 21–25; on bad faith, 231; BC Coudert investigation by, 177; on Communists fostering discontentment, 2; Dodd on, 277n36; ground rules set by, 79–80; interim report by, 217–18; on lack of fascism subversion hearings, 206; May Day parade attendance, use of, 183–86, 185f; membership list subpoenas and, 75–76; post-Coudert investigation, 237–38; at public hearings, 219; on public opinion, 26, 31–32; on role of Dewey Trial in investigation, 87; salary, 227–28; Seabury Commission comparison, 28–29; staff choices by, 80–81; subversion myths by, 32–35; witness handling by, 29–30, 42–48, 57–58, 188–91, 269n33

Winter Soldiers: The Story of a Conspiracy Against the Schools (Lerman), 256
Winwar, Frances (Francesca Vinciguerra), 37, 40, 168
Wise, Stephen, 200
Wolfe, Bertram, 97
Wolfson, Hilliard, 220, 226
Woll, Matthew, 90–91, 99, 164
Women's National Republican Club, 76
Woodson, Carter, 114
Works Progress Administration, 137
Wright, Harry, 210, 216
Writers Union, 39

Yale Divinity School, 143–44
Yates vs. United States (1957), 243
Yergan, Max, 221
Young Communist League (YCL): accusations against, 229–230; at Brooklyn College, 33, 44–45, 49–50, 229, 271–72n24; Canning (Edna) on, 178; Canning (William) on, 188–89; at City College of New York, 189, 229; at Harvard University, 49; recruitment for, 213

Zeichner, Otto, 214
Zeller, Belle, 182
Zitron, Abraham, 96–97
Zysman, Dale, 226

ESE SELECT TITLES FROM EMPIRE STATE EDITIONS

Andrew J. Sparberg, *From a Nickel to a Token: The Journey from Board of Transportation to MTA*

New York's Golden Age of Bridges. Paintings by Antonio Masi, Essays by Joan Marans Dim, Foreword by Harold Holzer

Daniel Campo, *The Accidental Playground: Brooklyn Waterfront Narratives of the Undesigned and Unplanned*

Gerard R. Wolfe, *The Synagogues of New York's Lower East Side: A Retrospective and Contemporary View, Second Edition*. Photographs by Jo Renée Fine and Norman Borden, Foreword by Joseph Berger

Howard Eugene Johnson with Wendy Johnson, *A Dancer in the Revolution: Stretch Johnson, Harlem Communist at the Cotton Club*. Foreword by Mark D. Naison

Joseph B. Raskin, *The Routes Not Taken: A Trip Through New York City's Unbuilt Subway System*

Phillip Deery, *Red Apple: Communism and McCarthyism in Cold War New York*

North Brother Island: The Last Unknown Place in New York City. Photographs by Christopher Payne, A History by Randall Mason, Essay by Robert Sullivan

Stephen Miller, *Walking New York: Reflections of American Writers from Walt Whitman to Teju Cole*

Tom Glynn, *Reading Publics: New York City's Public Libraries, 1754–1911*

Greg Donaldson, *The Ville: Cops and Kids in Urban America, Updated Edition*. With a new epilogue by the author, Foreword by Mark D. Naison

David Borkowski, *A Shot Story: From Juvie to Ph.D.*

Craig Saper, *The Amazing Adventures of Bob Brown: A Real-Life Zelig Who Wrote His Way Through the 20th Century*

R. Scott Hanson, *City of Gods: Religious Freedom, Immigration, and Pluralism in Flushing, Queens*. Foreword by Martin E. Marty

Dorothy Day and the Catholic Worker: The Miracle of Our Continuance. Edited, with an Introduction and Additional Text by Kate Hennessy, Photographs by Vivian Cherry, Text by Dorothy Day

Pamela Lewis, *Teaching While Black: A New Voice on Race and Education in New York City*

Mark Naison and Bob Gumbs, *Before the Fires: An Oral History of African American Life in the Bronx from the 1930s to the 1960s*

Robert Weldon Whalen, *Murder, Inc., and the Moral Life: Gangsters and Gangbusters in La Guardia's New York*

Joanne Witty and Henrik Krogius, *Brooklyn Bridge Park: A Dying Waterfront Transformed*

Sharon Egretta Sutton, *When Ivory Towers Were Black: A Story about Race in America's Cities and Universities*

Pamela Hanlon, *A Wordly Affair: New York, the United Nations, and the Story Behind Their Unlikely Bond*

Britt Haas, *Fighting Authoritarianism: American Youth Activism in the 1930s*

David J. Goodwin, *Left Bank of the Hudson: Jersey City and the Artists of 111 1st Street*. Foreword by DW Gibson

Nandini Bagchee, *Counter Institution: Activist Estates of the Lower East Side*

Carol Lamberg, *Neighborhood Success Stories: Creating and Sustaining Affordable Housing in New York*

Susan Celia Greenfield (ed.), *Sacred Shelter: Journeys of Homelessness and Healing*

Elizabeth Macaulay Lewis and Matthew McGowan (eds.), *Classical New York: Discovering Greece and Rome in Gotham*

Susan Opotow and Zachary Baron Shemtob (eds.), *New York after 9/11*

For a complete list, visit www.empirestateeditions.com.